STAND OUT 1

Evidence-Based Learning for Life, College, and Career

LESSON PLANNER

FOURTH EDITION

ROB JENKINS

STACI JOHNSON

NATIONAL
GEOGRAPHIC
LEARNING

Australia • Brazil • Canada • Mexico • Singapore • United Kingdom • United States

NATIONAL GEOGRAPHIC
LEARNING

National Geographic Learning,
a Cengage Company

**Stand Out 1: Evidence-Based Learning for Life,
College, and Career, Fourth Edition**
Rob Jenkins, Staci Johnson
Lesson Planner

Publisher: Sherrise Roehr

Executive Editor: Sarah Kenney

Development Editor: Katie Davis

Director of Global Marketing: Ian Martin

Heads of Regional Marketing:

  Charlotte Ellis (Europe, Middle East and Africa)

  Justin Kaley (Asia and Greater China)

  Irina Pereyra (Latin America)

  Joy MacFarland (US and Canada)

Senior Content Project Manager: Beth McNally

Media Researcher: Stephanie Eenigenburg

Senior Art Director: Brenda Carmichael

Operations Support: Hayley Chwazik-Gee,
  Katie Lee

Manufacturing Buyer: Terrence Isabella

Composition: MPS North America LLC

Lesson Planner
ISBN: 978-0-357-96420-0

National Geographic Learning
200 Pier 4 Boulevard
Boston, MA 02210
USA

Locate your local office at **international.cengage.com/region**

Visit National Geographic Learning online at **ELTNGL.com**
Visit our corporate website at **www.cengage.com**

Printed in China
Print Number: 01 Print Year: 2023

Acknowledgments

Mai Ackerman
Ventura College; Los Angeles Mission College, CA

Raul Adalpe
Tarrant County College, Paradise, TX

Mariam Aintablian
Los Angeles Valley College, Valley Glen, CA

Steven Amos
Norfolk Public Schools/Adult Education Services, VA

Ana Arieli
College of Southern Nevada, Las Vegas, NV

Rachel Baiyor
Literacy Outreach, Glenwood Springs, CO

Gregory Baranoff
Santa Barbara City College, Santa Barbara, CA

Valerie Bare
Chesterfield County Public Schools, VA

Dyani Bartlett
Edmonds College, Lynnwood, WA

Karin Bates
Intercambio Uniting Communities, Boulder, CO

Robin Bitters
Adult Learning Program, Jamaica Plain Community Center, Boston, MA

Emily Bryson
ELT Specialist, Author, Teacher, Teacher Educator, Graphic Facilitator, ESOL Lecturer

Janelle Cardenas
Tarrant County College, TX

Joyce Clement
Chesterfield County Public Schools, VA

Juan Corona
Antelope Valley Adult School, Palmdale, CA

Vasilika Culaku
Goodwill, King County, Seattle, WA

Melinda Dart
Chesterfield County Public Schools, VA

Lourdes Davenport
Tarrant County College, TX

Geisa Dennis
Orange County Public Schools, Orlando, FL

Katie Donoviel
English Skills Learning Center, UT

Reyye Esat Yalcin
Bilingual Education Institute, Houston, TX

Aimee Finley
Dallas College, Dallas, TX

Eleanor Forfang-Brockman
Tarrant County College, Fort Worth, TX

Martha Fredendall
Literacy Outreach, Glenwood Springs, CO

Maria Gutierrez
Miami Sunset Adult Education Center, Miami, FL

Anne Henderson
Goodwill, King County, Seattle, WA

Tracey Higgins
Edmonds College, Lynnwood, WA

Daniel Hopkins
Tarrant County College, TX

Fayne Johnson
Atlantic Technical College, Arthur Ashe Jr. Campus, Fort Lauderdale, FL

Angela Kosmas
City Colleges of Chicago, Chicago, IL

John Kruse
University of Maryland, Arnold, MD

Neskys Liriano
New York Mets, Port Saint Lucie, FL

Maria Manikoth
Evergreen Goodwill Job Training and Education Center, Everett, WA

Sean McCroskey
Goodwill, King County, Seattle, WA

Yvonne McMahon
Houston Community College, Houston, TX

Sarah Moussavi
Chaffey College, Rancho Cucamonga, CA

Xavier Munoz
Literacy Council of Northern Virginia, Falls Church, VA

Luba Nesterova
Bilingual Education Institute, Houston, TX

Melody Nguyen
Tarrant County College, Arlington, TX

Joseph Ntumba
Goodwill, King County, Seattle, WA

Sachiko Oates
Santa Barbara City College, Santa Barbara, CA

Liane Okamitsu
McKinley Community School for Adults, Honolulu, HI

Dana Orozco
Sweetwater Union High School District, Chula Vista, CA

Betty Osako
Mckinley Community School for Adults, Honolulu, HI

Dr. Sergei Paromchik
Adult Education Hillsborough County Public Schools, Tampa, FL

Ileana Perez
Robert Morgan Tech. College, Miami, FL

Carina Raetz
Academy School District 20, Colorado Springs, CO

Tom Randolph
Notre Dame Education Center, Lawrence, MA

Jody Roy
Notre Dame Education Center, Lawrence, MA

Andrew Sansone
Families for Literacy, Saint Peter's University, Jersey City, NJ

Lea Schultz
Lompoc Adult School and Career Center, Lompoc, CA

Jenny Siegfried
Waubonsee Community College, Aurora, IL

Daina Smudrins
Shoreline Community College, Shoreline, WA

Stephanie Sommers
Minneapolis Adult Education, Robbinsdale, MN

Bonnie Taylor
Genesis Center, RI

Yinebeb T. Tessema
Goodwill, King County, Seattle, WA

Dr. Jacqueline Torres
South Dade Senior High, Homestead, FL

Cristina Urena
Atlantic Technical College, Coconut Creek, FL

Marcos Valle
Edmonds College, Lynnwood, WA

Ricardo Vieira Stanton
Bilingual Education Institute, Houston, TX

Lauren Wilson
Shoreline Community College, Shoreline, WA

Pamela Wilson
Palm Beach County Adult and Community Education, FL

ROB JENKINS

STACI JOHNSON

We believe that there's nothing more incredible than the exchange of teaching and learning that goes on in an ESL classroom. And seeing the expression on a student's face when the light goes on reminds us that there's nothing more rewarding than helping a student succeed.

Throughout our careers, we have watched as students rise to challenges and succeed where they were not sure success was possible. Seeing their confidence grow and skills develop brings great joy to both of us, and it motivates us to find better ways to reach and support them. We are humbled to think that our contributions to the field over the last 20 years have made a small difference in both students' and teachers' lives. We hope our refinements in ongoing editions will further support their growth and success.

At its core, **Stand Out** has always prioritized robust, relevant content that will deliver student gains in the classroom; while that core mission has not changed, how the program achieves it has certainly evolved in response to a changing educational landscape. The basic principles that have made **Stand Out** successful have not changed. Students are challenged to collaborate and think critically through a well-organized series of scaffolded activities that lead to student application in each lesson. The popular first-of-their-kind lesson plans are still prominent. Features such as project-based learning, video, online practice, multilevel worksheets, and classroom presentation tools continue to support the core series. New to the fourth edition is explicit workplace exploration. A lesson in each unit has been added to explore different fields and careers, potential salaries, skills, and characteristics which workers might have to excel in potential jobs. Also new to the fourth edition, students will be introduced to "Life Online" in tips, activities, and video throughout the series. In addition, **Stand Out** will now be available in different digital formats compatible with different devices. Finally, **Stand Out** introduces a literacy level that will give access through a unique systematic approach to students who struggle to participate. We believe that with these innovations and features the fourth edition will bring success to every student.

STAND OUT MISSION STATEMENT

Our goal is to inspire students through challenging opportunities to be successful in their language learning experience, so they develop confidence and become independent lifelong learners preparing them for work, school, and life.

About the Series

The *Stand Out* series is designed to facilitate active learning within life-skill settings that lead students to career and academic pathways. Each Student's Book and its supplemental components in the seven-level series expose students to competency areas most useful and essential for the student community, with careful treatment of level-appropriate but challenging materials. Students grow academically by developing essential literacy and critical thinking skills that will help them find personal success in a changing and dynamic world.

The *Stand Out* Philosophy

Stand Out endeavors to meet adult language learners at their intellectual level, regardless of what their language level or educational level is. The series aims to develop life and language skills that are relevant and applicable for students now, while at the same time building a foundation that will lead to greater achievement and future success. We believe the *Stand Out* student community represents a vibrant and important part of the pattern in the fabric of our larger society, and we validate the variety of accents, stories, experience, and identities our student community has to share. We hope both the student and instructor communities using these materials will see themselves reflected in these materials, and be proud of what they see.

Integrated Skills

Stand Out now features six lessons per unit, which integrate all four skills in context and as appropriate to the lesson's objective, rather than separated into different sections of the unit. We believe that for real communication to occur, the classroom should mirror real life as much as possible. We also believe the recycling of skills should be emphasized. Students must learn and practice the same skills multiple times in various contexts to actually acquire them. Practicing a skill one time is rarely sufficient for acquisition and rarely addresses diverse student needs and learning styles.

Objective-Driven Activities

Every lesson in *Stand Out* is driven by a performance objective. These objectives have been carefully selected to ensure they are measurable, accessible to students at their particular level, and relevant to students and their lives. Good objectives lead to effective learning; effective objectives also lead to appropriate self-, student-, and program assessment which is increasingly required by state and federal mandates.

Lesson Plan Sequencing

Stand Out follows an established sequence of activities that provides students with the tools they need to practice and apply the skills required in the objective. A pioneer in Adult Education for introducing the Madeline Hunter WIPPEA lesson plan model into textbooks, *Stand Out* continues to provide a clear and easy-to-follow system for presenting and developing English language skills.

The WIPPEA model follows six steps:

- Warm up and Review
- Introduction
- Presentation
- Practice
- Evaluation
- Application

We would propose adding that the final "A" also stand for "assessment;" the final application activity of each sequence is a good tool for formative assessment for the teacher, and for self-assessment and reflection for the student.

Critical Thinking

Critical thinking has been defined in various ways and sometimes so broadly that any activity could be classified to meet the criteria. To be clear and to draw attention to the strong critical thinking activities in *Stand Out,* we define these activities as tasks that require learners to think deeper than the superficial vocabulary and meaning. Activities such as ranking, making predictions, analyzing, or solving problems, demand that students think beyond the surface. Critical thinking is highlighted throughout so the instructor can be confident that effective learning is going on.

New and Expanded!

Workforce Readiness

Adult Education in the United States is funded by the Department of Labor, and *Stand Out* has always had employment and career pathways as a central pillar of its curriculum. New to the fourth edition, *Stand Out* goes beyond reinforcing the language skills students will need to be successful in the workplace by highlighting transferable soft skills—many of which students may already have—in an aim to both validate the skills they already have and provide opportunities for upskilling. In addition to the dedicated Work units in each level, every unit now features one of the sixteen National Career Clusters in the new Lesson 6, inviting students to explore personal and educational requirements in different careers, potential earnings, and opportunities in their community, and thereby creating a link between the job they may have now and their career trajectory in the long term.

New! **Digital Literacy**

As we teach, learn, work, and interact more online and with our devices, it has become increasingly apparent that there is a gap in the digital literacy skills of many of our adult learners. *Stand Out* now strives to help address some of these gaps by offering explicit instruction on issues related to privacy and security, scams, and digital footprint, as well as etiquette and how-to tips for students (and instructors!) who may still be going to class online. This content area is supported in the Student's Book by a new Life Online feature and video, and a fully revamped and expanded digital experience on *Stand Out's* Spark platform.

Civics

Civics isn't just government; it's the school system, waiting in line at the DMV, the taxes on our grocery receipts, and our medical privacy. *Stand Out's* position is that civics is not limited to explicit instruction on systems of government, but that it is germane to every system and network students interact with in their local community. As such, *Stand Out* has always had a robust civics curriculum integrated into the topics covered in the series so students might be better aware of the resources available to them and logistics required of them as they build their lives here.

Learner-Centered, Cooperative, and Communicative Activities

Stand Out provides ample opportunities for students to develop interpersonal skills and to practice new vocabulary through graphic organizers and charts like Venn diagrams, graphs, classifying charts, and mind maps. Dialogues are used to prepare students for these activities in the lower levels and fewer dialogues are

To the Teacher

used at the higher levels, where students have already acquired the vocabulary and rudimentary conversation skills. Activities should provide opportunities for students to speak in near-authentic settings so they have confidence to perform outside the classroom.

New! Assessment

Stand Out Fourth Edition offers a completely new assessment experience, both in content and delivery. Now available for online and asynchronous delivery, the Spark platform offers a robust, completely rewritten, and fully customizable bank of assessment content that is aligned to CASAS Life and Work and the STEPS tests, as well as other important standards, such as CCRS and ELPS.

The *Stand Out* Assessment Suite is an ideal tool for summative assessment—assessment of learning—but just as, if not more, important to the *Stand Out* series is formative assessment—assessment for learning. Consider making use of these features of the series to offer additional progress checks and feedback for your students.

- **WIPPEA Model: Application Step** Can students perform the last activity in each section successfully? This is a great indicator that they have mastered the language objective for the lesson.
- **Review Section** This section, available in every unit, is a great temperature check for how students may perform on a unit test, and what they may want to review.
- **Team Project** This more open-ended task can give you a great window into how students can use the language extemporaneously and will also be a good measure of other areas of achievement, like teamwork, creativity, and effort.

We encourage you to use assessment to celebrate achievement rather than seek out deficits. All students will need additional support and review in many areas, and conditioning students to have a positive relationship with education will positively influence their resilience and motivation.

New! Literacy*

The new edition of *Stand Out* offers support for the most vulnerable and underserved segment of our student population: our literacy students. **Literacy Foundations** aims to build on the skills these adults already have in decoding the world around them through a context-supported ESL literacy curriculum, giving them the foundations they need to continue their literacy journey in a mainstream ESL classroom.

Components

The *Stand Out* series is a comprehensive one-stop destination for all student needs.

Stand Out Lesson Planners

The lesson planners go beyond merely describing activities in the Student's Book by providing teacher support, ideas, and guidance for the entire class period.

- **Standards Correlations** for CCRS, CASAS Competencies, and ELPS are identified for each lesson.
- **Pacing Guides** help with planning by giving instructors suggested durations for each activity and a selection of activities for different class lengths.
- **Teacher Tips** provide point-of-use pedagogical comments and best practices.
- **At-a-Glance** Lesson Openers provide the instructor with everything that will be taught in a particular lesson. Elements include the agenda, the goal, grammar, pronunciation, academic strategies, critical thinking elements, and correlations to standards.
- **Instructional Support** goes beyond what is shown in the Student's Book, providing teachers with guidance for implementation,

* Please note that the Literacy Foundations level will vary somewhat from this description in order to better achieve its specific literacy goals.

differentiation, expansion, and time management.

- **Listening Scripts** are integrated into the unit pages for easy access.

spark Platform

The Spark platform delivers all of the resources you need to be successful at every stage of teaching and learning with *Stand Out*.

For Students

- **Homework** Spark provides nearly fifty activities of additional Online Practice for each Student's Book unit, including CASAS activity types found on the STEPS test.
- **Digital Experience** A full Student's eBook is available on Spark, with audio and video available at point of use.
- **Media** All audio, the Life Skills video program, and the **New!** Life Online video program (replacing Video Challenge) are available at point of use in the Student's eBook.
- **Mobile-Compatible** Designed with your students in mind, all of this content is available for use on a mobile phone.

For Teachers

- **Classroom Presentation Tool** Available online and for offline use, the Classroom Presentation Tool integrates the Student's Book content with all media resources, interactive activities, and a host of new tools to help you deliver the class you want to your students.
- Completely revised **Assessment Suite** is aligned to CASAS and the new STEPS test.

- Robust **Reporting Functionality** in the Course Gradebook demonstrates achievement and informs for reteaching opportunities.
- **Downloadable Resources**, including multilevel worksheets for each lesson, **New!** word lists for Lesson 6 Career Clusters, **New!** digital literacy worksheets (a set of five worksheets for every two levels), audio and video scripts, rubrics for grading, and more, are available in the Teacher Resources tab.

We thank you, the instructor community, for your partnership and commitment to our students, and we welcome your feedback on how to better serve you and your students at any time.

Scope and Sequence

UNIT	LESSON 1	LESSON 2	LESSON 3
PRE-UNIT **Welcome** *Page 2*	**Goal:** Greet people **Pronunciation:** Contractions **Academic:** Focused listening	**Goal:** Say and write numbers **Academic:** Classify information **Writing:** Addresses and phone numbers	**Goal:** Follow instructions **Academic:** Make inferences **Life Online:** Tips for online learning **Grammar:** Imperatives
1 **Talking with Others** *Page 12*	**Goal:** Ask for and give personal information **Grammar:** Simple present: *Be* **Academic:** Make predictions; Do a survey	**Goal:** Describe people **Grammar:** Simple present: *Have* **Pronunciation:** /v/ **Academic:** Classify information	**Goal:** Describe family relationships **Academic:** Make predictions; Create a family tree **Grammar Review:** Simple present: *Be*
2 **Let's Go Shopping** *Page 38*	**Goal:** Identify places to shop **Life Online:** Interpreting online orders **Grammar:** Simple present: *Shop* **Academic:** Do a survey; Make a bar graph	**Goal:** Make purchases and read receipts **Grammar Review:** Simple present: *Be* **Academic:** Calculate amounts **Life Online:** Making online purchases; Credit card safety	**Goal:** Identify clothing **Grammar:** *Be* verb questions and answers **Academic:** Make inferences

Scope and Sequence

Life Online Video *Page 116*

LESSON 4	LESSON 5	LESSON 6	TEAM PROJECT	READING CHALLENGE
Goal: Compare prices **Academic:** Calculate totals; Make comparisons **Grammar:** Comparative adjectives: *Cheaper, More expensive* **Pronunciation:** Stress **Life Online:** Shopping for groceries online	**Goal:** Take and place orders **Academic:** Classify information; Focused listening **Grammar:** *Yes / No* questions and answers	**Workforce Goal:** Investigate food service jobs **Academic:** Interpret a bar graph; Calculate tips	**Goal:** Create a menu for a new restaurant **Soft Skill:** Collaboration—Brainstorming	*How to Stop Food Waste at Home* **Academic:** Interpret an infographic; Make inferences
Goal: Make appointments **Academic:** Make predictions; Focused listening **Life Online:** Using search filters **Grammar:** Present continuous	**Goal:** Identify furniture in a house **Academic:** Classify information **Grammar:** Prepositions	**Workforce Goal:** Identify employment opportunities in construction **Academic:** Interpret an infographic; Rank qualities	**Goal:** Plan a dream home **Soft Skill:** Presentation skills—Prepare and practice	*Risky Business* **Academic:** Infer meaning
Goal: Leave a phone message **Academic:** Focused listening **Writing:** Take notes **Grammar:** *Yes / No* questions with *can* **Pronunciation:** Intonation of *yes / no* questions	**Goal:** Write an email **Academic:** Read and interpret an email **Life Online:** Email greetings and closings **Grammar:** Present continuous; Simple present; Adverbs of frequency **Writing:** Compose an email	**Workforce Goal:** Identify employment opportunities at the post office **Academic:** Interpret an infographic; Reflect on preferences and personal qualities	**Goal:** Design a new city **Soft Skill:** Active listening—Asking questions	*Where Everyone Knows Your Name* **Academic:** Infer meaning; Classify pros and cons

Scope and Sequence

Life Online Video *Page 222*

LESSON 4	LESSON 5	LESSON 6	TEAM PROJECT	READING CHALLENGE
Goal: Ask for information **Grammar:** *Wh-* questions **Academic:** Interpret maps; Focused listening	**Goal:** Develop exercise goals **Academic:** Analyze a pie chart; Do a survey **Grammar:** Verb + infinitive **Writing:** Exercise goals	**Workforce Goal:** Identify employment opportunities in health care **Academic:** Interpret an infographic; Compare jobs	**Goal:** Create a role play about an emergency **Soft Skill:** Collaboration—Making polite suggestions	*The Best Medicine* **Academic:** Make predictions; Make inferences
Goal: Participate in a job interview **Academic:** Classify information; Identify strengths and weaknesses **Grammar Review:** *Yes / No* questions with *can* **Pronunciation:** Intonation of clarification questions **Life Online:** Online job interviews	**Goal:** Evaluate work and school performance **Grammar Review:** Simple present: *Be*; Adverbs of frequency; Simple past: *Be* **Academic:** Focused listening **Writing:** Write a self-evaluation	**Workforce Goal:** Identify employment opportunities in the landscaping industry **Academic:** Interpret a bar graph; Reflect on personal characteristics	**Goal:** Get a new job **Soft Skill:** Active listening—Asking for clarification	*How Many Jobs?* **Academic:** Do a survey; Investigate networking tools
Goal: Identify vocational preferences **Grammar:** Verb + infinitive; Verb + noun **Academic:** Reflect on preferences **Writing:** Work preferences	**Goal:** Develop goals **Grammar:** Future with *going to*; Future with *will* **Life Online:** Study habits; Spell checkers **Academic:** Focused listening; Classify information **Writing:** Goals	**Workforce Goal:** Identify employment opportunities in education **Academic:** Infer meaning; Reflect on work preferences	**Goal:** Set study goals **Soft Skill:** Presentation skills—Engaging the audience	*Learning Together* **Academic:** Reflect on learning; Express opinions

For other national and state specific standards, please visit the Spark platform.

Unit Walkthrough

NEW AND UPDATED IN *STAND OUT*, FOURTH EDITION

Now in its fourth edition, *Stand Out* is a seven-level, standards-based adult education program with a track record of real-world results. Close alignment to WIOA objectives and College and Career Readiness Standards provides adult students with language and skills for success in the workplace, college, and everyday life.

New Literacy level

**The Literacy level follows an instructional design that meets the needs of lower-level English learners.

Each unit opens with a dynamic image to introduce the theme and engage learners in meaningful conversations from the start.

Unit walkthrough pages are from *Stand Out* Level 3.

New 'Life Online' sections develop digital literacy skills.

An **updated video program** now features two 'Life Online' videos with related practice that aligns with workforce and digital literacy objectives.

Life ONLINE — Money In The Bank

Before You Watch

A Look at the photo. What is the woman in the photo doing? What type of things do you think she is doing on her phone? Is it safe for her to be using her phone in the subway?

B Check (✓) what is true for you. Then share your answers with a partner.

☐ 1. I shop online.
☐ 2. I order food online.
☐ 3. I check my bank account balance online.
☐ 4. I deposit checks online.
☐ 5. I pay my bills online.
☐ 6. I send money to my friends or family online.

C You are going to watch a video with advice about how to keep your money and information safe online. What tips do you think the video will give? Share with a partner.

116

While You Watch

D Watch the video. Check (✓) the things Alex talks about doing online.

☐ 1. making friends
☐ 2. shopping for shoes
☐ 3. ordering tacos
☐ 4. playing video games
☐ 5. buying shampoo
☐ 6. signing up for a new credit card
☐ 7. depositing checks
☐ 8. checking a bank account balance
☐ 9. paying bills
☐ 10. getting a debit card
☐ 11. sending money to friends and family
☐ 12. searching for ATMs

E Watch the video again. Complete the tips with the words you hear.

1. Never sign in to your _____ or enter your credit card number while using public wi-fi.
2. Don't give out your personal _____ over email or text.
3. Don't _____ on links in emails or texts if you don't know who sent them.
4. Use different _____ for different websites.
5. Check your _____ and bank account often to make sure there is nothing unusual.

After You Watch

F Read each sentence. Choose *T* if it is true and *F* if it is false.

1. In middle school, Alex wasn't allowed to use the internet.	T	F
2. Alex shops online and uses online banking because it's convenient.	T	F
3. Alex says the internet is very dangerous.	T	F
4. Seeing the lock icon next to a URL can help you decide if a website is safe.	T	F
5. Two-factor authentication can help keep your information safe even if someone has your password.	T	F
6. Alex says he won't shop online or use online banking in the future.	T	F

117

Digital literacy reinforces best practices around privacy, security, finances, and social media.

LESSON 2

The Bank, the Library, and the DMV

GOAL ▶ Interpret charts and compare information

A Discuss the following banking words with your classmates and teacher.

ATM	debit card	minimum deposit	secure banking
average daily balance	minimum daily balance	online banking	unlimited

B Riverview Bank offers three kinds of checking accounts. Interpret the website below.

Riverview BANK	Riverview Total Checking	Riverview Secure Banking	Riverview Premier Plus Checking
With a Riverview bank account, you'll enjoy state-of-the-art online banking and world-class customer service.			
Access to Riverview ATMs	yes	yes	yes
Online Banking, Online Bill Pay, and Mobile Banking	yes	yes	yes
Fees waived at non-Riverview ATMs	no	no	yes
Debit card	yes	yes	yes
Fees waived for checks	no	no paper checks	yes
Monthly service fee	$12 (fee waived if $500 in electronic deposits per month or $1,500 balance)	$4.95	$25 (fee waived if $15,000 total balance)

C Practice asking questions about the bank information above with a partner.

1. Can you do online bill pay with the _____ account?
2. What is the monthly service fee for the _____ account?
3. Do you get a debit card with the _____ account?
4. Can you use non–Riverview ATMs for free with the _____ account?

D DECIDE Listen to each person talk about their banking habits. Decide which account above would be best for each one of them. 🔊

Life ONLINE Watch the video at the end of the unit to learn about useful bank tips, including two-factor authentication and recognizing scams.

LESSON 2   95

Unit walkthrough pages are from *Stand Out* Level 3.

Unit Walkthrough

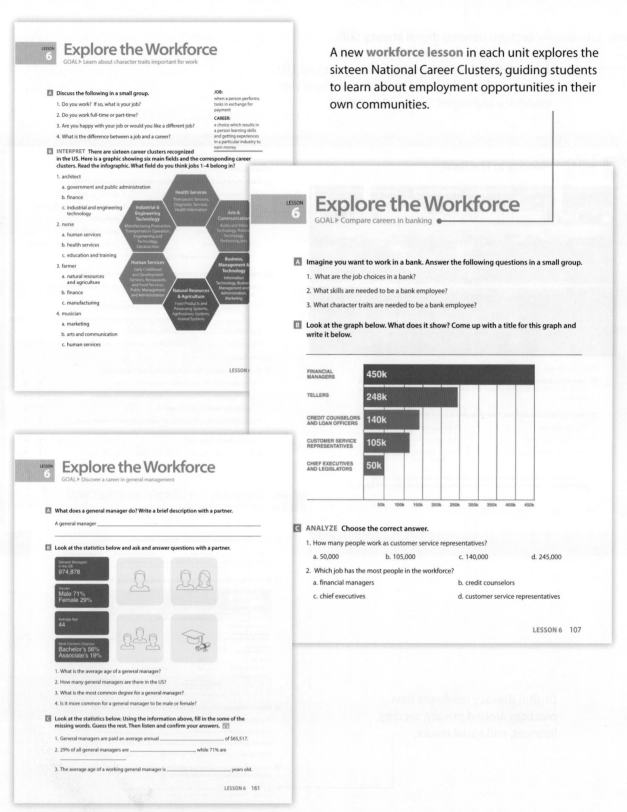

A new **workforce lesson** in each unit explores the sixteen National Career Clusters, guiding students to learn about employment opportunities in their own communities.

Unit walkthrough pages are from *Stand Out* Level 3.

The fully updated **Reading Challenge** will expose students to CASAS STEPS test question types.

Team projects now highlight transferable **Soft Skills**, such as collaboration, active listening, and presentation skills.

Team Project

Create a Community Brochure

SOFT SKILL ▶ Active listening

Imagine that a new family has moved into your neighborhood and you want to tell them all about your community. With your team, create a brochure about your community.

1. Form a team of four or five students. Choose a position for each member of your team.

Position	Job Description	Student Name(s)
Student 1: Leader	Check that everyone speaks English. Check that everyone participates.	
Student 2: Writer	Write information for brochure with help from the team.	
Student 3: Designer	Design brochure layout and add artwork.	
Students 4/5: City Representatives	Help writer and designer with their work.	

2. Make a list of everything you want to include in your brochure, for example: information about the library, banks, and other local services.

3. Create the text for your community brochure.

4. Create a map of your community. Then create artwork for your community brochure.

5. Present your brochure to the class.

Active Listening
Listen carefully
Listen carefully while each team is presenting. How is their presentation different than yours? How is it the same?

Public sculptures, like The Bean in Chicago, are great places for people to meet in towns and cities.

TEAM PROJECT   113

Reading Challenge

A PREDICT Look at the company's logo in the photo. What do you think it is a picture of? What types of food and drink do you think they serve at this café?

B Match the vocabulary word to its correct meaning.

_____ 1. brunch   a. money that a person gets if he or she loses his or her job

_____ 2. pandemic   b. evidence that something is true

_____ 3. unemployment c. a meal that combines breakfast and lunch

_____ 4. proof   d. a disease that happens to people all over the world

C Read the text.

D SEQUENCE Put the events in the correct order.

_____ Carolina collected unemployment.

___1___ Carolina lived in Guatemala City.

_____ Carolina lost her job.

_____ Carolina worked as a housekeeper.

_____ Carolina built her café.

_____ Carolina found a chef and business partner.

_____ Carolina crossed the border with her mother.

_____ Carolina opened Tikal Café.

E On a separate piece of paper, rewrite the sentences in D in the correct order, adding in extra details from the text. Sometimes, change the name Carolina to "she" to avoid too much repetition and add transitions like *such as, then, next,* etc.

EXAMPLE: Carolina lived in Guatemala City. In 2008, she came to the US with her mother. Then...

F EXPAND Imagine you are planning a visit to Brooklyn for brunch. What would you order?

62   UNIT 2

Rising to the Challenge

Tikal Café is a brunch and coffee shop located in Brooklyn, New York. If you go to its website, you will see delicious menu items such as Avocado Toast, Winter Porridge, a Walnut Pesto Quesadilla and Coconut Yogurt. You can drink Matcha, Iced Lavender Lattes, or Cold Brew Coffee. But what you won't see on the website is that the café is owned by an immigrant,
5 Carolina Hernandez from Guatemala.

Carolina is from Guatemala City, Guatemala, and came to the US with her mother in 2008. For over 10 years, she worked two to three jobs so she could save up enough money to open her own business. Sometimes, she worked 18-hour days. She used the money from her housekeeping job to survive and pay her bills. And she used the money from her food serving
10 job to save for her dream.

Unfortunately, when the pandemic hit in 2020, she lost all of her jobs. She was able to collect unemployment, but she wasn't happy. Carolina was a hard worker and wanted to work to earn her money, not sit on the couch and watch Netflix. So, she found a business partner, who is now the chef at the café, and picked out a location close to her home. She started with
15 an empty space and eventually built Tikal Café, a neighborhood spot where locals can come to enjoy a cup of coffee and a delicious meal. From housekeeper to restaurant owner—Carolina is living proof of the American Dream.

Carolina Hernandez's hard work made her dream come true.

READING CHALLENGE   63

Unit walkthrough pages are from *Stand Out* Level 3.

spark

Bring *Stand Out* to life with the Spark platform — where you can prepare, teach and assess your classes all in one place!

Manage your course and teach great classes with integrated digital teaching and learning tools. Spark brings together everything you need on an all-in-one platform with a single log-in.

Track student and class performance on independent online practice and assessment, including practice for CASAS assessments. The Course Gradebook helps you turn information into insights to make the most of valuable classroom time.

Set up classes and roster students quickly and easily on Spark. Seamless integration options and point-of-use support help you focus on what matters most: student success.

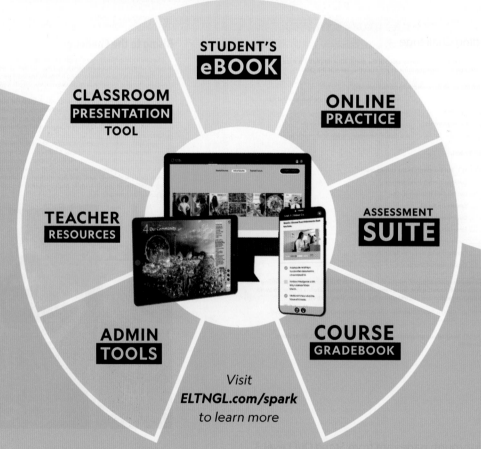

STUDENT'S eBOOK

CLASSROOM PRESENTATION TOOL

ONLINE PRACTICE

TEACHER RESOURCES

ASSESSMENT SUITE

ADMIN TOOLS

COURSE GRADEBOOK

Visit
ELTNGL.com/spark
to learn more

CASAS Competencies Chart

Pre-Unit	Welcome	
Lesson 1: Greet people	0.1.1, 0.1.4, 0.2.1
Lesson 2: Say and write numbers	0.1.2, 0.1.4, 0.2.2
Lesson 3: Follow instructions	0.1.5, 0.1.6, 0.1.7

Unit 1	Talking with Others	
Lesson 1: Ask for and give personal information	0.1.2, 0.1.4, 0.2.1
Lesson 2: Describe people	0.1.2, 0.1.3, 0.2.2, 1.1.4
Lesson 3: Describe family relationships	0.1.2, 0.1.5
Lesson 4: Express preferences	0.1.4, 0.1.5, 0.2.4
Lesson 5: Plan a schedule	0.1.2, 0.1.5, 2.3.1, 7.1.2
Lesson 6: Reflect on career options	0.1.2, 0.1.5, 4.1.3, 4.1.8
Review	2.3.1, 7.1.2
Team Project	0.1.2, 0.1.3, 0.2.1, 2.3.1, 4.8.1, 7.1.2
Reading Challenge	0.1.2, 0.1.5, 4.8.1, 7.4.4, 7.7.3

Unit 2	Let's Go Shopping	
Lesson 1: Identify places to shop	0.1.5, 1.2.3, 1.2.4, 1.2.6, 6.7.2, 7.7.3
Lesson 2: Make purchases and read receipts	0.1.2, 0.1.5, 0.2.2, 1.1.6, 1.6.4, 6.0.1, 6.0.2, 6.1.1, 7.7.3
Lesson 3: Identify clothing	0.1.2, 0.1.5, 1.2.1, 1.2.9, 6.1.1, 7.3.3
Lesson 4: Describe clothing	0.1.2, 0.1.5, 1.2.9
Lesson 5: Describe items in a store	0.1.2, 0.1.5, 1.1.6, 1.2.9, 1.4.1
Lesson 6: Identify employment opportunities in retail	0.1.2, 0.1.5, 4.1.3, 4.1.8, 4.1.9, 6.0.2, 6.7.1, 6.7.2, 7.4.4, 7.7.3
Review	0.1.2, 0.1.5, 1.1.6, 1.2.9, 1.6.4, 6.1.1
Team Project	0.1.2, 0.1.5, 1.3.3, 1.6.4, 4.8.1, 4.8.3, 4.8.6
Reading Challenge	0.1.5, 4.8.1, 6.7.4

Unit 3	Food	
Lesson 1: Identify common meals and foods	0.1.2, 0.1.5, 0.2.1, 1.2.8, 7.2.3
Lesson 2: Interpret grocery store ads	0.1.2, 0.1.5, 1.2.1, 1.2.4, 1.2.8, 7.2.3, 7.7.3
Lesson 3: Express needs and preferences	0.1.2, 0.1.5, 1.1.7, 1.2.8, 7.2.6
Lesson 4: Compare prices	0.1.2, 0.1.5, 1.2.2, 1.2.8, 1.3.1, 4.8.1, 6.0.5, 6.7.2, 7.7.3
Lesson 5: Take and place orders	0.1.2, 0.1.5, 1.2.8, 2.6.4, 7.2.3
Lesson 6: Investigate food service jobs	0.1.2, 0.1.5, 0.2.1, 4.1.3, 4.1.8, 4.1.9, 6.0.2, 6.0.5, 6.1.3, 6.7.1, 6.7.2, 6.7.4, 7.4.4, 7.7.3
Review	0.1.2, 0.1.5, 0.2.1, 1.1.7, 1.2.1, 1.2.2, 1.2.4, 2.6.4
Team Project	0.1.2, 0.1.5, 1.1.7, 1.2.1, 1.2.2, 1.2.4, 2.6.4, 4.8.1, 7.2.6
Reading Challenge	0.1.2, 0.1.5, 1.5.2, 6.7.4

Unit 4	Housing	
Lesson 1: Identify types of housing	0.1.2, 0.1.5, 0.2.1, 1.4.1, 6.7.4, 7.2.3
Lesson 2: Describe parts of a home	1.4.1, 4.8.1, 7.2.3
Lesson 3: Interpret housing ads	1.4.2, 6.1.1, 7.4.4, 7.7.3
Lesson 4: Make appointments	0.1.2, 0.1.5, 1.4.2, 4.8.1, 7.2.3, 7.4.4, 7.7.3
Lesson 5: Identify furniture in a house	0.1.2, 0.1.5, 1.4.1, 7.4.4, 7.7.3
Lesson 6: Identify employment opportunities in construction	0.1.2, 0.1.5, 4.1.3, 4.1.8, 4.1.9, 4.8.1, 6.1.3, 6.7.3, 7.2.3, 7.4.4, 7.7.3
Review	0.1.2, 0.1.5, 1.4.1, 1.4.2, 7.2.3
Team Project	0.1.2, 0.1.5, 1.4.1, 1.4.2, 4.8.1
Reading Challenge	0.1.2, 0.1.5, 1.4.1, 4.8.1

Unit 5	Our Community	
Lesson 1: Identify locations and services	0.1.2, 0.1.5, 2.5.1, 3.1.3, 6.7.2, 7.4.4, 7.7.3
Lesson 2: Give and follow street directions	0.1.2, 0.1.5, 1.9.1, 2.2.1, 2.2.2, 2.2.5, 7.2.3
Lesson 3: Describe locations in an airport	0.1.2, 0.1.5, 2.2.1, 2.2.7
Lesson 4: Leave a phone message	0.1.2, 0.1.5, 2.1.7, 2.1.8
Lesson 5: Write an email	0.1.2, 0.1.5, 0.2.3, 7.7.4
Lesson 6: Identify employment opportunities at the post office	0.1.2, 0.1.5, 4.1.3, 4.1.8, 4.1.9, 4.8.1, 7.4.4, 7.7.3
Review	0.1.2, 0.1.5, 0.2.1, 0.2.3, 1.9.1, 2.1.7, 2.1.8, 2.2.1, 7.7.4
Team Project	0.1.2, 0.1.5, 1.9.1, 4.8.1, 7.4.4, 7.7.3
Reading Challenge	0.1.2, 0.1.5, 2.5.8, 4.8.1, 7.4.4, 7.7.3

Unit 6	Health and Fitness	
Lesson 1: Identify parts of the body	0.1.2, 0.1.5, 3.6.1, 3.6.4
Lesson 2: Identify illnesses and health problems	0.1.2, 0.1.5, 3.6.2, 3.6.3, 7.2.3, 7.4.5
Lesson 3: Give advice	0.1.2, 0.1.3, 0.1.5, 3.3.1, 3.3.2, 3.3.4
Lesson 4: Ask for information	0.1.2, 0.1.5, 2.1.2, 2.2.1, 2.5.1, 7.4.4, 7.7.3
Lesson 5: Develop exercise goals	0.1.2, 0.1.5, 3.5.9, 6.7.4, 7.1.1
Lesson 6: Identify employment opportunities in health care	0.1.2, 0.1.5, 4.1.3, 4.1.8, 4.1.9, 6.7.3, 7.4.4, 7.7.3
Review	0.1.2, 0.1.5, 2.1.2, 2.5.1, 3.3.1, 3.3.2, 3.5.9, 3.6.1, 3.6.3
Team Project	0.1.2, 0.1.5, 2.5.1, 3.3.1, 3.3.2, 4.8.1, 7.3.3
Reading Challenge	0.1.2, 0.1.5, 3.5.9, 7.4.5

Unit 7	Work	
Lesson 1: Identify common occupations	0.1.2, 0.1.5, 4.1.8
Lesson 2: Interpret job information	0.1.2, 0.1.5, 4.1.3, 4.1.6, 4.1.8, 4.8.1, 7.4.4, 7.7.3
Lesson 3: Write your job history	0.1.2, 0.1.5, 4.1.2, 4.1.8, 7.4.4, 7.7.3
Lesson 4: Participate in a job interview	0.1.1, 0.1.2, 0.1.5, 0.1.6, 0.2.1, 4.1.5, 4.1.9, 4.6.1
Lesson 5: Evaluate work and school performance	4.1.9, 4.4.1, 4.4.4
Lesson 6: Identify employment opportunities in the landscaping industry	0.1.2, 0.1.5, 3.4.2, 4.1.3, 4.1.8, 4.1.9, 4.3.2, 6.7.2, 7.4.4, 7.7.3
Review	4.1.2, 4.1.3, 4.1.5, 4.1.6, 4.1.8, 4.4.1, 4.4.4, 4.6.1
Team Project	0.1.2, 0.1.5, 0.1.6, 4.1.2, 4.1.3, 4.1.5, 4.1.6, 4.1.8, 4.4.1, 4.8.1
Reading Challenge	0.1.2, 0.1.5, 4.1.9, 6.7.2, 7.4.4, 7.4.5, 7.7.3

Unit 8	Lifelong Learning	
Lesson 1: Evaluate study habits	6.1.1, 6.1.3, 7.2.3, 7.4.1, 7.4.3, 7.4.9
Lesson 2: Make a study guide	0.1.2, 0.1.5, 7.1.1, 7.1.4, 7.4.1, 7.4.3
Lesson 3: Identify learning opportunities	0.1.2, 0.1.5, 2.8.2, 7.1.1, 7.2.3, 7.4.4
Lesson 4: Identify vocational preferences	0.1.2, 0.1.5, 4.1.9, 7.1.1, 7.5.1
Lesson 5: Develop goals	2.3.1, 4.1.9, 7.1.1, 7.1.2, 7.4.1, 7.4.4, 7.7.3
Lesson 6: Identify employment opportunities in education	0.1.2, 0.1.5, 4.1.3, 4.1.8, 4.1.9, 6.7.4, 7.4.4, 7.7.3
Review	0.1.2, 0.1.5, 7.1.1, 7.1.4, 7.4.1, 7.4.9, 7.5.1
Team Project	0.1.2, 0.1.5, 4.8.1, 7.1.2, 7.1.4, 7.4.1, 7.4.3, 7.5.6
Reading Challenge	0.1.2, 0.1.5, 7.4.1, 7.4.3, 7.4.4, 7.4.5, 7.5.1

For more correlations, including ELPS, CCRS, and EL Civics, visit the Spark Platform.

About the Photo

The cover photos in *Stand Out* are intended to stimulate discussion about where students find themselves now and their aspirations for future employment. The different jobs and careers shown represent the wide variety of different paths students can take in their career journeys. *Stand Out* invites students to think about the life skills needed to communicate and participate successfully as members of their communities and in the workplace. Students are invited to explore the American workplace, culture, environment, and the numerous careers and jobs within in detail throughout the series with the aim of arming them with the tools they need to succeed.

Pulse Check

Before beginning any *Stand Out* course with your students, take a pulse check and use the opportunity at this early stage to ask about their preferred choice of names, titles, and pronouns. It is helpful to find out what you can about their specific needs before the course, with particular consideration for students whose mitigating circumstances may mean a tailored learning plan could be developed to help them

PRE-UNIT

Welcome

UNIT OUTCOMES
- ▶ Greet people
- ▶ Say and write numbers
- ▶ Follow instructions

2

UNIT OUTCOMES	GRAMMAR	VOCABULARY	EL CIVICS
• Greet people • Say and write numbers • Follow instructions	• The verb *be* • Imperatives	• Greetings • Numbers • Study words • Classroom commands	The skills students learn in this unit can be applied to all EL Civics competency areas, with a particular focus on the following: • Communication • Personal Identification

through the course. All students have barriers to learning, whether they are logistical, like work, family, connectivity, or commute, or connected to learning style or language apprehension, such as a fear of public speaking or making mistakes. They can also be related to issues of inclusivity, such as identity, health, physical mobility and ability, legal status, refugee status, and even trauma.

Take a moment at the beginning of your course to check in with your students privately, in person, or perhaps using a handout or questionnaire, to ask them (1) what their barriers to learning are and (2) if there is anything personal or sensitive that they would like to avoid talking about. Also ask how you can support them in navigating the classroom environment. This information will help you build a responsive course where you can adjust expectations, priorities, and tasks to maximize the value ratio of learning to time. It is also a great first step in creating community and trust to acknowledge that everyone has barriers to learning and that you, as their teacher, are there to support them on their journey toward success.

Welcome

- Introduce the unit. Greet students by saying *Hello* and *Hi*.
- Ask students to look at the photos. Elicit the greetings people say to each other when they meet for the first time. Write any useful vocabulary on the board.
- Discuss the unit outcomes with students. Ask them if they know anyone's phone number or any classroom instructions. Write any useful vocabulary on the board next to the vocabulary for greetings you elicited earlier.

Life Skills Focus

In this unit, students will learn how to greet people they meet for the first time. They will also learn how to ask for and give a specific piece of information.

The skills students learn in this unit can be applied to almost every area of EL Civics as they help students to function effectively within U.S. society.

Workplace Focus

All lessons and units in *Stand Out* include basic communication skills and interpersonal skills important for the workplace. They include *collecting and organizing information, making decisions and solving problems,* and *combining ideas and information.*

In Lesson 6 of each unit, one of the 16 National Career Clusters defined by the U.S. Department of Labor will be explored. This explicit workforce content delves into relevant information, from potential earnings to required skills and personal qualities. Instructors can take this opportunity to discuss the specifics of local employment opportunities in the students' own communities and beyond.

spark Resources

All resources for the unit are centrally located on the Spark platform and include: audio, video, multilevel worksheets, digital literacy worksheets, Online Practice, and Assessment Suite.

STEPS

CASAS COMPETENCIES	ELPS	CCRS
Lesson 1: 0.1.1, 0.1.4, 0.2.1 Lesson 2: 0.1.2, 0.1.4, 0.2.2 Lesson 3: 0.1.5, 0.1.6, 0.1.7	**S2:** Participate in level-appropriate oral and written exchanges of information, ideas, and analyses, in various social and academic contexts, responding to peer, audience, or reader comments and questions. **S10:** Demonstrate command of the conventions of standard English to communicate in level-appropriate speech and writing.	L1, L3, RI1, RI3, SL1, SL3

At-a-Glance Prep

Goal: Greet people
Grammar: *I'm*
Pronunciation: /m/
Academic Strategy: Focused listening
Vocabulary: Greetings

Agenda

☐ Greet each other.
☐ Practice greetings.
☐ Listen and write.
☐ Learn names.
☐ Talk to five classmates.

Resources

Heinle Picture Dictionary: Classroom, pages 18–19

Pacing

■ 1.5 hour classes ■ 2.5 hour classes
■ 3+ hour classes

Standards Correlations

CASAS: 0.1.1, 0.1.4, 0.2.1
CCRS: SL1, SL3
ELPS:

S2: Participate in level-appropriate oral and written exchanges of information, ideas, and analyses, in various social and academic contexts, responding to peer, audience, or reader comments and questions.

S10: Demonstrate command of the conventions of standard English to communicate in level-appropriate speech and writing.

Warm-up and Review   2–5 mins. ■■■

Shake hands and introduce yourself to students as they enter the classroom. Ask each student: *What is your name?* At this point, don't expect students to be able to produce this question.

BEST PRACTICE

Cultural Differences

Students may have a different concept of what is an appropriate greeting. In the U.S., we shake hands by firmly curling our fingers around the other person's hand and maintaining eye contact. It is important to teach this style of handshake by modeling it and explaining it verbally.

After greeting about ten students, ask the class if they remember the students' names you have just met. Point to each student and state their name. Encourage the class to help.

Introduction   2 mins. ■■■

Write the agenda on the board and state the goal: *Today, we will greet people.* Greet a student by saying *hi* and shaking their hand. Write *hi* and *hello* on the board and then point to the word *greetings* on the agenda.

Presentation 1   15 mins. ■■■

Ask students to open their books to page 3.

A Look at the photo. What do you see?

Have students look at the photo. Elicit any words they know related to what they can see. For example: *student, teacher, school,* etc. Write the words they suggest on the board. If they don't mention *greet* or *greeting*, point to the handshake and then to *greeting* on the board. Say: *The teacher is greeting the student.*

B Listen and read the conversation.

Tell students to read as they listen. Play the audio. Have students repeat the conversation as a class and practice the rhythm of the conversation. Divide the class in half and practice the conversation. One half takes the role of the teacher, the other the student; then switch and repeat.

Practice 1   5 mins. ■■■

Ask students to practice the conversation with several partners, using appropriate handshakes and eye contact. Encourage them to meet as many students as possible until you tell them to stop.

Evaluation 1   5 mins. ■■■

Observe students as they greet each other. You may also have students demonstrate in front of the class.

A Look at the photo. What do you see?

B Listen and read the conversation. 🎧

Teacher: Hi! Welcome to our class!

Student: Hello. Thank you!

Teacher: How are you?

Student: Fine! How are you?

C **Complete the conversations. Practice them with a partner.**
Answers may vary. Sample answers are given.

1. **Teacher:** _____Hi_____! Welcome to our class.

   Student: Hello. Thank you!

2. **Gabriela:** Hi! _____How are you_____?

   Jian: Fine, thanks. _____How are you_____?

3. **Teacher:** _____Hello_____. Welcome to our class.

   Student: Hi. Thank you!

D **Read the greetings.**

hi	hello	welcome	How are you?
good morning	good afternoon	good evening	

E **Listen. Complete the conversation.** 🎧

Jian: (1) _____Good morning_____! I'm Jian. What's your name?

Gabriela: (2) _____Hello_____. My name is Gabriela.

Jian: Nice to meet you, Gabriela. (3) _____How are you_____ today?

Gabriela: I'm fine, thanks! How are you?

Jian: I'm doing well. (4) _____Welcome_____ to our class!

Contractions 🎧
I am = I'm /m/

F **Listen and repeat.** 🎧

Hi! I'm Gabriela.
G-A-B-R-I-E-L-A.

Hello. I'm Jian.
J-I-A-N.

G **Listen and repeat.** 🎧

Aa Bb Cc Dd Ee Ff Gg Hh Ii
Jj Kk Ll Mm Nn Oo Pp Qq Rr
Ss Tt Uu Vv Ww Xx Yy Zz

Presentation 2   20–30 mins. ■■■□

Greet a few students again and say: *Welcome to our class*. Encourage students to say *thank you*. Write *thank you* on the board. Have students repeat the phrase until they feel comfortable saying it.

Note: Many students will have trouble pronouncing the *th* sound in *thank* properly. Including a mini lesson on the production of this sound may be useful. Explain that they should put the tongue between the teeth and push air past the tongue before moving on to the vowel sound.

BEST PRACTICE

Overcorrecting

As the instructor, it is very important to understand that students at this level will need repeated exposure to grammar, pronunciation, and vocabulary before they become proficient at using it on a daily basis. With pronunciation, students will have many opportunities to practice throughout the course. It is not productive to spend a lot of time on one concept or to spend too much time correcting students' pronunciation. Think of these mini lessons as students' initial exposure to the sounds particular to the English language.

C   Complete the conversations. Practice them with a partner.

Have students complete the sentences individually and compare answers with a partner. Make sure they understand that different options are possible. Monitor as students practice the conversations, providing help with pronunciation as needed.

D   Read the greetings.

Go over the greetings in the box with students. Have students repeat the greetings after you in preparation for the focused listening in **E**. Depending on the time of day, greet your students with the appropriate greeting: *good morning / afternoon / evening*. Use drawings, images, or clock times to help them understand each one.

Practice 2   10 mins. ■■□

E   Listen. Complete the conversation. 🎧

Read through the conversation with the class, eliciting possible words to complete it. Then play the audio as many times as needed.

Evaluation 2   7–10 mins. ■■□

Ask students to check each other's answers in **E** for spelling errors. At this level, students may have difficulty with peer-editing, but with repeated practice, they will become more accurate. Students may be uncomfortable at first with the task of finding mistakes in their peers' work. Stress the importance of spelling and methodically walk students through each word on the board.

Pronunciation   Contractions

Point out the pronunciation note and play the audio.

Students may avoid touching their lips together when pronouncing the /m/ in *I'm*. Help students pronounce the /m/ first in isolation and then as part of the phrase they are practicing. Don't single out students who are having problems with the target sound. After several students have made similar errors, go over the pronunciation of the sound again. You may want to have each student in turn say *I'm* just to be sure they understand that they must put their lips together. Again, be careful not to overcorrect.

Listening Script

A contraction is a short way of saying a group of words. Instead of saying I am, *we often say* I'm. */m/ I'm*

Presentation 3   15–20 mins. ■■■□

Wad up a piece of paper or bring a small soft ball into class and start a chain of questions. First, say: *My name's (your name)*. Then throw the ball to a student and help them to say the sentence substituting their name. Write the phrase on the board to help students see what they are saying. Next, ask the first student to throw the ball to another student. Students should continue the activity until everyone has had a chance to say the sentence.

F   Listen and repeat. 🎧

Play the audio. Tell students to read as they listen. Then play the audio again and have students repeat. Write the two names on the board and ask students to join you as you spell the two names while pointing to each letter.

G   Listen and repeat. 🎧

Write the alphabet across the board. Have students listen to and repeat each letter. Write *Gabriela* under the *G* on the board. Write *Jian* under the *J*.

Listening Techniques

Focused listening can be intimidating to some students. **H** will be challenging for students at this level because they will have to write information down instead of pointing to items as they hear them. Some focused listening activities can be made simpler by following these two tips:

1. Let students know that you will play the audio several times.
2. Allow students to discuss what they have gleaned from the audio between listenings.

Practice 3   5 mins. ■

H Listen. Complete the sentences 🎧

Read the items as a class. Then play the audio. Have students compare their answers with a partner. Play the audio again.

Listening Script

1. *Hi! I'm Ellen. E-L-L-E-N*
2. *Hello! My name is Cyrus. C-Y-R-U-S*
3. *How are you? I'm Ana. A-N-A*
4. *Hi! My name is Duong. D-U-O-N-G*

Evaluation 3   5 mins. ■

Ask volunteers to write the four names on the board from the practice activity under the corresponding letters in the alphabet.

Application   5–7 mins. ■■■

Point out the note about *yes / no* questions and play the audio. 🎧

Have students repeat the questions, using rising intonation. Make sure they understand when to use each question and explain that they will need to use these questions in **I**.

Listening Script

We use a rising intonation with yes / no *questions. They go up at the end.*
Can you spell that?
Can you speak slower, please?
Can you repeat that?

I Greet five people in your class. Ask them to spell their names. Write their names.

Model the activity with two students. Have them greet you (*Hi, I'm . . .*) and respond with a different *yes / no* question to each one. Write their names on the board. Then greet a student and elicit a *yes / no* question and respond spelling your name or saying it more slowly. Ask students to write the names they learn in the spaces provided.

Learner Persistence

Learner persistence is a term that describes students persisting in a program or a class. An instructor can do various things to improve persistence in the classroom. When students feel part of a community or feel comfortable in the classroom, there is a far greater chance that they will stay in the program. One way to build community is to make learning all the students' names a priority and to encourage students to do the same. Some techniques for learning names are described in this lesson.

Refer students to *Stand Out 1 Online Practice*, Pre-Unit, Lesson 1 on the Spark platform for more practice.

H Listen. Complete the sentences.

1. Hi! I'm _____ Ellen _____.

2. Hello! My name is _____ Cyrus _____.

3. How are you? I'm _____ Ana _____.

4. Hi! My name is _____ Duong _____.

I Greet five people in your class. Ask them to spell their names. Write their names.

Answers will vary.

1. _____

2. _____

3. _____

4. _____

5. _____

Yes / No Questions
Can you spell that?
Can you speak slower, please?
Can you repeat that?

Students shake hands to greet each other in English class.

LESSON 2

What's Your Number?

GOAL ▶ Say and write numbers

A Look at the photo. How many students are in the class? Who is the teacher?

B Read the paragraph. Underline the numbers.

Welcome to Ms. Smith's class. There are <u>12</u> students in the class. The students study for <u>six</u> hours every week. The school address is <u>19</u> Lincoln Street, Chicago, Illinois <u>60127</u>.

C Complete the chart about your class. Answers will vary.

Teacher's Name	
Number of Students	
Number of Hours	
Zip Code	

At-a-Glance Prep

Goal: Say and write numbers
Grammar: *is, are*
Academic Strategy: Classifying information
Vocabulary: Numbers, *hours, week, students, address, phone number, zip code*

Agenda
- ☐ Review names.
- ☐ Read a paragraph and complete a chart.
- ☐ Say and write numbers.
- ☐ Listen and write numbers.
- ☐ Learn how to say and write phone numbers, addresses, and zip codes.
- ☐ Ask for and write personal information.

Resources
Heinle Picture Dictionary: Numbers, pages 2–3; The Telephone, pages 16–17

Pacing
- ■ 1.5 hour classes   ■ 2.5 hour classes
- ■ 3+ hour classes

Standards Correlations
CASAS: 0.1.2, 0.1.4, 0.2.2
CCRS: SL1, SL3
ELPS:
S2: Participate in level-appropriate oral and written exchanges of information, ideas, and analyses, in various social and academic contexts, responding to peer, audience, or reader comments and questions.

Warm-up and Review   10–12 mins. ■■■
Write the alphabet across the board as you did in Lesson 1. Ask students to come to the board and write their names under the first letter of their first names. To help students understand the instructions, write a few students' names yourself. After students sit down, ask them to greet each other, practicing American-style handshakes and saying *hello*. Refer to the previous lesson to help students remember the vocabulary.

Introduction   5 mins. ■■■
Count the number of students' names under each letter. Count out loud and encourage students to count along with you. Under each letter, write the number of students whose name starts with that letter. State the goal: *Today, we will say and write numbers.*

Presentation 1   15 mins. ■■■
Write these words on the board: *students, hours,* and *week.* Help students understand the meaning of each word by saying and writing information about your class on the board. For example, *You study for 6 hours a week. We have 3 classes a week.*

Using a clock as a visual, say all the numbers from 1 to 12 and have students repeat them. Then count the number of students in the class out loud, encouraging students to count with you.

A Look at the photo. How many students are in the class? Who is the teacher?
Ask students to open their books and look at the photo. Have students describe what they see. Ask them to say how many students there are and who the teacher is.

B Read the paragraph. Underline the numbers. 🎧
This activity is still part of the presentation. At this stage, students are not expected to understand every word in the paragraph. The goal is to give students exposure to numbers within a text and to help them understand the general meaning.

Play the audio or read the paragraph out loud. Then ask questions such as: *What is the teacher's name? How many students are in the class?*

Workplace Focus
Exercise C: Collect and organize information.

Practice 1   3 mins. ■■■

C Complete the chart about your class.
To help students understand the chart format, complete the chart on the board using the information from the text in **B**. Then elicit your name to show students how they will complete the chart with information about their own class.

Evaluation 1   3 mins. ■■■
Observe students as they work. Check their charts.

Presentation 2

D Listen and practice saying the numbers 0 to 20. 🎧

After students have listened to the audio, call out different numbers and ask students to point to them in their books. Elicit the numbers from the photo at the bottom of the page.

Prepare students for focused listening by talking about things in the classroom and asking students to point to the numbers in the book. For example, you might say: *There are 18 desks in the classroom.* Help students understand that they don't have to know what a desk is to do the activity; they only need to recognize the numbers they hear.

BEST PRACTICE
Natural Speech

Natural speech is important in the classroom. Unnaturally slowing down or over-enunciating could make students frustrated when they listen to native speakers outside of the classroom and are unable to understand them. Help students learn the strategies they will use in such instances by speaking at an authentic pace and in a natural fashion.

Practice 2

15–20 mins. ■■□

E Listen and write the numbers you hear. Then spell them out. 🎧

Model the activity so students understand they have to spell each number too. Play the first item in the audio and answer it on the board together. Play Item b and have students complete individually. Then pause before Item c and explain that they will now hear conversations with numbers in them, but they don't need to understand everything. They only need to listen for and write the numbers. Give students time to write their answers before playing the audio again. Have students compare answers with a partner. Then play the audio again to check answers.

Listening Script

a. *five*
b. *eight*
c. **Student A:** *How many students are in your class?*
   Student B: *I think there are nine.*

d. **Student A:** *My class is bigger.*
   Student B: *Really? How many?*
   Student A: *We have 19 students.*
e. **Student B:** *How long is your class?*
   Student A: *It's two hours a day.*

BEST PRACTICE
Focused Listening

Focused listening is prevalent throughout the *Stand Out* series. The audio tracks are at an authentic speed and are filled with language students may not understand. The purpose of a focused listening task is to help students develop the ability to pull meaning out of complex and natural conversations by identifying key words.

It's important to remind students to listen for overall meaning every time you do a focused listening activity so they don't become frustrated and stop listening altogether.

F Listen and write the missing numbers. 🎧

In the second part of the practice, students are asked to put multiple numbers together. If they have problems, play the audio as many times as needed.

Evaluation 2

5 mins. ■■□

Write the short paragraph from **F** on the board with space for the answers. Ask volunteers to write their answers on the board.

BEST PRACTICE
Encourage Student Participation

Whether classes are quiet or not, always look for opportunities to encourage student participation. This doesn't have to be elaborate in planning. Rather, a simple twist can turn an ordinary activity into a more engaging one. Consider the following:

1. Whenever you need to write something on the board, ask yourself if one or more volunteers can do it instead.
2. When it comes to problem solving, fill-in-the-blank activities, and open-ended questions, have students work in pairs or groups to come up with answers before trying individual responses.

D **Listen and practice saying the numbers 0 to 20.** 🎧

0 zero / oh	6 six	11 eleven	16 sixteen
1 one	7 seven	12 twelve	17 seventeen
2 two	8 eight	13 thirteen	18 eighteen
3 three	9 nine	14 fourteen	19 nineteen
4 four	10 ten	15 fifteen	20 twenty
5 five			

E **Listen and write the numbers you hear. Then spell them out.** 🎧

a. _____5_____   _____five_____

b. _____8_____   _____eight_____

c. _____9_____   _____nine_____

d. _____19_____   _____nineteen_____

e. _____2_____   _____two_____

F **Listen and write the missing numbers.** 🎧

My name is Gabriela. My address is _____14_____ Main Street. The zip
code is _____06119_____. My phone number is _____401-555-7248_____.
There are _____nine_____ students in my class.
            (spell out)

Colorful mailboxes in Vancouver, Canada

G Read about Gabriela and Obinna.

Name: Gabriela Ramirez
Address: 14 Main Street
Zip code: 06119
Phone: 401-555-7248

Name: Obinna Kalu
Address: 333 Western Circle
Zip code: 75208
Phone: 469-555-3534

H **CLASSIFY** **Write the information in the chart.** Order of answers will vary.

~~2945 Broadway~~	617-555-2386	470-555-7869	72643
800-555-2675	9235 Sundry Way	46183	8 Palm Circle
213-555-5761	78231	9921 Johnson Street	33109

Address	Zip Code	Phone Number
2945 Broadway	78231	800-555-2675
9235 Sundry Way	46183	213-555-5761
8 Palm Circle	72643	617-555-2386
9921 Johnson Street	33109	470-555-7869

I **Complete the information about you and share with a partner. Listen and write your partner's information.** Answers will vary.

	You	Your Partner
1. The number of people in your family		
2. Your phone number		
3. Your address		
4. Your zip code		

Presentation 3

8–10 mins. ■■■

G Read about Gabriela and Obinna.

Do this activity as a class. Help students understand the new vocabulary, specifically *address, zip code,* and *phone number*. Ask questions about the information below the photos. Ask the class and individuals for answers.

Prepare students for the practice by writing addresses, zip codes, and phone numbers on the board and asking them to help you label them.

You can make a game of this by forming three teams of students. Have the teams line up in three lines facing the board. In front of each team on the board, write the three target items: *address, zip code,* and *phone number.* Then call out an address, zip code, or phone number. The first person in each line should slap the correct label. (Fly swatters work well here.) The first team to slap the correct word gets a point.

Workplace Focus
Exercise H: Collect and organize information.

Practice 3

5–10 mins. ■

H CLASSIFY Write the information in the chart.

Go over the chart with the class. Then point out the example. Say the first number in the box and ask: *Is this a zip code? Is it a phone number?* Have students tell you where to put it in the chart. Then have students complete the chart individually.

Evaluation 3

2–5 mins. ■

Ask students to compare answers. Then go over them as a class.

Application

10–15 mins. ■■■

I Complete the information about you and share with a partner. Listen and write your partner's information.

The goal here is to practice saying and writing numbers. Addresses will be the focus of another lesson; however, with the skills students learned in the first lesson, they should be able to give their addresses with the number and the name of the street. Students may not know how to spell their street names. Emphasize that the numbers are the most important part of the activity.

Model this activity by writing your information on the board and then saying: *There are (x) people in my family. My phone number is . . .,* etc. Have a student tell you their information and write it next to yours on the board. Have students complete their information in their books. Then refer them back to the text about Gabriela in **F** to help them give their information. Monitor as students complete the activity with a partner, providing help as needed.

After finishing this activity, it may be a logical next step to teach students how to write and spell their complete addresses.

Refer students to *Stand Out 1 Online Practice*, Pre-Unit, Lesson 2 on the Spark platform for more practice.

Instructor's Notes

_____

_____

_____

_____

_____

_____

_____

_____

_____

_____

_____

_____

_____

_____

_____

At-a-Glance Prep

Goal: Follow instructions
Grammar: Imperatives
Academic Strategy: Making inferences
Vocabulary: Classroom instructions

Agenda

☐ Review numbers.
☐ Complete instructions.
☐ Listen to new words.
☐ Listen and follow directions.
☐ Give and follow instructions with a partner.

Resources

Heinle Picture Dictionary: Listen, Read, Write,
pages 20–21

Pacing

■ 1.5 hour classes ■ 2.5 hour classes
■ 3+ hour classes

Standards Correlations

CASAS: 0.1.5, 0.1.6, 0.1.7
CCRS: L1, L3, RI1, RI3, SL1, SL3
ELPS:
S2: Participate in level-appropriate oral and written exchanges
of information, ideas, and analyses, in various social and academic
contexts, responding to peer, audience, or reader comments and
questions.

Warm-up and Review   10 mins. ■■■

Ask students to go to **I** in Lesson 2, page 8. Have them
find a different partner and do the activity again.

Introduction   5 mins. ■■■

Ask students to stand up. Model the action so that
they understand. Then ask them to turn right and
left as you model the actions. Then ask them to
turn around. Finally, ask them to sit down. Write the
agenda on the board and state the goal: *Today, we
will learn to follow instructions.*

Presentation 1   15–20 mins. ■■■

Students will learn the four words—*write, listen,
read,* and *speak*—through miming. Before students
open their books, act out the words several times.
Some students may call out the words. Write them
on the board. Then repeat the activity with *stand up,
sit down,* and *take out your books / pencil / paper.*

A Match the words to the photos.

Complete the activity as a class. Write the four
words on the board as headings to four columns.
Elicit / Provide additional vocabulary to go with
each word. For example, include *to music* under the
heading *listen.* Next, say the words and ask students
to act them out.

Practice 1   7–10 mins. ■■■

B INFER Listen. Point to the correct photo in A. You will point to some more than once.

Tell students to just listen the first time. Then play
the audio. Play the audio again and have students
point to the photos in **A**. Play the audio again,
pausing after each one and check which photo
students chose.

Listening Script

1. *I am very busy and have many things to do. I write
   everything I need to do in a notebook. It helps me
   stay organized.*
2. *I want to learn English quickly. I speak to my friends
   and my family in English for practice every day.*
3. *I like to listen to music. When I listen to music in
   English, I learn a lot.*
4. *I enjoy reading. I often read in my free time.*
5. *Here is the test paper. Write your answers in pencil,
   please.*
6. *I will find the information. I can look it up online.*

C Complete the instructions. Use the words from A.

Have students complete the activity individually
and then compare with a partner.

Evaluation 1   5 mins. ■■■

On the board, write the sentences with the blanks as
they appear in **C**. Have volunteers complete them.

D Read the tips for online learning. Then match the tips to the pictures.

Ask students to read the Life Online tips and
match them to the images individually. Check
answers as a class. If applicable, show students
these functions in a video calling software you use.
For more on video calling, see the *Stand Out Basic
and 1* digital literacy worksheets.

LESSON 3

Classroom Talk
GOAL ▶ Follow instructions

A Match the words to the photos.

listen	read	speak	write

1. _____write_____
2. _____listen_____
3. _____read_____
4. _____speak_____

B **INFER** Listen. Point to the correct photo in A. You will point to some more than once.
1. Picture 1; 2. Picture 4; 3. Picture 2; 4. Picture 3; 5. Picture 1; 6. Picture 3

C Complete the instructions. Use the words from A.

1. _____Write_____ your name on the paper.

2. _____Listen_____ to the audio and repeat.

3. _____Write_____ your answers on the board.

4. _____Read_____ the story and answer the questions.

5. _____Speak_____ with your partner about the picture.

D Read the tips for online learning. Then match the tips to the pictures. —— **Life**
ONLINE

__c__ 1. Learn to raise your hand.   a.

__a__ 2. Ask questions in the chat.   b. 👂

__b__ 3. Listen carefully to instructions.   c. ✋

E Match the instructions to the photos.

| Help Ana. | Open your book. | Sit down. | Take out a sheet of paper. |
| Listen carefully. | Read. | Stand up. | Write. |

1.

Open your book.

2.

Take out a sheet of paper.

3.

Read.

4.

Stand up.

5.

Write.

6.

Listen carefully.

7.

Help Ana.

8.

Sit down.

F Listen and follow the instructions. 🎧

Presentation 2   10–15 mins. ■■■

E   Match the instructions to the photos.

Go over the photos with the class and elicit any vocabulary students already know. Provide new vocabulary. Walk students through the matching activity and have them complete it individually. Check answers as a class.

Say the sentences and ask students to repeat them. Mime different actions and ask students to say the sentences, first as a group, and then individually.

Next, say the sentences and ask students to mime them.

Practice 2   7–10 mins. ■■

F   Listen and follow the instructions. 🎧

In this activity, play the audio several times. Ask students to follow the instructions as they listen.

Listening Script

Please stand up.
Please sit down.
Please read page one in your book.
Please listen carefully.
Please take out a sheet of paper.
Please write your name on the sheet of paper.

Evaluation 2   7–10 mins. ■■

Observe students miming the actions and following the instructions in **F**. In pairs, have students give each other instructions from **E**.

Instructor's Notes

_____
_____
_____
_____
_____
_____
_____
_____
_____
_____
_____
_____
_____
_____
_____
_____
_____
_____
_____
_____
_____
_____
_____

Presentation 3   10–15 mins. ■■■

Open and close a book in front of the class several times. Open the book and show students what page you are on. Show them the page and say the page number.

G   Read and listen to the conversation. 🎧

Play the audio. Play the audio again, pausing after each line so students can repeat it. Practice the conversation together. Help students use correct intonation, especially when they ask the clarification question.

Write the following clarification questions on the board: *Excuse me? Pardon me? What page? What did you say? Can you repeat that?* Say a sentence quickly so students can't understand it. Explain that they can ask for clarification by using one of these phrases.

Practice 3   7–10 mins. ■

H   Work with a partner. Give instructions for your partner to follow.

Model the activity with a student. Point to yourself and say: *Student A.* Then point to the student and say: *Student B.* Point to the *Student A* and *Student B* columns in the book. Give the first instruction and have the student do the action. Then have the student give you the first instruction from the Student B column.

Have students carry out the activity in pairs. Monitor and provide help as needed.

Evaluation 3   5 mins. ■

Ask volunteers to give instructions to the class.

Application   5-7 mins. ■■■

I   Work with a partner. Act out instructions for your partner to guess.

Model the activity with a student. First mime an action yourself for the student to guess, then have them mime an action for you.

Have students carry out the activity in pairs. Monitor and provide help as needed.

Refer students to *Stand Out 1 Online Practice*, Pre-Unit, Lesson 3 on the Spark platform for more practice.

Instructor's Notes

_____

_____

_____

_____

_____

_____

_____

_____

_____

_____

_____

_____

_____

_____

_____

_____

_____

_____

_____

_____

_____

_____

G Read and listen to the conversation. 🎧

Teacher: Please open your books to page 15.

Student: What page?

Teacher: Page 15. That's one, five.

Student: Thank you.

H Work with a partner. Give instructions for your partner to follow.

Student A:

1. Please take out your book.

2. Please open your book to page 62.

3. Please open to Unit 5, Lesson 2.

4. Please close your book.

5. Please take out a sheet of paper.

6. Please write your name.

7. Please stand up.

8. Please sit down.

Student B:

1. Please take out a sheet of paper.

2. Please write your name.

3. Please stand up.

4. Please sit down.

5. Please take out your book.

6. Please open your book to page 150.

7. Please open to Unit 3, Lesson 5.

8. Please close your book.

I Work with a partner. Act out instructions for your partner to guess.

EXAMPLE:

Student A:

Student B: Please listen carefully.

Talking with Others

About the Photo

This photo shows a campsite in the Joshua Tree National Park in California, U.S. The park is in the desert and is known for the distinctive Joshua trees and stunning rock formations. Many people come to the park to camp, hike, or simply relax and have fun. For some people, one of the attractions of the park is that there is limited cellphone service, so it offers an opportunity to fully disconnect from daily life and appreciate the beauty of nature.

- Introduce the unit. Ask students to talk with each other briefly about anything they feel like. Then ask what they talked about.
- Ask students to look at the photo and say what they see. Provide vocabulary as needed and write it on the board.
- Read and ask each question. Discuss the answers as a class.
- Ask volunteers to read the unit outcomes. Elicit vocabulary for each one and write it on the board. Give students an example for each.

Life Skills Focus

In this unit, students will learn how to introduce themselves and give information to people they meet for the first time. They will also learn how to describe people and family members, as well as express their preferences and plan a schedule.

12

UNIT OUTCOMES	GRAMMAR	VOCABULARY	EL CIVICS
• Ask for and give personal information	• Simple present: *Be*	• Personal information	The skills students learn in this unit can be applied to the following EL Civics competency area:
• Describe people	• *His / Her*	• Height, weight, hair colors and styles	
• Describe family relationships	• Simple present: *Have*	• Family	• Personal Information
• Express preferences	• Adjective order	• Entertainment	
• Plan a schedule	• Simple present: *Like*	• Clock times	
• Reflect on career options	• *From … to, at*	• Career fields and jobs	

UNIT OUTCOMES

▶ Ask for and give personal information
▶ Describe people
▶ Describe family relationships
▶ Express preferences
▶ Plan a schedule
▶ Reflect on career options

Look at the photo and answer the questions.

1. Where are these people?
2. How do you think they know each other?

People hold hands at a campground in Joshua Tree National Park, California, where phone service is limited.

1. Why do you think the people are holding hands?
2. Do they look upset that there isn't good phone service?
3. Many people go to national parks to get off of social media and spend time outside with friends and family. Does this sound interesting to you? What do you like to do in your free time?

13

Workplace Focus

All lessons and units in *Stand Out* include basic communication skills and interpersonal skills important for the workplace. They include *collecting and organizing information, making decisions and solving problems,* and *combining ideas and information.*

- In Unit 1, Lesson 6, *Explore the Workforce,* students will reflect on different career options and classify jobs according to career fields. Then they will identify their preferences. They will also analyze hourly rates and the job requirements for a photographer.
- In the Team Project, students practice the soft skill of collaboration as each of them participate and take on a role.
- A Life Online exercise in Lesson 5 raises awareness of how online calendars can be helpful.

spark Resources

All resources for the unit are centrally located on the Spark platform and include: audio, video, multilevel worksheets, digital literacy worksheets, Online Practice, and Assessment Suite.

─── STEPS ───

CASAS COMPETENCIES	ELPS	CCRS
Lesson 1: 0.1.2, 0.1.4, 0.2.1 Lesson 2: 0.1.2, 0.1.3, 0.2.2, 1.1.4 Lesson 3: 0.1.2, 0.1.5 Lesson 4: 0.1.4, 0.1.5, 0.2.4 Lesson 5: 0.1.2, 0.1.5, 2.3.1, 7.1.2 Lesson 6: 0.1.2, 0.1.5, 4.1.3, 4.1.8 Review: 2.3.1, 7.1.2 Team Project: 0.1.2, 0.1.3, 0.2.1, 2.3.1, 4.8.1, 7.1.2 Reading Challenge: 0.1.2, 0.1.5, 4.8.1, 7.4.4, 7.7.3	**S2:** Participate in level-appropriate oral and written exchanges of information, ideas, and analyses, in various social and academic contexts, responding to peer, audience, or reader comments and questions. **S9:** Create clear and coherent level-appropriate speech and text. **S10:** Demonstrate command of the conventions of standard English to communicate in level-appropriate speech and writing.	L1, L2, L3, RI1, RI2, RI3, SL1, SL3, SLK2, W1, W3

Where Are You From?

GOAL ▶ Ask for and give personal information

A **PREDICT** Look at the picture. Where is Roberto from?

GUATEMALA CITY

B **INTERPRET** Read about Roberto. Check your answer to **A**.

My name is <u>Roberto</u> <u>Garcia</u>. I'm a new student in this school. I'm from Guatemala City, <u>Guatemala</u>. I'm <u>43</u> years old and I'm <u>married</u>. I'm very happy in my new class.

C **CLASSIFY** Write the underlined words from **B** in the chart below.

First Name	Last Name	Country	Age	Marital Status
Roberto	Garcia	Guatemala	43	married

D Complete the sentences.

(age)   1. Roberto Garcia is _____43_____ years old.

(country)   2. He is from _____Guatemala_____.

(marital status)   3. He is _____married_____.

At-a-Glance Prep

Goal: Ask for and give personal information
Grammar: Simple present: *Be*
Academic Strategies: Focused listening, classifying information, doing a survey
Vocabulary: Personal information

Agenda

☐ Line up in alphabetical order.
☐ Give personal information.
☐ Talk about Roberto.
☐ Learn new vocabulary.
☐ Use the verb *be*.
☐ Ask for and give personal information.

Resources

Heinle Picture Dictionary: Nationalities, pages 44–45; Documents, pages 42–43

Pacing

■ 1.5 hour classes ■ 2.5 hour classes
■ 3+ hour classes

Standards Correlations

CASAS: 0.1.2, 0.1.4, 0.2.1
CCRS: L1, L2, L3, SL1, SL3
ELPS:

S2: Participate in level-appropriate oral and written exchanges of information, ideas, and analyses, in various social and academic contexts, responding to peer, audience, or reader comments and questions.

S10: Demonstrate command of the conventions of standard English to communicate in level-appropriate speech and writing.

Warm-up and Review   10–15 mins. ■■■

Write the alphabet across the board as you did in the Pre-Unit. Begin to write students' first names on the board under the appropriate letters. Ask three students to stand up. Show them how to form a line in alphabetical order by first name. Ask the class to help you add a few more students to the line. Then ask the class to complete the line by putting themselves in alphabetical order.

Introduction   5 mins. ■■■

Ask students to open their books and look at the picture of Roberto. Ask about Roberto. Students may not understand your questions at this point. Ask questions like: *Where is he from? Is he married? How old is he?* Write the agenda on the board and state

the goal: *Today, we will learn how to ask for and give personal information.*

BEST PRACTICE

Questioning Strategies

The questions in the introduction are based on what students will learn in this lesson. Students are not expected to answer them at this point, but a few students may be able to guess their meaning.

Give students twenty seconds before you help them answer questions, and ask each question more than once. If students are unable to respond, ask a follow-up *yes / no* question. For example, *Where is he from? Is he from China?* This process will allow students to give a yes or no response. After asking about a few different countries and eliciting negative responses, give students the answer by asking: *Is he from Guatemala?*

Presentation 1   10–15 mins. ■■■

On the board, write: *Where are you from?* Point to yourself and say: *I'm from . . .* Ask a few students where they are from. Expect one-word answers. Ask more students the same question. Follow up by asking the class: *Where's (Selma) from?*

A **PREDICT** **Look at the picture. Where is Roberto from?**

Look at the picture and answer the question together.

B **INTERPRET** **Read about Roberto. Check your answer to A.** 🎧

Read the paragraph with the class. Ask questions about Roberto: *Is Roberto married? How old is Roberto?* Then read it again, but insert your own information.

Workplace Focus

Exercise C: Collect and organize information.

Practice 1   10–15 mins. ■■■

C **CLASSIFY** **Write the underlined words from B in the chart below.**

Elicit / Provide the meaning of *age* and *marital status*. Check answers as a class.

D **Complete the sentences.**

Have students complete the activity individually.

Evaluation 1   3–5 mins. ■■■

Go over the answers to **D** as a class. Ask the class or individual students the questions about Roberto: *What's his name? Where is he from? Is he married? How old is he?*

Presentation 2

8–10 mins. ■■■□

The goal here is to help students understand the words associated with each idea. So, for example, if they are asked their marital status, they will be able to answer equally as well as if they are asked if they are married.

E Look at the photos and read the words.

Do this activity as a class. Have students look at the photos and help them understand the words *single*, *married*, and *divorced*. Write *marital status* on the board and point to the words in the book. Then review the word *age* and ask students to guess the age of each person in the photos. Finally, ask students to predict the country (You may write on the board: *country of origin*.) of each person in the photos.

Practice 2

5–7 mins. ■■□

F Match the questions with the answers.

This exercise reinforces what students have learned. Walk around the classroom and check students' answers as they work.

Workplace Focus

Exercise G: Collect and organize information.

G Listen and complete the missing information. 🎧

Show students what to listen for in this focused listening activity. Remind them that they don't need to understand every word. Play the audio twice. Give students time to finish writing, then play the audio again. Have students compare answers with a partner before playing the audio again.

BEST PRACTICE
Repeated Listening

It may be necessary with focused listening to play the audio more than once. You may ask students to compare answers with each other before you play an audio track again.

Note: Focused listening is at an authentic pace to help students learn the strategies they need to function outside of the classroom.

Listening Script

1. *Yan Wu is happy to be in the United States. She wants to learn English. She learned some English in her hometown of Shanghai, China. China is spelled:*

C-H-I-N-A. She wants to help other people in her family learn English. She is divorced, and she is 60 years old.

2. *Maha Khan is 28. She wants to learn English quickly. She watches TV and reads the news in English every day. She is single and is from Riyadh, Saudi Arabia. Saudi Arabia is two words. It is spelled: S-A-U-D-I space A-R-A-B-I-A.*

3. *Andre Paul is a student, and he is a salesperson. He works hard during the day and goes to school at night. He is 33 years old. He is married with three kids. Some of Andre's family live in his home country of Haiti. He talks to them on the phone once a week. Haiti is spelled: H-A-I-T-I.*

Evaluation 2

7–10 mins. ■■□

Check students' understanding by describing different things about the people in **G**. For example, say: *divorced*. Students should respond: *Yan*. You can also ask students to respond nonverbally by showing the number of fingers that correspond to picture 1, 2, or 3. After giving one-word descriptions, say complete sentences.

Finally, ask the four questions in **F** about each person in **G**, changing *you* to *he / she*. Then ask students to take on the role of the three students in **G** and ask each other the questions using *you*.

BEST PRACTICE
Monitoring Student Responses

An easy way to monitor student responses is to have students respond verbally with a word. Say: *married*. Students respond: *Andre*.

With the above method, however, more vocal students sometimes overwhelm students who need more time to think when asked for a verbal response. You may choose other ways for students to respond where they are less likely to "go along with the crowd." One such method could be to use 3-by-5 index cards with an answer choice on each. For example, each card could have different names (Yan, Maha, or Andre). Students then hold up the correct card after you give the cue. If you choose to use this method, have students create the cards themselves so they also get writing practice.

Another way is described in this lesson. Students will respond by showing the number of fingers that correspond to each picture. Start this method by first only saying the target word. Next, put the word in a sentence and then use all the words in a paragraph.

E **Look at the photos and read the words.**

single

divorced

married

F **Match the questions with the answers.**

___b___ 1. Where are you from?   a. Yes, I'm married.

___d___ 2. What's your name?   b. I'm from Guatemala.

___a___ 3. Are you married?   c. I'm 43 years old.

___c___ 4. How old are you?   d. Roberto

G **Listen and complete the missing information.** 🎧

1.

Name: _____Yan Wu_____
Age: _____60_____
Marital status: __divorced__
Country: _____China_____

2.

Name: _____Maha Khan_____
Age: _____28_____
Marital status: ____single____
Country: ____Saudi Arabia____

3.

Name: _____Andre Paul_____
Age: _____33_____
Marital status: ____married____
Country: _____Haiti_____

H Study the chart.

Simple Present: *Be*			
Subject	***Be***		**Example Sentence**
I	am	43 years old	I **am** 43 years old.
He / She	is	single from Venezuela	He **is** single. (Cumar **is** single.) She **is** from Venezuela. (Gabriela **is** from Venezuela.)
We / You / They	are	married 30 years old from Iran	We **are** married. (Sara and I **are** married.) You **are** 30 years old. They **are** from Iran. (Sara and Arash **are** from Iran.)

I Complete the sentences about the people.

Fabiana Silva
32 years old
single
Brazil

Rolando Perez
32 years old
divorced
Cuba

Ahmad Rahman
61 years old
married
Malaysia

(marital status) 1. Rolando _is divorced_____.

(marital status) 2. Ahmad _is married_____.

(marital status) 3. Fabiana _is single_____ and Rolando _is divorced_____.

(age) 4. Fabiana and Rolando _are 32 years old_____.

(age) 5. Ahmad _is 61 years old_____.

(country) 6. Ahmad _is from Malaysia_____.

J **SURVEY** Work in groups of four. Interview your group members. Complete the table.
Answers will vary.

What's your name?	Where are you from?	How old are you?	Are you married?

Presentation 3

10–15 mins. ■■■

H Study the chart.

Remember, at this stage, some students will have trouble understanding a chart like this one. Go over it carefully. Drill students by asking questions about the pictures below the chart and about themselves. Help students to use complete sentences. Write their responses on the board.

BEST PRACTICE

Drills

Drills can be a good way to help students become familiar with vocabulary, grammar structures, and proper pronunciation. They also help students to gain confidence, especially when performing together with their classmates. However, drills should not be the sole practice or method used to help students memorize something or acquire a grammar structure. Also, there are several ways to drill (choral repetition, substitution, build up, backward build-up, etc.). If particular drills are overused, there is a risk of losing the meaning of a structure.

Practice 3

5–7 mins. ■

I Complete the sentences about the people.

Ask students to complete the sentences in their books, then compare with a partner and copy them in their notebook.

Evaluation 3

3–5 mins. ■

Ask students to write their responses on the board and go over them as a class.

Workplace Focus

Exercise J: Interact appropriately with team members; Interpret and communicate information; Collect and organize information.

Application

5–7 mins. ■■■

J SURVEY Work in groups of four. Interview your group members. Complete the table.

Ask students to form groups or form them yourself to ensure a mixture of abilities in each group. Have students ask questions in a round-robin fashion and record answers. The round robin would work like

this: Student A asks Student B a question. Student B answers, and all students record the answer. Then Student B asks Student C, and so on. Demonstrate this several times before asking students to do it on their own. Monitor as groups work and provide help as needed.

When students have completed the chart, ask volunteers to share information they learned about their classmates. Correct use of the simple present as needed. If there are two students with the same information, encourage them to use *they*. For example: *Pedro and Jaime are from Mexico.*

Instructor's Notes

_____

_____

_____

_____

_____

_____

_____

_____

_____

_____

_____

_____

_____

_____

_____

At-a-Glance Prep

Goal: Describe people
Grammar: *His / Her,* simple present: *have,* adjective order
Pronunciation: /v/
Academic Strategies: Focused listening, classifying information
Vocabulary: hair and eye colors, hairstyles, height, weight

Agenda

☐ Review personal information.
☐ Learn about height, weight, age, hair and eye color.
☐ Describe people.
☐ Listen and practice a conversation.
☐ Describe hair.
☐ Complete a driver's license.

Resources

Heinle Picture Dictionary: Face and Hair, pages 32–33, Documents, pages 42–43

Pacing

■ 1.5 hour classes   ■ 2.5 hour classes
■ 3+ hour classes

Standards Correlations

CASAS: 0.1.2, 0.1.3, 0.2.2, 1.1.4
CCRS: L1, L2, L3, SL1, SL3
ELPS:
S2: Participate in level-appropriate oral and written exchanges of information, ideas, and analyses, in various social and academic contexts, responding to peer, audience, or reader comments and questions.
S10: Demonstrate command of the conventions of standard English to communicate in level-appropriate speech and writing.

Warm-up and Review   8–12 mins. ■■■

Ask a few students where they are from. Write their names and country of origin on the board. If you have a homogeneous group from one country, ask what city they are from. Take a class poll and create a graph. Put the number of students on the vertical axis and the countries, cities, or states on the horizontal axis. Have students copy the graph in their notebook.

Introduction   2 mins. ■■■

Write *tall* on the board. Direct three students to the front of the room. Ask the class which student is tall.

Help students understand. Have students form a line from shortest to tallest. State the goal: *Today, we will learn how to describe people.*

Workplace Focus

Exercise A: Collect and organize information; Perform basic computations;
Exercise B: Collect and organize information.

Presentation 1   15–20 mins. ■■■

Show the class your driver's license or other identification. Tell students that the card has important information on it such as your birth date and your height (if applicable). Remind them of the words *tall* and *short.*

A INTERPRET Look at Sayed's license. Complete the sentences.

Go over Sayed's license with the class. Check for understanding and prior knowledge. For example, ask what color Sayed's eyes are. Then complete the sentences together.

Point out the information about measuring height. Spend some time helping students understand the U.S. system of measurement and ways to write inches and feet. Many students will be familiar with the metric system. Show them how a foot equals 12 inches. Bring a tape measure, ruler, or yardstick into class to emphasize the point.

Elicit / Provide colors for hair and eyes. Have a few students describe their eye and hair color.

Go over the grammar note. Use *his* and *her* in sentences describing students in the class. Go over the pronunciation for *her.* Students may say it like *air.*

Practice 1   7–10 mins. ■■■

B Complete the sentences about Elena. Then take turns describing Luis with a partner.

Have students complete the sentences with a partner. Then check them as a class. Model describing Luis by saying: *Luis is 5 foot 6.* Have students continue the activity in pairs. Remind them that this part is to practice speaking, not writing.

Evaluation 1   7–10 mins. ■■■

Ask students to write sentences about Luis on the board and go over them as a class.

What Does He Look Like?

GOAL ▶ Describe people

A INTERPRET Look at Sayed's license. Complete the sentences.

Height
5'11" = five feet, eleven inches
When speaking, we usually say:
    She's five foot eleven.
    She's five-eleven.
6' = six feet
    He's six feet (tall).

1. Sayed is _____five-eleven_____. (height)

2. He is _____175_____ pounds.

3. His hair is _____black_____.

4. His eyes are _____brown_____.

5. He is _____(answer will vary)_____ years old.

6. His address is _____8220_____ State Street.

His / Her
Rolando
His hair is brown.
His eyes are brown.

Yan
Her hair is black.
Her eyes are brown.

B Complete the sentences about Elena. Then take turns describing Luis with a partner.

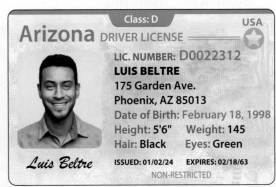

(height) 1. Elena is _____five-two / five foot two_____.

(weight) 2. She is _____120_____ pounds.

(hair) 3. Her _____hair is gray_____.

(eyes) 4. Her _____eyes are blue_____.

C **Study the chart.**

Simple Present: *Have*		
Subject	**Verb**	**Example Sentence**
I / You We / They	have	I **have** black hair. They **have** white hair.
He / She	has	He **has** brown eyes. She **has** blue eyes.

Pronunciation of /v/ 🎧
/v/ have
In English, the /v/ sound is different from the /b/ sound.
He is **very** tall.
Berries are my favorite fruit.

D **CLASSIFY** **Listen and complete the chart.** 🎧

Name	Height	Hair	Eyes	Age
1. Roberto	5'11"	brown	brown	43
2. Fabiana	5'1"	black	brown	32
3. Maha	5'8"	brown	brown	28
4. Alan	5'9"	red	green	55

E **Read and listen to the conversation.** 🎧

Student A: What does <u>Roberto</u> look like?

Student B: <u>He</u> has <u>brown</u> hair and <u>brown</u> eyes.

Student A: How tall is <u>he</u>?

Student B: <u>He</u> is <u>five</u> foot <u>eleven</u>.

Student A: Thank you.

Coworkers work together on a project.

Presentation 2

15–20 mins. ■■■

Write *have / has* and *am / are / is* on the board as headings for two columns. These words can be problematic when describing people because students may confuse them in similar expressions.

Ask questions about height, hair, eyes, and age. Refer to the licenses on the previous page if students are uncomfortable giving their ages. (Students at this level are not expected to use correct question form, so it isn't necessary to have them ask the questions.) Students will probably answer in short answers and not complete sentences. When they answer, write complete, correct sentences on the board using *have, has, am, are,* and *is*. After you have a good sample of sentences, circle all the verbs. Next, write *height, hair color, eye color,* and *age* as column headings on the board. Ask students to help put the words *am, are, is, have,* and *has* in the correct columns.

C Study the chart.

Go over the chart carefully. Ask students to create additional example sentences.

Pronunciation /v/ 🎧

Review the pronunciation of *have* while going over the grammar chart. Point out the information in the pronunciation note and play the audio. A good way to help students with the /v/ sound is to have them bite their lower lip. Make sure they don't hide their upper teeth with their upper lip. Ask them to smile and bring the corners of their mouths out and up, exposing their teeth.

Another way to teach this sound is to contrast it with /f/, which most students will be able to produce. Ask them to pronounce words that begin with /f/. Then show them how to make the /f/ voiced by activating the voice box.

Listening Script

To make the /v/ sound, touch your teeth to your bottom lip and push air out.
/v/ /v/ /v/ have
In English, the /v/ sound is different from the /b/ sound.
He is very tall.
Berries are my favorite fruit.
/v/ very, /b/ berry

Practice 2

15–20 mins. ■■■

The listening that follows is the first of a two-part practice. First, the vocabulary is reinforced in the audio. Then students will use *has* to describe people in a conversation.

Workplace Focus

Exercise D: Collect and organize information.

D CLASSIFY Listen and complete the chart. 🎧

Play the audio several times so students have an opportunity to hear all the information and complete the chart. Allow students to compare with a partner before checking the answers. Play the audio again for students to confirm their answers.

Listening Script

1. **Antonio:** *Excuse me. I am looking for my son, Roberto Garcia.*
   Mary: *I don't think I know him. What does he look like?*
   Antonio: *He has brown hair and brown eyes.*
   Mary: *And his height . . . how tall is he?*
   Antonio: *He is five foot eleven. And he is 43 years old.*
   Mary: *Oh, I think he's in Room 114.*
   Antonio: *Thanks!*
2. **Ana:** *Do you see my friend Fabiana over there?*
   Brad: *No, I don't see her.*
   Ana: *She has black hair and brown eyes. She's about five-one.*
   Brad: *Oh, I see her now. Is she around 30 years old?*
   Ana: *She is actually 32.*
3. **Mary:** *Excuse me. I am looking for Maha Khan. She is tall, maybe five-eight. She has brown hair and brown eyes. She is 28 years old. Have you seen her?*
   Brad: *No, sorry. I haven't seen her.*
4. **Alan:** *My name is Alan.*
   Mary: *Please describe yourself.*
   Alan: *I am five foot nine. I have red hair and green eyes. I am 55 years old.*

E Read and listen to the conversation. 🎧

Tell students to read as they listen. Play the audio. Play the audio again, pausing for students to repeat.

F **Practice the conversation in E with a partner. Then make new conversations with the information from D.**

Model both stages of this activity with students. Then put them in pairs to complete the activity. Monitor as they work, providing help as needed.

Evaluation 2   5–7 mins. ■■

Ask students to perform their conversations in front of the class.

Presentation 3   10–15 mins. ■■■

G **Look at the picture and read the words.**

Integrate the grammar from **C** as you go over the words. Flip through the book and ask students to find examples of different hairstyles and hair colors. Say: *He has blond hair* instead of *He is blond* to avoid confusion.

Draw students' attention to the note on adjectives and provide some additional examples from the picture in **G**. Then describe your own hair or a few students' hairstyles and point out that the color always goes right before the noun.

Practice 3   10–15 mins. ■

H **Work with a partner. Describe the people in the photo on the previous page.**

Have students look at the photo and as a class, describe one of the people. Put students in pairs to continue the descriptions. If time allows, encourage students to write down one of their descriptions.

I **With your partner, take turns describing the people in G and guessing who.**

Go over the example with the class. Then model the activity by describing a different person from **G** for students to guess. Monitor as students carry out the activity in pairs and provide help as needed.

Evaluation 3   7–10 mins. ■

Ask several students to describe one of the people in the photo on the previous page or from **G** for the class to guess.

Application   5–7 mins. ■■■

J **APPLY** **Complete the license with your information.**

Have students describe themselves by completing the driver's license. If time permits, have students share some of their information with a partner. They should omit what they don't feel comfortable sharing or use imaginary information. Then have pairs combine to form groups of four. Each student should share their partner's information with the other pair, using *his* or *her*.

Instructor's Notes

_____

_____

_____

_____

_____

_____

_____

_____

_____

_____

_____

_____

_____

_____

_____

_____

_____

F Practice the conversation in **E** with a partner. Then make new conversations with the information from **D**.

G Look at the picture and read the words.

John	Nadia	Luisa	Vincent	Roseline

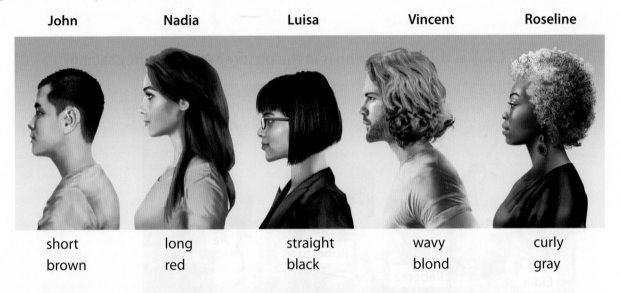

short	long	straight	wavy	curly
brown	red	black	blond	gray

H Work with a partner. Describe the people in the photo on the previous page.

I With your partner, take turns describing the people in **G** and guessing who.

Adjectives

Adjectives can go before nouns.
Always say colors just before the noun.

            1   2
Ana has **straight black** hair.

EXAMPLE: **Student A:** She has short straight hair. Who is she?
                    Student B: Luisa.

J APPLY Complete the license with your information. Answers will vary.

DRIVER LICENSE

Your Photo Here

Name:_____

Date of birth:_____

Height:_____ Weight:_____

Hair:_____ Eyes:_____

Address:_____

City:_____

State:_____ Zip Code:_____

Roberto's Family

GOAL ▶ Describe family relationships

A **PREDICT** Look at the picture. Who is in the picture? What are they saying?

B Listen to the conversation. 🎧

Roberto: Jie, this is my mother, my father, and my sister.

Rebecca: Nice to meet you, Jie. Where are you from?

Jie: Nice to meet you too! I'm from China.

Rebecca: Do your parents live here in the United States?

Jie: No. Right now they live in China.

C Match the words to the pictures of the people from **A**.

brother	friend	parents	sister	son

1. brother   sister

2. son   parents

3. friend   friend

At-a-Glance Prep

Goal: Describe family relationships
Grammar: The verb *be*
Academic Strategies: Predicting, focused listening
Vocabulary: Family

Agenda

☐ Review describing people.
☐ Describe family relationships.
☐ Learn family vocabulary.
☐ Listen for vocabulary in family trees.
☐ Ask questions about families.
☐ Make a family tree.

Resources

Heinle Picture Dictionary: Family, pages 26–27

Pacing

■ 1.5 hour classes   ■ 2.5 hour classes
■ 3+ hour classes

Standards Correlations

CASAS: 0.1.2, 0.1.5
CCRS: L1, L3, SL1, SL3, SLK2
ELPS:

S2: Participate in level-appropriate oral and written exchanges of information, ideas, and analyses, in various social and academic contexts, responding to peer, audience, or reader comments and questions.

S10: Demonstrate command of the conventions of standard English to communicate in level-appropriate speech and writing.

Warm-up and Review   10–12 mins. ■■■

Use a student volunteer or show a picture of a person and have the class describe them. Elicit the different colors for eyes, and the colors and types of hair, and have students spell them for you to write on the board.

Introduction   5–7 mins. ■■■

Write *brother* and *sister* on the board. Ask individual students how many brothers and sisters they have. Count the total number of brothers and sisters in the class, including yours. State the goal: *Today, we will learn how to describe family relationships.*

Presentation 1   15–20 mins. ■■■

Draw a family tree on the board. Start with your parents. Draw a line from the parents to a child

(you). Make sure you present *parents* as one of the vocabulary words. Add brothers and sisters. Ask for help describing your family relationships to see what vocabulary students might already know. You may choose to add grandchildren. You are demonstrating what you hope students will be able to do by the end of class, so include vocabulary that you think will be most useful.

A PREDICT   Look at the picture. Who is in the picture? What are they saying?

Look at the picture together and elicit descriptions of the people. For example: *She has long, black hair.* Ask: *How old / tall is he / she?* and encourage students to guess heights and ages. Next, ask the questions in the direction line.

B   Listen to the conversation.

Play the audio with books closed. Have students just listen. Play the audio a second time and ask students to write down any family vocabulary they hear. Play the audio a third time. This time, have students follow along in their books and underline the family vocabulary.

BEST PRACTICE
Eliciting Information

Whenever possible, we suggest that you elicit as much information from students as they can give. By doing this, you will create a student-centered classroom. This method will also help you assess what students already know. Students are much more engaged when they are actively contributing to the lesson instead of passively listening to the teacher.

Practice 1   3–10 mins. ■■■

C   Match the words to the pictures of the people from A.

Have students complete the activity individually, then compare with a partner. Extend this activity by writing sentences on the board. Ask students to complete them in their notebooks. For example:

Roberto is Lidia's brother. Lidia is _____.

Evaluation 1   5 mins. ■■■

Walk around and check students' work.

Presentation 2

10–15 mins. ■■■

D Discuss the words with your classmates and teacher.

Reinforce what students have already learned by using the family tree you created on the board to go over the new vocabulary. Elicit / Explain what the prefix *grand-* means and how it is combined with other family words. It might be helpful to point out that *child* and *parent* are gender neutral.

Go over the picture and the family tree in **E** with students. Discuss them using the target vocabulary in the box. Without listening, students will not know the relationships for sure. Encourage them to guess and predict what the audio will say.

BEST PRACTICE

Predicting

An important part of listening is anticipating what will be heard. Predicting is an academic skill that students will begin to develop at this level. Predicting will help students focus on what they are listening for and be more prepared to pick out the target information.

Workplace Focus

Exercise E: Collect and organize information; Combine ideas and information.

Practice 2

5–7 mins. ■■

E PREDICT Look at the picture and write the names on the family tree. Then listen to check your answers. 🎧

Before students listen, have the class predict names to go on each line of the family tree by looking at the picture. Play the audio twice. Then have students compare answers with a partner. Play the audio again and check answers as a class.

Listening Script

My name is Roberto Garcia. I am very happily married. My wife's name is Silvia. This is a picture of my family. The older man and woman in the picture are my parents. My mother's name is Rebecca and my father's name is Antonio. I have one sister, Lidia, and one brother, Julio. The girl and the boy are my children, Carla and Juan.

Evaluation 2

3 mins. ■■

Ask questions such as: *Who is Silvia?* Students might answer: *She is Roberto's wife.*

Instructor's Notes

_____

_____

_____

_____

_____

_____

_____

_____

_____

_____

_____

_____

_____

_____

_____

_____

_____

_____

_____

_____

D **Discuss the words with your classmates and teacher.**

father	son	brother	grandson	uncle
mother	daughter	sister	granddaughter	aunt
parent(s)	husband	grandfather	grandparent(s)	nephew
child/children	wife	grandmother	grandchild(ren)	niece

E **PREDICT** **Look at the picture and write the names on the family tree. Then listen to check your answers.** Placement of answers may vary.

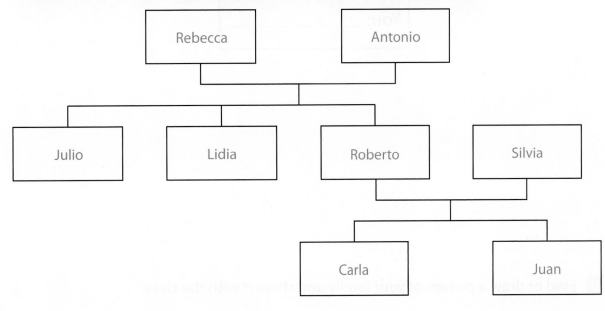

F Practice the conversation with a partner. Then make new conversations using the information about Roberto's family from **E**.

Student A: Who is Silvia?

Student B: Silvia is Roberto's wife. Who are Antonio and Rebecca?

Student A: They are Roberto's parents.

Be
He **is** Roberto's brother.
They **are** Roberto's children.

G **CREATE** Complete the family tree for your family. Use the family tree from **E** as a model. Answers will vary.

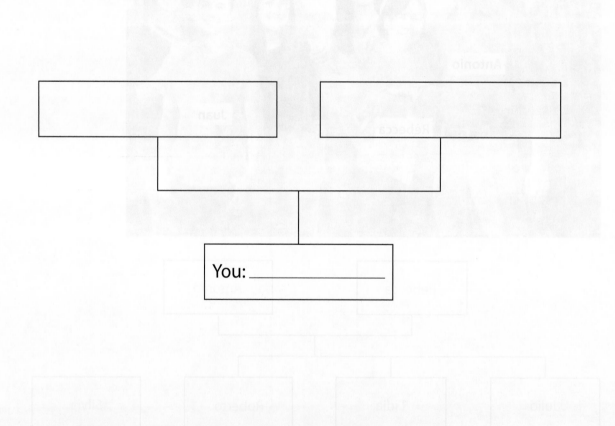

You: _____

H Find or draw a picture of your family and share it with the class.

Presentation 3
10–15 mins. ■■■

On the board, write: *Who is . . . ?* Help students understand what kind of information is required in response to a question that begins with this phrase. Review the singular and plural forms of the verb *be* in the note.

Practice 3
5–7 mins. ■

F Practice the conversation with a partner. Then make new conversations using the information about Roberto's family from E.

Read the conversation and have students repeat. Model the conversation with a student. Then model a new conversation with the student, asking about a different person in Roberto's family. Remind students that they need to go back to the picture and family tree in **E**. Make sure students use good intonation in their practice.

> **Pronunciation   Prominence**
>
> Show students which words get emphasis in a particular sentence. Usually, the question word will receive emphasis. Also, the names of people get more emphasis than the verb *be*, which gets no emphasis.

Evaluation 3
2 mins. ■

Observe students as they perform the conversations about Roberto's family.

Application
5–7 mins. ■■■

Workplace Focus
Exercise G: Collect and organize information; Combine ideas and information.

G CREATE Complete the family tree for your family. Use the family tree from E as a model.

Show students how it is possible for them to add to the family tree above (grandparents), to the sides (siblings), and below (children and grandchildren). Ask students to describe their family to a partner or to a group after they complete their family trees.

H Find or draw a picture of your family and share it with the class.

Show a picture of your family and describe them to the class. For example: *This is my mother, Elise.*

This is . . ., etc. Elicit and write on the board: *This is my . . .* Then have students show their pictures and describe their families. Depending on the size of your class, this can be done as a whole-class activity or in small groups or pairs.

As an extension, students can describe each person in their family. Again, model this with your own family picture. (*My brother is 6 foot three. He has gray hair and blue eyes.*) Elicit the vocabulary for describing people and have students write it on the board before they begin.

Instructor's Notes

_____

_____

_____

_____

_____

_____

_____

_____

_____

_____

_____

_____

_____

_____

At-a-Glance Prep

Goal: Express preferences
Grammar: Simple present: *like*
Academic Strategies: Interpreting Venn diagrams, making comparisons
Vocabulary: Entertainment

Agenda

☐ Write a paragraph about family.
☐ Listen to things people like.
☐ Use *like*.
☐ Read about people's likes.
☐ Complete a Venn diagram.

Resources

Heinle Picture Dictionary: Daily Activities, pages 34–35

Pacing

■ 1.5 hour classes   ■ 2.5 hour classes
■ 3+ hour classes

Standards Correlations

CASAS: 0.1.4, 0.1.5, 0.2.4
CCRS: L1, L2, L3, SL1, SL3, W3
ELPS:

S2: Participate in level-appropriate oral and written exchanges of information, ideas, and analyses, in various social and academic contexts, responding to peer, audience, or reader comments and questions.

S9: Create clear and coherent level-appropriate speech and text.

S10: Demonstrate command of the conventions of standard English to communicate in level-appropriate speech and writing.

Warm-up and Review   15–20 mins. ■■■

Write a paragraph on the board about your family. Keep it simple and short. This will be a model for students. It might look something like this:

My Family
My name is Jim Smith. My parents are John and Judy. I have three brothers. I love my family.

Ask students to copy the paragraph, or if you feel they can do it, ask them to rewrite the paragraph with their own personal information.

Introduction   2 mins. ■■■

Write the word *like* on the board. Mention something that you like. Ask students what they like. Make a list on the board. State the goal: *Today, we will learn how to express preferences.*

Presentation 1   10–12 mins. ■■■

Ask students to open their books and go over the meaning of each new vocabulary item in **A**. Draw a Venn diagram on the board. Make a list of the items on the page you like. Ask a student for the items they like. Record the information in the Venn diagram. You can also have students draw a Venn diagram in their notebooks so they can do the activity along with you. Use this activity to prepare students for the focused listening.

Practice 1   10–20 mins. ■■■

A **Listen. Put an *R* by things Roberto likes and an *S* by things Silvia likes. Roberto and Silvia both like some of them.**

Play the audio twice. Then have students compare answers with a partner. Play the audio again and check answers as a class. Play the audio again as needed.

Listening Script

Roberto and Silvia are happily married. Roberto likes movies, gaming, and books. Silvia likes parks, restaurants, and music. They both like sports, social media, and TV.

This activity can be expanded by asking students to complete a Venn diagram for Roberto and Silvia.

Workplace Focus

Exercise B: Collect and organize information.

B **Complete the sentences.**

Have students complete this activity individually.

Evaluation 1   7–10 mins. ■■■

Ask volunteers to write their completed sentences on the board.

I Like Sports and Music

GOAL ▶ Express preferences

A Listen. Put an *R* by things Roberto likes and an *S* by things Silvia likes. Roberto and Silvia both like some of them. 🎧

1. movies _____ R

2. music _____ S

3. sports _____ R S

4. gaming _____ R

5. social media _____ R S

6. TV _____ R S

7. books _____ R

8. restaurants _____ S

9. parks _____ S

B Complete the sentences. Order of answers may vary.

1. Roberto likes _____ movies _____.

2. Roberto likes _____ gaming _____.

3. Roberto likes _____ books _____.

4. Silvia likes _____ music _____.

5. Silvia likes _____ restaurants _____.

6. Silvia likes _____ parks _____.

7. They both like _____ sports _____.

8. They both like _____ social media _____.

9. They both like _____ TV _____.

C Study the chart.

Simple Present: *Like*			
Subject	**Verb**	**Noun**	**Example Sentence**
I / You We / They	like	social media gaming music books	I **like** social media. You **like** gaming. We **like** music. They **like** books.
He / She	likes	parks restaurants	He **likes** parks. She **likes** restaurants.

D Complete the sentences with *like* or *likes*. Then listen and check your answers. 🎧

1. Antonio _____likes_____ social media.

2. Rebecca _____likes_____ parks.

3. Antonio and Rebecca _____like_____ movies.

4. We _____like_____ gaming.

5. The students _____like_____ books.

6. I _____like_____ music.

7. My mother _____likes_____ restaurants.

8. My brother _____likes_____ sports.

E **INTERPRET** Read the Venn diagram about Roberto's children.

Carla likes ...   **Carla and Juan like ...**   **Juan likes ...**

restaurants   movies   sports

books   music   social media

_____   _____   _____

_____   _____   _____

Presentation 2

C Study the chart.

As you go over the chart, show students that other verbs follow the same rule as *like(s)*. Students are only working with *like* in this lesson, but you can use it as an introduction to the simple present. Drill students on the verb forms.

D Complete the sentences with *like* or *likes*. Then listen and check your answers.

Complete the activity as a class. Play the audio for students to check the answers.

E INTERPRET Read the Venn diagram about Roberto's children.

Discuss the Venn diagram. Ask questions with *who*, for example: *Who likes sports? Who likes music?*

BEST PRACTICE

Diagrams

Getting students familiar with common types of diagrams and graphic organizers is useful as they may encounter these in their future academic or professional lives. Be mindful that some students may understand diagrams more intuitively than others, so it is important to clearly explain what is being shown and how the visual elements of the diagram help illustrate the relationship between the information presented. As a form of review or consolidation, this explanation should be elicited as much as possible.

Instructor's Notes

Practice 2

15–20 mins. ■■□

F Read the statements about the Venn diagram in E. Choose *True* or *False*.

Explain the meaning of *true* and *false* by using example sentences from previous lessons, perhaps about physical appearance. (*Roberto has red hair.* = false, *Roberto has brown hair.* = true) Do the first item together and then have students complete the exercise individually. Check answers as a class.

G COMPARE Write sentences about the Venn diagram in E and say them to a partner.

Ask students to write their sentences individually. Then ask them to read their sentences to a partner. Monitor as students work, providing help as needed.

Evaluation 2

7–10 mins. ■■□

Ask for volunteers to write sentences about the Venn diagram on the board.

Presentation 3

5–10 mins. ■■■

Review the grammar chart on the previous page again and drill once more. Point out the different verb forms in the Venn diagram in **H**.

BEST PRACTICE

Grammar Exposure

Students at this level are not always ready to acquire certain grammar points, such as the third person singular in the simple present. While it is wise to expose them to these particular structures, experience suggests that they will not be able to internalize all of it yet. Focus mainly on the goal of the lesson and not on a lengthy discussion about a grammar point. Nevertheless, at times it is necessary to briefly explain a concept if students ask for clarification.

Workplace Focus

Exercise H: Interact appropriately with team members; Interpret and communicate information; Collect and organize information; Complete tasks as assigned;
Exercise I: Interpret and communicate information.

Practice 3

15–20 mins. ■□□

H COMPARE Talk to a partner and complete the diagram. Ask: *What things do you like?*

Model this activity with a student by copying the Venn diagram on the board and completing your likes. Then ask the student: *What things do you like?* Write a couple of answers in the diagram. Have the class help you identify which items go in the middle of the diagram.

Put students in pairs and make sure they understand that they both need to ask the question and complete their diagram with their partner's likes.

Evaluation 3

5 mins. ■□□

Observe as students carry out the activity. Check students' work.

Application

5–7 mins. ■■■

I Introduce your partner to your classmates.

Read the example as a class. Then model the activity by introducing the student you modeled **H** with. Give students time to prepare what they want to say. Remind them they can say: *We both like . . .,* as well as *He / She likes . . .* Provide help as they prepare their introductions. Tell them to refer to the example for help.

Students can introduce their partner in small groups or to the whole class depending on the size of your class.

F Read the statements about the Venn diagram in E. Choose *True* or *False*.

1. Carla likes sports.   True   (False)

2. Carla and Juan like books.   True   (False)

3. Juan likes social media.   (True)   False

4. Carla and Juan like movies.   (True)   False

5. Juan likes restaurants.   True   (False)

G COMPARE Write sentences about the Venn diagram in E and say them to a partner.

1. Carla likes restaurants _____.

2. Carla likes books _____.

3. Carla and Juan like movies _____.

4. Carla and Juan like music _____.

5. Juan likes sports _____.

6. Juan likes social media _____.

H COMPARE Talk to a partner and complete the diagram. Ask: *What things do you like?*
Answers will vary.

I like ...	We both like ...	My partner likes ...
_____	_____	_____
_____	_____	_____
_____	_____	_____
_____	_____	_____
_____	_____	_____
_____	_____	_____

I Introduce your partner to your classmates.

EXAMPLE: This is my friend Faheem. He is interested in many things.
Faheem likes movies and books. He also likes sports and gaming.

When Do You Study?

GOAL ▶ Plan a schedule

A Look at Tuan's schedule. Match the activities to the start times by writing the letters.

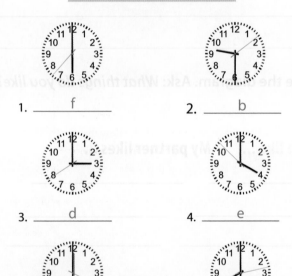

◀ **December** ▶

Su	Mo	Tu	We	Th	Fr	Sa
1	2	3	4	5	6	7
8	9	10	11	12	13	14
15	16	17	18	19	20	21
22	23	24	25	26	27	28
29	30	31				

▼ My Calendars

☑ Personal
☑ School
☑ Work

1. ___f___   2. ___b___

3. ___d___   4. ___e___

5. ___c___   6. ___a___

DECEMBER 12		
8 a.m.	Exercise	a.
9 a.m.		
10 a.m.	Practice English in class	b.
11 a.m.		
12 p.m.	Eat lunch with Omar	c.
1 p.m.		
2 p.m.		
3 p.m.	Watch kids at soccer practice	d.
4 p.m.	Do homework	e.
5 p.m.		
6 p.m.	Work	f.
7 p.m.		
8 p.m.		
9 p.m.		

B Read. Look at the online calendar in **A** and complete the paragraph. 🎧 **Life** ONLINE

Online calendars can help you stay organized and remember the things you need to do. You can use online calendars to see activities in different parts of your life. Tuan has three different calendars: ___Personal___, ___School___, and ___Work___.

At-a-Glance Prep

Goal: Plan a schedule
Grammar: Prepositions of time: *from . . . to, at*
Academic Strategies: Focused listening, creating a schedule
Vocabulary: Clock times, routine activities

Agenda

☐ Review *like* in a corners activity.

☐ Talk about schedules and times.

☐ Listen for information about schedules and times.

☐ Write your own schedule.

☐ Ask about your partner's schedule.

Resources

Heinle Picture Dictionary: Time, pages 4–5; Calendar, pages 6–7

Pacing

■ 1.5 hour classes   ■ 2.5 hour classes
■ 3+ hour classes

Standards Correlations

CASAS: 0.1.2, 0.1.5, 2.3.1, 7.1.2
CCRS: L1, L2, L3, RI1, RI2, SL1, SL3
ELPS:
S10: Demonstrate command of the conventions of standard English to communicate in level-appropriate speech and writing.

Warm-up and Review   10–15 mins. ■■□□

Do a corners activity, explained below, to warm students up as well as to review Lesson 4. Take a class poll and ask students what they like to do in their free time based on the vocabulary they learned in the previous lesson. From the list, categorize the items into four groups. For example, you may choose outdoor activities, such as sports, or indoor activities, such as reading.

Next, assign a category to each corner of the room. Ask students to choose a corner and go there. Then ask students to share with their new group what, specifically, they like to do in that category. To facilitate this activity, write: *What do you like?* on the board.

In a virtual class, this could be done by having students identify which category they like best in the chat and then placing students in breakout rooms by category to discuss further.

Introduction   5–7 mins. ■■■□

With their books closed, ask students in groups to compile a list of what makes a good student. Provide vocabulary as needed to help students express their ideas. Then discuss the lists with the class. If students didn't think of coming to school every day, add this. Suggest that a schedule will help them learn English. State the goal: *Today, we will learn how to plan a schedule.*

Presentation 1   15–20 mins. ■■■□

Tell students what you do every day and write your schedule on the board. Include times. This schedule will be referred to throughout the entire lesson. Point to the clock in the room and ask students what it is. Then do the same with a watch so students understand that we use two different words in English. Write *clock* and *watch* on the board.

Write on the board: *When do we practice English?* Ask the question and see what students say. Write on the board: *We practice English in class from (the starting time) to (the ending time).*

A Look at Tuan's schedule. Match the activities to the start times by writing the letters.

Point out the calendar with the month and the highlighted day, as well as the schedule for that day. Go over the clocks and elicit / provide the times. Write each one on the board. Go through the activities in the schedule. You can have students mime each one to check their understanding. Point out the color coding for the three different calendars. Then have students complete the activity with a partner. Check answers as a class.

Ask students if any of them use a calendar on their phone or computer. You can also elicit or discuss some benefits of using an online calendar.

Practice 1   7–10 mins. ■■■□

B Read. Look at the online calendar in A and complete the paragraph.

Ask students to read and complete the paragraph. Play the audio for students to check their answers. Play the audio again as needed.

C Complete the sentences.

Point out the information about prepositions of time in the note. Then have students complete the sentences individually. Have them compare with a partner before checking as a class.

Evaluation 1
5–7 mins. ■■■□

Ask students to practice the sentences with a partner. Observe as they practice. Write these questions on the board and ask students:
When does Tuan exercise?
When does he practice English in class?
When does he do homework?
When does he work?

Workplace Focus

Exercise D: Interpret and communicate information; Exercise E: Collect and organize information.

Presentation 2
15–20 mins. ■■■□

Refer back to your personal schedule that you developed on the board. Ask students questions about it. For example: *When do I leave for work?*

D Look at the clocks. Write the times.

Do this activity as a class. Then ask students to briefly discuss in groups how long they think Lidia eats breakfast for. Write on the board: *Lidia eats breakfast from 6:45 to _____.* Have the groups report and get a class consensus. Complete the sentence on the board. Do the same for the other activities Lidia does.

E Write Lidia's schedule.

Do this activity as a class. Prepare students for the focused listening activity they will do in **F** by doing a quick practice with times in sentences. For example, you might say: *I eat lunch from 12:30 to 1:00.*

Practice 2
10–15 mins. ■■□□

F Listen and write Aisha's schedule. 🎧

Go over the activities in Aisha's schedule. Say them so students are aware of the pronunciation. Remind students that they don't need to understand everything. They should focus on the activities and the times.

Tell students to just listen first and play the audio. Play the audio several more times, pausing for students to finish writing. See Best Practice: Focused Listening for more ideas on how to make listening texts accessible for students at this level.

Listening Script

Aisha is a good student. She wants to learn English so she can get a better job. She has a regular schedule and follows it every day. She eats breakfast every morning from 6:00 to 6:30. She usually eats cereal, but sometimes she has eggs. Directly after she eats, she does her homework from 6:30 to 7:00. Then she usually reads in English from 7:00 to 7:15. After that, she writes in her journal from 7:15 to 7:45. She practices English in class from 8:30 to 10:30 a.m. Monday through Friday.

BEST PRACTICE
Focused Listening

Stand Out includes many exercises with audio at the beginning levels to improve students' developing listening skills. It is imperative that students don't get discouraged because most of the listening is in context. Stress to students that the tasks will help them begin to understand every word, but for now, completing the tasks by picking out the target information is sufficient.

In listening activities like the one in **F**, it is a good idea to play the audio once and ask students to listen for the information, but to refrain from writing anything down. At this level, when students are writing, many of them will not be able to listen to the information coming up. So, it is a good strategy to play the audio in five parts, isolating the five pieces of information. You may need to play the audio several times to help students hear what the task requires.

C Complete the sentences.

1. Tuan exercises from ___8:00___ to ___9:00___.

2. He practices English in class from ___9:30___ to ___11:30___.

3. He does homework from ___4:00___ to ___5:00___.

4. He works from ___6:00___ to ___10:00___.

Prepositions of Time

from 8:00 **to** 9:00
(start)   (finish)

at 10:00 a.m.

D Look at the clocks. Write the times.

1. Lidia eats breakfast at ___6:45___.

2. Lidia eats lunch at ___1:15___.

3. Lidia practices English in class at ___2:25___.

4. Lidia writes in a journal at ___7:50___.

E Write Lidia's schedule.

Time	Activity
6:45	She eats breakfast.
1:15	She eats lunch.
2:25	She practices English in class.
7:50	She writes in a journal.

F Listen and write Aisha's schedule. 🎧

Start Time	End Time	Activity
6:00	6:30	Aisha eats breakfast.
6:30	7:00	Aisha does homework.
7:00	7:15	Aisha reads in English.
7:15	7:45	Aisha writes in a journal.
8:30	10:30	Aisha practices English in class.

G Write sentences about Aisha's schedule.

1. Aisha _____ eats breakfast _____ from ___ 6:00 ___ to ___ 6:30 ___.
2. Aisha _____ does homework _____ from ___ 6:30 ___ to ___ 7:00 ___.
3. Aisha _____ reads in English _____ from ___ 7:00 ___ to ___ 7:15 ___.
4. Aisha _____ writes in a journal _____ from ___ 7:15 ___ to ___ 7:45 ___.
5. Aisha _____ practices English in class _____ from ___ 8:30 ___ to ___ 10:30 ___.

H CREATE Add your daily activities to the schedule. Use A as a model. Answers will vary.

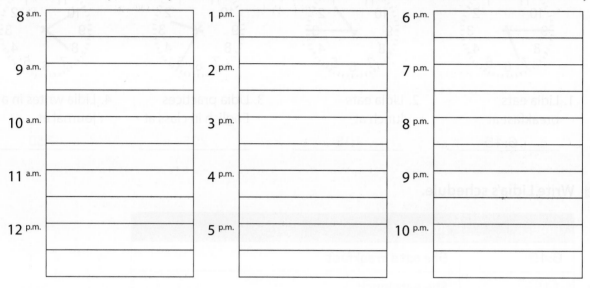

I Talk to a partner about their activities and add them to the schedule. Ask: *When do you . . . ?* Answers will vary.

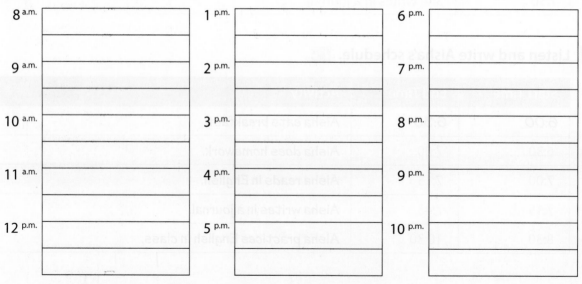

J Report the information about your partner to a group.

G Write sentences about Aisha's schedule.

Have students complete this activity individually. Remind them to refer back to **F** as needed.

Evaluation 2   7–10 mins. ■■

Ask volunteers to write the sentences on the board so that students can check their answers.

Presentation 3   7–10 mins. ■■■

Write *morning, afternoon,* and *night* across the board. Then, under each one, write *from* _____ *to* _____. Ask students to come up to the board and write the times they believe go with each word.

Some cultures consider the starting time of morning, afternoon, and night differently. For example, many people from Spanish-speaking countries may consider 7:00 p.m. as the afternoon and translate it as *la tarde*. Elicit students' opinions and teach them the standard for the U.S.

Look back at your personal schedule on the board. Ask students what you do in the morning, in the afternoon, and at night. Show them that they can also say *in the evening*.

Practice 3   10–15 mins. ■

H CREATE Add your daily activities to the schedule. Use A as a model.

Go over the times in the schedule and ask a few students: *What do you do at (8:00)?* Have students work individually to complete the chart.

Evaluation 3   5–7 mins. ■

Check students' information. Ask them questions such as: *What do you do in the morning?*

Workplace Focus

Exercise I: Collect and organize information; Complete tasks as assigned; Interact appropriately with team members;
Exercise J: Interpret and communicate information.

Application   10–15 mins. ■■■

I Talk to a partner about their activities and add them to the schedule. Ask: *When do you . . . ?*

Model the activity by asking a student about two or three activities and writing them in the schedule in your book (or copy the schedule on the board and write them there). Put students in pairs to carry out the activity. Make sure they ask for and listen to the information from their partner and do not merely copy from their partner's book. Monitor and model the question again for students as needed.

J Report the information about your partner to a group.

Have students look at the sentences about Aisha's schedule in **G** again. Then model the activity by reporting the schedule from the student you modeled **I** with. Assign students to groups of four to carry out the activity. Monitor and provide help as needed.

Instructor's Notes

_____
_____
_____
_____
_____
_____
_____
_____
_____
_____
_____
_____
_____
_____
_____
_____

At-a-Glance Prep

Goal: Reflect on career options

Agenda

- ☐ Learn about jobs and career fields.
- ☐ Reflect on work preferences.
- ☐ Interpret a bar graph about photographers' pay.
- ☐ Read about job requirements for photographers.
- ☐ Search for jobs that interest you.

Pacing

- ■ 1.5 hour classes ■ 2.5 hour classes
- ■ 3+ hour classes

Standards Correlations

CASAS: 0.1.2, 0.1.5, 4.1.3, 4.1.8

CCRS: L1, L2, L3, RI1, RI2, RI3, SL1, SL3, SLK2, W1, W3

ELPS:

S5: Conduct research and evaluate and communicate findings to answer questions or solve problems.

S9: Create clear and coherent level-appropriate speech and text.

In this lesson, students are introduced to the concept of a career field, the larger category that contains multiple of the 16 National Career Clusters by the U.S. Department of Labor. Students are asked to match jobs to the appropriate fields and consider which fields interest them most. They are then presented with information on photographer careers, part of the art and communication field. They will interpret data on pay rates and read about job requirements. Throughout the series, careers from a variety of clusters will be introduced, and students will study and research them.

Warm-up and Review   10–15 mins. ■■■

Write *Jobs* on the board and have students help you to brainstorm different jobs. Write their ideas on the board. If necessary, get them started by writing *teacher*. Explain that in this unit they learned how to give personal information and plan a schedule, both of which are useful when looking for a job. Introduce the concept of a career field by saying: *I am a teacher. I work in the field of education.*

Introduction   5–10 mins. ■■■

Ask students about their jobs. Expect that some students won't be working. They may be homemakers or may be full-time students. Mention that *homemaker* and *student* are possible answers to the question *What do you do?* Tell them that throughout *Stand Out*, they will investigate many job possibilities. Write the goal on the board: *Today we will reflect on career options.* Provide vocabulary support for *reflect* and *options* as needed.

Presentation 1   10–15 mins. ■■■

A **Listen and repeat the job titles.**

Have students look at the photos and share any words or ideas related to each job that they know, such as: *camera, wood, medicine, food,* or *restaurant.* Write them on the board.

Play the audio. Ask students for other words they hear related to each job. Play the audio again. Say the jobs and have students repeat them.

Listening Script

a. *photographer: A photographer takes pictures.*
b. *carpenter: A carpenter makes things out of wood.*
c. *pharmacist: A pharmacist prepares medications.*
d. *chef: A chef prepares meals at a restaurant.*
e. *customer service representative: A customer service representative helps customers.*
f. *pest control worker: A pest control worker sprays insecticide.*

Practice 1   20–25 mins. ■■■

B **CLASSIFY Write the letters from A in the chart to match the jobs to the fields. Look up words you don't know or ask your teacher.**

Have students look at the chart. Elicit what the term *career fields* refers to. Direct them to online dictionaries or provide dictionaries in the classroom to look up the new words. After they complete the activity, have students compare answers with a partner.

See Best Practice: Dictionary Skills on the following page for suggestions on building effective dictionary skills.

Explore the Workforce

GOAL ▶ Reflect on career options

A **Listen and repeat the job titles.** 🎧

a. photographer

b. carpenter

c. pharmacist

d. chef

e. customer service
representative

f. pest control worker

B **CLASSIFY** Write the letters from **A** in the chart to match the jobs to the fields. Look up words you don't know or ask your teacher.

CAREER FIELDS					
Health	Art and Communication	Human Services	Natural Resources	Business	Industry
doctor	actor	social worker	fisher	administrative assistant	construction worker
nurse	dancer	food service manager	farmer	office manager	machine repairperson
dentist	graphic designer	tutor	conservationist	accountant	auto mechanic
c	**a**	d	f	e	b

C Work in a group. Take turns telling the group what career field you like.

> EXAMPLE: **Student A:** I like art and communication. What do you like?
>
> **Student B:** I like business.

D Study the jobs with your classmates and teacher. Then complete the chart.

electrician	home health aide	teacher
environmental scientist	salesperson	writer

Field	Job
Health	home health aide
Art and Communication	writer
Human Services	teacher
Natural Resources	environmental scientist
Business	salesperson
Industry	electrician

E **REFLECT** Check (✓) your work preferences. Then share with a partner. Answers will vary.

☐ I like to work outside.

☐ I like to work with my hands.

☐ I like to work alone.

☐ I like to work with others.

☐ I like to make new things.

☐ I like to think of new ideas.

☐ I like to help others.

☐ I like to work at a desk.

☐ I like to work at the same time every day.

☐ I like to solve problems.

F **REFLECT** Write true sentences about yourself. Use the words below. Answers will vary.

creative	hardworking	motivated
friendly	honest	organized

I am _____ .

I _____ .

_____ .

C Work in a group. Take turns telling the group what career field you like.

Model the conversation with a student. Then have two students model it. Put students in pairs to talk about their career field preferences. Monitor and provide help as needed. For additional practice, have students switch partners.

D Study the jobs with your classmates and teacher. Then complete the chart.

Go over the jobs together. Encourage students to look up the ones that nobody can explain or give an example for. Have students work with a partner to complete the chart. Call on different pairs to share one of their answers. Copy the chart on the board and add the jobs.

Evaluation 1   5–10 mins. ■■■

Go over the answers to **D** as a class. Then ask students to suggest other jobs for each field.

Presentation 2   10–15 mins. ■■■

E REFLECT Check (✓) your work preferences. Then share with a partner.

Elicit when we use *like*. Then go over the work preferences together and clarify any vocabulary questions. Share some of your work preferences that would be familiar to students from having worked with you. For example: *work with others, think of new ideas*. Have students check their preferences before they share with a partner.

Practice 2   10–15 mins. ■■□

For shorter classes, have students do **F** for homework.

F REFLECT Write true sentences about yourself. Use the words below.

Write two true sentences about yourself on the board. Elicit or have students look up the meaning of the words you chose. Go over the rest of the words together. Then have students write their sentences individually.

Evaluation 2   10–15 mins. ■■□

Observe students as they work. Make corrections to their sentences in **F** as needed.

BEST PRACTICE
Dictionary Skills

Helping students use a dictionary effectively is important, which is why it is useful to focus specifically on dictionary use at this level. Effective dictionary use will enable students to become more autonomous learners and less dependent on the teacher to explain everything.

Students need to be aware that a word may have more than one meaning; therefore, it is important to always check the context of the word they are looking for so that they can identify which of the meanings is the most appropriate.

They should also be encouraged to check what words are commonly used with the new word.

Instructor's Notes

_____
_____
_____
_____
_____
_____
_____
_____
_____
_____
_____
_____
_____
_____
_____
_____
_____

Presentation 3 · 20–25 mins. ■■■

Tell students that in Lesson 6 of each unit, they will explore different jobs so they have a better idea about what is expected in the workplace in the United States. In this lesson, they will learn about a career as a photographer. Have students look at the photo of a photographer on page 29. Elicit any words related to the career of a photographer that students might know and write them on the board.

G INTERPRET Read the graph. How much do photographers make?

Help students interpret the graph by explaining what each axis tells us. Remember that students may only just be becoming familiar with this kind of graph. Point out the example sentence and have students identify where on the graph they can find this information. Elicit a sentence about entry-level photographers using *between*. Put students in pairs to say the three other sentences about the graph. When they have finished, call on three students to share their sentences. Check them as a class.

Practice 3 · 15–20 mins. ■

Ask students in shorter classes to do Practice 3 for homework.

H Read about the job requirements for photographers and follow the instructions.

Go over the job requirements together, having students use dictionaries as needed to confirm meanings of new concepts. Then have students identify what they are able to do from the list of requirements. Discuss whether anyone in the group is a photographer or would like to be. Have students share anything they would like to learn in the future.

I Go online and search for any jobs that interest you. What is the pay?

Help students get started with their searches. Suggest search engines and search terms they could use. For example, they should include the town, city, or zip code they could work in and the career field or a specific type of job they'd like to have.

Evaluation 3 · 5–10 mins. ■

Monitor as students are carrying out their searches and provide help as needed. When they have found one or two options, have them share the information with a partner. As a group, compare what levels of pay they found and encourage them to share job requirements. If time allows, refer students back to their work preferences in **E** and their descriptions of themselves in **F**, and help them relate the jobs they found to those.

BEST PRACTICE

Online Research

In *Stand Out*, we often encourage online research. While we hope that students will do this on their own regularly to expand their knowledge and to help them learn, we also recognize that some guidance would be advisable in the classroom itself.

Help students access search engines. Show them how to choose the best keywords for their searches. Help them refine searches by using quotation marks and limiting the number of words they use. Show them how they can access information online.

Also, internet searches are frequently part of the application stage in *Stand Out* lessons. Again, we hope students carry this application beyond the classroom, but it is imperative that they do application activities in class as well so their efforts can be monitored and participation of all students can be ensured. In the authors' view, the application is the most important part of the lesson.

See the Life Online Video after Unit 4, titled *Searching for Answers*, for more tips on effective use of search engines.

G INTERPRET Read the graph. How much do photographers make?

EXAMPLE: Student photographers make **between** $50 and $100 an hour.

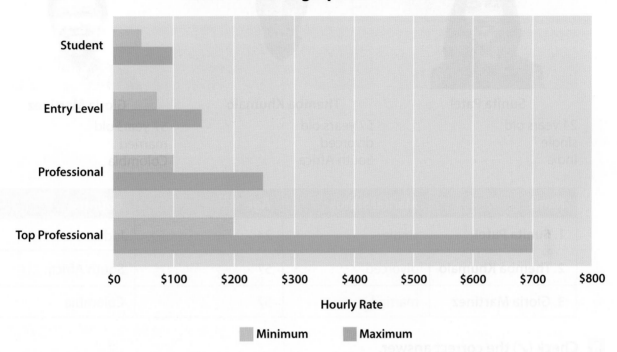

Rates for Photographers in the United States

(Hourly Rate axis: $0 $100 $200 $300 $400 $500 $600 $700 $800)

Categories: Student, Entry Level, Professional, Top Professional

Minimum | Maximum

H Read about the job requirements for photographers and follow the instructions.

Answers will vary.

1. Check (✓) the things you can do now.

2. Underline anything you want to learn.

PHOTOGRAPHERS WANTED

Take photos for customers
- work inside and outside
- take photos for families and businesses
- use photography equipment
- talk with customers

Edit photos
- use computer programs

Deliver final product to customers
- deliver photos on time
- use email

Roscoe's Photo Shop: **976-555-3542**

I Go online and search for any jobs that interest you. What is the pay?

Review

A Complete the chart about Sunita, Themba, and Gloria.

Sunita Patel	Themba Khumalo	Gloria Martinez
24 years old	57 years old	57 years old
single	divorced	married
India	South Africa	Colombia

Name	Marital Status	Age	Country
1. Sunita Patel	single	24	India
2. Themba Khumalo	divorced	57	South Africa
3. Gloria Martinez	married	57	Colombia

B Check (✓) the correct answer.

1. My name _____ Sunita.

   ☐ am   ☑ is   ☐ are

2. I _____ from India.

   ☑ am   ☐ is   ☐ are

3. Themba _____ from South Africa.

   ☐ am   ☑ is   ☐ are

4. Themba and Gloria _____ 57 years old.

   ☐ am   ☐ is   ☑ are

5. Sunita and Gloria _____ brown eyes.

   ☐ has   ☑ have   ☐ are

6. Gloria _____ brown hair.

   ☑ has   ☐ have   ☐ is

7. Sunita _____ 24 years old.

   ☐ has   ☐ have   ☑ is

Learner Log	I can ask for and give personal information.
	☐ Yes ☐ No ☐ Maybe

At-a-Glance Prep

Goal: All unit goals
Grammar: All unit grammar
Academic Strategies: Reviewing, evaluating, developing study skills
Vocabulary: All unit vocabulary

Agenda

☐ Discuss unit goals.
☐ Complete the review.
☐ Evaluate and reflect on progress.

Pacing

■ 1.5 hour classes   ■ 2.5 hour classes
■ 3+ hour classes

Standards Correlations

CASAS: 2.3.1, 7.1.2
CCRS: L1, L2, L3, RI1, RI2, W3
ELPS:
S9: Create clear and coherent level-appropriate speech and text.

Warm-up and Review   15–20 mins. ■■■

Ask students to write their schedule on a 3-by-5 index card. Tell them not to put their name on it. Collect the cards and pass them out again to different students. Ask them to find the author of their card by asking questions. Write the questions on the board and demonstrate how to do this activity by practicing with a few students. The questions will be based on the card: *When do you (eat breakfast)? What time do you (eat lunch)?*

Introduction   2 mins. ■■■

Write all the goals from Unit 1 on the board. Show students the first page of the unit and say the six goals. Explain that today they will review the whole unit.

Note: Depending on the length of the term, you may decide to have students do the Practice for homework and then review student work as either the warm-up or another class activity.

Presentation   10–15 mins. ■■■

This will serve as the Presentation for all three pages of the review. Quickly go to the first page of Lessons 1–5. Discuss the goal of each. Ask simple questions to remind students of what they have learned.

Workplace Focus

Exercise A: Collect and organize information.

Practice 1   15–20 mins. ■■■

A Complete the chart about Sunita, Themba, and Gloria.

Elicit sentences about each person to review *He / She is . . .* Then have students complete the chart. Students can work in pairs if you are doing the Review in class.

B Check (✓) the correct answer.

Have students complete the activity individually.

Evaluation 1   15–20 mins. ■■■

Go around the classroom and check on students' progress. Help individuals as needed. If you see consistent errors among several students, interrupt the class and give a mini lesson or review to help students feel comfortable with the concept.

Learner Log   10–15 mins. ■■■

Write *learner log* on the board and explain to students that this is a place where you keep track of what you have learned. Tell them that they will do a learner log at the end of each unit. Point out the log at the bottom of the page.

Have students read the statement at the bottom of the page and show them that they need to check one of the boxes. Have them complete the log. If students answer *no* or *maybe,* encourage them to set themselves a goal to practice. Show them where they can find more practice activities.

BEST PRACTICE

Learner Logs

Learner Logs function to help students in many different ways:

1. They serve as part of the review process.
2. They help students to gain confidence and to document what they have learned. Consequently, students see that they are progressing in their learning.
3. They provide students with a tool that they can use over and over to check and recheck their understanding of the target language. In this way, students become independent learners.

Practice 2   20–25 mins. ■■■

BEST PRACTICE

Recycling / Review

The Review and the Team Project that follows are part of the recycling / review process. Students at this level often need to be reintroduced to concepts to solidify what they have learned. Many concepts are learned and forgotten while learning other new concepts. This is because students learn but are not necessarily ready to acquire language concepts.

Therefore, it is very important to review and to show students how to review on their own. It is also important to recycle the new concepts in different contexts.

C Match the questions and answers.

Have students complete the activity individually. Then have students practice asking and answering the questions with their own information.

D What is the relationship? Complete the sentences.

Elicit / Review family words. Then have students complete the sentences.

E Read the paragraph and complete the family tree. 🎧

Play the audio and tell students to listen as they read. Have students read the text again and complete the family tree.

Evaluation 2   20–25 mins. ■■■

Go around the classroom and check on students' progress. Help individuals as needed. If you see consistent errors among several students, interrupt the class and give a mini lesson or review to help students feel comfortable with the concept.

Learner Log   5-10 mins. ■■■

Have students read the statements and remind them that they need to check one of the boxes for each one. Have them complete the log. If students answer *no* or *maybe*, encourage them to set themselves a goal to practice. Show them where they can find more practice activities.

Instructor's Notes

C **Match the questions and answers.**

___d___ 1. What's your name?

___f___ 2. Where are you from?

___b___ 3. How old are you?

___e___ 4. What is your weight?

___a___ 5. How tall are you?

___c___ 6. Are you married?

a. six-two

b. 28

c. Yes, I am.

d. Ernesto Hernandez

e. 195 pounds

f. El Salvador

D **What is the relationship? Complete the sentences.**

1. Silvia is Juan's mother; Juan is Silvia's _____son_____.

2. Juan is Carla's brother; Carla is Juan's _____sister_____.

3. Roberto is Carla's father; Carla is Roberto's _____daughter_____.

E **Read the paragraph and complete the family tree.** 🎧 Placement of answers may vary.

Agus and Sri are married. They have three children. Dewi is 15, Endang is 17, and Haji is 22. Haji is married. His wife's name is Dian. They have a baby named Siti.

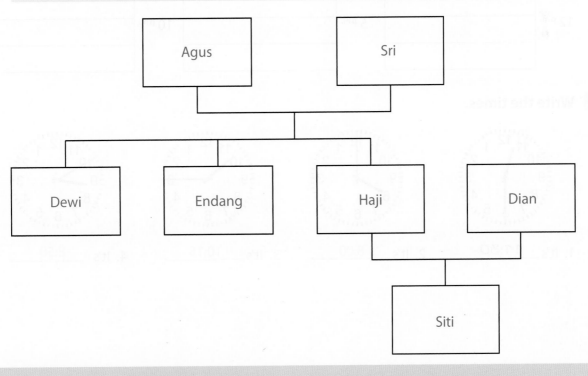

Learner Log	I can describe people.	I can describe family relationships.
	☐ Yes ☐ No ☐ Maybe	☐ Yes ☐ No ☐ Maybe

Review

F **Complete the sentences with the correct form of *like*.**

1. Patty _____likes_____ movies.

2. Omar and Kim _____like_____ sports.

3. We _____like_____ parks.

4. They _____like_____ social media.

5. I _____like_____ books.

6. She _____likes_____ restaurants.

G **Write your schedule for today.** Answers will vary.

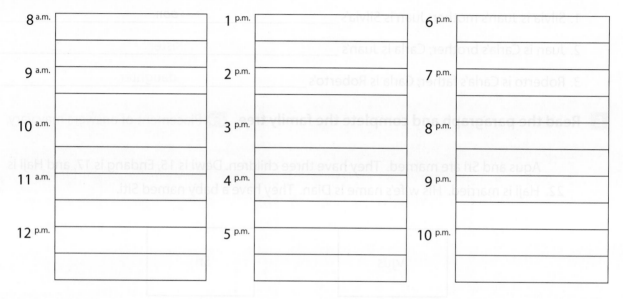

8 a.m.		1 p.m.		6 p.m.	
9 a.m.		2 p.m.		7 p.m.	
10 a.m.		3 p.m.		8 p.m.	
11 a.m.		4 p.m.		9 p.m.	
12 p.m.		5 p.m.		10 p.m.	

H **Write the times.**

1. It's ___11:30___.   2. It's ___8:00___.   3. It's ___10:15___.   4. It's ___8:50___.

Learner Log

I can express preferences.
☐ Yes ☐ No ☐ Maybe

I can plan a schedule.
☐ Yes ☐ No ☐ Maybe

Practice 3

F Complete the sentences with the correct form of *like*.

Tell students some things you like; then elicit examples from several students. Provide new vocabulary for them as needed and write it on the board. Write the name of each student and one or two things they like. Then call on different students to say what other students like using the information on the board. Be sure to elicit examples with *likes* and *like*. For example: *Lin likes restaurants. Katia likes parks. Lin and Katia like social media.* Then have students complete the sentences.

G Write your schedule for today.

Review times by having students say the times in the schedule. Then have students say what they do from 8:00 to 10:00, at 1:00, etc., to review the prepositions of time. Have students complete the schedule. If students are working on the Review in the classroom, have them talk about their schedule with a partner and find any activities / times they have in common. Remind them of the question *When do you . . . ?*

H Write the times.

Have students complete the times individually. Ask them what they do at those times.

Evaluation 3

20–25 mins. ■■■

Go around the room and check on students' progress. Help individuals as needed. If you see consistent errors among several students, interrupt the class and give a mini lesson or review to help students feel comfortable with the concept.

Ask students what their favorite lesson or page in the unit was and why.

Learner Log

5–10 mins. ■■■

Have students read the statements and remind them that they need to check one of the boxes for each one. Have them complete the log. If students answer *no* or *maybe*, encourage them to set themselves a goal to practice. Show them where they can find more practice activities.

Instructor's Notes

_____

_____

_____

_____

_____

_____

_____

_____

_____

_____

_____

_____

_____

_____

_____

_____

_____

_____

_____

_____

_____

_____

_____

_____

_____

_____

Standards Correlations

CASAS: 0.1.2, 0.1.3, 0.2.1, 2.3.1, 4.8.1, 7.1.2

CCRS: L1, L3, RI1, SL3

ELPS:

S3: Speak and write about level-appropriate complex literary and informational texts and topics.

S7: Adapt language choices to purpose, task, and audience when speaking and writing.

S8: Determine the meaning of words and phrases in oral presentations and literary and informational text.

Workplace Focus

Collect and organize information; Complete tasks as assigned; Interact appropriately with team members; Combine ideas and information; Interpret and communicate information; Make decisions; Exercise leadership roles.

Soft Skill: Collaboration
Participation

Explain that collaboration means working with others and that this is a very important skill in the workplace. Projects can be completed more easily and effectively when people collaborate. This is because each person brings different ideas, experiences, and skills to the project. Tell students they will practice this skill by making sure everyone participates and leads one step of the project.

Warm-up and Review   10 mins

Review items in the Review section of the unit and make sure all have recorded their progress in the Learner Log.

Introduction   10 mins.

Tell students that in this project they will design a profile for an imaginary person that will include the person's personal information (name, birth date, age, height, etc.).

Presentation   10–15 mins.

1.   Form a team with four or five students. Choose a position for each member of your team.

Place students in teams of four or five. Have students choose their positions in the group. To do this, go through each step of the project and explain the role of the person who will lead that step. Make sure they understand that although each person has a specific task, they will work together on each step.

The team leader has the responsibility of making sure everyone participates and speaks English.

In **Step 2**, the writer will create the profile, but all team members will contribute information and suggestions. In **Step 3**, the scheduler will create the schedule with help from the rest of the team. Go over the model conversation in **Step 3** to show how each person should lead their particular step. The organizer(s) can lead the discussion of how to present the profile in **Step 4**. In **Step 5**, all students will give the presentation as a team.

Be aware of who volunteers for which position so that, throughout the different units, you can enourage students to try different roles.

Practice / Evaluation / Application   1-2 hours

2.   Create a profile sheet. Complete the profile, including first and last names, birth date, age, home country, marital status, height, hair and eye color, and things the person likes.

If necessary, create a model profile sheet on the board for students to refer to.

3.   Create a weekly schedule for your imaginary person. Think about their work, school, and personal life.

Refer students back to the schedules on pages 26 and 28 for examples if necessary.

4.   Prepare a presentation to tell the class about your person. Practice as a group.

5.   Present your profile to the class.

When students give their presentations, be sure to assign the rest of the class a task to carry out as they listen.

Create a Profile

SOFT SKILL ▶ Collaboration

In this project, you will work together to create a profile for an imaginary person.

1. Form a team with four or five students. Choose a position for each member of your team.

Position	Job Description	Student Name
Student 1: **Team Leader**	Check that everyone speaks English. Check that everyone participates.	
Student 2: **Writer**	Complete the profile with help from the team.	
Student 3: **Scheduler**	Make a schedule with help from the team.	
Students 4/5: **Organizer(s)**	Organize the presentation with help from the team.	

2. Create a profile sheet. Complete the profile, including first and last names, birth date, age, home country, marital status, height, hair and eye color, and things the person likes.

3. Create a weekly schedule for your imaginary person. Think about their work, school, and personal life.

Team Leader: OK, so now we need to make a schedule. Carlos, you're the scheduler, so you can lead this part.

Scheduler: That's right. Thanks! Let's start with work. What is our person's work schedule? Any ideas?

4. Prepare a presentation to tell the class about your person. Practice as a group.

5. Present your profile to the class.

COLLABORATION:
Participation
Every student on your team has a job to do. Make sure each person participates and leads part of the project.

When collaborating with a group, it's important for everyone to participate.

Reading Challenge

About the Photo

This photo shows a man and a dog who look a lot alike. Research has shown that people may be more likely to choose a pet that looks similar to them and that there are even similarities between the personalities of owners and their pets. Some photographers have done series of portraits showing people and their look-alike pets.

Read the title out loud. Tell students they are going to read about how pets sometimes look like their owners. Clarify the meaning of *pet*. Ask questions such as: *Who has a pet? Is it a dog? a cat? What is your pet's name?*

A Check (✓) the information that describes you best today.

Go over the items in the chart. Encourage students to use dictionaries to look up any words they are not familiar with and that nobody in the class can explain. Then have students identify the ones that describe them. Call on students to share their answers.

B Work in a group. Describe yourself to the group.

Point out the example; then describe yourself. Put students into groups of four to share their descriptions. Remind students of the order of adjectives they learned in the unit: hair length → hair style → hair color

C Complete the sentences with the words.

Elicit any ideas students may have about the words before

Reading Challenge

A Check (✓) the information that describes you best today. Answers will vary.

Hair			Expressions
☐ very long hair	☐ curly hair	☐ red hair	☐ calm
☐ long hair	☐ wavy hair	☐ blond hair	☐ happy
☐ short hair	☐ straight hair	☐ brown hair	☐ sad
☐ very short hair		☐ black hair	☐ serious
☐ no hair		☐ other	☐ confused

B Work in a group. Describe yourself to the group.

EXAMPLE: I have long straight black hair and I am happy today.

C Complete the sentences with the words.

beard	calm	expression	owner	personality	pets

1. He is the _____owner_____ of a new car.
2. She is not nervous. She is very _____calm_____.
3. Haroun is fun to spend time with. He has a good _____personality_____.
4. Paula is smiling. She has a happy _____expression_____ on her face.
5. Many people have dogs and cats as _____pets_____.
6. My father has a lot of hair on his face. His _____beard_____ is very long.

D Read the text. Circle any words you don't know.

E Choose the best answer.

1. What is interesting about the man and his dog?
   - a. They are calm and happy.
   - b. They look the same.
   - c. They have short hair.
2. What is the man's expression?
   - a. no hair
   - b. serious
   - c. sad
3. Why do dogs and their owners sometimes look the same?
   - a. People find pets that look like them.
   - b. They have beards.
   - c. They are confused.

F In the text, underline three ways that the dog and its owner are the same.

G COMPARE Work in a group. Search online for pets that look like their owners. Take turns describing them.

36 UNIT 1

---

discussing their meanings as a class. Have students complete the sentences individually, then compare with a partner. Check answers as a class.

D Read the text. Circle any words you don't know.

Tell students that they don't need to understand every word, just the main ideas.

CASAS FOR READING
0.1.2, 0.1.5, 4.8.1, 7.4.4, 7.7.3

CCRS FOR READING
RI1, RI2, RI3

Does My Dog Look Like Me?

Look at the man and his dog. Do you see anything interesting? The dog has short hair. The man has no hair. The man has a black and gray beard. The dog does too! They both have round* faces. They even have the same expression. Some people say that dogs often look like their owners. Maybe people find pets that look like them. But what about personality? Research*

5 shows that dogs and their owners can have the same personalities too. A calm, happy owner usually has a calm, happy dog. Do you agree? Do you know any dogs and owners that look the same?

---

round shaped like a circle
research study that is done to find and report new information about something

READING CHALLENGE 37

READING STRATEGIES

Understanding Main Ideas

Explain to students that when they read, they will usually come across new words. If they stop to look up all of these words, they may become frustrated and also lose the gist of the text. It's important to help them realize that they can understand the main ideas of a text without understanding every single word. **E** and **F** should help them see this.

Students should circle words they don't know but wait to look them up. After they read the first time, play the audio as they read again. Point out the glossary below the text and make sure students understand its purpose.

Ask students to share what they understood. This could be a word, a phrase, or an idea.

E Choose the best answer.

Have students answer the questions individually, then compare with a partner. Check answers as a class. Then go over the meanings of the words students have circled. Write them on the board and see if other students can explain them.

Suggest to students that they keep a vocabulary notebook that they can add new words to each lesson.

F In the text, underline three ways that the dog and its owner are the same.

Have students do this individually before they compare with a partner. Then check the answers as a class.

G COMPARE Work in a group. Search online for pets that look like their owners. Take turns describing them.

Help students think of effective search terms. Monitor as they conduct their search and help as needed.

About the Photo

Photojournalist Jackie Molloy took this photo. Molloy is based in New York City, where this photo was taken. The photo shows the window of an iconic department store on 5th Avenue. The window display entices customers with an excess of bright, neon-colored cookies and cakes. Extravagant window displays like this are especially common in New York during the winter holidays and attract tourists and locals alike.

- Introduce the unit by reading the title out loud. Go over the unit outcomes.
- Have students look at the photo and discuss the first two questions in pairs.
- Ask a volunteer to read the text about the photo out loud. Then discuss the three questions as a class.

Life Skills Focus

In this unit, students will learn the necessary skills for identifying and making purchases when shopping for goods. They will also learn how to describe items and interpret proof of their purchases.

2 Let's Go Shopping

38

UNIT OUTCOMES	GRAMMAR	VOCABULARY	EL CIVICS
• Identify places to shop • Make purchases and read receipts • Identify clothing • Describe clothing • Describe items in a store • Identify employment opportunities in retail	• Simple present: *Shop* • Questions and answers with *be* • Singular and plural nouns • Possessive adjectives • Adjectives • Simple present: *Want*	• Types of stores and products they sell • Money • Clothing • Colors • Adjectives of size, age, pattern • Retail jobs	The skills students learn in this unit can be applied to the following EL Civics competency areas: • Banking • Community Resources

39

UNIT OUTCOMES

▸ Identify places to shop

▸ Make purchases and read receipts

▸ Identify clothing

▸ Describe clothing

▸ Describe items in a store

▸ Identify employment opportunities in retail

Look at the photo and answer the questions.

1. What clothing do you see in the photo?

2. What do you think you can buy at this store?

The window of Bergdorf Goodman, a department store in New York City, is filled with brightly colored cookies and cakes for the holiday shopping season.

1. Do you think this store sells cookies and cakes?

2. Why do you think this store decorates its window with such bright colors?

3. Do you want to go to this store? Why or why not?

Workplace Focus

All lessons and units in *Stand Out* include basic communication skills and interpersonal skills important for the workplace. They include *collecting and organizing information, making decisions and solving problems,* and *combining ideas and information.*

• In Unit 2, Lesson 6, *Explore the Workforce,* students will identify jobs in the retail field. They will analyze statistics related to retail positions. They will also analyze a job advertisement and reflect on the characteristics of an effective salesperson, and relate these to themselves.

• In the Team Project, students practice the soft skill of disagreeing politely while collaborating to complete the project.

• Life Online activities in Lessons 1 and 2 raise awareness about online shopping and form filling.

spark Resources

All resources for the unit are centrally located on the Spark platform and include: audio, video, multilevel worksheets, digital literacy worksheets, Online Practice, and Assessment Suite.

— STEPS —

CASAS COMPETENCIES	ELPS	CCRS
Lesson 1: 0.1.5, 1.2.3, 1.2.4, 1.2.6, 6.7.2, 7.7.3 Lesson 2: 0.1.2, 0.1.5, 0.2.2, 1.1.6, 1.6.4, 6.0.1, 6.0.2, 6.1.1, 7.7.3 Lesson 3: 0.1.2, 0.1.5, 1.2.1, 1.2.9, 6.1.1, 7.3.3 Lesson 4: 0.1.2, 0.1.5, 1.2.9 Lesson 5: 0.1.2, 0.1.5, 1.1.6, 1.2.9, 1.4.1 Lesson 6: 0.1.2, 0.1.5, 4.1.3, 4.1.8, 4.1.9, 6.0.2, 6.7.1, 6.7.2, 7.4.4, 7.7.3 Review: 0.1.2, 0.1.5, 1.1.6, 1.2.9, 1.6.4, 6.1.1 Team Project: 0.1.2, 0.1.5, 1.3.3, 1.6.4, 4.8.1, 4.8.3, 4.8.6 Reading Challenge: 0.1.5, 4.8.1, 6.7.4	S2: Participate in level-appropriate oral and written exchanges of information, ideas, and analyses, in various social and academic contexts, responding to peer, audience, or reader comments and questions. S9: Create clear and coherent level-appropriate speech and text. S10: Demonstrate command of the conventions of standard English to communicate in level-appropriate speech and writing.	L1, L2, L3, RI1, RI2, RI3, SI1, SL3, W1, W3

Shopping
GOAL ▶ Identify places to shop

A Study the words. As a class, make a list of stores you know for each type.

online stores

specialty stores

big-box stores

B Match the words to the pictures.

| clothing | electronics | food | medicine | shoes |

Products	Places to Shop		
1. ___food___	online	a market	a big-box store
2. ___shoes___	online	a shoe store	a big-box store
3. ___electronics___	online	an electronics store	a big-box store
4. ___clothing___	online	a clothing store	a big-box store
5. ___medicine___	online	a pharmacy	a pharmacy inside a big-box store

At-a-Glance Prep

Goal: Identify places to shop
Grammar: Simple present: *Shop*
Academic Strategies: Focused listening, doing a survey, making a bar graph
Vocabulary: Types of stores and products

Agenda

- ☐ Identify places to shop for different items.
- ☐ Identify items you can buy at a big-box store.
- ☐ Interpret an online order.
- ☐ Use the simple present.
- ☐ Make a bar graph.

Resources

Heinle Picture Dictionary: Shops and Stores, pages 48–49

Pacing

- ■ 1.5 hour classes ■ 2.5 hour classes
- ■ 3+ hour classes

Standards Correlations

CASAS: 0.1.5, 1.2.3, 1.2.4, 1.2.6, 6.7.2, 7.7.3
CCRS: L1, L2, L3, RI1, RI2, SL1, SL3
ELPS:
S5: Conduct research and evaluate and communicate findings to answer questions or solve problems.
S10: Demonstrate command of the conventions of standard English to communicate in level-appropriate speech and writing.

Warm-up and Review   7–10 mins. ■■■

Write *$500* on the board. Ask students what they would buy with that amount of money. Tell them what you would buy. Write *shopping* on the board. Ask students what their favorite store is and write the stores on the board as students call them out.

Ask students to work in groups and add more stores to the list. Go over the list as a class.

Introduction   5–7 mins. ■■■

Write on the board different items, such as *apples, a T-shirt, a book, a hamburger.* Ask students where they buy these things. Refer to the stores listed on the board and add others. State the goal: *Today, we will identify places to shop.*

Presentation 1   10–15 mins. ■■■

Ask students where the stores they mentioned in the Warm-Up are. For example, ask: *Is this store downtown? Is it in a mall? Is it online?*

A Study the words. As a class, make a list of stores you know for each type.

Have students look at the pictures and tell you what they see. Help them understand the difference between the types of stores. In pairs, have students identify examples for each one, then share them. Make a list for each type as a class. Some stores might be in more than one list.

Practice 1   10–15 mins. ■■■

B Match the words to the pictures.

Have students complete the activity individually, using a dictionary to look up new words as needed.

Evaluation 1   3–5 mins. ■■■

Go over the answers to **B**.

Instructor's Notes

_____

_____

_____

_____

_____

_____

_____

_____

_____

_____

_____

Presentation 2

15–20 mins. ■■■

C Choose where you shop for the items in the chart in B. Compare with a partner.

Point out the three options for each item in the chart in **B** and tell students to circle where they shop for each item. Put students in pairs to share and discuss their answers. Monitor and ask: *Do you shop at the same type of store?*

D As a class, make a list of other things you can buy at a big-box store.

Elicit the names of some big-box stores students might be familiar with. Write them on the board. Then have students help you create a list of items you can buy at these stores. Remind them that *food*, *shoes*, *electronics*, *clothing*, and *medicine* have already been mentioned. Help them with new vocabulary as needed and encourage them to add new words that are useful to them to their vocabulary notebooks.

Practice 2

15–20 mins. ■■□

E PREDICT Guess where Noor buys each product. Then listen and choose the correct place. 🎧

Tell students they are going to listen to a telephone conversation about where Noor shops. Remind them to listen for the details they need and not try to understand everything. Go over the items so they know which parts of the conversation they need to pay attention to. Introduce the word *groceries*. Then play the first few lines of the audio (stop after *fresh produce*). Choose the first answer together. Then play the whole conversation. Give students time to circle their answers before playing the audio again. Have students compare with a partner. Then play the audio a final time, stopping after each item to help students as needed.

This may be a good opportunity to mention that if students get survey calls, they don't have to answer the questions and they should not give out any personal information.

Listening Script

Caller: *Hello, I'd like to speak to Noor Hassan.*

Noor: *This is she. How can I help you?*

Caller: *I am with Harrington Consumer Reports. We are doing a survey to see where people shop. Do you have a few minutes?*

Noor: *Sure.*

Caller: *Thank you. My first question is, Do you shop for groceries online, at your local market, or at a big-box store?*

Noor: *Well, that is hard to say. If I only have food to buy, I usually go to the market. My market has very fresh produce.*

Caller: *Very good. What about shoes? Do you go to a big-box store for those?*

Noor: *No, they don't have many choices. I shop at a shoe store so I can try the shoes on.*

Caller: *Have you bought a laptop in the past few years?*

Noor: *I have. I buy all my electronics online. Then I can find exactly what I need.*

Caller: *And clothing? Do you buy clothing online?*

Noor: *Most of the time, I shop for clothing at big-box stores. It's so much cheaper.*

Caller: *And finally, do you get your medicine at a pharmacy?*

Noor: *I do. I go to a small pharmacy on my street.*

Caller: *Thanks for all this information. Have a good day.*

BEST PRACTICE

Mini Lessons

Within a lesson, there are opportunities to teach different concepts, either as an introduction to future concepts or as a quick review of concepts students have already been exposed to. Sometimes, students ask specific questions. If you can respond in a short explanation or mini lesson, it might be more beneficial than tabling the discussion for another time. Be careful not to allow the lesson plan to restrict you to the point where you are not meeting students' specific needs.

F INTERPRET Read the online order. Answer the questions in a group.

Have students look at the picture and information and tell you what they see. Assist them in understanding any new vocabulary, such as: *order*, *cart*, *quantity*, *discount code*, etc. Then put them in groups to complete the activity.

Evaluation 2

3–5 mins. ■■□

Go over the answers to **F** as a class. Ask students if they like shopping online and why or why not. Ask if they use discount codes when they shop online.

C Choose where you shop for the items in the chart in **B**. Compare with a partner.

D As a class, make a list of other things you can buy at a big-box store.

Answers will vary.

_____   _____

_____   _____

E PREDICT Guess where Noor buys each product. Then listen and choose the correct place.

Products		Places to Shop	
1. food	a. online	(b.) a market	c. a big-box store
2. shoes	a. online	(b.) a shoe store	c. a big-box store
3. a laptop	(a.) online	b. an electronics store	c. a big-box store
4. clothing	a. online	b. a clothing store	(c.) a big-box store
5. medicine	a. online	(b.) a pharmacy	c. a pharmacy inside a big-box store

F INTERPRET Read the online order. Answer the questions in a group ——— **Life** ONLINE

🛒 **Your Cart**

Casper Ideal 15.6" Laptop – 8GB Memory

In Stock

Quantity

[− | 1 | +]   **$479.99**

SAVE20 [Apply]

Discount code applied!

Order Summary

Subtotal:	$479.99
Shipping:	Free
Discount:	-$20.00
Estimated Sales Tax:	$33.35
Total:	**$493.34**

[Checkout]

1. What is the total price of the order? $493.34

2. Before buying something online, it's a good idea to look for discount codes you can use to save money. How much is the discount here? $20.00

3. How many laptops are in the order? 1

4. What do you click to pay? Checkout

G Study the chart.

Simple Present: *Shop*		
Subject	**Verb**	**Example Sentence**
I / You We / They	shop	I **shop** for shoes at big-box stores. You **shop** for bread at the market. We **shop** for laptops at an electronics store. They **shop** for books online.
He / She	shops	He **shops** for shoes at a shoe store. She **shops** for dresses at clothing stores.

H Complete the sentences with the correct form of *shop*. Then listen and check your answers. 🎧

1. Noor _____ shops _____ for electronics online.

2. They _____ shop _____ for food at a market.

3. We _____ shop _____ for sneakers at a shoe store.

4. He _____ shops _____ for soda at a big-box store.

5. I _____ shop _____ for books online.

I SURVEY How many of your classmates shop in different types of stores? Make a bar graph. Answers will vary.

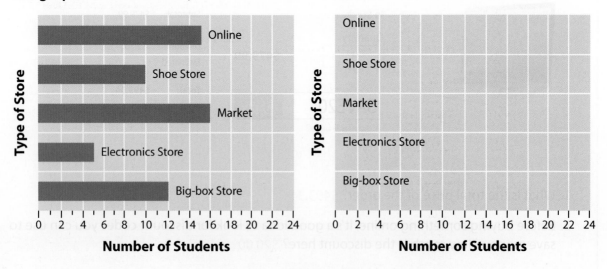

J Go online. Find the names of three online stores that you like. Report them to the class.

BEST PRACTICE

Teaching the Logic of the Book

Take opportunities throughout the term to help students understand the logic of the textbook. Students who understand why they are doing different activities and how activities relate to one another will have more confidence in the process.

Near the beginning of the book, help students see how the goals relate to the lessons and that each lesson is a one-day activity. Soon students will be anticipating the next lesson and understanding the purpose of the goal. At the end of each lesson, ask students if they feel they have accomplished the goal and can do what is asked of them even outside of the classroom.

Presentation 3   10–15 mins. ■■■

G Study the chart.

Remember that at this stage, some students will have trouble understanding a chart like this one. Go over it together carefully. Point to students as you say each example to remind them of the different pronouns. For example, point to yourself and a group of students and say: *We shop for laptops at an electronics store.* Elicit / point out the change in the verb form for *he / she*. If students are ready, elicit further examples from them.

BEST PRACTICE

Drills

Drills can be a good way to help students become familiar with vocabulary, grammar structures, and proper pronunciation. They also help students to gain confidence, especially when performing together with their classmates. However, drills should not be the sole practice or method used to help students memorize something or acquire a grammar structure. There are several ways to drill (choral repetition, substitution, build-up, backward build-up, etc.). If particular drills are overused, there is a risk of losing the meaning of a structure.

Practice 3   5–7 mins. ■

H Complete the sentences with the correct form of *shop*. Then listen and check your answers. 🎧

Ask students to complete the sentences and then to copy them into a notebook. Play the audio for students to check their answers. Show students how *look for* might work in place of *shop for* in these sentences. Have students write new sentences in their notebooks using *look for* with different items and places.

Evaluation 3   5–7 mins. ■

Ask several students to write one of their new sentences using *look for* on the board. Check the sentences as a class and make corrections together as needed.

Application   15–20 mins. ■■■

Workplace Focus

Exercise I: Collect and organize information.

I SURVEY How many of your classmates shop in different types of stores? Make a bar graph.

Look at the example graph and have students answer questions about the data presented. Write on the board: *How many students shop _____?* Put students in five groups and assign each group a type of store to ask the rest of the class about. Show them how to get the attention of the class, phrase a question, and ask for a vote. Each group should ask the class at least one question. Make students aware that they should pay attention to the answers to other students' questions and take notes so they will have numbers for all five types of stores at the end.

After all the groups have asked their questions, have them complete their graphs together.

J Go online. Find the names of three online stores that you like. Report them to the class.

Help students decide how they are going to look for online stores. Ask: *What do you write?* Monitor as they are searching. Depending on your class size, have students report their information in pairs, small groups, or to the whole class. Encourage them to try to say why they chose the stores. Don't worry about accurate expression at this point. Help them with vocabulary as needed.

At-a-Glance Prep

Goal: Make purchases and read receipts
Grammar: Questions and answers with *be*
Academic Strategies: Focused listening, calculating
Vocabulary: Money, amounts, bills, coins

Agenda

- ☐ Discuss neighborhood stores.
- ☐ Read receipts and listen to amounts.
- ☐ Ask for prices.
- ☐ Count U.S. money.
- ☐ Identify credit card information.
- ☐ Complete an online order form.

Resources

Heinle Picture Dictionary: Money and Shopping, pages 8–9

Pacing

- ■ 1.5 hour classes   ■ 2.5 hour classes
- ■ 3+ hour classes

Standards Correlations

CASAS: 0.1.2, 0.1.5, 0.2.2, 1.1.6, 1.6.4, 6.0.1, 6.0.2, 6.1.1, 7.7.3
CCRS: L1, L3, SL1, SL3
ELPS:

S2: Participate in level-appropriate oral and written exchanges of information, ideas, and analyses, in various social and academic contexts, responding to peer, audience, or reader comments and questions.

S10: Demonstrate command of the conventions of standard English to communicate in level-appropriate speech and writing.

Warm-up and Review   8–10 mins. ■■■

Write the names of several local stores on the board. Use high-end and lower-end department stores. Ask students which are more expensive. Use a money gesture or take out some bills to make the point. Then ask students which store is their favorite.

Introduction   2 mins. ■■■

Write *How much?* on the board and ask students how much different items might cost at a store. State the goal: *Today, we will learn to make purchases and read receipts.*

Presentation 1   15–20 mins. ■■■

Write *item*, *price*, *tax*, and *total* on the board. Ask students what each word means. They might not

be able to explain the words well, but allow them to try. Draw a receipt on the board. Ask students to help you fill it out. Then ask students to open their books and read the receipts.

A INTERPRET Look at the receipts. What are the totals? What is the tax?

Go over the receipts. Ask questions such as: *How much are the oranges? How much is the tablet?*

Workplace Focus

Exercise B: Perform basic computations.

B How much is the total for the clothing, electronics, and food?

Work with the class to figure out the total. If you like, make it a competition where the first student to get the correct total is the winner. Do the math on the board to ensure that all students know how to do it. You might also ask for the total before taxes and the total of different quantities of the items.

Practice 1   30–35 mins. ■■■

C Listen and choose the amounts you hear.

Review numbers by eliciting 1–30. Tell students to listen and pay attention to the numbers. Play the audio twice and then have students compare with a partner. Play the audio one or more times and check answers.

Listening Script

EXAMPLE: How much is it? It's $22.50.
1. *That's $34.15.*
2. *Here's $33.00.*
3. *That comes to $15.70.*
4. *The total cost is $77.95.*

D Listen and write the prices.

Go over the items and have students guess how much each one costs. Tell them they are going to listen to conversations between customers and salespeople. Remind them to listen for the prices. Play the first conversation twice and ask students for the answer. Have them write it in their books. Then play the rest of the audio. Give students time to complete their answers before checking with a partner. Then play the audio a final time and check answers as a class.

Note: The listening script for **D** and guidance for **E** are on the following page.

Making Purchases

LESSON 2

GOAL ▶ Make purchases and read receipts

A **INTERPRET** Look at the receipts. What are the totals? What is the tax?

Martin's	
Shirt............... 2 @ $17.98 -	$35.96
Sneakers	$64.98
Subtotal..........................	$100.94
Tax...................................	$8.08
TOTAL	$109.02
Customer Copy	

Hero Electronics	
Headphones......................	$24.99
8-inch Tablet..................	$109.99
Subtotal..........................	$134.98
Tax...................................	$10.80
TOTAL	$145.78
No Returns Without Receipt	

All Day Food Mart	
Bread	$3.50
Cheese	$5.62
Oranges @1.99 a pound.......	$3.98
Potato Chips	$4.60
TOTAL	$17.70
THANK YOU for shopping at All Day.	

B How much is the total for the clothing, electronics, and food?

$109.02 (clothing) + $145.78 (electronics) + $17.70 (food) = _____ $272.50 _____

C Listen and choose the amounts you hear. 🎧

EXAMPLE: $2.15   ($22.50) $22.15

1. ($34.15) $34.50 $45.50   2. $13.00   ($33.00) $43.00

3. $.57 $57.00   ($15.70)   4. $19.75 $17.90   ($77.95)

D Listen and write the prices. 🎧

1. vacuum:
_____ $89.99 _____

2. washing machine:
_____ $450.00 _____

3. candy bars:
_____ $2.50 _____

4. paper:
_____ $6.50 _____

5. phone:
_____ $999.99 _____

E Work with a partner. Practice asking about prices. Use the information in D.

Student A: Excuse me, how much <u>is</u> the <u>vacuum</u>?

Student B: <u>$89.99</u>.

Student A: Thank you.

The Verb *Be*

How much **is** the vacuum?

How much **are** the candy bars?

LESSON 2   43

F Match the words to the pictures.

a dime	a nickel	a penny	a ten-dollar bill
a five-dollar bill	a one-dollar bill	a quarter	a twenty-dollar bill

1. _____a penny_____ 2. _____a nickel_____ 3. _____a dime_____ 4. _____a quarter_____

5. _____a one-dollar bill_____

6. _____a five-dollar bill_____

7. _____a ten-dollar bill_____

8. _____a twenty-dollar bill_____

G Write the amount.

a. 2 one-dollar bills, 1 five-dollar bill, 2 quarters, 1 nickel: $ _____7.55_____

b. 1 twenty-dollar bill, 1 ten-dollar bill, 1 five-dollar bill, 2 dimes, 3 pennies: $ _____35.23_____

c. 1 ten-dollar bill, 1 five-dollar bill, 3 quarters, 1 nickel, 2 pennies: $ _____15.82_____

d. 2 twenty-dollar bills, 3 one-dollar bills, 2 quarters, 2 nickels, 4 pennies: $ _____43.64_____

H CALCULATE What bills and coins do you need for these items? Tell a partner.

a. $75.05   b. $26.99   c. $43.71

Practice 1 (continued)
Listening Script

1. **Customer:** *Excuse me. How much is the vacuum?*
   Salesperson: *It's $89.99 on sale.*
   Customer: *Thanks, I'll take it.*

2. **Customer:** *Excuse me, can you help me? I'm looking for a washing machine.*
   Salesperson: *This is a good brand.*
   Customer: *Is that right? OK, how much is it?*
   Salesperson: *It's four hundred and fifty dollars.*
   Customer: *Four hundred and fifty dollars? That much?*
   Salesperson: *I'm afraid so.*

3. **Customer:** *I just want these candy bars.*
   Salesperson: *That will be $2.50, please.*
   Customer: *Here you go—two dollars and fifty cents.*

4. **Customer:** *I want to buy a ream of white paper.*
   Salesperson: *The paper is over there. It's $6.50.*
   Customer: *Thank you.*

5. **Customer:** *Every time I buy a cell phone, I get a bad one. Maybe I should buy an expensive one.*
   Salesperson: *How about this one for $999.99?*

E Work with a partner. Practice asking about prices. Use the information in D.

Go over the grammar note with students, reminding them of the singular and plural forms of the verb *be*. Model the conversation with a student. Help them with the pronunciation of *dollars* and make sure they pronounce the final *s*. Show students how to substitute a different item from **D** in the conversation. Then have students ask you how much something is. This activity can also be expanded to include the items on the receipts in **A**. Put students in pairs and monitor as they practice.

BEST PRACTICE
Conversation Cards

Another way to do pair work when substitution is involved is to use conversation cards.

1. Pass out 3-by-5 index cards to each student.
2. List the vocabulary on the board, numbering each word.
3. Count students off by the number of words and have them write the word that goes with their

number. For example, if there are 32 students and 8 vocabulary words. You would count students off by 8 and each word would be written four times.

4. Collect the cards and randomly distribute them again.
5. Students are to find other students with the same word on their card. They discover this by practicing the conversation. The student uses the word on their card in the conversation.
6. When students find matches, they write the classmates' names on the card. They continue until they find all the matches.

Evaluation 1   7–10 mins. ■■■

Ask students to perform their conversations in front of the class.

Presentation 2   7–10 mins. ■■■

F Match the words to the pictures.

Do this activity with the class. Review all the coins and bills. If possible, display real bills and coins in the classroom. Be prepared to discuss who and what is pictured on each bill and coin if students are interested.

Workplace Focus

Exercise G: Perform basic computations; Interpret and communicate information.

Practice 2   10–15 mins. ■■

G Write the amount.

Have students complete this activity individually, then compare with a partner. Check answers as a class.

H CALCULATE What bills and coins do you need for these items? Tell a partner.

Ask students to work individually at first and then to compare items in pairs. Bring in real ads if you wish to extend the activity.

Evaluation 2   5–7 mins. ■■

Write an amount on the board and ask individuals to decide what bills and coins they will need. You might extend this by writing some prices on the board and asking individuals to write the bills and coins they think would work.

Presentation 3

I Review the credit card information. Write the correct letter.

Go over the information with students. Then have them look at the credit card and match the information with what they see on the card. Check answers as a class.

Practice 3

J Complete the online form with your name and address and the credit card information from I. Then answer the questions.

Life ONLINE

Remind students about online shopping and how they have to give some personal information to complete their order. Go over the information required on the form. Then have students complete the form individually. Have them compare with a partner and answer the questions in pairs. Check answers as a class. Find out who has already had to fill out an online form similar to this. Have them share their experiences.

K Read about credit card safety. Do you save your credit card number on your phone or computer? Why or why not? 🎧

Help students understand the questions and share their answers. Help with the vocabulary they need to express their ideas. Read the title and elicit or explain the meaning of *tips*. Then play the audio and tell students to read as they listen. Although the text is short, it may still be challenging for students, so remind them that, as with listening, they don't need to understand every single word. Have them read it again and then discuss the tips as a class to check understanding. Ask questions as prompts. For example: *What shows you a website is safe?*, etc.

Evaluation 3

Review the elements of a credit card by drawing one on the board and having students label it without looking in their books.

Application

Give students different online scenarios and ask them to identify whether they are safe or not safe. For example: You buy something online and there is no lock symbol next to the web address. (Not safe) You save your credit card number on your phone, but your phone has a strong password. (Safe)

Instructor's Notes

_____
_____
_____
_____
_____
_____
_____
_____
_____
_____
_____
_____
_____
_____
_____
_____
_____
_____
_____

I Review the credit card information. Write the correct letter.

_c_ 1. card number

_a_ 2. chip

_b_ 3. CVV number

_d_ 4. expiration date

a.

b.

BANK NAME

)))

Your Name

Your Name   123

1234 5678 0912 3456   c.

VALID THROUGH
06/28   d.

J Complete the online form with your name and address and the credit card information from I. Then answer the questions.

Answers will vary.

1. How much is shipping?
   Free

2. When will the computer be delivered?
   Tomorrow, June 24

3. Are the billing and the shipping information the same?
   Yes

◄ ► ↻   +   🔒 www.superst0p.com

Getting your order

Product

Casper Ideal
15.6" Laptop –
8GB Memory

Shipping

| Delivery: Tomorrow, June 24 | |
| NEXT DAY | **FREE** |

Shipping Address

First Name [   ]   Last Name [   ]

Address [   ]

City [   ]   State [   ]   Zip Code [   ]

☑ Use as billing address

Payment Information

Credit or Debit Card Number

[   ]

Expiration Date   CVV

Month: [   ]   Year: [   ]   [   ]

☐ Save my card for future purchases

Place your order

K Read about credit card safety. Do you save your credit card number on your phone or computer? Why or why not? 🎧

Here are some online credit card safety tips:

- Look for the lock symbol (🔒) next to the website address. This means the website is safe for typing your credit card information.
- Never save your credit card information on a phone or computer that isn't yours.
- If you do save your card on your phone or computer, make sure it has a good password.
- Never send your credit card information over email.

Buying New Clothes

GOAL ▶ Identify clothing

A **INTERPRET** Write the correct letter under each item of clothing. Then listen for the missing prices. 🎧

a. suit

b. T-shirt

c. ties

d. baseball cap

e. sweater

f. dress

g. socks

h. hat

i. sneakers

j. blouse

k. coat

l. skirt

YOUR DEPARTMENT STORE

DRESS FOR LESS

1. g ONLY $12

8. h $ 38 ONLY

5. k $84 ONLY

9. f $ 48 ONLY

2. d $12 ONLY

10. c $22 ONLY

11. l $ 35 ONLY

6. a $285 ONLY

3. e $36 ONLY

4. i $33 ONLY

7. b $17 ONLY

12. j $24 ONLY

B **CLASSIFY** In a group, complete the chart with the clothing from **A**. Add other clothing words that you know. Answers will vary. Sample answers provided.

Women's	Men's	Both
dress	suit	socks
skirt	ties	baseball cap
hat		coat
blouse		sweater
		sneakers
		T-shirt

At-a-Glance Prep

Goal: Identify clothing
Grammar: *Be* verb: questions and answers
Academic Strategies: Interpreting and classifying
information, focused listening, making inferences
Vocabulary: Clothing

Agenda

☐ Interpret receipts.
☐ Learn clothing words.
☐ Classify clothing items.
☐ Ask for prices.
☐ Read about Nilda.

Resources
Heinle Picture Dictionary: Clothes, pages 104–105

Pacing

■ 1.5 hour classes   ■ 2.5 hour classes
■ 3+ hour classes

Standards Correlations

CASAS: 0.1.2, 0.1.5, 1.2.1, 1.2.9, 6.1.1, 7.3.3
CCRS: L1, L2, L3, RI1, RI2, SL1, W1, W3
ELPS:
S2: Participate in level-appropriate oral and written exchanges
of information, ideas, and analyses, in various social and academic
contexts, responding to peer, audience, or reader comments and
questions.
S10: Demonstrate command of the conventions of standard
English to communicate in level-appropriate speech and writing.

Warm-up and Review   15–20 mins. ■■□

Bring in some receipts or find online prices for five
items that students will recognize. On the board,
write: *How much is the _____?* Write the five items on
the board. Ask students to work in groups to come
up with a price for each item. Then pass out the
receipts or show students the prices online and see
which group was the closest to the correct amounts.

Introduction   5–7 mins. ■■□

Ask students again where they shop for clothing.
Help them understand the words *cheap* and
expensive. State the goal: *Today, we will identify
clothing.*

Presentation 1   15–20 mins. ■■■

With books closed, ask students to stand up. Ask
them to point to items of clothing they are wearing
as you say them. For example, you might say *socks*
and students would point to their socks. Use colors
too if you feel your students are ready. This activity
will help you to see what students already know.

Instruct the class to study the picture in **A**. Go over
the vocabulary. Point to students wearing articles of
clothing similar to those in the picture.

A INTERPRET Write the correct letter under each item of clothing. Then listen for the missing prices. 🎧

Do this activity as a class, but elicit the names of
the items of clothing in the ad from the students.
Then play the audio and have them write the prices.
Play the audio again then have students compare
answers. Review the question, *How much is / are . . . ?*
and check the answers by asking different students
the question.

Listening Script

*We have many good deals at Dress for Less. Be sure to
come in. Socks are $12, ties are $22, and suits are $285.
Our dresses are $48, and our skirts are $35! We have
great deals on sweaters at $36, and women's hats are
$38. Don't miss our great deals!*

Workplace Focus

Exercise B: Collect and organize information.

Practice 1   5–10 mins. ■■■

B CLASSIFY In a group, complete the chart with the clothing from A. Add other clothing words that you know.

Do one or two items as a class. Then ask students
to complete this activity in groups. When they
finish, explain different ways to classify the same
information. Ask the groups to reclassify the
clothing words by casual and formal, above and
below the waist, and singular and plural.

Evaluation 1   5 mins. ■■■

Ask group representatives to write their
classifications on the board.

Presentation 2

C Study the charts.

Go over the charts as a class. Have students look back at the previous page. Ask questions about prices and show them how you use *How much is . . .* and *How much are . . .* It is important that students know that money is implied in the question. This will help them better understand *How many . . .* when it is presented later.

Do a chain drill where Student A asks Student B a question. Student B responds and then asks Student C a new question, etc.

BEST PRACTICE

Drills

Drills can be a good way to help students become familiar with vocabulary, grammar structures, and pronunciation. They also help students to gain confidence, especially when performing together with their classmates. However, drills should not be the sole practice or method used to help students memorize something or acquire a grammar structure. There are several ways to drill (choral repetition, substitution, build-up, backward build-up, etc.). If particular drills are overused, there is a risk of losing the meaning of a structure.

D Practice the conversation with a partner.

Practice the conversation as a group. Divide the class in half to be Student A and Student B. Then switch roles. Say an item and have the class insert the new item and its price. Put students in pairs to practice. Monitor and help with pronunciation and the correct use of *is / are*, as needed.

Workplace Focus

Exercise E: Interpret and communicate information.

Practice 2   5–7 mins.

E Make new conversations with your partner. Use the price information from A.

Model a new conversation with a student, having them ask you how much the sweater is so they understand that Student B needs to look back at **A** for the price. Put students in A-B pairs. Monitor as they practice, providing help with pronunciation and the correct form of *be*. This is an information-gap

activity, so be sure that students who are asking the questions refrain from looking at the previous page where the prices are.

BEST PRACTICE

Facilitating Information-Gap Activities

Information-gap activities are activities that allow one student to give new information to another. In the *Stand Out* approach, there are many opportunities to do this type of activity.

Sometimes the nature of the activity is difficult to understand for some students. There are several things to do to help students.

1. Model the activity several times with several different students.
2. Make sure students know who is A and who is B. To do this, ask all As to stand up. Check to make sure all students understand.
3. Monitor the practice. If a pair of students is having trouble, do the exercise with them.
4. Do the activity in groups of four with at least one student who can direct the others. In groups of four, one pair goes first and the other pair listens. Then the other pair performs.

Evaluation 2   3–5 mins.

Ask students to demonstrate the conversation in front of the class.

Instructor's Notes

_____

_____

_____

_____

_____

_____

_____

_____

C Study the charts.

Be Verb (Questions)			
Question Words	**Be**	**Singular or Plural Noun**	**Example Question**
How much (money)	is	the dress the suit	How much **is** the dress? How much **is** the suit?
How much (money)	are	the socks the ties	How much **are** the socks? How much **are** the ties?

Be Verb (Answers)		
Singular or Plural Noun or Pronoun	**Be**	**Example Answer**
It	is	It **is** $48. It's $48. (The dress **is** $48.) It **is** $285. It's $285. (The suit **is** $285.)
They	are	They **are** $12. They're $12. (The socks **are** $12.) They **are** $22. They're $22. (The ties **are** $22.)

D Practice the conversation with a partner.

Student A: How much <u>is the dress</u>?

Student B: <u>It's $48</u>.

E Make new conversations with your partner. Use the price information from **A**.

Student A asks Student B:

1. $ <u>   48   </u>

3. $ <u> $36   </u>

5. $ <u> $22 / $44 </u>

Student B asks Student A:

2. $ <u> $285   </u>

4. $ <u> $33   </u>

6. $ <u> $35   </u>

F INFER Read about Nilda. What is her problem? 🎧

Nilda shops at Dress for Less. It is a clothing store on Main Street. The prices are good, but she only has $75. She needs clothes for a party. She needs a new blouse, a skirt, and a hat. She has a problem.

G Choose *Yes* or *No*. Look at the prices in **A**.

1. Nilda shops at Lang's department store.	Yes	(No)
2. Nilda has $75.	(Yes)	No
3. Nilda can buy a blouse, a skirt, and a hat.	Yes	(No)

H Look at the ad in **A**. You have $75. What different items can you buy? Write the items and their prices. Share your answers with a group. Answers will vary.

_____   _____   _____

_____   _____   _____

I INVESTIGATE Research clothing stores online. What can you buy for $100?

A *secondhand* store sells clothes that aren't new. These stores are usually less expensive than other clothing stores.

Presentation 3

Ask students to look at the photo. Talk about the photo and elicit what kind of store the woman is in, what she is buying, etc. Point out the caption and make sure students understand what a secondhand store is.

Write any words that may be new to students on the board.

Practice 3

F INFER Read about Nilda. What is her problem? 🎧

Tell students to read as they listen. Play the audio. Ask: *What does Nilda need? How much money does she have?* Tell students to read the text again and tell you what her problem is.

G Choose *Yes* or *No*. Look at the prices in A.

Have students complete the activity individually, then compare with a partner.

Evaluation 3

Check the answers to **G** as a class.

Workplace Focus

Exercises H and I: Perform basic computations; Interpret and communicate information.

Application

H Look at the ad in A. You have $75. What different items can you buy? Write the items and their prices. Share your answers with a group.

Tell students to go back to **A** and work out what they can buy with their $75. After they have written their list with the prices, put them into small groups to share their choices. Monitor as they discuss.

I INVESTIGATE Research clothing stores online. What can you buy for $100?

Elicit names of clothing stores students like and write them on the board. Then have students choose which ones they would like to look up online. Monitor as they carry out their searches and help as needed. Remind them to factor taxes and shipping costs into the total. Have students share with a partner what they can buy with their $100. Encourage them to say which store or stores they used.

Instructor's Notes

_____

_____

_____

_____

_____

_____

_____

_____

_____

_____

_____

_____

_____

_____

_____

_____

_____

_____

_____

_____

_____

_____

_____

_____

At-a-Glance Prep

Goal: Describe clothing
Grammar: Singular and plural, possessive adjectives
Academic Strategies: Classifying and comparing information
Vocabulary: Clothing, colors

Agenda

☐ Decide what Nilda can buy.
☐ Describe clothing.
☐ Identify colors.
☐ Use plurals.
☐ Use possessive adjectives.
☐ Describe classmates' clothing.

Resources

Heinle Picture Dictionary: Colors, pages 10–11; Describing Clothes, pages 110–111

Pacing

■ 1.5 hour classes   ■ 2.5 hour classes
■ 3+ hour classes

Standards Correlations

CASAS: 0.1.2, 0.1.5, 1.2.9
CCRS: L1, L2, L3, SL1, SL3
ELPS:

S2: Participate in level-appropriate oral and written exchanges of information, ideas, and analyses, in various social and academic contexts, responding to peer, audience, or reader comments and questions.

S5: Conduct research and evaluate and communicate findings to answer questions or solve problems.

Warm-up and Review   10–15 mins. ■■■

Look back at **H** in Lesson 3. Ask students to do the activity again in groups, but this time ask them to decide what Nilda can buy for $100. Have the groups report to the class.

Introduction   5–7 mins. ■■■

Ask students to stand up. Do a modified *stand up and share* activity. Ask students with various color items of clothing to sit down. Observe how much students know about colors. For example, you might say: *All students wearing a white shirt, please sit down.* State the goal: *Today, we will describe clothing.*

Presentation 1   15–20 mins. ■■■

With the students' books closed, write the items that Nilda and Musa are wearing in **A** on the board.

Make sure students know what each word means. Show examples from the class when possible. Practice the pronunciation of the words.

When identifying clothing that students in the class are wearing, ask students what color the items are. This activity will help you identify how much students already know.

A Listen and point to the clothing you hear in the conversation. 🎧

Have students open their books and look at the pictures of Nilda and Musa. Go over the colors with them. Say one of the items of clothing and have students point to it. For example: *Musa is wearing a red T-shirt.* Tell them they will listen to Nilda and Musa talking about clothes. Play the audio. Play the audio again and ask students to point to each item when they hear it. Play the audio again as needed.

Listening Script

Musa: *Nilda, what are you wearing on the first day of classes?*
Nilda: *I think I'll wear a white top. How about you?*
Musa: *I'll wear my red T-shirt. And I think I will go casual and wear shorts.*
Nilda: *Nice. I'm wearing my blue pants with a black belt.*
Musa: *Sounds great! You won't miss me. I'll be wearing a blue baseball cap and brown sandals.*

Ask students questions, such as: *What color is Musa's T-shirt?* Encourage students to respond with a complete sentence: *It's red.* Respond by reiterating the vocabulary: *That's right. His shirt is red.* Write the exchange on the board. Help students see when to use *are* and *is*.

Remind students about plurals and work with their pronunciation to prepare them for **B**.

Practice 1   7–10 mins. ■■■

B CLASSIFY Complete the chart with the words from the picture. Then add more clothing words.

Go over the example. Then have students complete the chart with a partner. Check answers as a class by having students complete the chart on the board.

Evaluation 1   7–10 mins. ■■■

Have students ask one another questions using the exchange you wrote on the board after **A**. Observe their conversations.

What Color Is Your Shirt?
GOAL ▶ Describe clothing

A Listen and point to the clothing you hear in the conversation. 🎧

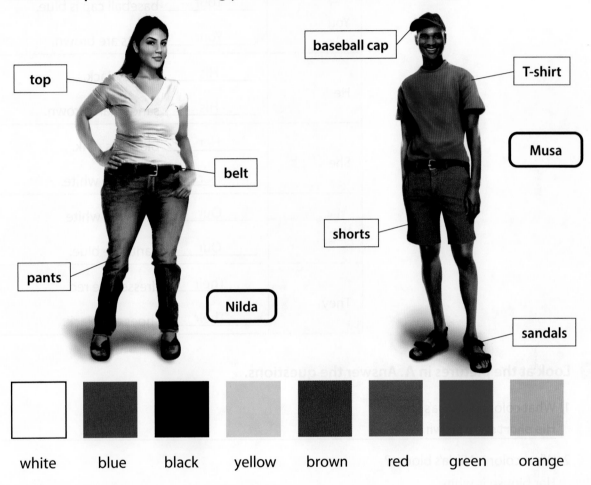

baseball cap

T-shirt

top

Musa

belt

shorts

pants

Nilda

sandals

white blue black yellow brown red green orange

B CLASSIFY Complete the chart with the words from the picture. Then add more clothing words.

Singular	Plural		Plural Only
T-shirt	T-shirts		pants
top	tops		shorts
belt	belts		sandals
baseball cap	baseball caps		

C Complete the chart with words from the box.

her	my	their
his	our	your

Pronoun	Possessive Adjectives
I	_My_ shirt is blue. _My_ shoes are black.
You	_Your_ baseball cap is blue. _Your_ shorts are brown.
He	_His_ belt is black. _His_ sandals are brown.
She	_Her_ blouse is pink. _Her_ shoes are white.
We	_Our_ shirts are white. _Our_ pants are blue.
They	_Their_ dresses are red. _Their_ shoes are black.

D Look at the pictures in A. Answer the questions.

1. What color are Musa's shorts?
   His shorts are brown.

2. What color is Nilda's blouse?
   Her blouse is white.

3. What color are Nilda's and Musa's belts?
   Their belts are black.

4. What color are Nilda's pants?
   Her pants are blue.

5. What color is Musa's T-shirt?
   His T-shirt is red.

6. What color are Nilda's and Musa's shoes?
   Their shoes are brown.

Presentation 2   10–15 mins. ■■□

C Complete the chart with words from the box.

Have students complete the chart individually or with a partner to see how familiar they are with possessive adjectives. Some students might be confused by the fact that the possessive adjective does not reflect whether the noun is singular or plural. Clarify as needed. Also, make sure they understand that the form of the *be* verb is determined by the subject.

BEST PRACTICE

Contrastive Analysis

Possessive adjectives are treated differently in different languages. For example, *his*, *her*, and *your* in English all translate to the same word in Spanish, which can be very confusing. In Portuguese, possessive adjectives reflect the gender and number of the noun they modify. In Korean, possessive adjectives are often avoided altogether, and names or titles are used instead. These differences can cause problems for students. If you are aware of language differences, sometimes it will prompt additional instruction. If the students in your class all speak the same language, knowledge of their first language can be even more useful.

Practice 2   10–15 mins. ■■

D Look at the pictures in A. Answer the questions.

This activity is similar to what students did orally in Presentation 1, except now they are using possessive adjectives.

You can turn this exercise into an information-gap activity by having students practice in pairs. One student asks the questions while the other looks at page 49 and answers. Monitor and help them use possessive adjectives appropriately.

Evaluation 2   3–5 mins. ■■
Briefly quiz students on possessive adjectives. This can be done by saying a pronoun and having students respond with the appropriate possessive adjective.

Instructor's Notes

Presentation 3
7–10 mins. ■■■

Ask a female and a male volunteer to come forward. Ask students to help you describe their clothes, and write sentences on the board. For example, you might write: *His shirt is red. Her pants are blue.*

Workplace Focus
Exercise E: Interpret and communicate information.

Practice 3
15–20 mins. ■

E COMPARE Work with a partner. Talk about your and your classmates' clothes. Then write sentences.

Go over the instructions and the chart. Then put students in pairs. Monitor and clarify any doubts about completing the chart. Make sure students are using the possessive adjectives and plural noun forms correctly.

F With a different partner, describe your classmates by their clothes. Let your partner guess who the classmates are.

Model the activity by describing a student's clothes and having another student guess who it is. Then assign students to new partners. Have them use the information in **E** in their conversations.

Evaluation 3
10 mins. ■

Observe the activity. Provide feedback as needed on students' use of possessive adjectives and plural forms.

Workplace Focus
Exercise G: Collect and organize information.

Application
7–10 mins. ■■■

G CLASSIFY Work in a group. Make lists of your classmates' clothes by color.

Copy the chart on to the board and change the example to someone in the class. Elicit another example and write it in the correct column. Put students in groups of three or four and have them complete the chart in their books. Set a time limit of 3–5 minutes. Then have a volunteer from each group write some of their answers on the board. Correct any mistakes as a class.

Instructor's Notes

_____

_____

_____

_____

_____

_____

_____

_____

_____

_____

_____

_____

_____

_____

_____

_____

_____

_____

_____

_____

_____

_____

_____

_____

_____

E COMPARE Work with a partner. Talk about your and your classmates' clothes. Then write sentences. Answers will vary.

My	His
My shirt is _____	His shirt is _____
My shoes are _____	_____
My _____	_____
_____	_____
_____	_____

Your	Her
Your shirt is _____	Her shirt is _____
_____	_____
_____	_____
_____	_____
_____	_____

Our	Their
Our _____	Their _____
_____	_____
_____	_____
_____	_____
_____	_____

F With a different partner, describe your classmates by their clothes. Let your partner guess who the classmates are.

Student A: His shirt is blue.

Student B: Pedro?

G CLASSIFY Work in a group. Make lists of your classmates' clothes by color.

Answers will vary.

Red	Blue	Green	Black
Carolina's sweater			

A Large TV or a Small TV?

GOAL ▶ Describe items in a store

A Write a word for each photo.

1. Do you want a small laptop or a large desktop computer?

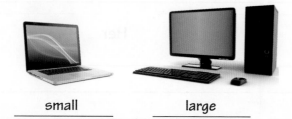

small   large

2. Do you want a new house or an old house?

new   old

3. Do you want a new car or a used car?

used   new

4. Do you want a striped shirt or a plaid shirt?

striped   plaid

5. Do you want a large blouse or a medium blouse?

large   medium

6. Do you want a small T-shirt or a medium T-shirt?

medium   small

B CLASSIFY Complete the chart with words from A.

Size	Age	Pattern
large	new	striped
medium	old	plaid
small	used	

At-a-Glance Prep

Goal: Describe items in a store
Grammar: Simple present: *Want*
Pronunciation: Contrastive stress
Academic Strategies: Focused listening, classifying information
Vocabulary: Adjectives of size, age, and pattern

Agenda

☐ Find the student based on description of clothes.
☐ Describe store items.
☐ Use adjectives.
☐ Practice a conversation.
☐ Use the verb *want*.
☐ Write a new conversation.

Resources

Heinle Picture Dictionary: Opposites, pages 14–15

Pacing

■ 1.5 hour classes ■ 2.5 hour classes
■ 3+ hour classes

Standards Correlations

CASAS: 0.1.2, 0.1.5, 1.1.6, 1.2.9, 1.4.1
CCRS: L1, L2, L3, RI1, SL1, SL3, W1, W3
ELPS:

S2: Participate in level-appropriate oral and written exchanges of information, ideas, and analyses, in various social and academic contexts, responding to peer, audience, or reader comments and questions.

S9: Create clear and coherent level-appropriate speech and text.

Warm-up and Review   7–10 mins. ■■□

Ask students to write what they are wearing on an index card, for example, *blue shirt, black pants*. Tell students not to write their name on the card. Collect and redistribute the cards randomly. Ask students to find who the card was written by.

Introduction   5–7 mins. ■■□

Use items from the classroom, for example, a pencil, a book, a backpack, and a chair. Line the items up in the front of the classroom and, with the help of students, put them in order from the smallest to the largest. State the goal: *Today, we will describe items in a store.*

Presentation 1   15–20 mins. ■■■

Compare the items you used in the introduction. Don't use comparative adjectives here. Say: *The pencil is small and the book is big.* Make these comparisons until students can do them with you.

A Write a word for each photo.

Do this activity with the class. Practice asking the questions after you fill in the words below the photos. For example, ask: *Do you want a striped shirt or a plaid shirt?* Make sure you show students how adjectives come before the noun. Once they are comfortable with one-word answers, encourage them to answer with both the adjective and the noun.

> **Pronunciation   Stress**
>
> For the questions in this activity, the adjectives get the stress because they are showing the difference between the two choices. *Do you want a STRIPED shirt or a PLAID shirt?* Help students to respond by stressing the adjective to show their preference: *a PLAID shirt.*
>
> One way to practice emphasizing this information is to ask students to stand when they say the adjective and sit when they say the noun. Another idea is to have half of the class say the adjective and the other half of the class follow with a noun.

Ask students to ask and answer the questions in pairs, emphasizing the adjectives in both the questions and the answers. Finally, make sure they understand *size*, *age*, and *pattern* in preparation for the practice.

Practice 1   5–7 mins. ■■□

B CLASSIFY Complete the chart with words from A.

Have students complete the activity individually.

Evaluation 1   5–7 mins. ■■□

Write the three categories on the board: *size*, *age*, and *pattern*. Have volunteers come up and fill in the categories. Discuss their answers as a class.

Presentation 2 15–20 mins. ■■■

C Look at the picture. Where is Liping? What does he want to buy?

Look back at **A**. Ask students if there is anything on the page that they really want. Write the word *want* on the board. Elicit or explain the meaning of *want*. Then ask students to look at the picture in **C**. Ask them to cover up everything under the picture with a piece of paper. Have students answer the questions. Then ask questions about details in the picture. For example, you could ask: *Are the TVs new or old?*, *small or large?*, etc.

D Listen to the conversation with your books closed. What does Liping want? 🎧

With the lower half of the page still covered, ask students to listen to the conversation. Ask students again: *What does Liping want to buy?* Have them call out the answer. Play the audio again and ask students to read as they listen.

> #### Pronunciation   Stress 🎧
> Point out the pronunciation note on stress and play the audio. Have students repeat the conversation.

Listening Script

In English, we use stress to show the difference between two choices. When you stress a word, you say it louder and longer than usual.
A: *Do you want a big TV or a small TV?*
B: *I want a small TV.*

Have students listen to the audio from **D** a final time to see if they can hear the stress on the adjectives.

E Practice the conversation in D with a partner.

At this point, you want students to place stress on the appropriate words. Drill students as a class on the conversation, using correct stress. Then have them practice in pairs.

To extend the exercise, show students how to substitute information from **A** into the conversation.

BEST PRACTICE
Conversation Preparation

There are many opportunities in *Stand Out* for students to have conversational exchanges. The conversations help students manipulate new vocabulary, think critically about what to substitute, and practice pronunciation. To prepare students to do the substitutions and to help them with pronunciation, consider the following steps:

1. Do a choral drill where students repeat what you say.
2. Take the role of Student A and have students in unison take the role of Student B.
3. Switch roles.
4. Ask part of the class to be A and part to be B.
5. Take the role of A and ask a student to be B.
6. Take the role of B and ask a different student to be A.
7. Ask two or three pairs to demonstrate.

This may appear to be more than you think is needed; however, remember your goal is to help all of your students be successful. You don't want to start the practice before everyone understands exactly what to do.

Practice 2 5–7 mins. ■■

F Make new conversations with your partner. Use the conversation in D and the information below.

Go over the instructions and the information for students A and B carefully. Model the activity with a student, taking first the salesperson role and then the customer role. Then put students in pairs to carry out the conversations. Monitor and help as needed. Remind students to emphasize the adjectives.

Evaluation 2 5–7 mins. ■■

Ask students to demonstrate their conversations in front of the class.

C Look at the picture. Where is Liping? What does he want to buy?

D Listen to the conversation with your books closed. What does Liping want? 🎧
He wants to buy a small TV.

Liping:	Excuse me. I want a <u>TV</u>.
Salesperson:	<u>A **big** TV</u> or <u>a **small** TV?</u>
Liping:	I want <u>a **small** TV</u>.
Salesperson:	OK, how about this one?
Liping:	Yes, that's good. How much is it?
Salesperson:	It's <u>$135</u>.
Liping:	I'll take it!

Stress 🎧

A: Do you want a **BIG** TV or a **SMALL** TV?
B: I want a **SMALL** TV.

E Practice the conversation in **D** with a partner.

F Make new conversations with your partner. Use the conversation in **D** and the information below.

Student A is the customer.
Student B is the salesperson.

1. blouse	medium / small	$24
2. laptop	large / small	$899
3. refrigerator	new / used	$410
4. shirt	small / medium	$18

Student B is the customer.
Student A is the salesperson.

5. car	used / new	$18,000
6. house	old / new	$500,000
7. sweater	striped / plaid	$42
8. dress	large / medium	$33

G Study the chart.

Simple Present: *Want*		
Subject	**Verb**	**Example Sentence**
I / You / We / They	want	I **want** a large TV.
He / She	wants	He **wants** a new house.

H Listen to the conversations and choose the correct answers. 🎧

1. a. a small TV   b. a big TV   c. a new TV

2. a. a new house   b. an old house   c. a small house

3. a. a small shirt   b. a medium shirt   c. a large shirt

4. a. a new car   b. an old car   c. a used car

I Complete the sentences with the correct form of *want*. Use the information about the people from **H**.

1. He _____ wants _____ a small TV.

2. They _____ want an old house _____.

3. She _____ wants a medium shirt _____.

4. They _____ want a new car _____.

J Work with a partner. Write a conversation like the ones in **H**. Present it to the class.

Can you describe the hats in this photo?

54 UNIT 2

Presentation 3

7–10 mins. ■■■

Have students look at the items in **A** and **F** again and say what they want. Write sentences on the board using student names. For example, write: *Van wants a large TV.* You might also write: *I want a new laptop.* Ask the students who responded to read the sentences from the board out loud.

Next, underline *want* and *wants*. Circle the third person singular *s* in *wants*.

G Study the chart.

Go over the chart and elicit further examples from students.

Practice 3

10–15 mins. ■

H Listen to the conversations and choose the correct answers. 🎧

Tell students they are going to listen to four different conversations. Play the first conversation and choose the answer as a class. Play the rest of the audio. Have students compare answers with a partner. Then play the audio again, pausing after each conversation to confirm answers. Play the audio again as needed.

Listening Script

1. **Liping:** *Excuse me. I want a TV.*
   Salesperson: *A big TV or a small TV?*
   Liping: *I want a small TV.*
   Salesperson: *OK, how about this one?*
   Liping: *Yes, that's good. How much is it?*
   Salesperson: *It's $135.*
   Liping: *I'll take it!*

2. **Emily:** *We need to move.*
   Steve: *I know. What do you want? Do you want a new house or an old house?*
   Emily: *Well, I'm not sure. They both have benefits. I guess I want an old one.*
   Steve: *OK, we want an old house, right?*
   Emily: *Right.*

3. **Nancy:** *I am here to buy a shirt for my friend Gabriela.*
   Salesperson: *OK, do you know her size?*
   Nancy: *She needs a medium, I think.*
   Salesperson: *All right. Step over here, and we'll see what we can find in a medium.*

4. **Ivan:** *I want a new car.*
   Natasha: *I want a new car too.*
   Ivan: *They're expensive.*

Natasha: *How can we afford it?*
Ivan: *I guess we want a new car, but we'll have to wait to buy one.*

Evaluation 3

5–7 mins. ■

I Complete the sentences with the correct form of *want*. Use the information about the people from H.

Refer students back to the chart in **G**. Then have them complete the sentences individually. Check answers as a class.

Application

10–15 mins. ■■■

J Work with a partner. Write a conversation like the ones in H. Present it to the class.

Students can use the conversation in **D** as a model. Monitor and help as needed. Allow students time to practice before they present to the class.

Instructor's Notes

_____

_____

_____

_____

_____

_____

_____

_____

_____

_____

_____

At-a-Glance Prep

Goal: Identify employment opportunities in retail

Agenda

☐ Interpret graphs.

☐ Read about job requirements in retail.

☐ Reflect on the characteristics of a salesperson.

☐ Search for job openings online.

Pacing

■ 1.5 hour classes   ■ 2.5 hour classes

■ 3+ hour classes

Standards Correlations

CASAS: 0.1.2, 0.1.5, 4.1.3, 4.1.8, 4.1.9, 6.0.2, 6.7.1, 6.7.2, 7.4.4, 7.7.3

CCRS: L1, L3, RI1, RI3, SL1, SL3, W1, W3

ELPS:

S7: Adapt language choices to purpose, task, and audience when speaking and writing.

S8: Determine the meaning of words and phrases in oral presentations and literary and informational text.

In this lesson, students are introduced to employment opportunities in the retail field. They will learn about the different positions available in retail, compare salaries, and identify the areas in retail that pay the most. Students will also look at a retail job ad and consider the characteristics of a good salesperson, while reflecting on their own characteristics. Finally, students will carry out an online search to find retail positions available in their area.

Warm-up and Review   10–15 mins. ■■■

Write *salesperson* on the board and have students explain where this person works and what they do. Refer them back to the conversations in Lesson 5 if necessary. Then ask about other people who work in stores and elicit or provide the words *cashier* and *manager*. Write them on the board with *salesperson* and explain that these jobs are all in *retail*. Provide examples from another area if necessary. For example: *doctor, nurse, therapist* are all in the health field.

Introduction   5–10 mins. ■■■

Ask students about their jobs. Tell them that throughout *Stand Out*, they will investigate many job possibilities. Write the goal on the board: *Today, we will identify employment opportunities in retail.*

Presentation 1   15–20 mins. ■■■

A INTERPRET   Read the graph.

Go over the graph together, having students tell you what they see. At this point, it isn't important that they use the correct terms, rather that they say whatever they can about the graph. Encourage students to look up the positions that they are not familiar with, such as *marketing manager* and *purchasing agent*.

B Answer the questions about the graph.

Have students answer the questions with a partner. Then go over them as a class. Clarify any vocabulary questions students still have from the graph or exercise items.

Practice 1   20–25 mins. ■■■

C Practice saying the numbers.

Have students say what each number represents in the graph. Say the numbers and have the class repeat them several times. Write the numbers on the board. Then point to each number and have the class and individual students say the number. Repeat until you feel students are comfortable with the format for saying numbers. Write other numbers from the graph on the board to continue practicing.

Refer to Best Practice: Large Numbers on page 57a for more practice with large numbers.

D Work with a partner. Ask and answer questions about the graph in A.

Point out the questions and have students repeat them after you. Model the activity by having a student ask you each of the questions. Then ask the student: *How much does a marketing manager make a year? How many marketing manager positions are there?* Have the class help with the answers as needed. Put students in pairs to talk about the graph. Monitor and help with question formation and numbers as needed.

Explore the Workforce

GOAL ▶ Identify employment opportunities in retail

A INTERPRET Read the graph.

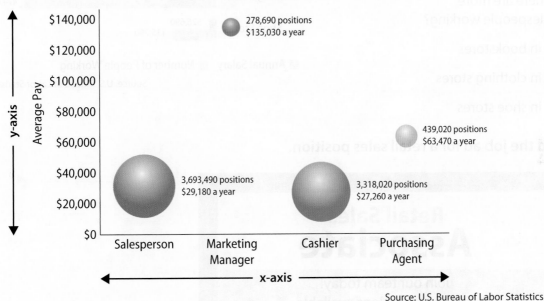

Retail Positions in the U.S. (2021)

278,690 positions
$135,030 a year

439,020 positions
$63,470 a year

3,693,490 positions
$29,180 a year

3,318,020 positions
$27,260 a year

Salesperson   Marketing Manager   Cashier   Purchasing Agent

y-axis — Average Pay

x-axis

Source: U.S. Bureau of Labor Statistics

B Answer the questions about the graph.

1. What information is on the y-axis?

   (a.) pay   b. job titles   c. number of positions

2. What information is on the x-axis?

   a. pay   (b.) job titles   c. number of positions

3. What other information is in the graph?

   a. job locations   b. work schedule   (c.) number of positions

C Practice saying the numbers.

29,**180**   twenty-nine thousand, **one hundred eighty**

278,**690**   two hundred seventy-eight thousand, **six hundred ninety**

3,318,**020**   three million, three hundred eighteen thousand, **twenty**

D Work with a partner. Ask and answer questions about the graph in A.

EXAMPLES: How *much* does a salesperson make a year?
How *many* salesperson positions are there?

E **INTERPRET** **Read the graph and answer the questions.**

1. What type of store pays the most for salespeople?

   a. bookstores

   b. clothing stores

   (c.) jewelry stores

2. Where are more salespeople working?

   a. in bookstores

   (b.) in clothing stores

   c. in shoe stores

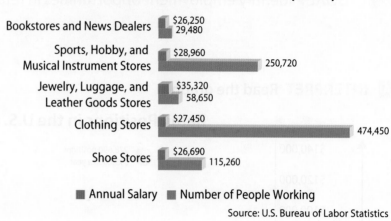

Retail Sales Positions in the U.S. (2021)

Bookstores and News Dealers — $26,250 / 29,480

Sports, Hobby, and Musical Instrument Stores — $28,960 / 250,720

Jewelry, Luggage, and Leather Goods Stores — $35,320 / 58,650

Clothing Stores — $27,450 / 474,450

Shoe Stores — $26,690 / 115,260

■ Annual Salary   ■ Number of People Working

Source: U.S. Bureau of Labor Statistics

F **Read the job ad for a retail sales position.**

Retail Sales
Associate

Join our team today!
Full-time positions available

Qualifications:
- High school diploma or equivalent (GED or HiSET)
- 18 years or older
- Dependable
- Enthusiastic
- Good communication skills
- No experience required

G **Match the words to the descriptions.**

__b__ 1. enthusiastic   a. I come on time every day. I always do my work.

__a__ 2. dependable   b. I love to work. I am happy all the time.

__c__ 3. good communication skills   c. I speak clearly and listen carefully.

H **Talk to a partner. Can you do the job described in F? Why or why not?**

BEST PRACTICE

Graphs

Developing an awareness and understanding of graphs is an important skill for the workplace. Depending on the position, students may be exposed to different kinds of graphs or may be required to create graphs themselves as part of their responsibilities. Therefore, it is important to give them time to understand the different elements of a graph and what information they are giving. This is especially important at this level, where students may only just be getting used to the format of graphs as there may be cultural differences. In addition to the Lesson activities, asking basic comprehension questions about the graphs to check understanding is a useful step to include.

E INTERPRET Read the graph and answer the questions.

This time, ask students to study the graph and answer the questions individually. Have them compare and discuss their answers with a partner.

Evaluation 1   5–10 mins. ■■■

Go over the answers to **E** as a group and ask further questions about the graph to check students' understanding. For example: *What are the blue lines? What is the number 474,450?*, etc. Then ask students which area of retail they want to work in.

Presentation 2   10–15 mins. ■■■

F Read the job ad for a retail sales position.

Go over the ad together. Elicit or explain what *full-time* refers to and what the difference is between *full-* and *part-time*. Ask students if they work full- or part-time. Ask questions about the age and experience required for the position.

Practice 2   15–20 mins. ■■

For shorter classes, have students do **G** for homework.

G Match the words to the descriptions.

Encourage students to use dictionaries to help them with this activity if necessary. Have them compare with a partner. Then check answers as a class. Ask a few students: *Are you dependable / enthusiastic? Do you have good communication skills?*

H Talk to a partner. Can you do the job described in F? Why or why not?

Put students in pairs to discuss the questions. Remind them that they need to explain the reasons for their answers.

Evaluation 2   7–10 mins. ■■

Observe students as they discuss the job and their skills in pairs.

Instructor's Notes

_____

_____

_____

_____

_____

_____

_____

_____

_____

_____

_____

_____

_____

_____

_____

Presentation 3
10–15 mins. ■■□□

I Read about what makes a good salesperson. 🎧

Tell students to read as they listen. Play the audio. Ask students to read the text again and underline the words that describe a good salesperson. Have students call out the words, and write them on the board. Check students' understanding.

Practice 3
15–20 mins. ■■

Ask students in shorter classes to do **J** for homework.

J REFLECT Check (✓) the words that describe you.

Have students complete the activity individually.

K Work with a partner. Practice the conversation. Then create new conversations with your own information. Use phrases from the box.

Point out the example and go over the phrases in the box. Then model the conversation with a student. Have two students model the conversation before putting students in pairs. Monitor and help as needed.

L Choose a job title from A. Go to a job search site online and see if there are any openings within 25 miles of your school or home.

Help students get started with their searches. Share some job search sites that they can use.

Evaluation 3
5–10 mins. ■■

Monitor as students are carrying out their searches and help as needed. When they have found one or two options, have them share the information with a partner. As a class, compare the levels of pay they found and the job requirements.

BEST PRACTICE

Large Numbers

Saying large numbers in English can be quite complicated for students. Provide further practice for students whenever possible:

Have each student write five large numbers on a piece of paper. In pairs, students switch papers and say each other's numbers.

Write large numbers randomly on the board. Divide the class into teams and have each team stand in a line one behind the other in front of the board. Say one of the numbers and the team member who touches the correct number on the board first wins the point for their team.

Have students search online for different jobs and record the pay to share with the class. You could do this on a daily basis. For example, assign a day to each student to have a large number to say to the class and say what it is and where it is from (e.g., annual pay for a computer technician from www.compujobsearch.com).

Instructor's Notes

_____

_____

_____

_____

_____

_____

_____

_____

_____

_____

_____

_____

_____

I Read about what makes a good salesperson. 🎧

- Good salespeople are sociable. *Sociable* means they like to talk and work with customers.
- Good salespeople are compassionate. *Compassionate* means they understand how people feel.
- Good salespeople are supportive. *Supportive* means they like to help others.

J **REFLECT** Check (✓) the words that describe you. Answers will vary.

☐ sociable ☐ compassionate ☐ supportive

K Work with a partner. Practice the conversation. Then create new conversations with your own information. Use phrases from the box.

Student A: Are you <u>compassionate</u>?

Student B: <u>Yes, I am.</u> What about you?

Student A: <u>Yes. I am very compassionate.</u>

Yes, I am.
I am very sociable / compassionate / supportive.
I am a little sociable / compassionate / supportive.
Not really.

L Choose a job title from A. Go to a job search site online and see if there are any openings within 25 miles of your school or home.

A retail sales associate helps a customer in a clothing store.

Review

A Listen and write the prices in Column 1. 🎧

Item	1. How much is it?	2. Where can you buy it?	3. Describe it.
a.	$899	an electronics store a big-box store	small, gray, and black
b.	$168		
c.	$18.95		
d.	$58.98		
e.	$459.99		
f.	$33.99		
g.	$17		
h.	$34.50		

B Complete Columns 2 and 3 in the table in **A** with your ideas.   Answers will vary.

Learner Log	I can identify places to shop.	I can describe items in a store.
	▢ Yes ▢ No ▢ Maybe	▢ Yes ▢ No ▢ Maybe

At-a-Glance Prep

Goal: All unit goals
Grammar: All unit grammar
Academic Strategies: Focused listening, reviewing, evaluating, developing study skills
Vocabulary: All unit vocabulary

Agenda

☐ Discuss unit goals.
☐ Complete the review.
☐ Evaluate and reflect on progress.

Pacing

■ 1.5 hour classes   ■ 2.5 hour classes
■ 3+ hour classes

Standards Correlations

CASAS: 0.1.2, 0.1.5, 1.1.6, 1.2.9, 1.6.4, 6.1.1
CCRS: L1, L2, L3, RI1, RI2, W3
ELPS:
S9: Create clear and coherent level-appropriate speech and text.

Warm-up and Review   10–15 mins. ■■■

Ask additional students to perform their conversations from the previous lesson in front of the class.

Introduction   2–5 mins. ■■■

With students' help, write all the goals from Unit 2 on the board. Show students the first page of the unit and mention the six goals. Explain that today they will review the whole unit.

Presentation   10–15 mins. ■■■

This presentation will cover all three pages of the review. Quickly go to the first page of each lesson. Discuss the goal of each. Ask simple questions to remind students of what they have learned.

Workplace Focus

Exercise A: Collect and organize information.

Practice 1   15–20 mins. ■■■

A Listen and write the prices in Column 1.

Go through the list, eliciting the name of each item. Ask: *How much is the TV?* Tell students to just listen the first time. Then play the audio. Play the audio two more times, giving students time to complete their answers each time. Have students compare answers with a partner. Then play the audio once more for students to confirm their answers.

Listening Script

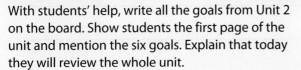

The TV is $459.99.   *The shoes are $58.98.*
The laptop is $899.   *The dictionary is $18.95.*
The shirt is $34.50.   *The sweater is $33.99.*
The vacuum is $168.   *The shorts are $17.*

B Complete Columns 2 and 3 in the table in A with your ideas.

Go over the example. Then elicit other kinds of stores and adjectives to describe items. Have students complete the table. This can be done in pairs.

Evaluation 1   10–15 mins. ■■■

Go around the classroom and check on students' progress. Help individuals as needed. If you see consistent errors among several students, interrupt the class and give a mini lesson or review to help students feel comfortable with the concept.

BEST PRACTICE

Learner Logs

Learner Logs function to help students in many different ways:

1. They serve as part of the review process.
2. They help students to gain confidence and to document what they have learned. Consequently, students see that they are progressing in their learning.
3. They provide students with a tool that they can use over and over to check and recheck their understanding of the target language. In this way, students become independent learners.

Learner Log   5–10 mins.

Have students read the statements and complete the log. If students answer *no* or *maybe*, encourage them to set themselves a goal to practice. Show them where they can find more practice activities.

Practice 2

15–20 mins. ■■□□

Workplace Focus

Exercise C: Perform basic computations.

C Read the receipts. Answer the questions.

Tell students to go over the receipts carefully and answer the questions. Have them compare answers with a partner.

D Write the numbers of bills and coins you need to purchase the shoes at Shoe Emporium in C.

Review bills and coins and then have students work out the answer. Have volunteers write their answers on the board and discuss any differences.

E Write the word for each item.

Have students complete the activity. Ask what color each item is. Then elicit other items of clothing and colors and write them on the board.

Evaluation 2

10–15 mins. ■■■□

Go around the classroom and check on students' progress. Help individuals as needed. If you see consistent errors among several students, interrupt the class and give a mini lesson or review to help students feel comfortable with the concept.

Learner Log

5–10 mins.

Have students read the statements and complete the log. If students answer *no* or *maybe*, encourage them to set themselves a goal to practice. Show them where they can find more practice activities.

BEST PRACTICE

Recycling / Review

The review and the project that follows are part of the recycling and review process. Students at this level often need to be reintroduced to concepts to solidify what they have learned. Many concepts are learned and forgotten while learning other new concepts. This is because students learn but are not necessarily ready to acquire language concepts. Therefore, it becomes very important to review and to show students how to review on their own. It is also important to recycle the new concepts in different contexts.

Instructor's Notes

C Read the receipts. Answer the questions.

Martin's	
Shirt .... 2 @ $27.98	
Subtotal $55.96	
Tax $4.48	
TOTAL $60.44	
Customer Copy	

ELECTRONICS SURPLUS	
Magi 70-inch TV $789.55	
Subtotal......................... $789.55	
Tax.................................. $63.16	
TOTAL $852.71	
Customer Copy	

SHOE EMPORIUM	
Black sneakers $44.95	
Subtotal........................... $44.95	
Tax $3.60	
TOTAL $48.55	
Customer Copy	

1. How many shirts are on the receipt from Martin's? ___two___

2. How much is the Magi TV from Electronics Surplus without tax? ___$789.55___

3. What is the total of all three receipts?

   ___$60.44___ + ___$852.71___ + ___$48.55___ = ___$961.70___

D Write the numbers of bills and coins you need to purchase the shoes at Shoe Emporium in C. Answers may vary. Example answers included.

___2___ twenty-dollar bill(s)   ___1___ five-dollar bill(s)   ___2___ quarter(s)   _____ dime(s)

_____ ten-dollar bill(s)   ___3___ one-dollar bill(s)   ___1___ nickel(s)   _____ pennies

E Write the word for each item.

1. ___shirt / top / blouse___   2. ___sandals___   3. ___skirt___

Review

F **Describe the pictures. Use** *his*, *her*, **or** *their*.

Rowena

Yadiel

1. What color is Rowena's hat? _Her hat is brown._

2. What color is Yadiel's cap? _His cap is green._

3. What color are Yadiel's shorts? _His shorts are blue._

4. What color is Rowena's dress? _Her dress is yellow._

5. What color are Rowena's and Yadiel's shoes? _Their shoes are black._

6. What color is Yadiel's T-shirt? _His T-shirt is white._

G **Write sentences about things you want in Unit 2.** Answers will vary.

1. _I want a new vacuum._

2. _____

3. _____

4. _____

5. _____

H **Talk to a partner. Write sentences about things your partner wants in Unit 2.**

Answers will vary.

1. _Eduardo wants a red car._

2. _____

3. _____

4. _____

5. _____

Learner Log I can describe clothing.
  ☐ Yes ☐ No ☐ Maybe

Practice 3   15–20 mins. ■■■

F **Describe the pictures. Use *his*, *her*, or *their*.**

Tell students to read the questions and answer them to describe the people in the pictures.

G **Write sentences about things you want in Unit 2.**

Tell students to go back through the unit to review the different items, then write their sentences.

Workplace Focus

Exercise H: Interpret and communicate information; Interact appropriately with team members.

H **Talk to a partner. Write sentences about things your partner wants in Unit 2.**

Make sure students talk to each other and don't just copy the sentences. Point out the change from *want* to *wants* when they write about their partner.

Evaluation 3   10–15 mins. ■■■

Go around the room and check on students' progress. Help individuals as needed. If you see consistent errors among several students, interrupt the class and give a mini lesson or review to help students feel comfortable with the concept.

Learner Log   5–10 mins.

Have students read the statement and complete the log. If students answer *no* or *maybe*, encourage them to set themselves a goal to practice. Show them where they can find more practice activities.

Instructor's Notes

_____

_____

_____

_____

_____

_____

_____

_____

_____

_____

_____

_____

_____

_____

_____

_____

_____

_____

_____

_____

_____

_____

_____

_____

Standards Correlations

CASAS: 0.1.2, 0.1.5, 1.3.3, 1.6.4, 4.8.1, 4.8.3, 4.8.6

CCRS: L1, L3, SL1, SL3

ELPS:

S3: Speak and write about level-appropriate complex literary and informational texts and topics.

S7: Adapt language choices to purpose, task, and audience when speaking and writing.

Workplace Focus

Combine ideas and information; Make decisions; Exercise leadership roles; Complete tasks as assigned; Interact appropriately with team members; Interpret and communicate information.

Soft Skill: Collaboration
Disagreeing Politely

Explain how in the workplace, collaboration is a very important skill. Projects can be developed and completed more easily and effectively when people work together, when they collaborate. However, when collaborating, it's important that if you disagree with others' ideas, you do so politely and suggest another idea. Tell students they will practice this skill as they carry out the steps of the project.

Warm-up and Review   10 mins.

Go over the items in the review section of the unit and make sure all have recorded their progress in the learner logs.

Introduction   10 mins.

Let students know that in this lesson they will be creating a big-box store and performing a role-play.

Presentation   10–15 mins.

1. Form a team of four or five students. In your team, you need:

Place students in teams of four or five. Have students choose their positions in the group. To do this, go through each step in the project and explain the role of the person who will lead that step. Make sure they understand that they will complete one step before going to the next and that although each person has a specific task, they will work together on each step. Point out the note about disagreeing politely when collaborating.

In **Step 2**, the team leader can manage the discussion of the name for their store. Then in **Step 3**, the architect will draw the floor plan, but all team members will contribute ideas and suggestions. In **Step 4**, the sales manager will lead the activity to decide products and prices. Go over the model conversation in **Step 4**. The sales manager will also make the price tags and receipts in **Step 6** with help from the team. In **Step 5**, the writers will write the role-play, but all team members will contribute ideas and help with the language. All members will participate in the role-play in **Step 7**.

Be aware of who volunteers for which position so that in the course of the different units, you can encourage students to try different roles.

Practice / Evaluation / Application   1–2 hours

2. Choose a name for your big-box store.

3. Draw a floor plan of your store.

4. Make a list of ten things your store sells. Include prices. Where are the items located on your floor plan?

5. Prepare a role-play in which a customer or customers come to your store to buy things and ask questions about items. The roles can include customers, a salesperson, a cashier, and a manager.

6. Make price tags and receipts for the items the customers buy in the role-play.

7. Practice the role-play and perform it for the class.

Plan a Big-Box Store

SOFT SKILL ▶ Collaboration

In this project, you will create a big-box store and perform a role-play for the class.

1. Form a team of four or five students. In your team, you need:

Position	Job Description	Student Name
Student 1: **Team Leader**	Check that everyone speaks English. Check that everyone participates.	
Student 2: **Architect**	With help from the team, draw a floor plan.	
Student 3: **Sales Manager**	With help from the team, list some of the items in your store and their prices. Create some price tags and receipts.	
Students 4/5: **Writers**	With help from the team, write a role-play to perform for the class.	

2. Choose a name for your big-box store.

   _____

3. Draw a floor plan of your store.

4. Make a list of ten things your store sells. Include prices. Where are the items located on your floor plan?

   Student A: I think $15.00 is a good price for a shirt.

   Student B: Maybe, but I think it can be more. What do others think?

   Student B: Candy can be in the back of the store.

   Student A: I'm sorry, but I disagree. I think we want people to see the candy when they are checking out. Can we have it in the front?

5. Prepare a role-play in which a customer or customers come to your store to buy things and ask questions about items. The roles can include customers, a salesperson, a cashier, and a manager.

6. Make price tags and receipts for the items the customers buy in the role-play.

7. Practice the role-play and perform it for the class.

COLLABORATION:
Disagreeing Politely
Be careful when you disagree. Always be polite and give other suggestions. Never say: "That's a bad idea."

Reading Challenge

About the Photo

This photo was taken by photojournalist Mel Melcon for a story about Avalon Nursery and Ceramics. Maria Lopez, an immigrant from Mexico, started the business in an empty lot in South L.A. more than 35 years ago. Maria's story of hard work and struggle to make her business the success it is today is truly inspiring. As seen in the photo, Maria's family is very involved in the business and helps out a lot. Here we see Maria's daughter-in-law Wendy Lopez hanging up holiday wreaths she made.

Have students look at the photo. Ask where the woman is and who they think she is. Discuss as a class.

A INTERPRET Read the pie charts and answer the questions.

Explain that pie charts are like graphs. They show us information about something. Ask students to look at the charts and read the titles. Check their understanding of *population* and *business owners*. Then have them study the charts and answer the questions with a partner. Check the answers as a class.

B Write the word for each picture.

Say the words in the box and complete the activity together.

Reading Challenge

A INTERPRET Read the pie charts and answer the questions.

1. What percentage of the population of the United States are immigrants? 14.1%

2. What percentage of U.S. business owners are immigrants? 21.7%

Immigrant Population in the United States
Immigrants 14.1%
Born in the U.S. 85.9%

Business Owners in the United States
Immigrants 21.7%
Born in the U.S. 78.3%

B Write the word for each picture.

| jungle | nursery | plant |

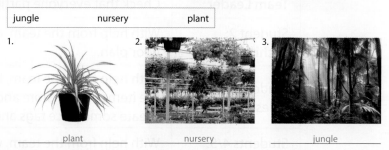

1. ___plant___   2. ___nursery___   3. ___jungle___

C Read the text. Underline any words you don't know.

D Complete the sentences with information from the text.

1. Around ___eight million___ people work at immigrant-owned businesses in the U.S.

2. Maria Lopez is from ___Mexico___. She moved to Los Angeles in 1987.

3. Sometimes Maria's family calls her ___nursery___ "the jungle" because there are so many plants there.

E What is each paragraph about? Choose the main idea.

Paragraph #1:

a. the number of small businesses in the United States

b. immigrant-owned businesses in the United States *(circled)*

Paragraph #2:

a. Maria Lopez and her business *(circled)*

b. Maria's family

F Work as a class. Make a list of immigrant-owned businesses in your community.

62   UNIT 2

CASAS FOR READING
0.1.5, 4.8.1, 6.7.4

CCRS FOR READING
L1, L3, RI1, RI2, RI3

READING STRATEGIES

Thinking Aloud

After completing a reading, students can usually recall key details or apply newly acquired knowledge by thinking aloud. Ask students to talk through an exercise in groups or pairs before going directly back to the reading to find an answer. Tell students to get in the habit of speaking their responses and then checking the answers against the reading once they have completed an exercise.

Business Is Good!

1 Starting your own business is not easy, but millions of immigrants do it and many are successful. One in five business owners in the United States is an immigrant; that is a big number! With these businesses come a lot of jobs: Around eight million people in the U.S. work at immigrant-owned businesses.

2 Maria Lopez is an immigrant. She came with her kids to the U.S. from Mexico in 1987. Maria owns a nursery in a busy part of Los Angeles, California, that she opened more than 35 years ago. She has a lot of plants. Her family calls the nursery "the jungle." Maria's family often helps out at the nursery. Her daughter-in-law, Wendy Lopez, whom you can see in the photo, makes colorful holiday wreaths to sell. Maria's business is very successful. Visiting L.A.? Go to Avalon Nursery and Ceramics. Say hello!

Wendy Lopez hangs holiday wreaths that she made at Avalon Nursery and Ceramics in Los Angeles.

READING CHALLENGE   63

F Work as a class. Make a list of immigrant-owned businesses in your community.

Write the list on the board and have students say what each business sells or what service it provides. Ask students which ones they go to often, don't go to, etc.

C Read the text. Underline any words you don't know.

Remind students not to worry about understanding everything and to focus on the main ideas. Tell them to underline any new words and continue reading.

D Complete the sentences with information from the text.

Have students complete this activity with a partner. Tell them to talk about the answers before looking at the text again. See the **Reading Strategies** note for more information on how talking through what students remember can be useful for their recall and understanding.

E What is each paragraph about? Choose the main idea.

Make sure students know what *paragraph* means. Point out the paragraph numbers in the reading. Then go over the options for each paragraph and have students choose their answers. Ask students to read the text again to confirm. Then ask students to look back at the words they underlined and see if there are any that they now understand from the context. Have students call out any words they are still unsure about and write them on the board. Cross out any that other students can explain and have students use dictionaries to find the remaining words in pairs or small groups and explain them to the class.

3 Food

About the Photo

This photo shows a colorful array of fresh fruits and vegetables. Produce of different colors provides different vitamins and nutrients. For example, orange fruits and vegetables are high in vitamins A, C, and K. Experts recommend we eat one from each color group (purple, red, orange, yellow, green) every day as a part of a healthy and balanced diet.

- Introduce the unit. Have students look at the photo. Then ask the questions. Discuss them as a class. Write the names of the fruits and vegetables students mention on the board.

- Go over the unit outcomes. Elicit any vocabulary that students already know related to each outcome. Write it on the board.

Life Skills Focus

In this unit, students will learn how to identify various foods and interpret grocery store advertisements and menus. They will also learn how to compare prices and to become informed consumers.

Workplace Focus

All lessons and units in *Stand Out* include basic communication skills and interpersonal skills important for the workplace. They include

UNIT OUTCOMES	GRAMMAR	VOCABULARY	EL CIVICS
• Identify common meals and foods	• Simple present: *Like*	• Meals	The skills students learn in this unit can be applied to the following EL Civics competency areas:
• Interpret grocery store ads	• Questions and answers with *Be*	• Foods	
• Express needs and preferences	• Simple present (multiple verbs)	• Quantities and containers	
• Compare prices		• Expensive, cheap	• Consumer Economics
• Take and place orders	• Comparative adjectives: *cheaper, more expensive*	• Menu sections	• Health and Nutrition
• Investigate food service jobs		• Food service jobs	
	• *Yes / no* questions and answers		

UNIT OUTCOMES

▶ Identify common meals and foods

▶ Interpret grocery store ads

▶ Express needs and preferences

▶ Compare prices

▶ Take and place orders

▶ Investigate food service jobs

Look at the photo and answer the questions.

1. What foods do you see?
2. Which of these foods do you like or dislike?
3. Are there any foods in the photo you haven't eaten before?
4. Many doctors say it is healthy to "eat the rainbow." A *rainbow* is all the different colors. What do you think "eat the rainbow" means and why is it good for you?
5. What meals can you make using the fruits and vegetables from the photo?

collecting and organizing information, making decisions and solving problems, and *combining ideas and information.*

In Unit 3, Lesson 6, *Explore the Workforce,* students will investigate food service jobs. They will analyze statistics related to restaurant positions and read about the responsibilities of different positions. They will also learn about tipping and then reflect on the characteristics of a good server and relate these to themselves.

• In the Team Project, students practice the soft skill of brainstorming while collaborating to complete the project.

• Life Online notes and exercises in Lessons 3 and 4 raise awareness about using apps to manage shopping lists and the pros and cons of online grocery shopping.

spark Resources

All resources for the unit are centrally located on the Spark platform and include: audio, video, multilevel worksheets, digital literacy worksheets, Online Practice, and Assessment Suite.

STEPS

CASAS COMPETENCIES	ELPS	CCRS
Lesson 1: 0.1.2, 0.1.5, 0.2.1, 1.2.8, 7.2.3 Lesson 2: 0.1.2, 0.1.5, 1.2.1, 1.2.4, 1.2.8, 7.2.3, 7.7.3 Lesson 3: 0.1.2, 0.1.5, 1.1.7, 1.2.8, 7.2.6 Lesson 4: 0.1.2, 0.1.5, 1.2.2, 1.2.8, 1.3.1, 4.8.1, 6.0.5, 6.7.2, 7.7.3 Lesson 5: 0.1.2, 0.1.5, 1.2.8, 2.6.4, 7.2.3 Lesson 6: 0.1.2, 0.1.5, 0.2.1, 4.1.3, 4.1.8, 4.1.9, 6.0.2, 6.0.5, 6.1.3, 6.7.1, 6.7.2, 6.7.4, 7.4.4, 7.7.3 Review: 0.1.2, 0.1.5, 0.2.1, 1.1.7, 1.2.1, 1.2.2, 1.2.4, 2.6.4 Team Project: 0.1.2, 0.1.5, 1.1.7, 1.2.1, 1.2.2, 1.2.4, 2.6.4, 4.8.1, 7.2.6 Reading Challenge: 0.1.2, 0.1.5, 1.5.2, 6.7.4	S1: Construct meaning from oral presentations and literary and informational text through level-appropriate listening, reading, and viewing. S7: Adapt language choices to purpose, task, and audience when speaking and writing. S9: Create clear and coherent level-appropriate speech and text. S10: Demonstrate command of the conventions of standard English to communicate in level-appropriate speech and writing.	L1, L2, L3, RI1, RI2, RI3, SL1, SL3, W1, W3

What's for Lunch?

GOAL ▶ Identify common meals and foods

A Look at the picture. Where is Dave? What foods do you see? Then read about Dave. 🎧

I'm Dave Chen. I'm an English teacher in Florida. I like to eat! I eat a big breakfast in the morning at around seven, a small lunch at noon, and a big dinner at about six o'clock.

B Practice the conversation with a partner.

Mario: What time do you eat <u>breakfast?</u>

Dave: Oh, at about <u>7:00 a.m.</u> How about you?

Mario: I eat breakfast at <u>8:00 a.m.</u>

C **SURVEY** Ask four students: *What time do you eat breakfast, lunch, and dinner?*

Answers will vary.

Name	Breakfast	Lunch	Dinner
Dave	7:00 a.m.	12:00 p.m.	6:00 p.m.
(You)			

At-a-Glance Prep

Goal: Identify common meals and foods
Grammar: Simple present: *Like*
Academic Strategies: Doing a survey, predicting, classifying information
Vocabulary: Meals and food

Agenda

☐ Talk about favorite meals.
☐ Identify meals and common foods.
☐ Learn new food vocabulary.
☐ Write what you like to eat.

Resources

Heinle Picture Dictionary: Food, pages 82–103

Pacing

■ 1.5 hour classes ■ 2.5 hour classes
■ 3+ hour classes

Standards Correlations

CASAS: 0.1.2, 0.1.5, 0.2.1, 1.2.8, 7.2.3
CCRS: L1, RI1, RI3, SL1, SL3
ELPS:

S1: Construct meaning from oral presentations and literary and informational text through level-appropriate listening, reading, and viewing.

S8: Determine the meaning of words and phrases in oral presentations and literary and informational text.

Warm-up and Review   10–15 mins. ■■■

Write the word *favorite* on the board. Tell students what your favorite meal is. Write the words *breakfast, lunch,* and *dinner* on the board and above them write *meals.* Ask students what their favorite meal is and take a class poll. You may need to explain in more detail what each meal is by using a clock to indicate the approximate time each meal is usually eaten.

Introduction   5 mins. ■■■

Ask students what they had for their most recent meal. Give this information about yourself to help explain and write the foods you had on the board. Add the foods students mention. State the goal: *Today, we will identify common meals and foods.*

Stating the Goal

We always suggest that you state the goal and write it on the board for all students to see. It is also important to revisit the goal at the end of the lesson so students can see that they learned something new. This will give them confidence. Revisiting the goals in the review and in the project is also important.

Presentation 1   10–15 mins. ■■■

Ask students to open their books and to cover up the reading about Dave. Discuss the picture. Write *food* on the board and ask students to identify any foods they can. If they are unable to tell what the foods are, ask them to make guesses.

A Look at the picture. Where is Dave? What foods do you see? Then read about Dave. 🎧

Discuss the questions as a class. Have students read the text on their own. Then play the audio and have students listen as they read along. Discuss any new words. Review the names for meals that students learned in the warm-up.

Practice 1   7–10 mins. ■■■

B Practice the conversation with a partner.

Model the conversation with a student. Then ask students to practice the conversation in pairs. Have students take turns practicing each role.

Workplace Focus

Exercise C: Collect and organize information.

C SURVEY Ask four students: *What time do you eat breakfast, lunch, and dinner?*

Have students complete the survey with information for themselves and then ask four of their classmates. Draw the survey form on the board and ask volunteers to share some of their personal information with the class by filling in the survey. Then add information that is true for you.

Evaluation 1   3–5 mins. ■■■

Go over the chart on the board and, as a class, discuss differences in meal schedules.

Presentation 2

10–15 mins. ■■■□

D Study the food words.

Go over the food words. Have students repeat them to practice the pronunciation. Take another class poll and find out about students' preferences. Ask which food they like best. Take the top four choices and do a corners activity. Each corner is one of the four top choices. Once students have formed groups in the different corners, ask them to make a list of foods that go along with the food that they chose. Students may use dictionaries or rely on other members of the group to make the list.

BEST PRACTICE

Corners

A corners activity is a cooperative-learning technique where the instructor assigns different attributes or qualities to the four corners of the room. For example, in this case, the instructor might assign each corner one of the following: *hamburger, spaghetti, roast beef,* and *toast.* Then the teacher asks students to go to the corner of their choice and perform some kind of task. This could involve writing a sentence using new vocabulary or asking and answering discussion questions.

In virtual classes, breakout rooms can be used to accomplish something similar.

Remind students again about the three meals. Ask individuals what they eat for breakfast, lunch, and dinner.

BEST PRACTICE

Asking Individuals

Educators debate whether or not to call on individuals who have not volunteered to speak in class. Some feel that students could be intimidated and leave the course.

One of the most important things the instructor can do is to develop a community in the class where students are comfortable about participating and not afraid to make mistakes. It should be a place where students feel they will get help from the instructor and other students and won't be left embarrassed or unsatisfied. When students feel comfortable, they are less likely to feel intimidated when called on and will be more open to learning.

Calling on individuals serves several purposes. First, students who ordinarily are timid about participating get more comfortable and may become more likely to volunteer in the future. Second, students don't know when they will be asked to participate, so they stay alert in the class. Third, students get a better sense of their classmates' abilities and personalities, which promotes community. Fourth, the information in the class should come from many different sources. Finally, the instructor gets a better feel for the students' level and how much the group as a whole understands and can produce.

Workplace Focus

Exercise E: Collect and organize information.

Practice 2

10–15 mins. ■■□

E PREDICT What do you think Dave eats for breakfast, lunch, and dinner? Complete the diagram with the foods from D.

Ask students to do this activity in groups of three or four. Help students understand that at this point all answers are acceptable, but ultimately, students will be listening to what Dave actually eats and checking their answers.

Evaluation 2

10 mins. ■■

F Listen to Dave and check your answers in E. 🎧

Play the audio two or three times and have students check their work by putting a checkmark by each item in the cluster diagram. Ask which groups predicted correctly.

Listening Script

Hello, my name is Dave. I am a teacher at Alexander Community College. I eat lunch here. They have a cafeteria. I teach all day, so I can eat here for all three meals. For breakfast before class, I eat eggs, cereal, and toast. For lunch after my first class, I eat a hamburger and french fries. Sometimes, I eat a sandwich for lunch instead of a hamburger. For dinner, I either have pasta, roast beef, or fried chicken. Pasta is my favorite.

D Study the food words.

cereal	french fries	a hamburger	roast beef	toast
eggs	fried chicken	pasta	a sandwich	

E **PREDICT** What do you think Dave eats for breakfast, lunch, and dinner? Complete the diagram with the foods from **D**.

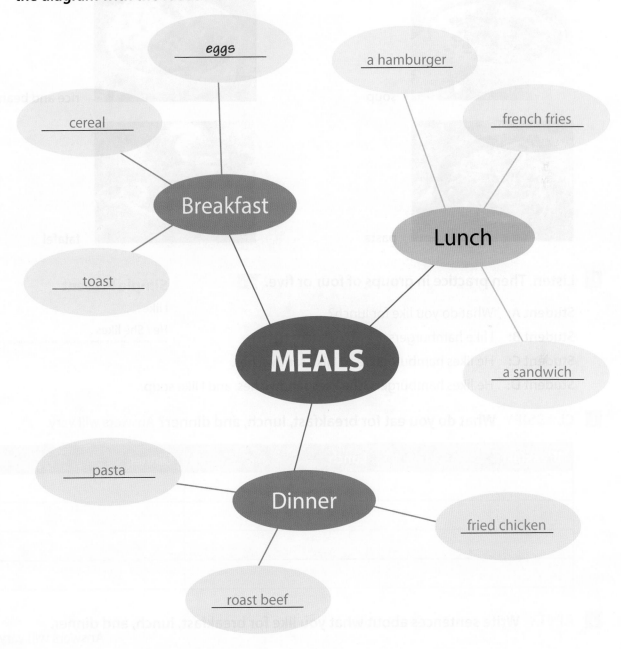

F Listen to Dave and check your answers in **E**. 🎧

G Practice the conversation with a partner. Then make new conversations with the food words.

Mario: What do you like for lunch?

Jim: I like <u>turkey sandwiches</u>. How about you?

Mario: I like <u>tacos</u>.

soup

rice and beans

pasta

falafel

H Listen. Then practice in groups of four or five. 🎧

Student A: What do you like for lunch?

Student B: I like hamburgers.

Student C: He likes hamburgers, and I like sandwiches.

Student D: He likes hamburgers, she likes sandwiches, and I like soup.

Simple Present

I **like** . . .

He / She **likes** . . .

I CLASSIFY What do you eat for breakfast, lunch, and dinner? Answers will vary.

Breakfast	Lunch	Dinner

J APPLY Write sentences about what you like for breakfast, lunch, and dinner.

Answers will vary.

1. I like _____ for breakfast.

2. _____ for lunch.

3. _____ .

Presentation 3   10–15 mins. ■■■

Ask different individuals what they like for breakfast, lunch, and dinner again. Go over the grammar note on the simple present. Remind students that the third-person singular form of the verb has an *s*.

Look over the photos on the page with students and discuss the meals. Ask students to tell you what their first, second, and third choice would be for lunch.

G   Practice the conversation with a partner. Then make new conversations with the food words.

Go over the conversation as a class. Practice the intonation of the question. Ask students to briefly practice it with a partner to get the feel of the exchange. Then model the same conversation with different food. Have students continue practicing using the different food words.

Workplace Focus

Exercise H: Interact appropriately with team members; Interpret and communicate information.

Practice 3   10–15 mins. ■

H   Listen. Then practice in groups of four or five. 🎧

Tell students to read the conversation as they listen. Then model the conversation with three students. Do another round with them so students see that Student B becomes Student A and asks the question. Have students do the activity four or five times so each person in the group can ask the question. Remind them throughout the activity to clearly pronounce the third-person singular *s* and to adjust the pronouns as needed to describe the students in their group.

Evaluation 3   5–7 mins. ■
Observe groups doing the activity.

Application   10–15 mins. ■■■

I   CLASSIFY   What do you eat for breakfast, lunch, and dinner?

Have students complete the chart. Provide help with vocabulary as needed.

J   APPLY   Write sentences about what you like for breakfast, lunch, and dinner.

Monitor as students write their sentences. If time allows, have students talk about their meal preferences with a partner and take notes. Then have them report their partner's preferences to the class. Remind them about the third-person singular *s* if necessary.

Instructor's Notes

_____

_____

_____

_____

_____

_____

_____

_____

_____

_____

_____

_____

_____

_____

_____

_____

_____

At-a-Glance Prep

Goal: Interpret grocery store ads
Grammar: Questions and answers with *be*
Academic Strategies: Interpreting information, focused listening, analyzing information
Vocabulary: Food, quantities, and containers

Agenda

☐ Talk about fruits and vegetables.
☐ Read grocery store ads.
☐ Listen to Mario and Lucy.
☐ Learn quantities and containers.
☐ Ask *How much?*
☐ Make a grocery store ad.

Resources

Heinle Picture Dictionary: Measurements and Containers, pages 96–97; Fruits and Nuts, pages 82–83; Vegetables, pages 84–85.

Pacing

■ 1.5 hour classes   ■ 2.5 hour classes
■ 3+ hour classes

Standards Correlations

CASAS: 0.1.2, 0.1.5, 1.2.1, 1.2.4, 1.2.8, 7.2.3, 7.7.3
CCRS: L1, L2, L3, RI1, RI2, RI3, SL1, SL3, W1, W3
ELPS:
S5: Conduct research and evaluate and communicate findings to answer questions or solve problems.
S9: Create clear and coherent level-appropriate speech and text.

Warm-up and Review   10–15 mins. ■■■

Ask students in groups to list on the board all the fruits and vegetables they know without using dictionaries. Make sure that the list includes *tomatoes, carrots,* and *avocados.*

Introduction   2 mins. ■■■

Refer to the list on the board and ask students how much they think a few of the items cost. Help them by guessing a few of the prices yourself. Use the phrase *a pound* when appropriate. State the goal: *Today, we will interpret grocery store ads.* Show how *ad* is a short version of *advertisement.*

Presentation 1   20–30 mins. ■■■

Go over the fruits and vegetables on the board and ask the class to come up with a price for each item. Ask questions such as: *How much are the apples?*

A INTERPRET Read the weekly specials. Then answer the questions with a partner.

Go over the items in order by asking different students: *How much is / are . . . ?* Compare the prices the students assigned to *avocados, tomatoes,* and *carrots* with the prices at Puente Market. Then have students answer the questions.

In **B**, students will listen for the vocabulary from **A**. To prepare for the focused listening, ask additional questions about the ad: *How much is the milk? What costs $4.20? What costs $1.25?*

Practice 1   10–15 mins. ■■■

B Listen to Mario and his wife Lucy make a shopping list. What do they need to buy? Check (✓) the correct items in A. 🎧

Point out that students should check the box next to *Add to list.* Play the audio several times. Ask students to discuss their answers in groups or pairs between plays.

Listening Script

Mario: *We need to go shopping. We're out of a few things.*
Lucy: *I'll open my shopping app and make a list.*
Mario: *Good idea. Well, I know we need ground beef. We really need carrots and tomatoes too.*
Lucy: *OK, I'll add those to the list … ground beef, carrots … and tomatoes.*
Mario: *Let's buy some soda too.*
Lucy: *OK. Oh, look. Avocados are on sale. Let's buy three.*
Mario: *That sounds good!*
Lucy: *Can you think of anything else?*
Mario: *No, I think that's it.*
Lucy: *OK. I have ground beef, carrots, tomatoes, soda, and avocados on the list.*

Evaluation 1   10–15 mins. ■■■

C Write sentences about what Mario and Lucy need.

Ask four students to write a sentence each on the board.

How Much Is It?

GOAL ▶ Interpret grocery store ads

A INTERPRET Read the weekly specials. Then answer the questions with a partner.

1. How much is the pasta? ___$1.98___

2. How much is the peanut butter? ___$3.25___

3. How much are the tomatoes? ___$1.50___

4. How much are the avocados? ___$1.25___

B Listen to Mario and his wife Lucy make a shopping list. What do they need to buy? Check (✓) the correct items in **A**. 🎧

C Write sentences about what Mario and Lucy need.

1. _They need ground beef._

2. _They need carrots._

3. _They need tomatoes._

4. _They need soda._

5. _They need avocados._

D INTERPRET Read the weekly specials. What prices look good to you?

FOOD CITY — Click ⊞ to add to your list.   WEEKLY SPECIALS

| BREAD | GROUND BEEF | PEANUT BUTTER | CUCUMBERS | ORANGES | FRESHLY BAKED COOKIES | MUSTARD | POTATO CHIPS |
| $1.98 a loaf | $4.30 a pound | $3.25 a jar | $.89 each | $2.39 a pound | $2.75 a box | $1.89 a jar | $2.75 a bag |

| PASTA | TOMATOES | MILK | AVOCADOS | APPLES | SODA | CARROTS | YOGURT |
| $2.20 a package | $1.75 a pound | $4.50 a gallon | $1.50 each | $1.49 a pound | $2.14 a bottle | $1.00 a package | $.79 each |

E ANALYZE Complete the chart with information from D.

Product	Container or Quantity	Price
cookies	box	$2.75
potato chips	bag	$2.75
soda	bottle	$2.14
avocados	each	$1.50
cucumbers	each	$.89
yogurt	each	$.79
milk	gallon	$4.50
mustard	jar	$1.89
peanut butter	jar	$3.25
bread	loaf	$1.98
pasta	package	$2.20
carrots	package	$1.00
tomatoes	pound	$1.75
ground beef	pound	$4.30
oranges	pound	$2.39
apples	pound	$1.49

Presentation 2

10–15 mins. ■■■

In this presentation, students will scan information and continue to learn quantity and container vocabulary. The practice will be for students to engage in a process of elimination to complete a chart. They will need to use all the vocabulary to do it. Therefore, spend some time making sure students understand the new vocabulary.

Workplace Focus

Exercise D: Interpret and communicate information; Combine ideas and information.

D INTERPRET Read the weekly specials. What prices look good to you?

Go over the items and clarify any vocabulary doubts. Ask questions about the items: *How much are the apples? What costs $2.75?* At this point, encourage students to say the price and the container or quantity in their answers.

Practice 2

10–15 mins. ■■

E ANALYZE Complete the chart with information from D.

Students will use the clues to complete the chart. Do the first two or three items with them so they get the idea. Encourage students to work in pairs or groups to do this activity so they have an opportunity to speak.

BEST PRACTICE

Critical Thinking

It is important to help students think critically about topics. It gives them more of an ability to apply learning and serves as a "hook" to future learning. Students who think critically will develop better organizational and academic skills and learn better and faster. There are many ways to provide this kind of activity. Below is a list of activities that develop critical thinking skills:

- using graphic organizers—students complete charts and graphs based on given information
- categorizing and classifying information
- reading charts and graphs
- doing open-ended projects with no one correct answer
- applying instruction to their daily lives
- problem solving

Many cooperative-learning techniques will stimulate critical thinking skills.

Evaluation 2

7–10 mins. ■■▲

Review students' charts.

Instructor's Notes

_____

_____

_____

_____

_____

_____

_____

_____

_____

_____

_____

_____

_____

_____

_____

_____

_____

_____

_____

_____

_____

_____

Presentation 3   10–15 mins. ■■■

Go over the ad in **D** again. Ask: *How much is the milk? How much are the carrots?* Write the questions on the board and ask students why in the first question you use *is* and in the second you use *are*. Draw a three-column chart on the board. Write all the new food vocabulary in the first column. The second column will be labeled *Question,* and students must decide whether to use *How much is* or *How much are*. The third column will contain the subject and the verb of the answer (*It is / They are*).

F   Study the charts.

Go over the charts. Then have students complete the third column of the chart you wrote on the board in groups. For example:

Item	Question	Answer
carrots	How much are	They are / They're
milk	How much is	It is / It's

Practice 3   10–15 mins. ■

G and **H** are information-gap activities. Only the student giving the answers should look at **D**. Ask students to record their answers on a separate sheet of paper.

G   Make conversations with a partner. Student A asks questions. Student B looks at the ad in D to answer. Ask about peanut butter, tomatoes, milk, and cookies.

Put students in A-B pairs. Then have the A students cover the previous page. Model the conversation with one of the A students. Next have a pair model the conversation. Ask students to continue with the conversations. When the A students have asked about their four items, have pairs move on to **H**.

H   Make conversations with a partner. Student B asks questions. Student A looks at the ad in D to answer. Ask about bread, potato chips, soda, and apples.

Tell the B students to cover the ad in **D**. This time the B students ask questions and the A students answer.

Evaluation 3   7–10 mins. ■

Observe students as they do **G** and **H**.

Workplace Focus

Exercise I: Combine ideas and information.

Application   20–25 mins. ■■■

I   DESIGN   Work in a group. Decide the weekly specials at your local market. Design an ad on a separate piece of paper.

Go over the instructions and put students in groups to design their ads. Tell them to first think of a list of items, then the prices before they design the ad. When they are ready, have each group show their ad to the class. For further practice with the questions, if time allows, have groups ask each other how much their different items are.

J   Look online for weekly specials at a grocery store. Are the prices in the ad in D more expensive or cheaper?

Elicit the names of local grocery stores and write them on the board. Then check students' understanding of *expensive* and *cheap*. Have them choose a store to look up online. They can work in pairs or small groups to do this. When they are ready, have students share what they found out with the class. Encourage them to give examples of specific items that are more expenisve or cheaper.

Instructor's Notes

_____

_____

_____

_____

_____

_____

_____

_____

_____

_____

_____

F Study the charts.

Be Verb (Questions)	
How much **is**	the bread? the peanut butter?
How much **are**	the tomatoes? the potato chips?

Be Verb (Answers)	
The bread **is** (It's)	$1.98 a loaf.
The peanut butter **is** (It's)	$3.25 a jar.
The tomatoes **are** (They're)	$1.75 a pound.
The potato chips **are** (They're)	$2.75 a bag.

G Make conversations with a partner. Student A asks questions. Student B looks at the ad in **D** to answer. Ask about peanut butter, tomatoes, milk, and cookies.

EXAMPLE:

Student A: How much is the peanut butter?

Student B: It's $3.25 a jar.

H Make conversations with a partner. Student B asks questions. Student A looks at the ad in **D** to answer. Ask about bread, potato chips, soda, and apples.

EXAMPLE:

Student B: How much are the potato chips?

Student A: They're $2.75 a bag.

I **DESIGN** Work in a group. Decide the weekly specials at your local market. Design an ad on a separate piece of paper.

J Look online for weekly specials at a grocery store. Are the prices in the ad in **D** more expensive or cheaper?

What Do We Need?

GOAL ▶ Express needs and preferences

A Look at the photo. When you're out of the house, do you usually pack a lunch or eat out?

Eat out

eat out = eat at a restaurant

B Read about Abdul. 🎧

My name is Abdul. I study at North Creek Adult School. It is very expensive to eat out every day, so I bring my lunch to school. My wife and I go to the store every Saturday. We buy bread and meat for sandwiches.

C Read the statements. Choose *True* or *False*.

1. Abdul buys his lunch at school.	True	(False)
2. Abdul and his son go to the store every Saturday.	True	(False)
3. Abdul and his wife buy bread and meat for sandwiches.	(True)	False

D Listen to the conversation between Abdul and his wife Laila. Check (✓) the foods they need from the supermarket. 🎧

Shopping List

_____ beef   ✓ jelly

_____ carrots   ✓ peanut butter

_____ cheese   ✓ tuna fish

✓ chicken   _____ turkey

Life ONLINE

Shopping Apps There are apps you can use to make shopping lists on your smartphone. This way, you can save your list and share it with others. Some apps can also help you find the best prices for the items on your list. In fact, you sometimes need a membership or an app to get sale prices.

At-a-Glance Prep

Goal: Express needs and preferences
Grammar: Simple present
Pronunciation: Plural -s
Academic Strategy: Focused listening
Vocabulary: Food, containers

Agenda

☐ Talk about sandwiches.
☐ Read about Abdul.
☐ Learn food container vocabulary.
☐ Express needs and wants.
☐ Read a shopping list.

Resources

Heinle Picture Dictionary: Measurements and Containers, pages 96–97

Pacing

■ 1.5 hour classes   ■ 2.5 hour classes
■ 3+ hour classes

Standards Correlations

CASAS: 0.1.2, 0.1.5, 1.1.7, 1.2.8, 7.2.6
CCRS: L1, L2, L3, RI1, RI2, SL1, SL3
ELPS:
S2: Participate in level-appropriate oral and written exchanges of information, ideas, and analyses, in various social and academic contexts, responding to peer, audience, or reader comments and questions.

Warm-up and Review   10–15 mins. ■■■

Write *sandwich* on the board. Ask groups to list on the board as many types of sandwiches as they can. Find out which sandwich is the class favorite.

Introduction   7–10 mins. ■■■

Make a two-column chart on the board. Label the first *needs* and the second *wants / preferences*. Say: *I want ice cream for breakfast.* Write *ice cream* in the *wants* column. Explain that our *preferences* are things we like or want. Then say: *I need water.* Write *water* in the *needs* column. Give other examples and ask students to figure out which column to write it in. State the goal: *Today, we will express needs and preferences.*

Presentation 1   20–25 mins. ■■■

A Look at the photo. When you're out of the house, do you usually pack a lunch or eat out?

Ask students to say what they see in this packed lunch. If appropriate, show them your packed lunch and explain that you bring your lunch with you, or tell them that you *eat out*. Go over the vocabulary note and say where you eat lunch on work days. Then have students share what they do. If students pack a lunch, ask what they usually bring. Take a class poll to see how many people pack a lunch and how many eat out.

B Read about Abdul.

Have students read the text individually. Ask some comprehension questions. For example: *Is Abdul a student? Does he buy lunch at school?*, etc.

C Read the statements. Choose *True* or *False*.

Do this as a class. Ask students to correct the false sentences and make them true.

Practice 1   10–15 mins. ■■■

D Listen to the conversation between Abdul and his wife Laila. Check (✓) the foods they need from the supermarket.

Play the audio two or three times. Allow students to compare answers between listenings.

Evaluation 1   5–7 mins. ■■■

Go over students' answers.

Listening Script

Abdul: *It is too expensive to buy food at school every day. I have the same sandwiches every week. Maybe we should buy something different, but I need something healthy.*
Laila: *OK. What do you have in mind?*
Abdul: *Well, I thought I might try tuna fish. It is delicious.*
Laila: *Yes, they say fish is good for you too. What about chicken?*
Abdul: *Chicken is OK, but I don't have time to prepare it.*
Laila: *We can buy it in slices. You don't need to prepare it.*
Abdul: *Great. I also need peanut butter and jelly.*
Laila: *Yes, we do need both. We are completely out.*

Note: The Life Online note is addressed on page 73a.

Presentation 2 15–20 mins. ■■■

This presentation will further reinforce the new vocabulary and prepare students to express their needs.

E Study the words for food containers. Match the words to the pictures.

Do this activity with the class and make sure students understand the vocabulary.

Workplace Focus

Exercise F: Interpret and communicate information; Interact appropriately with team members.

F Work in a group. Discuss what other foods go in each container.

Ask students to brainstorm in a group. Give them around three minutes. You may also suggest that they look back at the ads in Lesson 2 to help them. Ask the groups for their answers and encourage them to respond in sentences such as: *We have a can of soup and a bottle of oil.*

Pronunciation   Plural -s 🎧

Point out the pronunciation note on the plural *-s*. Play the audio. Then play it again and have students repeat each plural form.

The final *-s* in plural nouns is sometimes omitted by students, especially if final consonants are not emphasized in their native languages. Show students how the final *-s* in these words can be voiced by asking them to put two fingers on their voice box and feeling the vibration.

Explain that container words, such as those in **E** and **F**, are often followed by *of*. When they are followed by *of*, the /z/ links to the *o* in *of*. So, for example, students should practice pronouncing: *bottle-zof* and *boxe-zof*.

Overemphasizing a sound is OK for demonstration as long as you also demonstrate the sound in context with appropriate emphasis.

Remember that most students need to be exposed several times to pronunciation and grammar concepts before they acquire them.

Practice 2 7–10 mins. ■■

G Create sentences using words from F. Then read your sentences to a partner.

Go over the example. Then have students complete the sentences individually. When they are ready, put them in pairs for the second part of the activity. Remind them to focus on their pronunciation of the plural *-s*.

Evaluation 2 10–15 mins. ■■

After completing the sentences, ask students to close their books. Write a name on the board and then give students a dictation with sentences about what the person needs using the vocabulary from **F**. Say each sentence twice. The first time, students should just listen and then repeat the sentence. The second time, they should write. Pause between sentences to give them time to write. Say each sentence a third time if necessary. Then ask volunteers to write the sentences on the board.

BEST PRACTICE

Dictation

Dictation can be a very good activity for encouraging writing accuracy and developing listening skills. At this level, students have a limited vocabulary, so it often makes sense to give a dictation of a text or sentences that students have already seen.

When doing a dictation activity, be aware that, at this level, students have difficulty listening and writing at the same time. And yet the minute you start speaking, students will probably start writing. This is not a productive way to do dictation.

Teach students to listen to the sentence, repeat the sentence, and then write the sentence. The first time you read the dictation text, have students just listen and then ask them to repeat the text in unison. Finally, ask them to write what they have heard and repeated. After they are confident that they understand the text, ask students to repeat it to themselves silently instead of out loud.

E Study the words for food containers. Match the words to the pictures.

bag	bottle	box	~~can~~	jar	package

1. a ___can___ of beans

2. a ___bottle___ of water

3. a ___package___ of cheese

4. a ___box___ of cookies

5. a ___jar___ of mustard

6. a ___bag___ of potato chips

F Work in a group. Discuss what other foods go in each container. Answers will vary.

Container	Food
can / cans	soup, coffee
bottle / bottles	
package / packages	
box / boxes	
jar / jars	
bag / bags	

Plural -s 🎧

The plural -s makes three different sounds.

/z/	/s/	/ɪz/
jars	chips	packages
bags	snacks	boxes
cans		

G Create sentences using words from F. Then read your sentences to a partner.
Answers will vary.

1. Alicia needs three cans of ___soup___ .

2. She needs four bottles of _____ .

3. She needs two packages of _____ .

4. _____ three boxes of _____ .

5. _____ .

6. _____ .

H Study the chart.

Simple Present		
Subject	**Verb**	**Example Sentence**
I / You We / They	eat like need want make	I **eat** tacos for lunch. You **like** eggs for breakfast. We **need** three cans of corn. They **want** three boxes of cookies. I **make** sandwiches for lunch.
He / She	eats likes needs wants makes	He **eats** pizza for dinner. She **likes** tomato soup. He **needs** three pounds of apples. She **wants** two bottles of water. She **makes** dinner every night.

I Read.

← Notes
Shopping List

6 bottles of water

3 cans of soup

1 jar of jelly

3 packages of cheese

J Complete the sentences with the correct form of the verbs in parentheses and the correct container. Then listen and check your answers. 🎧

1. Abdul _____needs_____ (need) one _____jar_____ of jelly.

2. They _____like_____ (like) soup for dinner.

3. Abdul _____eats_____ (eat) sandwiches at school.

4. Laila _____makes_____ (make) sandwiches for lunch.

5. They _____want_____ (want) three _____packages_____ of cheese.

K Make a list of things you need at the store. Tell a partner what you need.

Presentation 3   15–20 mins. ■■■■

Rewrite the sentences from the dictation on the board. Then write, for example: *I _____ three cans of beans.* Have students complete the sentence. Ask them to rewrite the remaining sentences using *you, we,* and *they.*

Underline the third-person singular *-s* in the original dictation sentences and show students how the verbs in the new sentences don't take an *-s.*

H   Study the chart.

Go over the chart carefully. If you think students are comfortable with the verb forms, elicit further examples about themselves and their family and friends. Model by saying something about your family or friends.

I   Read.

Ask students to read the shopping list. Then ask questions. For example: *What do they need? How many packages of cheese?*, etc.

Practice 3   10–15 mins. ■

J   Complete the sentences with the correct form of the verbs in parentheses and the correct container. Then listen and check your answers. 🎧

Make sure students see that the sentences they are completing directly relate to the shopping list. Have students complete the sentences individually. Then play the audio and have students check their answers.

Evaluation 3   10–15 mins. ■

Ask students to write the sentences on the board. Underline the third person singular *-s.*

Workplace Focus

Exercise K: Interpret and communicate information.

Application   10–15 mins. ■

K   Make a list of things you need at the store. Tell a partner what you need.

Make sure students write their list first. Then put them in pairs. Students should listen and write their partner's list. When they have finished, have students tell the class or a small group their partner's list.

Instructor's Notes

_____

_____

_____

_____

_____

_____

_____

_____

_____

_____

_____

_____

_____

_____

_____

_____

_____

_____

_____

_____

_____

At-a-Glance Prep

Goal: Compare prices

Grammar: Comparative adjectives

Pronunciation: Stress

Academic Strategies: Evaluating, calculating, making comparisons, focused listening

Vocabulary: Food, *cheaper, more expensive*

Agenda

☐ List foods.

☐ Complete a graph.

☐ Compare prices.

☐ Read about Sonia.

☐ Listen for prices.

☐ Discuss stores.

Resources

Heinle Picture Dictionary: Supermarket, pages 98–99

Pacing

■ 1.5 hour classes   ■ 2.5 hour classes

■ 3+ hour classes

Standards Correlations

CASAS: 0.1.2, 0.1.5, 1.2.2, 1.2.8, 1.3.1, 4.8.1, 6.0.5, 6.7.2, 7.7.3

CCRS: L1, L2, L3, RI1, RI2, RI3, SL1, SL3, W1, W3

ELPS:

S1: Construct meaning from oral presentations and literary and informational text through level-appropriate listening, reading, and viewing.

S5: Conduct research and evaluate and communicate findings to answer questions or solve problems.

Warm-up and Review   15–20 mins. ■■■

On the board, elicit all the new vocabulary used in this unit thus far. Make sure students know what each word means. Make a four-column chart on the board with the following headings: *fruits, vegetables, meat,* and *drinks*. In groups, have students make a similar chart and put all the items in the appropriate columns. Ask volunteers from the groups to fill out the chart on the board.

BEST PRACTICE

Group Participation

There are many ways to encourage all students to participate in groups. It helps when students are working on a written task if they work on one chart for the entire group and not their own individual ones. One student is the writer and the others make suggestions.

Introduction   5–7 mins. ■■■

Ask students to look at the grocery store ads in Lesson 2. Ask which store they think is better and why. Students may determine that the prices at one store are cheaper than at the other. State the goal: *Today, we will compare prices.*

Presentation 1   15–20 mins. ■■■

A EVALUATE Read Abdul's shopping list. Look at the specials for Puente Market and Food City in Lesson 2. Which store do you think is cheaper for Abdul?

Take a class poll about which store they think is cheaper for Abdul.

Workplace Focus

Exercise B: Collect and organize information; Combine ideas and information.

B CALCULATE Calculate the prices of the items on Abdul's shopping list. Then calculate the total for each store.

Study the chart as a class and help students understand what information is missing and how to complete it. Have them complete the chart with a partner. Make sure they are getting the prices from the two stores in Lesson 2. Copy the chart on the board, and when pairs have finished calculating, have them call out the numbers for you to complete the chart.

Practice 1   10–15 mins. ■■■

C COMPARE Complete the graph with the prices from B.

Go over the graph with the class. Then have students fill in the columns for carrots, avocados, and pasta based on the information they collected in **B**.

Evaluation 1   5–7 mins. ■■■

Go over the completed graph as a class. Ask which store is cheaper for Abdul.

What's Cheaper?

GOAL ▶ Compare prices

A **EVALUATE** Read Abdul's shopping list. Look at the specials for Puente Market and Food City in Lesson 2. Which store do you think is cheaper for Abdul?

Puente Market is cheaper.

Notes

Shopping List

2 packages of pasta

2 pounds of tomatoes

3 avocados

3 packages of carrots

B **CALCULATE** Calculate the prices of the items on Abdul's shopping list. Then calculate the total for each store.

	Puente Market	Food City
Tomatoes	$3.00	$3.50
Carrots	$3.75	$3.00
Avocados	$3.75	$4.50
Pasta	$3.96	$4.40
Total Cost:	$14.46	$15.40

C **COMPARE** Complete the graph with the prices from **B**.

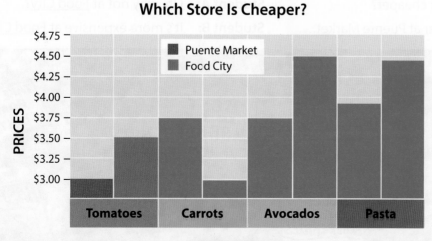

Which Store Is Cheaper?

D Study the charts.

Cheaper	Question	Answer
Singular	Where is pasta **cheaper**?	It's **cheaper** at Puente Market.
Plural	Where are carrots **cheaper**?	They're **cheaper** at Food City.

More Expensive	Question	Answer
Singular	Where is pasta **more expensive**?	It's **more expensive** at Food City.
Plural	Where are carrots **more expensive**?	They're **more expensive** at Puente Market.

E Complete the sentences. Then listen and check your answers. 🎧

Stress 🎧
Where are **carrots cheaper**?
They're **cheaper** at **Food City**.

1. Soda is $2.14 at Food City and $2.99 at Puente Market.
   Soda is _____more expensive_____ at Puente Market.

2. Avocados are $1.50 at Food City and $1.25 at Puente Market. Avocados are _____cheaper_____ at Puente Market.

3. Tomatoes are $1.75 at Food City and $1.50 at Puente Market. Tomatoes are _____cheaper_____ at Puente Market.

4. Pasta is $2.20 at Food City and $1.98 at Puente Market. Pasta is _____more expensive_____ at Food City.

F Practice the conversations with a partner. Then make new conversations using the foods and prices from **C**.

Student A: I need some <u>ground beef</u>.
Where <u>is it</u> cheaper?

Student B: It's cheaper at <u>Puente Market</u>.

Student B: I buy <u>pasta</u> at <u>Puente Market</u>.

Student A: Oh, why not at <u>Food City</u>?

Student B: It's more expensive at <u>Food City</u>.

Fruit for sale at a market in Seattle, Washington

BEST IN THE MARKET

TAKE SOME HOME WE PACK TO GO!!

SWEET STRAWBERRIES 2 FOR $7.00 $4 EA

SWEET LOCAL BLUEBERRIES 2 FOR $5.00 $3 EA

RASPBERRIES 2 FOR $9.00 $5 EA

Presentation 2

Review the difference between questions that start with *How much is* and *How much are*. Ask when to use each phrase with the words on the shopping list in **A**. Also, remind students how to use *it is* and *they are*.

Write *cheap* and *cheaper* on the board. Add *expensive* and *more expensive*. Explain these new words by talking about the prices in **B**. Also, point out the word *at* (as in *at* Puente Market). Ask questions and see how much students understand before they open their books. It is helpful to work with students and allow them to think about the concepts before you give them all the information in a chart. In this way, students will understand the charts better.

D Study the charts.

Go over the examples in the charts and have students repeat both the questions and the answers. Repeat the questions with other items.

Pronunciation   Stress 🎧

There is a rhythm to English that is similar to some languages and very distinct from others. Speakers of different languages vary which words they emphasize to show rhythm in discourse. However, in English, important words are stressed regularly, and words that answer a specific question are also given emphasis. Syllables with less emphasis are generally spoken quickly, whereas words with more emphasis are lengthened.

Direct students to the pronunciation note on stress. Play the audio. Then play it again, pausing for students to repeat the question and the answer. Remind students that stress means saying a word louder and / or longer than usual. Explain that question words, nouns, verbs, and adjectives give meaning to a sentence, so we say these words louder and longer.

In teaching stress, an instructor might have students clap along with the stress pattern several times before they attempt to produce an utterance so they have a general feel for the rhythm.

Ask students to say only the syllables that receive more emphasis. In this case, they might say: *Where-car-cheap*.

Once students are comfortable with the rhythm, say the question and ask them to repeat it.

Listening Script

Stress the words that give meaning to the sentence.
Where are **carrots cheaper**?
They're **cheaper** at **Food City**.

Practice 2

E Complete the sentences. Then listen and check your answers. 🎧

Have students complete the activity individually, then compare with a partner. Play the audio for students to check their answers.

F Practice the conversations with a partner. Then make new conversations using the foods and prices from C.

Have students repeat each line of the conversations after you. Then divide the class in half and practice the conversations chorally with half the class being A, the other half B, then switching roles. Model each conversation with a student before you put students in pairs. Monitor as they practice and help with pronunciation as needed. Remind students to switch roles so they practice both parts of the conversation.

Evaluation 2

Ask for volunteers to demonstrate their conversations for the class.

Instructor's Notes

_____

_____

_____

_____

_____

_____

_____

_____

Presentation 3 15–20 mins. ■■■

G INTERPRET Read the paragraph about Sonia. Underline words you don't know. 🎧

Tell students to read as they listen. Play the audio. Have students read the paragraph again and underline new vocabulary. Go over the vocabulary questions, eliciting explanations from other students wherever possible.

H Read the statements. Choose *True* or *False*.

Have students complete the activity individually, then compare with a partner. Check answers as a class.

Practice 3 10–15 mins. ■

I COMPARE Listen to Sonia ask about prices. Complete the chart. 🎧

Prepare students for focused listening by having them look at the chart. Ask them to predict what information they will listen for.

You may need to play the audio several times. Allow students to discuss their answers in groups between listenings.

Listening Script

Sonia: *Excuse me. Does this store do price matching? If I find a cheaper price at a different store, can you give me the same price here?*

Salesperson: *Yes, we do. Do you have an ad?*

Sonia: *Yes. It says right here that at Puente Market, bananas are ninety-two cents a pound. Here at Food City, they are ninety-eight cents.*

Salesperson: *That looks right. We can give you that price.*

Sonia: *Here are more examples. Puente Market is always cheaper.*

Salesperson: *Let's see. You're right. Oranges at Puente Market are $2.20 a pound and at Food City, they cost $2.39 a pound. Pears at Puente Market are $1.29 a pound. Here at Food City, they are $1.59.*

Sonia: *Look at this! Apples are $1.49 at Food City and only $1.31 at Puente Market.*

Salesperson: *Wow. It looks like we need to change a lot of prices!*

Evaluation 3 5–10 mins. ■

J Shopping for groceries online has advantages and disadvantages. Read. Then add your own ideas.

Life ONLINE

Go over the chart and check that students understand each pro and con. As a class, think of other pros and cons. Write them on the board.

K Work in a group. Ask each member of the group if it is better to shop for groceries online or at the store. Where do they shop and why?

Have groups report their answers to the class and determine which way of grocery shopping is more popular. Ask volunteers to share more information about the stores or online services they use and why.

Application 10–15 mins. ■■■

L As a class, choose one food item. Choose two stores in your neighborhood or go online. Compare prices. Which store is cheaper?

Have students suggest items. Take a poll to decide which of their suggestions they will research. Elicit the names of local grocery stores and write them on the board. Then have students carry out the research in pairs. Tell them to write the prices they find and then report which store is cheaper.

G **INTERPRET** Read the paragraph about Sonia. <u>Underline</u> words you don't know. 🎧

> I shop at Food City. They have a lot of different fruits and vegetables there. The fruit is cheaper at Puente Market, but there aren't many choices. Food City has good specials too. It is also near my home.

H Read the statements. Choose *True* or *False*.

1. Sonia shops at Puente Market.   True   (False)

2. The fruit at Food City is more expensive.   (True)   False

3. Food City has a lot of choices.   (True)   False

I **COMPARE** Listen to Sonia ask about prices. Complete the chart. 🎧

Fruit	Price at Puente Market	Price at Food City
bananas	$.92	$.98
oranges	$2.20	$2.39
pears	$1.29	$1.59
apples	$1.31	$1.49

J Shopping for groceries online has advantages and disadvantages. Read. Then add your own ideas. Answers will vary.

Life ONLINE

Shopping for Groceries Online	
Advantages	Disadvantages
You can compare prices from home.	You pay more for delivery.
You can save money on gasoline.	Sometimes the driver makes mistakes.
You can save time.	You can't see the food before you buy it.

K Work in a group. Ask each member of the group if it is better to shop for groceries online or at the store. Where do they shop and why?

L As a class, choose one food item. Choose two stores in your neighborhood or go online. Compare prices. Which store is cheaper?

LESSON 5

Buying Lunch

GOAL ▶ Take and place orders

A **CLASSIFY** Look at the menu. Write *Beverages*, *Side Orders*, and *Sandwiches*.

Jim's Lunch Truck

Sandwiches	Side Orders	Beverages
Hamburger $5.00	French Fries $2.00	Milk $3.00
Cheeseburger............. $5.50	Fruit Cup $2.00	Orange Juice $3.50
Hot Dog $3.00	Green Salad $3.25	Soda $3.50
Grilled Cheese............. $3.50		Bottled Water.............. $ 3.00
Turkey........................... $ 4.00		

B Listen and write the prices you hear in the menu in **A**. 🎧

C Practice the conversation with a partner. Then make new conversations using the menu from **A**.

Sebastian: Hi! I want a <u>turkey sandwich</u>, please.
Server: Do you want a side order?
Sebastian: Yes, a <u>green salad</u>.
Server: Great! Do you want a drink?
Sebastian: <u>A bottle of water</u>, thanks.

Singular	Plural
a burger	two burgers
a salad	three salads
	french fries

D Look at the menu in **A**. Talk to your classmates and teacher. What do you like to eat? What is cheap?

At-a-Glance Prep

Goal: Take and place orders
Grammar: *Yes / no* questions and answers
Academic Strategies: Classifying information, focused listening
Vocabulary: Food, menu sections

Agenda

☐ Guess prices.
☐ Read a menu.
☐ Listen and write prices.
☐ Listen to restaurant orders.
☐ Ask and answer *yes / no* questions.
☐ Place your own lunch order.

Resources

Heinle Picture Dictionary: Order, Eat, Pay, pages 102–103

Pacing

■ 1.5 hour classes   ■ 2.5 hour classes
■ 3+ hour classes

Standards Correlations

CASAS: 0.1.2, 0.1.5, 1.2.8, 2.6.4, 7.2.3
CCRS: L1, L2, L3, SL1, SL3
ELPS:

S2: Participate in level-appropriate oral and written exchanges of information, ideas, and analyses, in various social and academic contexts, responding to peer, audience, or reader comments and questions.

S10: Demonstrate command of the conventions of standard English to communicate in level-appropriate speech and writing.

Warm-up and Review   10–15 mins. ■■□

Play a game. Write the food items from the grocery store ads in Lesson 2 on the board in random order under a heading for each store (*Puente Market* or *Food City*). Split the class into two teams. Team 1 guesses the price of an item. Team 2 guesses if the item is cheaper than Team 1 has said or more expensive. If the price is exactly right, Team 1 receives a point. If Team 2 successfully determines that the price is cheaper or more expensive than Team 1's guess, they get a point.

Introduction   5–7 mins. ■■□

Ask students what restaurants they like. Ask what their favorite foods to order are. Ask if they order in English. State the goal: *Today, we will learn to take and place orders.*

Presentation 1   15–20 mins. ■■■

A CLASSIFY Look at the menu. Write *Beverages, Side Orders, and Sandwiches.*

Make sure students understand the meaning of the different categories. Go over the items in the menu as a class. Then elicit where the headings go.

Workplace Focus

Exercise B: Collect and organize information.

B Listen and write the prices you hear in the menu in A. 🎧

Have students look at the photo on page 79. Point out the food truck employee and the customer. Ask: *What does he want?* Tell students they are going to listen to a conversation at a food truck. Remind students they don't need to understand everything. Tell them to focus on the prices they need to complete the menu. Play the audio twice. Then have students compare with a partner. Play the audio again to check answers.

Note: The listening script for **B** is on page 79a.

Workplace Focus

Exercise C: Interpret and communicate information.

Practice 1   10–15 mins. ■■■

C Practice the conversation with a partner. Then make new conversations using the menu from A.

Practice the conversation with the whole class. Then model it with a student. Ask for different items from the menu. Then switch roles. Point out the plural forms in the chart. Put students in pairs to practice.

Evaluation 1   3–5 mins. ■■■

Ask volunteers to perform a conversation for the class.

Presentation 2   7–10 mins. ■■■

D Look at the menu in A. Talk to your classmates and teacher. What do you like to eat? What is cheap?

Write on the board: *I like...* and *cheap - cheaper*. Tell the students what you like. Then say: *Grilled cheese is cheap.* Elicit an item that is cheaper. Encourage students to talk about the menu. Make sure everyone says something.

Listening Script

Sebastian: *Hi! I want a turkey sandwich, please.*
Server: *Do you want a side order?*
Sebastian: *Yes, a green salad.*
Server: *Great! Do you want a drink?*
Sebastian: *A bottle of water, thanks.*
Server: *Great, that's a turkey sandwich for $4.00, a green salad for $3.25, and a bottle of water for $3.00. Is that right?*
Sebastian: *Perfect.*
Server: *That will be $10.89 with tax.*
Sebastian: *Here you go!*

BEST PRACTICE

Inside / Outside Circle

At this level, students are asked to perform short conversations often to provide practice. This is necessary because they don't have an extended vocabulary to discuss things freely yet. It is a good idea to provide different ways to approach pair practice. In the previous unit, students used conversation or substitution cards. This can work again here. Another approach is *inside / outside circle*. Students stand in two circles, one circle inside the other. Both circles contain the same number of students. The students in the outer circle face the students in the inner one. They perform the conversation once, and then one of the circles rotates so each student has a new conversation with another student. This activity continues until you feel students have gotten enough practice.

Workplace Focus

Exercise E: Combine ideas and information; Collect and organize information.

Practice 2   10–15 mins. ■■□

E **Listen and write each person's order. Write the menu sections and prices from A. Which order is the most expensive?** 🎧

Go over the first two columns in the chart. Then play the audio, pausing after Manny's order and pointing to the items and sections in the chart. Have students listen and complete the first columns only for Tran's and Delia's orders. Play the audio twice. Then have students compare with a partner and complete the second column. Play the audio again as needed to confirm the answers. Finally, have students add the prices from the menu and calculate the totals. Have them do this in pairs if they feel more comfortable.

Listening Script

1. **Manny:** *I want a cheeseburger, a green salad, and an orange juice, please.*
   Server: *No orange juice today. Would you like milk or soda?*
   Manny: *A soda, please.*
   Server: *OK, two minutes. Next.*

2. **Tran:** *I'll have a grilled cheese sandwich, please.*
   Server: *OK. Anything else?*
   Tran: *And a fruit cup too.*
   Server: *Of course. What about a drink?*
   Tran: *No, thanks.*
   Server: *OK. That's a grilled cheese sandwich and fruit cup, right?*
   Tran: *That's right. Thanks.*

3. **Delia:** *I want some milk, please, and a hot dog.*
   Server: *Do you want mustard?*
   Delia: *No, thanks. Just french fries.*
   Server: *OK. A hot dog, no mustard, french fries, and a milk coming up.*

Evaluation 2   7–10 mins. ■■□

Check to see that everyone got the same totals and have students say which order is the most expensive. If students ask about the use of *most*, explain briefly that we use *more* to compare two things and *most* to compare more than two.

Instructor's Notes

_____

_____

_____

_____

_____

_____

_____

_____

_____

_____

E Listen and write each person's order. Write the menu sections and prices from **A.**
Which order is the most expensive?

1. Manny's order

Item	Section	Price
cheeseburger	sandwiches	$5.50
green salad	side orders	$3.25
soda	beverages	$3.50
	Total	$12.25

2. Tran's order

Item	Section	Price
grilled cheese	sandwiches	$3.50
fruit cup	side orders	$2.00
	Total	$5.50

3. Delia's order

Item	Section	Price
milk	beverages	$3.00
hot dog	sandwiches	$3.00
french fries	side orders	$2.00
	Total	$8.00

A man buys lunch
from a food truck in
Richmond, Virginia.

F **Study the chart.**

Yes / No Questions and Answers		
Question	***Yes***	***No***
Do you want a hamburger?	Yes, I do.	No, I don't.
Do they want sandwiches?	Yes, they do.	No, they don't.
Does he want a sandwich?	Yes, he does.	No, he doesn't.
Does she want a hot dog?	Yes, she does.	No, she doesn't.

G **Read the orders.**

José
Sandwich: turkey
Side order: salad
Beverage: water

Fatimah
Sandwich: cheeseburger
Side order: french fries
Beverage: water

Beatrice
Sandwich: hot dog
Side order: french fries
Beverage: orange juice

H **Answer the questions.**

1. Does José want a salad? _____ Yes, he does. _____

2. Does Beatrice want orange juice? _____ Yes, she does. _____

3. Do José and Fatimah want orange juice? _____ No, they don't. _____

4. Do José and Fatimah want water? _____ Yes, they do. _____

5. Do Fatimah and Beatrice want turkey sandwiches? _____ No, they don't. _____

6. Does Beatrice want a cheeseburger? _____ No, she doesn't. _____

I **Look at the menu in A. Choose your order. Then practice taking an order with a partner. Use the conversation in C as a model.** Answers will vary.

Item	Section	Price

J **Go to a food truck or restaurant and order your lunch in English.**

Presentation 3
10–15 mins. ■■■

Role-play taking food orders with volunteers in front of the class. Use the menu in **A**. Ask some *yes / no* questions such as: *Do you want a side order? Do you want a drink?*

BEST PRACTICE

Conversations in *Stand Out*

In the lower levels of *Stand Out*, there are various things that might be considered conversation.

1. There are controlled conversations where students merely read and repeat what is on the page. The purpose of these types of activities is to help students with pronunciation features and to help them become accustomed to new vocabulary. It is not necessary for students to memorize the conversations.
2. Similarly, conversations with substitutions can be useful to help students think critically and manipulate the text.
3. Role play activities should not be scripted. Students use the language they know and take on the roles of different characters. The language requirements are limited by the context of the role play.
4. Finally, we have open-ended discussions. Such discussions can be difficult at this level, but students will find that in groups they can successfully convey ideas even with limited vocabulary.

F Study the chart.

Help students with pronunciation and intonation. Explain the different ways to answer the same *yes / no* questions in the affirmative and in the negative.

Practice 3
15–20 mins. ■

G Read the orders.

Have students read the orders. Then ask a few questions. For example: *Does Fatimah want a soda? Does Beatrice want a hot dog?*

H Answer the questions.

Have students write the answers individually, then compare with a partner. Check answers as a class.

I Look at the menu in A. Choose your order. Then practice taking an order with a partner. Use the conversation in C as a model.

Have students complete their own order first. Refer students back to **C** and model the activity with a student. Take their order. Prompt the student to tell you what they want. Then ask about a side order. Prompt the student to continue the conversation as needed. Write the order in your chart. Put students in pairs to practice taking and placing orders. If time allows, review the third-person singular by having students report their partner's order. For example: *Mila wants a turkey sandwich and a green salad, and she wants an orange juice.*

Evaluation 3
5–7 mins. ■

Call on different pairs to perform a conversation for the class.

Application
10–15 mins. ■■■

J Go to a food truck or restaurant and order your lunch in English.

Have students report back in the following class. They can do this in pairs, small groups, or as a whole class, depending on the number of students. Encourage them to share where they went and what they ordered. At this stage, they might not be able to use the simple past, but that's OK. Write on the board: *Where? Food? Drink?* as prompts.

At-a-Glance Prep

Goal: Investigate food service jobs

Agenda
- ☐ Interpret a graph.
- ☐ Read about restaurant positions.
- ☐ Calculate tips.
- ☐ Reflect on the characteristics of servers.
- ☐ Evaluate your personal characteristics.
- ☐ Search for job openings online.

Pacing
- ■ 1.5 hour classes   ■ 2.5 hour classes
- ■ 3+ hour classes

Standards Correlations

CASAS: 0.1.2, 0.1.5, 0.2.1, 4.1.3, 4.1.8, 4.1.9, 6.0.2, 6.0.5, 6.1.3, 6.7.1, 6.7.2, 6.7.4, 7.4.4, 7.7.3

CCRS: RI1, RI2, RI3, SL1, SL3, W1, W3

ELPS:

S2: Participate in level-appropriate oral and written exchanges of information, ideas, and analyses, in various social and academic contexts, responding to peer, audience, or reader comments and questions.

S5: Conduct research and evaluate and communicate findings to answer questions or solve problems.

In this lesson, students are introduced to food service jobs. They will compare salaries for different restaurant positions. Students will also read about opportunities to grow in the food service area and about tipping. They will learn about the qualities of a good server and reflect on their own characteristics. Finally, students will carry out an online search for restaurant positions available in their area.

Warm-up and Review   10–15 mins. ■■□

Write *server* on the board and have students explain where this person works and what they do. Refer students back to the conversations in Lesson 5 if necessary, but explain that a server usually comes to your table at a restaurant and takes your order. Then ask about other people who work in restaurants. Write any other restaurant jobs students know on the board. For example: *chef, cook, manager.*

Introduction   5–10 mins. ■■■

Find out if any of the students have food service jobs. Remind them that throughout *Stand Out*, they will investigate many job possibilities. Write the goal on the board: *Today, we will investigate food service jobs.*

Presentation 1   15–20 mins. ■■■

A INTERPRET Read the graph.

Go over the graph together, having students tell you what they see. Remember that it isn't important that they use the correct terms, rather that they say whatever they can about the graph. Encourage students to look up the positions that they are not familiar with. Review large numbers by writing *$44,484* on the board and asking the class to say it. Then call on different students to say other numbers in the graph.

B Choose the correct words to complete the sentences.

Have students complete the sentences individually, then compare with a partner. Go over the answers as a class. Clarify any vocabulary questions students still have about the graph or the items.

Practice 1   15–20 mins. ■■□

C Study the chart.

Say each word and its example sentence. Help students understand the meaning. Provide further examples and write them on the board.

BEST PRACTICE

Writing Ideas and Examples

When students are contributing ideas, such as in the Warm-up, Review, and Introduction stages, it's important to write these on the board so they are visible for other students. There are a number of reasons for this. Firstly, it can confirm what students heard. Secondly, if it involves a new word, they can see how it is spelled. Thirdly, seeing the words that are being called out may encourage other students to participate since it helps them understand what they are being asked to do. Similarly, when you give examples, write them on the board so you can be sure students have understood what you said. Some students need to see things as well as hear them, when possible, to clarify their understanding.

Explore the Workforce

GOAL ▶ Investigate food service jobs

A INTERPRET Read the graph.

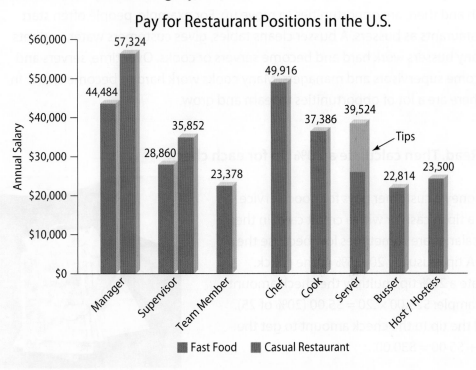

Pay for Restaurant Positions in the U.S.

B Choose the correct words to complete the sentences.

1. In the graph, fast food is **blue** / **orange**.

2. The salaries in the graph are for a **month** / **year**.

3. Chefs at casual restaurants usually make **over** / **under** $50,000.

C Study the chart.

Estimating Words	
under	Fast-food team members make **under** $25,000 a year. ($23,378)
almost	Fast-food supervisors make **almost** $29,000 a year. ($28,860)
just over	Restaurant managers make **just over** $57,000 a year. ($57,324)
over	Hosts make **over** $23,000 a year. ($23,500)

D Practice the conversation with a partner. Then make new conversations.

Student A: How much do <u>fast-food supervisors</u> make a year?

Student B: They make <u>under $30,000</u> a year.

E Read about positions in restaurants. <u>Underline</u> any words you don't know. 🎧

> There are many different restaurant jobs. For these jobs, you don't always need to know a lot of English and there are opportunities to move up. For example, people often start working in restaurants as bussers. A busser cleans tables, gives customers water, and sets the tables. Many bussers work hard and become servers or cooks. Over time, servers and hosts can become supervisors and managers. Many cooks work hard to become chefs. In restaurants, there are a lot of opportunities to learn and grow.

F CALCULATE Read. Then calculate a 20% tip for each check. 🎧

> A tip is money a customer pays for good service. You can give a tip in cash or with a credit card. In the U.S., servers' salaries are sometimes low because they also get tips. A tip is usually 20–25% of the check.
> To calculate a 20% tip, multiply the check amount by .20. For example: $25.00 x .20 = $5.00 (20% of 25).
> Then add the tip to the check amount to get the total: $25.00 + $5.00 = $30.00.

1.
Check amount: $25.00

Tip: ___$5.00___

Total: ___$30.00___

2.
Check amount: $55.00

Tip: ___$11.00___

Total: ___$66.00___

3.
Check amount: $40.00

Tip: ___$8.00___

Total: ___$48.00___

4.
Check amount: $35.50

Tip: ___$7.10___

Total: ___$42.60___

G Read the diagram.

H Work with a partner. Use the sentences from the box to talk about yourself.

I am friendly.	I can learn the menu quickly.
I am helpful.	I speak clearly.

Student A: Tell me about yourself.

Student B: I _____.

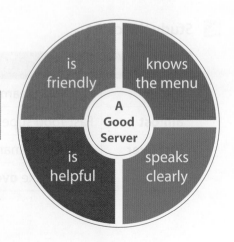

A Good Server
- is friendly
- knows the menu
- is helpful
- speaks clearly

D Practice the conversation with a partner. Then make new conversations.

Say each line of the conversation and have students repeat it after you. Then practice the conversation by dividing the class in half. Model with a student. Then ask the student: *How much do fast food team members make?* Have the class help with the answer if necessary. Make sure the student uses one of the words from the chart in **C**. Put students in pairs to ask and answer questions about the pay for each position. Remind them to switch roles. Monitor and help with numbers as needed. Make sure students are using *under*, *almost*, *just over*, *over*.

Evaluation 1   5–10 mins. ■■■

Have several pairs perform a conversation for the class.

Presentation 2   10–15 mins. ■■■

E Read about positions in restaurants. Underline any words you don't know. 🎧

Ask students to read as they listen. Play the audio. Write *busser* on the board and ask what a busser does. To check their understanding of how you can learn and grow in restaurants, have students complete the following diagram with information from the text:

busser → ☐ → ☐

Repeat for *server* and *cook*.

BEST PRACTICE

Graphic Organizers

Having students complete graphic organizers such as flow charts, Venn diagrams, and charts after they have read a text is a good way to help them process what they have read and demonstrate their understanding.

Practice 2   15–20 mins. ■■

For shorter classes, have students do **F** for homework.

F CALCULATE   Read. Then calculate a 20% tip for each check. 🎧

Ask students to read as they listen. Play the audio. Ask questions to check students' understanding. For example: *What is a tip? How much is a tip?* Clarify

any vocabulary questions or doubts about the text. Then have students calculate the tips with a partner.

Evaluation 2   5–10 mins. ■■■

Check answers as a class by having students write their calculations on the board.

Presentation 3   10–15 mins. ■■■

G Read the diagram.

Go over the diagram as a class and check students' understanding.

H Work with a partner. Use the sentences from the box to talk about yourself.

Put students in pairs to talk about themselves. Remember to switch pairs sometimes so students don't always work with the same partner.

Instructor's Notes

_____

_____

_____

_____

_____

_____

_____

_____

_____

_____

_____

_____

_____

Practice 3

15–20 mins. ■

Ask students in shorter classes to do **I** and **K** for homework.

I REFLECT Check (✓) how true the statements are about you. These are often true for servers in restaurants.

Go over the statements and encourage students to try to explain why servers need to have these characteristics. The photo at the bottom of the page can be used to help illustrate some of the items. Make sure they understand that 10 means very true and 1 means not true at all. Have students complete the activity individually.

J Practice the conversations with a partner. Then make new conversations with the information from I.

Model the first conversation with a student. Then have two students model the second conversation before putting students in pairs. Monitor and help as needed.

K INVESTIGATE Choose a job title from A. Go to a job search site online and see if there are any openings within 25 miles of your school or home.

Help students get started with their searches. Help them decide which kind of position they want to look for. Then share some job search sites that they can use.

Evaluation 3

5–10 mins. ■

Monitor as students are carrying out their searches and help as needed. When they have all found one or two options, have them share the information with a partner or the class.

Instructor's Notes

I **REFLECT** Check (✓) how true the statements are about you. These are often true for servers in restaurants. Answers will vary.

	not true									very true
	1	2	3	4	5	6	7	8	9	10
1. I like to work on a team.										
2. I am a good listener.										
3. I am friendly.										
4. I like people.										
5. I like to help people.										
6. I like to work inside.										

J Practice the conversations with a partner. Then make new conversations with the information from I.

Student A: What do you have for "I like to work on a team"?

Student B: I have 7. What do you have?

Student A: I have 3. I usually like to work alone.

Student B: What do you have for "I am a good listener"?

Student A: I have 7. What about you?

Student B: I have 10. I think I'm a very good listener.

K **INVESTIGATE** Choose a job title from A. Go to a job search site online and see if there are any openings within 25 miles of your school or home.

A good server is friendly and helpful.

Review

A **Write the names of the foods and drinks in the chart. Are they for breakfast, lunch, or dinner? Add more foods to each list.** Answers will vary.

Breakfast	Lunch	Dinner

B **Work with a partner. Ask the questions and write your partner's answers.** Answers will vary.

1. What do you eat for breakfast? _____

2. What do you eat for lunch? _____

3. What do you eat for dinner? _____

C **Write foods you like for each meal.** Answers will vary.

Breakfast	Lunch	Dinner

D **Complete the sentences.** Answers will vary.

1. I _____ like toast _____ for breakfast.

2. My partner _____ for breakfast.

3. I _____ for lunch.

4. My partner _____ for lunch.

5. I _____ for dinner.

6. My partner _____ for dinner.

Learner Log	I can identify common meals and foods.
	☐ Yes ☐ No ☐ Maybe

At-a-Glance Prep

Goal: All unit goals
Grammar: All unit grammar
Academic Strategies: Reviewing, evaluating, developing study skills
Vocabulary: All unit vocabulary

Agenda
☐ Discuss unit goals.
☐ Complete the review.
☐ Evaluate and reflect on progress.

Pacing
■ 1.5 hour classes ■ 2.5 hour classes
■ 3+ hour classes

Standards Correlations
CASAS: 0.1.2, 0.1.5, 0.2.1, 1.1.7, 1.2.1, 1.2.2, 1.2.4, 2.6.4
CCRS: L1, RI1, RI3, SL1, SL3
ELPS:
S2: Participate in level-appropriate oral and written exchanges of information, ideas, and analyses, in various social and academic contexts, responding to peer, audience, or reader comments and questions.
S10: Demonstrate command of the conventions of standard English to communicate in level-appropriate speech and writing.

Warm-up and Review   7–10 mins. ■■■
Ask individuals what they like to eat. Make a list on the board of all the vocabulary students can come up with from the unit.

Introduction   5 mins. ■■■
Write all the goals from Unit 3 on the board. Show students the first page of every lesson so they understand that today they will review the whole unit.

Presentation   10–15 mins. ■■■
This presentation will cover all three pages of the review. Quickly go to the first page of each lesson. Discuss the goal of each. Ask simple questions to remind students of what they have learned.

Practice 1   15–20 mins. ■■■

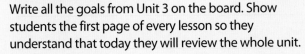
A **Write the names of the foods and drinks in the chart. Are they for breakfast, lunch, or dinner? Add more foods to each list.**
Have students complete the activity individually or with a partner.

B **Work with a partner. Ask the questions and write your partner's answers.**
Have students work in pairs to ask and answer the questions. Provide further meal vocabulary as needed. Have students write their answers.

C **Write foods you like for each meal.**
Encourage students to write more than one option in each column.

D **Complete the sentences.**
Make sure students understand that they need to use their answers from **B** and **C** to complete the sentences.

Evaluation 1   10–15 mins. ■■■
Go around the classroom and check on students' progress. Help individuals as needed. If you see consistent errors among several students, interrupt the class and give a mini lesson or review to help students feel comfortable with the content.

Learner Log   5–10 mins.
Have students read the statement and complete the log. If students answer *no* or *maybe*, encourage them to set themselves a goal to practice. Show them where they can find more practice activities.

BEST PRACTICE
Learner Logs
Learner Logs function to help students in many different ways:

1. They serve as part of the review process.
2. They help students to gain confidence and to document what they have learned. Consequently, students see that they are progressing in their learning.
3. They provide students with a tool that they can use over and over to check and recheck their understanding of the target language. In this way, students become independent learners.

Practice 2

E **Read the weekly specials and complete the chart.**

Have students read the ad. Then ask them a few *How much is / are . . .?* questions before they complete the chart.

F **Work with a partner. Take turns asking questions about the specials in E. Ask: *How much is . . .?* or *How much are . . .?***

Make sure students take turns asking and answering so that they practice both.

G **Complete the sentences with the container words and the correct form of the verbs.**

Have students complete the sentences individually, then compare with a partner.

Evaluation 2

15–20 mins. ■■■

Go around the classroom and check on students' progress. Help individuals as needed. If you see consistent errors among several students, interrupt the class and give a mini lesson or review to help students feel comfortable with the content.

BEST PRACTICE

Recycling / Review

The review and the project that follows are part of the recycling and review process. Students at this level often need to be reintroduced to concepts to solidify what they have learned. Many concepts are learned and forgotten while learning other new concepts. This is because students learn but are not necessarily ready to acquire language concepts.

Therefore, it becomes very important to review and to show students how to review on their own. It is also important to recycle the new concepts in different contexts.

Learner Log

5–10 mins.

Have students read the statements and remind them that they need to check one of the boxes. Have them complete the log. If students answer *no* or *maybe*, encourage them to set themselves a goal to practice. Show them where they can find more practice activities.

Instructor's Notes

_____
_____
_____
_____
_____
_____
_____
_____
_____
_____
_____
_____
_____
_____
_____
_____
_____
_____
_____
_____
_____
_____
_____
_____

E Read the weekly specials and complete the chart.

Swift Mart

Click + to add.

+ BREAD	+ GROUND BEEF	+ JELLY	+ CUCUMBERS
$2.25 a loaf	$3.98 a pound	$2.75 a jar	$.55 each

+ PASTA	+ COOKIES	+ WHOLE MILK	+ POTATO CHIPS
$1.25 a package	$2.55 a box	$3.25 a gallon	$3.15 a bag

Product	Container or Quantity	Price
bread	loaf	$2.25
cucumbers	each	$.55
pasta	package	$1.25
milk	gallon	$3.25
potato chips	bag	$3.15

F Work with a partner. Take turns asking questions about the specials in E. Ask: *How much is . . . ?* or *How much are . . . ?*

G Complete the sentences.

~~bottle~~	box	jar	pound

1. Sebastian _____needs_____ (need) a _____bottle_____ of water.

2. Amani _____wants_____ (want) a _____box_____ of cookies.

3. Amani _____needs_____ (need) a _____pound_____ of oranges.

4. Sebastian _____likes_____ (like) potato chips.

5. They both _____want_____ (want) a _____jar_____ of peanut butter.

H Read the menus. Then choose *R* for Rudolf's Café or *A* for Allen's Home Cooking.

Rudolf's Café

Lunch Menu

SANDWICHES

Turkey... $5.75
Tuna.. $4.75
Hamburger..................................... $4.50

SIDE ORDERS

Salad... $3.98
Soup... $2.75
French Fries................................... $2.50

BEVERAGES

Soda... $2.50
Milk.. $2.00
Coffee.. $2.50

ALLEN'S Home Cooking

Lunch Menu

SANDWICHES

Turkey... $5.50
Cheese.. $3.25
Hamburger..................................... $5.95

SIDE ORDERS

Salad... $4.75
French Fries................................... $2.95

BEVERAGES

Soda... $3.00
Milk.. $2.25
Coffee.. $3.00

1. Which is cheaper—a hamburger at Rudolf's Café or at Allen's Home Cooking? Ⓡ A

2. Which is more expensive—a salad at Rudolf's or at Allen's? R Ⓐ

3. Which is cheaper—coffee at Rudolf's or at Allen's? Ⓡ A

4. Which is more expensive—soda at Rudolf's or at Allen's? R Ⓐ

I With a partner, make a conversation about one of the menus in H. Answers will vary.

Student A: Hello. Can I take your order?

Student B: Yes, I want _____.

Student A: Great. Do you want a side order?

Student B: _____.

Student A: Do you want a drink?

Student B: _____. I want _____.

Student A: OK. Thank you.

J Practice the conversation with your partner.

Learner Log   I can compare prices. ☐ Yes ☐ No ☐ Maybe   I can take and place orders. ☐ Yes ☐ No ☐ Maybe

Practice 3

15–20 mins. ■■□

H **Read the menus. Then choose *R* for Rudolf's Café or *A* for Allen's Home Cooking.**

Have students answer the questions individually.

I **With a partner, make a conversation about one of the menus in H.**

Make sure students complete the conversation fully.

J **Practice the conversation with your partner.**

Encourage students to practice a few times with their books open and then try having the conversation without looking in their books.

Evaluation 3

15 mins. ■■□

Go around the room and check on students' progress. Help individuals as needed. If you see consistent errors among several students, interrupt the class and give a mini lesson or review to help students feel comfortable with the concept.

Learner Log

5–10 mins.

Have students read the statements and remind them that they need to check one of the boxes. Have them complete the log. If students answer *no* or *maybe*, encourage them to set themselves a goal to practice. Show them where they can find more practice activities.

Instructor's Notes

_____
_____
_____
_____
_____
_____
_____
_____
_____
_____
_____
_____
_____
_____
_____
_____
_____
_____
_____
_____
_____
_____
_____
_____

Standards Correlations

CASAS: 0.1.2, 0.1.5, 1.1.7, 1.2.1, 1.2.2, 1.2.4, 2.6.4, 4.8.1, 7.2.6
CCRS: L1, L3, RI1, SL1, SL3, W3
ELPS:
S3: Speak and write about level-appropriate complex literary and informational texts and topics.
S8: Determine the meaning of words and phrases in oral presentations and literary and informational text.

Workplace Focus

Combine ideas and information; Manage money; Make decisions; Exercise leadership roles; Complete tasks as assigned; Interact appropriately with team members; Interpret and communicate information.

Soft Skill: Collaboration
Brainstorming

Explain that in the workplace, collaboration is a very important skill and that brainstorming is something team members often need to do in order to get a lot of different ideas to choose from. Help students understand that brainstorming is a part of the process in which they should not judge others' ideas or think too critically. Instead, they should focus on being creative and encouraging their team members. Tell students they will practice this skill in Steps 2 and 3 of the project.

Warm-up and Review   10 mins.

Review items in the review section of the unit and make sure all have recorded their progress in the learner logs.

Introduction   10 mins.

Let students know that in this lesson they will be creating a menu for a new restuarant.

Presentation   10–15 mins.

1. Form a team of four or five students. In your team, you need:

Place students in teams of four or five. Have students choose their positions in the group. To do this, go through each step in the project and explain the role of the person who will lead that step. Make sure they understand that they will complete one step before going to the next and that although each person has a specific task, they will work together on each step.

In **Step 2**, the team leader can manage the discussion of the name for the restaurant and write down the ideas suggested. Then in **Steps 3** and **4**, the chef will manage the brainstorming, note-taking, and decision-making process for the menu. In **Step 5**, the advertising agent will create the ad, but all team members will contribute ideas. In **Step 6**, the trainers will write the conversation, but all team members will make suggestions and help with the language. All members will participate in the presentation in **Step 7**.

As you go through what the different positions are at this level, it might be easier to ask one volunteer from each team to stand after each description. Be aware of who volunteers for which position so that in the course of the different units, you can encourage students to try different roles.

Practice / Evaluation / Application   1–2 hours

2. Choose a name for your restaurant.

Draw students' attention to the Soft Skill note. Explain that in this step and the next, they will need to brainstorm a list of ideas before choosing the ones they like the best.

3. Make a list of foods your restaurant serves.

Go over the example conversation. Assign students the B and C parts and read it aloud with them. Point out that *maybe* and *how about . . . ?* are useful phrases for presenting ideas.

4. Design the restaurant menu.

5. Create an advertisement for your restaurant, giving some prices.

6. Write a conversation between a server and customers.

7. Present your menu, advertisement, and conversation to the class.

8. Compare prices on your menu with prices from other teams' menus.

Create a Menu for a New Restaurant

SOFT SKILL ▶ Collaboration

In this project, you will create a menu for a new restaurant (including foods and prices) and an ad for your restaurant. You will also write a conversation between a server and customers in your restaurant as the server takes their orders.

1. Form a team of four or five students. In your team, you need:

Position	Job Description	Student Name
Student 1: **Team Leader**	Check that everyone speaks English. Check that everyone participates.	
Student 2: **Chef**	With help from the team, write a list of foods for the menu. Design the menu.	
Student 3: **Advertising Agent**	With help from the team, make an ad for your restaurant with a few prices.	
Students 4/5: **Trainers**	With help from the team, write a conversation between a server and customers in a restaurant.	

2. Choose a name for your restaurant.

3. Make a list of foods your restaurant serves.

Student A: What can we serve?

Student B: Maybe burgers and fries.

Student A: OK, I can write that down.

Student C: How about fish?

Student A: OK. I can write everything down and then we can decide what to do.

4. Design the restaurant menu.

5. Create an advertisement for your restaurant, giving some prices.

6. Write a conversation between a server and customers.

7. Present your menu, advertisement, and conversation to the class.

8. Compare prices on your menu with prices from other teams' menus.

COLLABORATION:
Brainstorming
Brainstorming means thinking of many new ideas as a group. It's important to write down everyone's ideas before making a choice.

About the Photo

Infographics use images and short text to provide important information in an accessible format for any reader. In this case, the objective of the infographic is to inform readers about what food waste is and why it is a problem, and then provide practical ideas for individuals to help avoid food waste.

- Have students look at the images in the infographic and say what they see. Write the vocabulary on the board. Then ask: *What do you think the text is about?* The idea here is just that students make predictions about the content, not that they read the text.

A INTERPRET Read the pie charts. Do you think there is enough food for everyone in the United States?

Go over the pie charts with the class and remind them how they are like graphs and represent numerical information. Elicit what each one shows and what the percentages represent. Then discuss the question.

B Match the words to the photos.

Have students do this activity individually. Encourage them to use a dictionary if they need to. Have them compare with a partner. Then check answers as a class.

C Read the infographic about food waste. 🎧

Have students read the infographic and circle the words from **B**. Ask: *What is the infographic telling us?*

Reading Challenge

A INTERPRET Read the pie charts. Do you think there is enough food for everyone in the United States?

U.S. Food Produced

Food not used (wasted) 40%

U.S. Population

Population that doesn't have enough food 12%

B Match the words to the photos.

| donate | expiration date | food waste | ugly food |

1. ___food waste___ 2. ___ugly food___ 3. ___donate___ 4. ___expiration date___

C Read the infographic about food waste.

D INFER Match the quotes to the ways of stopping food waste.

___d___ 1. "Ugly tomatoes make the best sauce!"   a. Donate extra food.

___c___ 2. "7/17… Hmm, will we use all this milk before Friday?"   b. Plan your meals every week.

___a___ 3. "I bought too many cans of beans. Can you bring some to the community center?"   c. Learn about dates.

___b___ 4. "This week, we're having chicken on Monday, pasta on Tuesday, and tacos on Wednesday."   d. Buy ugly food.

E Check (✓) three things you can do to stop food waste in your life. *Answers will vary.*

- ☐ Buy only what I need.
- ☐ Buy ugly food.
- ☐ Store food correctly.
- ☐ Give extra to pets.
- ☐ Plan my meals.
- ☐ Donate food.
- ☐ Learn about dates.
- ☐ Use in my garden.

F Write sentences with your choices from **E**. Then share your sentences in a group.

EXAMPLE: I can plan my meals every week.

___Answers will vary.___

CASAS FOR READING

0.1.2, 0.1.5, 1.5.2, 6.7.4

CCRS FOR READING

L1, L2, L3, RI1, RI2, RI3, W1, W3

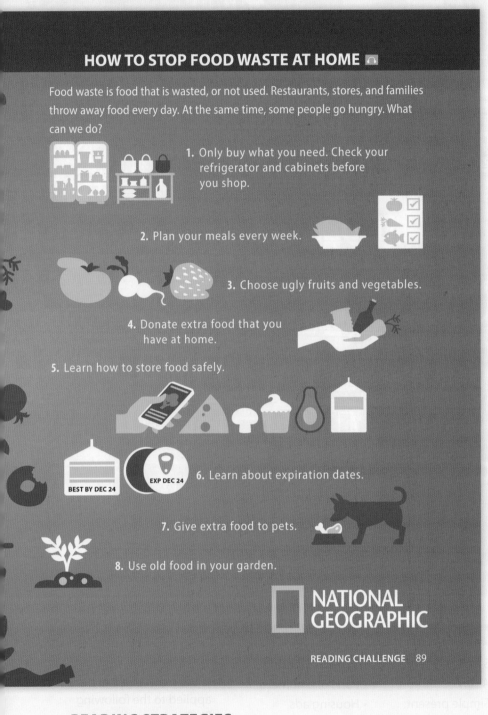

HOW TO STOP FOOD WASTE AT HOME

Food waste is food that is wasted, or not used. Restaurants, stores, and families throw away food every day. At the same time, some people go hungry. What can we do?

1. Only buy what you need. Check your refrigerator and cabinets before you shop.

2. Plan your meals every week.

3. Choose ugly fruits and vegetables.

4. Donate extra food that you have at home.

5. Learn how to store food safely.

6. Learn about expiration dates.

BEST BY DEC 24   EXP DEC 24

7. Give extra food to pets.

8. Use old food in your garden.

NATIONAL GEOGRAPHIC

READING CHALLENGE   89

D INFER Match the quotes to the ways of stopping food waste.

Remind students that *infer* means to understand something that isn't written in the text. Have students do this activity with a partner. Read each quote and check understanding as you confirm answers with the class.

E Check (✓) three things you can do to stop food waste in your life.

Ask students to do the activity individually. Tell them to think about which things are easy for them and which ones are more difficult and why.

F Write sentences with your choices from E. Then share your sentences in a group.

Point out the example. Then have students write their sentences. Encourage them to write more about their choices if they can. Monitor and help as needed. Put students in groups to share their sentences. Ask them to report back to the class on similarities and differences in their choices.

READING STRATEGIES

Visual Support

Students need to know that it is important to pay attention to any images, graphs, and diagrams that are in a text. These visual representations of the content of the text can help them understand the text itself when they come across new vocabulary.

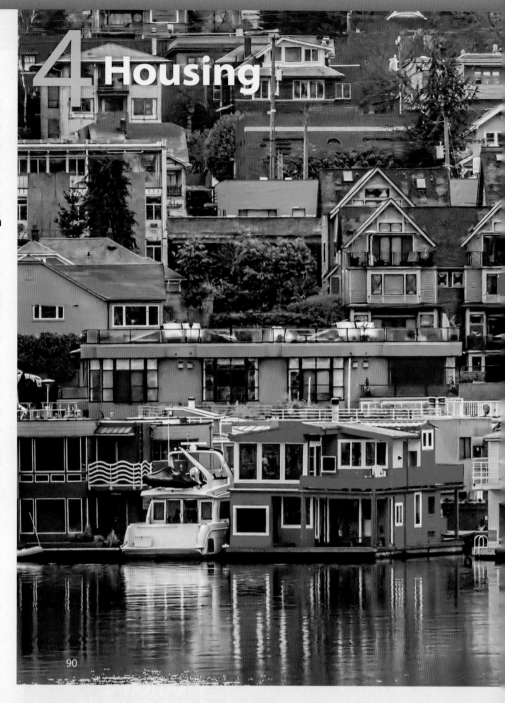

4 Housing

About the Photo

This photo shows the different types of housing on Lake Union in Seattle, Washington. The photo was taken at sunrise, and the colorful houses are reflected in the lake. What's interesting to see is how the different types of housing are all together, with houseboats right on the lake, then behind them a mixture of houses, townhouses and apartments. Often, there are areas of a town or city where you will mostly find either apartments or houses, rather than both mixed together.

- Introduce the unit by reading the title. Ask students to look at the photo. Ask them where they think it is. Then have them answer the first two questions with a partner.
- Ask a volunteer to read the description of the photo out loud. Ask students to look at the photo again and discuss the remaining questions as a class.

Life Skills Focus

In this unit, students will learn how to identify different types of housing and different parts of a house. They will also learn how to research homes, look at housing ads, and make appointments for viewing homes.

90

UNIT OUTCOMES	GRAMMAR	VOCABULARY	EL CIVICS
• Identify types of housing • Describe parts of a home • Interpret housing ads • Make appointments • Identify furniture in a house • Identify employment opportunities in construction	• Simple present: *Live* • *A / an* • Simple present: *Have* • *Yes / no* questions • Present continuous • Prepositions of location	• Types of housing • Parts of a home • Housing ads • Appointments • Furniture • Jobs in construction	The skills students learn in this unit can be applied to the following EL Civics competency areas: • Consumer Economics • Housing

UNIT OUTCOMES

▸ Identify types of housing
▸ Describe parts of a home
▸ Interpret housing ads
▸ Make appointments
▸ Identify furniture in a house
▸ Identify employment opportunities in construction

Look at the photo and answer the questions.

1. What kinds of buildings do you see?
2. Are there buildings like these in your city or town?

On Lake Union in Seattle, Washington, there are houses, townhouses, apartment buildings, and houseboats.

1. What colors are the houseboats in the photo?
2. Why do you think people choose to live on houseboats?
3. Which home in the photo do you like? Why?

Workplace Focus

All lessons and units in *Stand Out* include basic communication skills and interpersonal skills important for the workplace. They include *collecting and organizing information, making decisions and solving problems,* and *combining ideas and information.*

- In Unit 4, Lesson 6, *Explore the Workforce*, students will identify jobs in construction. They will interpret an infographic with the different steps for building, the jobs involved, and levels of pay. They will also read about carpenters' pay and learn about the qualities a carpenter needs to have. Then they will reflect on their own work preferences.
- In the Team Project, students practice the soft skill of preparing for a presentation.
- Life Online features in Lessons 3 and 4 raise awareness about fake housing ads online and using filters when searching for housing.

spark Resources

All resources for the unit are centrally located on the Spark platform and include: audio, video, multilevel worksheets, digital literacy worksheets, Online Practice, and Assessment Suite.

91

STEPS

CASAS COMPETENCIES	ELPS	CCRS
• Lesson 1: 0.1.2, 0.1.5, 0.2.1, 1.4.1, 6.7.4, 7.2.3 • Lesson 2: 1.4.1, 4.8.1, 7.2.3 • Lesson 3: 1.4.2, 6.1.1, 7.4.4, 7.7.3 • Lesson 4: 0.1.2, 0.1.5, 1.4.2, 4.8.1, 7.2.3, 7.4.4, 7.7.3 • Lesson 5: 0.1.2, 0.1.5, 1.4.1, 7.4.4, 7.7.3 • Lesson 6: 0.1.2, 0.1.5, 4.1.3, 4.1.8, 4.1.9, 4.8.1, 6.1.3, 6.7.3, 7.2.3, 7.4.4, 7.7.3 • Review: 0.1.2, 0.1.5, 1.4.1, 1.4.2, 7.2.3 • Team Project: 0.1.2, 0.1.5, 1.4.1, 1.4.2, 4.8.1 • Reading Challenge: 0.1.2, 0.1.5, 1.4.1, 4.8.1	**S2:** Participate in level-appropriate oral and written exchanges of information, ideas, and analyses, in various social and academic contexts, responding to peer, audience, or reader comments and questions. **S5:** Conduct research and evaluate and communicate findings to answer questions or solve problems. **S9:** Create clear and coherent level-appropriate speech and text.	L1, L2, L3, RI1, RI2, RI3, SL1, SL3, W1, W3

LESSON 1

A House or an Apartment?

GOAL ▶ Identify types of housing

A INTERPRET Read the business card. Answer the questions.

1. What is the name of the company?

   Irving Properties

2. What is the name of the agent?

   Angela Alvarez

3. What is her phone number?

   (214) 555-3375

4. What is her email?

   angela@irvingreal.com

Irving Properties

- Houses
- Condos
- Townhouses
- Apartments
- Mobile Homes

Rental Agent
Angela Alvarez
(214) 555-3375
angela@irvingreal.com

B Label the housing types in the graph. Then listen and write the number of units for each type. 🎧

condo = condominium

Types of Housing
Irving, Texas

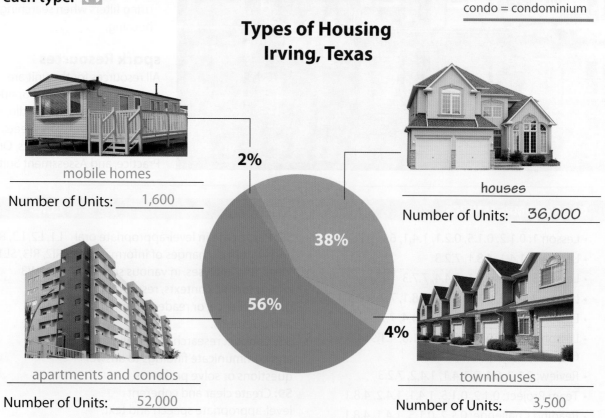

mobile homes

Number of Units: 1,600

houses

Number of Units: 36,000

apartments and condos

Number of Units: 52,000

townhouses

Number of Units: 3,500

2%

38%

56%

4%

Data from the U.S. Census Bureau

At-a-Glance Prep

Goal: Identify types of housing
Grammar: Simple present: *Live, a / an*
Pronunciation: /v/
Academic Strategies: Interpreting information, focused listening, doing a survey, making a pie chart
Vocabulary: Types of housing

Agenda

☐ Read a business card.
☐ Read a pie chart.
☐ Use the simple present.
☐ Talk about housing.
☐ Write a paragraph.
☐ Complete a pie chart.

Resources

Heinle Picture Dictionary: Housing, pages 62–81

Pacing

■ 1.5 hour classes ■ 2.5 hour classes
■ 3+ hour classes

Standards Correlations

CASAS: 0.1.2, 0.1.5, 0.2.1, 1.4.1, 6.7.4, 7.2.3
CCRS: L1, L2, L3, RI1, RI2, RI3, SL1, SL3, W1, W3
ELPS:
S5: Conduct research and evaluate and communicate findings to answer questions or solve problems.
S10: Demonstrate command of the conventions of standard English to communicate in level-appropriate speech and writing.

Warm-up and Review   10–15 mins. ■■■

Pass out index cards to every student. Have them write their address, city, and home country on the card. Make sure they don't write their name on the card. Model this by creating a card with your information. Explain that students who don't want to write their address may write *private information*.

Collect the cards and randomly pass them out to all students. Ask students to find the author of the card by asking the *yes / no* questions that you have written on the board:

1. *Is your address (address)? Yes, it is. / No, it's not.*
2. *Do you live in (city)? Yes, I do. / No, I don't.*
3. *Are you from (home country)? Yes, I am. / No, I'm not.*

Demonstrate with a couple of students. Give one of them your card so you can model both negative and affirmative answers.

Introduction   5 mins. ■■■

Survey students to find out who lives in an apartment, a house, or a condominium. State the goal: *Today, we will identify types of housing.*

Presentation 1   15–20 mins. ■■■

Ask students how many people live in your town or city. Ask if it is a big or small city or town. Then ask about the size of their city or town in their home country. Ask them about the housing there: *Do more people live in houses or apartments?*

A INTERPRET Read the business card. Answer the questions.

Have students look at the card. Make sure they understand what it is. Pass around other business cards for them to look at if possible. Use the images in **B** to help students understand the different types of housing, and explain *rental agent* if necessary. Then have students answer the questions individually. When checking the answers, have students say the phone number and spell out the email as you write them on the board.

Practice 1   10–15 mins. ■■■

B Label the housing types in the graph. Then listen and write the number of units for each type.

Go over the pie chart as a class to make sure students understand what it shows. Practice saying the percentages and number of units for houses. Say a few more large numbers to review hundreds and thousands.

Tell students that they are going to hear someone talking about housing in Irving. Remind them that they don't need to understand everything. They should listen for the types of housing and the numbers. Play the audio twice. Then have students compare answers.

Note: The listening script for **B** is on page 93a.

Evaluation 1   5 mins. ■■■

Check the answers to **B** and make sure students can say the types of housing and numbers correctly.

Listening Script

Irving, Texas, is a thriving community near Dallas. There is a lot to do and friendly people to meet.

Irving has many different housing options. There are approximately 36,000 houses in the city, and even more apartments and condos—around 52,000. There are also about 3,500 townhouses in Irving. Finally, there are nearly 1,600 mobile homes in the area. Irving is a wonderful place to live.

Presentation 2   20–30 mins. ■■■□

C Study the chart.

Review the simple present with students. Focus on the third-person singular *s*. First, do a choral drill where students repeat what you say. Next, do a transformation drill where you say a sentence, perhaps in the first person, and then give students a different pronoun to use in place of the pronoun you used.

When you feel comfortable with the students' grasp of the structure, introduce the pronunciation.

Pronunciation   /v/ 🎧

Direct students' attention to the pronunciation note. Play the audio and have students repeat what they hear.

Remember that many languages don't have the /v/ sound. Some have similar sounds that are not written with the letter *v*, which often causes confusion.

One approach is to teach the articulation points. Explain that the top teeth touch the bottom lip. The same articulation points are used to create /f/, which many students will already be able to pronounce because many languages have this sound. Ask students to pronounce a /f/ sound. Then ask students to put two fingers on their voice boxes and have them vibrate it as when they pronounce /m/. This should help them differentiate between the /f/ and /v/ sounds.

Listening Script

/v/ /v/ live, live
We live in an apartment.

D Read about the people and their homes.

Have students read about each person. Continue your presentation of the verb chart in **C** by asking specific questions about the three people in this exercise. For example: *Does Saud live in a townhouse?*

Practice 2   15–20 mins. ■■□

E Practice the conversation with a partner. Then make new conversations with information from D.

Prepare students to practice the conversation by using the steps mentioned in previous lessons:

1. Teacher reads; students repeat.
2. Teacher is Saud; students are Wei.
3. Teacher is Wei; students are Saud.
4. Teacher is Saud; student volunteer is Wei.
5. Teacher is Wei; student volunteer is Saud.
6. Student volunteer is Saud; another student volunteer is Wei.

Work on the rhythm of the sentences and questions. Point out the note about *a* and *an* and remind students about the use of indefinite articles. Then put students in pairs to practice. Monitor and make sure they are using different information for each conversation.

BEST PRACTICE

Conversation Strategies

In *Stand Out*, we have suggested a few ways to do these substitution practices, including the following:

- Students work in pairs.
- Students use conversation or substitution cards.
- Students practice the conversation in an inside / outside circle activity.

Sometimes inside / outside circle activities take up too much room in the class. If this is the case, try forming two lines in the class that face one another. Students pair up with the person across from them. After students have practiced the conversation at least one time, ask one line to shift. The student at one end of the line will go to the other end of the line.

Evaluation 2   5–7 mins. ■■□

Ask volunteers to perform the conversation in front of the class.

C Study the chart.

Simple Present: *Live*		
Subject	**Verb**	**Example Sentence**
I / You We / They	live	I **live** in a house. You **live** in an apartment. We **live** in a condo. They **live** in a mobile home.
He / She	lives	He **lives** in a house. She **lives** in an apartment.

Pronunciation of /v/ 🎧
/v/   live

D Read about the people and their homes.

Saud

Housing: apartment
Address: 23 Hart Rd., Unit 2
City: Irving
State: Texas

Silvia

Housing: mobile home
Address: 13 Oak St.
City: Irving
State: Texas

Wei

Housing: house
Address: 15092 Arbor Lane
City: Irving
State: Texas

E Practice the conversation with a partner. Then make new conversations with information from D.

Saud: Do you live in a house, an apartment, or a mobile home?

Wei: I live in <u>a house</u>.

Saud: Where do you live?

Wei: My address is <u>15092 Arbor Lane</u>.

Saud: Where does <u>Silvia</u> live?

Wei: <u>She</u> lives at <u>13 Oak St.</u>

Saud: That's close by.

a / an
a house
an apartment

F INTERPRET Read the paragraph. Where do Saud's sister and brothers live? 🎧

> Saud and his family are from Iraq. Saud lives in an apartment in Irving, Texas. His sister also lives in Irving. She lives in a townhouse. Saud's brothers live in a small house in Los Angeles, California. Their parents live in a condominium in Iraq.

G Write a paragraph about where you and your family live. Use the paragraph in **F** as a model. Then talk with a partner. Write a new paragraph about your partner.

H SURVEY Ask four classmates what type of housing they live in. Share your information with the class. Answers will vary.

Name	Type of Housing
Saud	Saud lives in an apartment.

I CREATE Combine your information from H with the rest of the class and make a pie chart. Answers will vary.

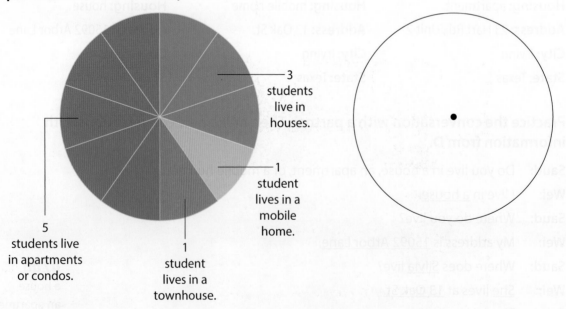

3 students live in houses.

1 student lives in a mobile home.

5 students live in apartments or condos.

1 student lives in a townhouse.

Presentation 3

10–15 mins. ■■■

Write a paragraph about yourself or someone you know on the board. For example:

Mary is from Portugal. She lives in an apartment. Her parents live in Lisbon, Portugal. They live in a condominium.

Study the paragraph with students. Show them the third-person singular *s* and the third-person plural with no *s*.

F INTERPRET Read the paragraph. Where do Saud's sister and brothers live?

Tell students to read as they listen. Play the audio. Then ask students to answer the question individually. Check the answer and have students underline the information in the text. Then ask: *Where do his parents live?*

Practice 3

20–30 mins. ■

G Write a paragraph about where you and your family live. Use the paragraph in F as a model. Then talk with a partner. Write a new paragraph about your partner.

Point out your paragraph on the board and the one about Saud in the book. Then ask a few students: *Where do you live? Where does your family live? Where does your sister / brother live?* Explain that they will write about their family. It will take some students a long time to do this activity. Monitor and help as needed.

When students are ready, put them in pairs to talk about where their families live. Then have them write a paragraph about their partner's family. If time allows, have them tell someone else about their partner's family.

BEST PRACTICE

Student Writing

Depending on your personal preference and purpose, you may want to do one of two things with student writing in a practice like this one.

One idea would be to give students a certain amount of time. Once that time is up, collect all work whether students have finished or not. This method will provide you with a sense of the true level of students' writing, and you can adjust your teaching appropriately.

Another way would be to ask all students to take time at home to do the activity and turn it in during the next class period. This will generate more polished work, and students may learn a lot by having more time to work.

Evaluation 3

5–7 mins. ■

Ask a few students to read their paragraphs out loud, or collect all the paragraphs and look them over.

Workplace Focus

Exercise H: Interpret and communicate information.

Application

20–25 mins. ■■■

H SURVEY Ask four classmates what type of housing they live in. Share your information with the class.

Elicit the question students need to ask: *Do you live in a . . . ?* Refer them back to the conversation in E if necessary.

After they complete the chart for four classmates, ask students to talk to more classmates or to look at someone else's chart to get the information for other classmates.

Workplace Focus

Exercise I: Interact appropriately with team members; Combine ideas and information.

I CREATE Combine your information from H with the rest of the class and make a pie chart.

Look at the example pie chart together. Then have students divide the empty circle according to the number of students in the class. Demonstrate this by drawing the pie chart on the board. Then ask: *How many people live in houses?* Have students tell you how many segments to color on the board.

One way to help students combine the information they gathered from their pie chart is to make four categories on the board for the four different housing types and elicit sentences from students about their classmates. For example: *Juan lives in a condo.* Then you can list the students names under the different categories until all students are accounted for.

Have students complete their pie chart themselves. When they're ready, ask for a volunteer to complete the chart on the board.

At-a-Glance Prep

Goal: Describe parts of a home
Grammar: Simple present: *Have*
Academic Strategies: Interpreting information, focused listening, doing a survey
Vocabulary: Parts of a home

Agenda
- ☐ Make a pie chart.
- ☐ Listen for number of bedrooms and bathrooms.
- ☐ Describe what people do at home.
- ☐ Learn about the parts of a home.
- ☐ Ask questions about your partner's home.

Resources
Heinle Picture Dictionary: Housing, pages 68–75

Pacing
- ■ 1.5 hour classes   ■ 2.5 hour classes
- ■ 3+ hour classes

Standards Correlations
CASAS: 1.4.1, 4.8.1, 7.2.3
CCRS: L1, L3, SL1, SL3, W1, W3
ELPS:

S2: Participate in level-appropriate oral and written exchanges of information, ideas, and analyses, in various social and academic contexts, responding to peer, audience, or reader comments and questions.

S10: Demonstrate command of the conventions of standard English to communicate in level-appropriate speech and writing.

Warm-up and Review   10–15 mins. ■■■
Draw an empty pie chart on the board. Take a class poll and complete the pie chart with the housing everyone in the class wants to live in in the future.

Introduction   10–15 mins. ■■■
Ask students to write all the rooms in a home they can think of. Don't allow dictionary use: the idea is to see what students already know. Write their ideas on the board. State the goal: *Today, we will describe parts of a home.*

Presentation 1   10–15 mins. ■■■

A INTERPRET Study the house floor plan. How many bedrooms and bathrooms are there?
Look at the floor plan with students. Help them understand that a floor plan looks at the rooms in a house as if from above. Point out features of the plan such as doors, walls, and windows that may not be clear to students. Ask the question in the direction line.

Workplace Focus
Exercise B: Collect and organize information.

Practice 1   30–45 mins. ■■■

B Listen and complete the chart. 🎧
Write *Irving Properties* on the board and ask students what it is the name of. Refer them back to Lesson 1 if necessary. Elicit the name of the rental agent and what she does. Tell students they are going to listen to conversations between Angela and people who are looking for housing. Go over the chart and ask students what information they need to listen for. Play the audio a few times. If students have trouble, play each conversation separately and check the answers together.

Note: The listening script for **B** is on page 96a.

C Practice the conversation with a partner. Then make new conversations with information from B.
Practice the conversation with the class and then with individuals. Model using different information from **B**. Put students in pairs to practice.

Evaluation 1   5–10 mins. ■■■
Have students perform one of their conversations for the class.

Does It Have a Yard?

GOAL ▶ Describe parts of a home

A **INTERPRET** Study the house floor plan. How many bedrooms and bathrooms are there?

There are two bedrooms
and two bathrooms.

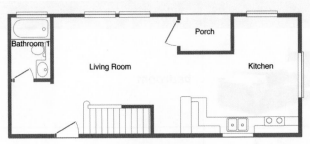

FIRST FLOOR

SECOND FLOOR

Floor Plan 1127 Sq. Ft. Total

B Listen and complete the chart. 🎧

Name	Bedrooms	Bathrooms
1. Saud	three	two
2. Silvia	two	one
3. Wei	four	two
4. Felipe	one	one

C Practice the conversation with a partner. Then make new conversations with information from **B**.

Student A: How many bedrooms does <u>Saud</u> want?

Student B: <u>He</u> wants <u>three</u> bedrooms.

Student A: And how many bathrooms?

Student B: <u>Two</u>.

D Study the words.

bathroom	bedroom	dining room	kitchen	living room

E Work in a group. Write the names of the rooms that match the activities. Use the words from **D**.

Activity	Room
1. People sleep in this room.	*bedroom*
2. People take showers in this room.	bathroom
3. People watch TV in this room.	living room
4. People eat dinner in this room.	dining room
5. People make dinner in this room.	kitchen

F IDENTIFY Practice the conversation with a partner. Then use the questions to make new conversations.

Student A: Where do people make breakfast?
Student B: People make breakfast in the kitchen.

1. Where do people sleep?

2. Where do people take showers?

3. Where do people watch TV?

4. Where do people eat dinner?

5. Where do people make lunch?

Listening Script

1. **Angela (agent):** *Hello, this is Irving Properties. How can I help you?*
   Saud: *Hello, I'm looking for an apartment to rent for my family. I checked online, but I'm not sure what is still available.*
   Angela: *OK. How many bedrooms do you need?*
   Saud: *I need three bedrooms and two bathrooms.*
   Angela: *I think we can help you. We have a three-bedroom, two-bath available now.*

2. **Angela:** *Hello, how can I help you?*
   Silvia: *Hi, we're interested in the small house on Market Street.*
   Angela: *The one with two bedrooms and one bathroom, right?*
   Silvia: *Yes, that's right. Is it still available?*
   Angela: *Yes, it is.*
   Silvia: *Great! How much is the rent?*
   Angela: *It's only $1,800 a month.*
   Silvia: *$1,800 a month? This is going to be more difficult than I thought.*

3. **Angela:** *Hello, what can I do for you?*
   Wei: *Hello, I don't see any large properties on your website. Do you have any properties for a big family?*
   Angela: *Well, let's see . . .*
   Wei: *I think I need a house with four bedrooms.*
   Angela: *OK. We have one on Foley Lane with four bedrooms and two bathrooms.*
   Wei: *That's perfect! How much is the rent?*
   Angela: *$3,000 a month.*
   Wei: *Can we come and look at it?*
   Angela: *Yes, of course.*

4. **Angela:** *Hello, this is Irving Properties. How can I help you?*
   Felipe: *What do you have in terms of one-bedroom apartments?*
   Angela: *We have a one-bedroom apartment on Sycamore Street.*
   Felipe: *OK. How much is the rent?*
   Angela: *It's $1,400 a month, plus utilities.*
   Felipe: *Is it one-bathroom too?*
   Angela: *Yes, that's right. One bathroom and one bedroom.*

Presentation 2
10–15 mins. ■■□

Elicit the names of rooms in a house from students to see what they already know. Write them on the board.

D Study the words.

Go over each word, having students repeat to practice the pronunciation. At this point, don't focus on the meaning as students will do that in **E**.

Workplace Focus

Exercise E: Interact appropriately with team members.

E Work in a group. Write the names of the rooms that match the activities. Use the words from D.

Students should work in groups to complete this activity because it may be too challenging for individual work. Encourage them to use dictionaries if necessary. After groups have finished the task, discuss the vocabulary, including *sleep, shower, watch, oven, dining room set*, etc.

> **Pronunciation   Distinguishing Words**
> Sometimes comparing one word with another word with only one or two distinguishing factors can help students hear the difference between two words. One way to drill students is to write the two words at opposite ends of the board. Ask students to point to each word when they hear it. Say the words randomly and see how many students have caught on. Then say the words in sentences and, finally, in a paragraph. Try this with *bedroom* and *bathroom*.

Practice 2
15–20 mins. ■■□

F IDENTIFY Practice the conversation with a partner. Then use the questions to make new conversations.

Model the conversation with a few students. Then go over the questions and have students repeat them. Put students in pairs to ask and answer the questions. Then have them switch roles so they practice both questions and answers. See the Best Practice: Conversation Chain note on page 97a for an alternative way of practicing conversations.

Evaluation 2
5–10 mins. ■■□

At some point during the activity, ask students to cover the top part of the page so they can't see the answers to the questions. Observe how students do.

BEST PRACTICE

Conversation Chain

Another strategy for conversation practice is a conversation chain. Do this activity in a group of four. Have Student A ask one question to Student B. Everyone will listen as Student B responds. Then Student B asks Student C the next question, and so on.

Presentation 3   15–20 mins. ■■■

G **Work in a group. Match the parts of the picture to the words by writing the letters.**

Ask students to first try doing this activity on their own. Give them only five minutes. Then ask them to work with a partner for five more minutes. Finally, ask them to work in a group and complete the task.

Practice 3   10–15 mins. ■

Write the words *inside* and *outside* on the board. Ask students to identify which places are inside the house and which are outside. In pairs, have students draw a two-column chart on a piece of paper and classify the items.

Evaluation 3   7–10 mins. ■

Draw the columns on the board and ask volunteers to come to the board and complete the chart.

Application   10–15 mins. ■■■

Before doing **H**, remind students about the forms of *have*. Point out the grammar note next to the table.

Workplace Focus

Exercise H: Interpret and communicate information.

H **SURVEY** **Ask your classmates the questions in the chart. When you find someone that says "Yes," write their name. Then share what you learned with a group.**

Go over the questions as a class. Have students repeat them and clarify understanding. Model the activity by asking several students the same question and writing the name of the person who says "yes" in your chart. Monitor as students ask and answer the questions. When they have completed their charts, put them in groups to share their information. Remind them about when to use *live / lives* and *have / has*. Provide examples using information about students in the class. For

example: *Mia and Luka have two bathrooms. Luka has a yard.* Monitor as students talk. Help with verb forms and pronuciation of the parts of a home.

Extension Activity: Ask students to make a Venn diagram with a partner about the rooms in their homes. Model this activity with a student and record the information in a Venn diagram on the board.

Instructor's Notes

_____

_____

_____

_____

_____

_____

_____

_____

_____

_____

_____

_____

_____

_____

_____

_____

_____

_____

_____

_____

G **Work in a group. Match the parts of the picture to the words by writing the letters.**

__d__ 1. stairs __m__ 2. swimming pool __a__ 3. bathroom __f__ 4. living room

__g__ 5. kitchen __j__ 6. garage __e__ 7. hall __c__ 8. balcony

__b__ 9. bedroom __l__ 10. deck __h__ 11. front porch __i__ 12. front yard

__n__ 13. backyard __k__ 14. driveway

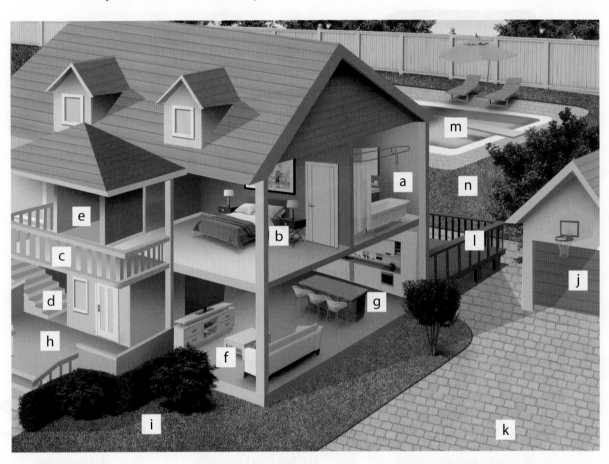

H **SURVEY** **Ask your classmates the questions in the chart. When you find someone that says "Yes," write their name. Then share what you learned with a group.**

Question	Name	
Do you live near a swimming pool?		*Have*
Do you have two bathrooms?		I **have** . . .
Do you have one bedroom?		He / She **has** . . .
Do you have a yard?		
Do you have parking?		
Do you have noisy neighbors?		

LESSON
3

Look Online

GOAL ▶ Interpret housing ads

A **PREDICT** Look at the picture. What is Saud reading? Why?

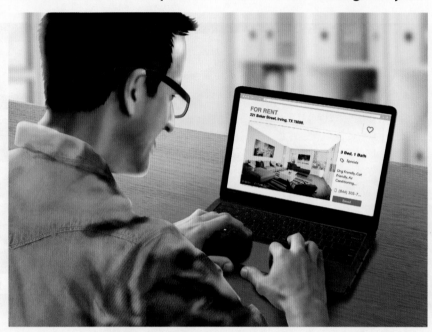

B **INTERPRET** Read the ads and label each *house*, *apartment*, or *townhouse*.

1.

AVAILABLE

2 bed, 3 bath townhouse
Gated community, near
schools and parks.

$2,000 / month

Contact Agent

____townhouse____

2.

HOME FOR RENT

$2,600 / month
3 bed, 2 bath house
155 Cherry Tree Lane
Irving, TX 75016
AC, garage, pool, utilities included

Contact Agent

____house____

3.

Roommate Wanted

Furnished 2 bed, 2 bath apartment
$1,000 / month per person
818 Sundry Ave
Irving, TX 27802
Sunny balcony, no pets.

Contact Agent

____apartment____

C Complete the sentences about the ads from **B**.

1. The house has ____three____ bedrooms and ____two____ bathrooms.

2. The apartment has ____two bedrooms and two bathrooms____.

3. The townhouse ____has two bedrooms and three bathrooms____.

4. The house ____has____ two ____bathrooms____.

At-a-Glance Prep

Goal: Interpret housing ads
Grammar: *Yes / no* questions
Pronunciation: Intonation of *yes / no* questions
Academic Strategies: Making predictions,
    interpreting information, calculating costs
Vocabulary: Housing ads, utilities

Agenda

☐ Interpret housing ads.
☐ Calculate move-in costs.
☐ Listen to identify ads.
☐ Answer questions about housing ads.
☐ Create a housing ad.

Resources

Heinle Picture Dictionary: Finding a place to live,
    pages 64–65

Pacing

■ 1.5 hour classes   ■ 2.5 hour classes
■ 3+ hour classes

Standards Correlations

CASAS: 1.4.2, 6.1.1, 7.4.4, 7.7.3
CCRS: L1, RI2, SL1, W1, W3
ELPS:
S5: Conduct research and evaluate and communicate findings to answer questions or solve problems.
S9: Create clear and coherent level-appropriate speech and text.

Warm-up and Review   10–15 mins. ■■■

In pairs, have students first list types of housing, then the rooms in a home, and finally, other parts of a house. Set a time limit of 2–3 minutes. Have students call out words on their lists and write them on the board. Check understanding by asking questions. For example: *Where do people make dinner? Is a balcony inside or outside?*, etc.

Introduction   5 mins. ■■■

Tell students that you are looking for a new place to live. Ask them where you might go to find housing. Answers might include the internet, friends, and an agency. State the goal: *Today, we will interpret housing ads.*

Presentation 1   25–30 mins. ■■■

Write *ad* on the board and have students explain what it means. Refer them back to the grocery store ads in Unit 3. Then add the word *housing*. Elicit what a housing ad would be for and what information it would have. Write students' ideas on the board. Show some housing ads from the internet if possible.

BEST PRACTICE

Realia

Using realia is often effective in the ESL classroom. Effective examples of realia can be challenging to find; however, whenever real-world examples can be brought to class to help students understand and associate them with target vocabulary, they can be very beneficial.

A   PREDICT   Look at the picture. What is Saud reading? Why?

Ask students to open their books and look at the picture. Discuss the questions in the direction line as a class.

Workplace Focus

Exercise B: Collect and organize information.

B   INTERPRET   Read the ads and label each *house*, *apartment*, or *townhouse*.

Go over the housing ads with students. Have them guess at the meanings of the abbreviations and any new vocabulary before explaining.

Workplace Focus

Exercise C: Collect and organize information.

Practice 1   5–7 mins. ■■■

C   Complete the sentences about the ads from B.

Have students complete the activity individually, then compare with a partner.

Evaluation 1   7–10 mins. ■■■

Ask volunteers to write the sentences on the board. Insist on uppercase letters at the beginning of sentences and periods at the end.

Presentation 2

12–15 mins. ■■■

Read through the ad in **D** with students. Ask pertinent comprehension questions, such as: *Is it a house or an apartment? How many bedrooms does it have?* Go over any new vocabulary, such as *spacious, remodeled, gated,* and *security deposit.* Elicit what *water paid* means. Write *utilities* on the board. Ask students what the word means. Clarify the definition after they answer by discussing the note next to **D**.

D CALCULATE **Read the housing ad. What is the move-in cost with a dog?**

Tell students to read the ad again, and clarify any vocabulary doubts. Allow them to do the calculation with a partner if they want to. Check the answer on the board as a class. Have students tell you the numbers that need to be added together, then do the calculation.

BEST PRACTICE

Presentation and Practice

There is a distinct difference between presenting new material and practicing it. In the presentation stage, the instructor explains the new material and walks students through all the information they will need later in the practice stage. It is certainly teacher-directed but should involve students by eliciting any prior knowledge they might have that will help them understand the new ideas, or encouraging them to make guesses or predictions. The classroom can be both student-centered and teacher-directed.

In the practice stage, the instructor encourages students to "try out" the new structures and vocabulary, while often making mistakes. The teacher prepared and initiated the activities, but they are not as controlled by the teacher as in the presentation stage since students are producing the new language themselves.

Practice 2

10–12 mins. ■■

E **Read the ads. Then listen and write the letter of the correct ad for each description.** 🎧

Ask students to read the ads and briefly discuss any new vocabulary. Then play the audio several times. Give students time to write their answers and compare with a partner.

Listening Script

1. *This is a large three-bedroom townhouse with a lot of good features. There is a pool. All utilities are included, and it's near elementary and middle schools. Come and see it. You won't be sorry.*

2. *This apartment is the best out there. It has three bedrooms, and it's only $2,500 a month. It's on the second floor, so you can enjoy a beautiful balcony. First and last month's rent are required for move-in.*

3. *This great apartment is far from city traffic. Hot summers are no problem. We have air-conditioning, and we pay the electric bill. Request a tour today.*

4. *This is a bargain! One thousand dollars a month to lease this one-bedroom, one-bath apartment. No pets please! Available September 1st.*

If possible, have students go online, look at three or four ads, and report the content to the class.

Evaluation 2

3 mins. ■■

Go over the answers to **E**.

Instructor's Notes

_____

_____

_____

_____

_____

_____

_____

_____

_____

_____

_____

_____

D **CALCULATE** Read the housing ad. What is the move-in cost with a dog?

The move-in cost is $4,475.

Apartment for RENT

192 Oliver Ave., Apt. 5, Irving, TX 75014

*$2,000 a month

*1,000 sq. ft.

Request a tour

- Spacious two-bedroom, two-bathroom apartment
- Water paid, remodeled kitchen
- Gated community with pool and large grass area, near schools and parks
- Pets are allowed with an additional $50 of rent per month.
- Application fee is $175.
- Move in with first, last, and $200 security deposit

Utilities:

gas

water

electricity

E Read the ads. Then listen and write the letter of the correct ad for each description.

a.

FOR RENT

3 bed, 2 bath apt.
AC, balcony
$2,500 / mo
First and last required
for move-in.

Request a tour

b.

AVAILABLE 9/1

$1,000 / mo
1 bed, 1 bath apartment
No pets

Request a tour

c.

APT. FOR RENT

2 bed, 3 bath apt.
$2,100 / mo
AC, electric included
First, last, and security
deposit for move-in.

Request a tour

d.

HOME FOR RENT

3 bed, 3 bath townhouse
Pool, utilities included
Near schools
$3,500 / mo

Request a tour

1. __d__   2. __a__   3. __c__   4. __b__

F Study the chart.

Yes / No Questions	
Question	**Answer**
Does it have three bedrooms?	Yes, it does. No, it doesn't.
Does it have air-conditioning?	Yes, it does. No, it doesn't.

Intonation 🎧

Yes / No Questions

Does it have three bedrooms?

Does it have air-conditioning?

G **INTERPRET** Read the ad and answer the questions.

CONDO FOR RENT

3 bed, 2 bath, $3,500 / mo
22954 Kensington Place
Irving, TX 75062
Pool, AC, utilities included

Contact owner

Life
ONLINE

Housing Ads
Be careful when looking for housing online.
1. Never pay rent before seeing the home and signing
   a lease.
2. If the rent is much lower than any other place
   and the home looks too good to be true, the ad is
   probably fake.

1. Does the home have four bedrooms?   No, it doesn't.

2. Does it have a pool?   Yes, it does.

3. Does it have two bathrooms?   Yes, it does.

4. Does it have furniture?   No, it doesn't.

5. Does it have air-conditioning?   Yes, it does.

H Check (✓) the items for your home. Share the information with a partner.
Answers will vary.

_____ pets allowed   _____ utilities paid   _____ balcony   _____ garage

_____ air-conditioning   _____ near a school   _____ near a park

I **CREATE** Write an ad for a home.

J Look online to find a home that is good for you.

Presentation 3
15–20 mins. ■■■

Look at the housing ads in **E** once again. Ask *yes / no* questions similar to the questions in **G**, but don't let students know that you are asking those particular questions. Accept short and long answers.

F Study the chart.

Say each question and focus students' attention on the short answer forms.

Pronunciation

Intonation of *Yes / No* Questions 🎧

Draw students' attention to the pronunciation note. Go over the rising intonation of *yes / no* questions. Play the audio and have students repeat each question, focusing on the appropriate intonation. Elicit appropriate answers to the questions.

Listening Script

Yes / no questions have a rising intonation. They go up at the end.
Does it have three bedrooms?
Does it have air-conditioning?

Practice 3
5–7 mins. ■

G INTERPRET Read the ad and answer the questions.

Ask students to do this activity on their own, then compare answers with a partner.

Read the information with the class. Help them understand the new vocabulary, such as *sign a lease*, *too good to be true*, and *fake*.

Life ONLINE

Evaluation 3
7–10 mins. ■

Ask volunteers to write their short answers to **G** on the board. Be sure to ask other students for help correcting capitalization errors and pointing out where commas or periods are missing.

Have students work in pairs and peer-edit their partner's work.

Workplace Focus

Exercise H: Interpret and communicate information.

Application
25–30 mins. ■■■

H Check (✓) the items for your home. Share the information with a partner.

Tell students to check the items that match their current homes or homes they want in the future. Then put them in pairs to share. Have students report back to the class about their partner's home.

I CREATE Write an ad for a home.

This activity can be done in pairs or small groups if students prefer. Tell them to imagine a home and make a list of the features it has. Remind them to use the example ads they've seen in the lesson to help them turn their list into a housing ad on a separate piece of paper. When they have finished, have them share their ads with the class. Take a poll to see which home is the most popular for renting.

J Look online to find a home that is good for you.

Ask students to write a list of what they want and need in a home. Ask: *Do you want a house or an apartment? How many rooms do you need?*, etc. Then have students go online and search for an ad that matches their needs. Suggest rental sites they can look at to help them. When they're ready, have them describe the best option they found to a partner. For example: *It is a condo. It has two bedrooms.*, etc. Write a few sentences as prompts on the board if necessary. Monitor and help as needed.

At-a-Glance Prep

Goal: Make appointments
Grammar: Present continuous
Academic Strategies: Make predictions, focused
   listening, ranking
Vocabulary: Appointment phrases

Agenda

☐ Ask questions about housing ads.
☐ Learn the steps to finding a home.
☐ Learn about filters.
☐ Listen and ask for information.
☐ Use the present continuous.

Resources

Heinle Picture Dictionary: Finding a Place to Live,
   pages 64–65

Pacing

■ 1.5 hour classes   ■ 2.5 hour classes
■ 3+ hour classes

Standards Correlations

CASAS: 0.1.2, 0.1.5, 1.4.2, 4.8.1, 7.2.3, 7.4.4, 7.7.3
CCRS: RI1, RI2, RI3, SL1, SL3
ELPS:

S2: Participate in level-appropriate oral and written exchanges
of information, ideas, and analyses, in various social and academic
contexts, responding to peer, audience, or reader comments and
questions.

S10: Demonstrate command of the conventions of standard
English to communicate in level-appropriate speech and writing.

Warm-up and Review   10–15 mins. ■■□

Ask students to come up with questions to ask
when calling about renting an apartment. Write
on the board: *How much is the rent?* Students most
likely won't construct such questions correctly, but
encourage them to try. Then write your corrected
versions of their questions on the board. Ask students
to turn back to **G** on page 100 and look at the
questions again. Write each question on the board.

Introduction   5 mins. ■■□

Write *housing ads* on the board. Ask students what
they should do after they find a home in an ad.
Accept all answers. State the goal: *Today, we will
learn how to make appointments.*

Presentation 1   20–25 mins. ■■■

A PREDICT Look at the picture. Who is
Saud talking to? Read his plan. 🎧

Have students look at the picture. Ask them to
describe what they can see. Tell them to listen as they
read. Play the audio. Ask: *What is Saud's plan for?* Then
answer the question in the direction line together.

B Read about using filters to look for a home online. 🎧

Tell students to read the text. Then clarify any
vocabulary doubts together. Remind students
to try to guess the meaning of new words from
the context. The image in **C** will also help. Then
play the audio and have students listen as they
read to help them with intonation and the
pronunciation of new vocabulary.

Practice 1   5–7 mins. ■■■

C Work in a group. Look at the
example from Saud's search and
answer the questions.

Make sure students understand that this is from
the web page Saud is using to look for housing
online in **A**. Put students in groups to go over
the information and answer the questions.

Evaluation 1   5 mins. ■■■

Check the answers to **C**. Ask several students
what options they would choose with the filters.

BEST PRACTICE

Group Responses

An interesting approach to getting the whole class
involved in discussions is to have students give a group
response. Ask students to form small groups of no more
than three or four. Assign each group a name or number.
Write each group name or number on a small piece of
paper and place all the pieces in a bowl or small box.
When you ask a question, instruct groups to first discuss
on their own and come up with a group response. Then
select a name or number to signal that it is that group's
turn to give their response. Repeat this action, randomly
giving groups a chance to share with the class.

When Can I See It?

GOAL ▶ Make appointments

A **PREDICT** Look at the picture. Who is Saud talking to? Read his plan. 🎧

1. Decide where I want to live.
2. Decide how many bedrooms and bathrooms I need.
3. Look online.
4. Talk to an agent, the manager, or the owner.
5. Make an appointment.
6. See the apartment.

B Read about using filters to look for a home online. 🎧

Life
ONLINE

Many real estate apps or websites have filters to make your online search easier. With filters, you can choose the type of home you want, the number of bedrooms and bathrooms, and the rent amount. This way you only see homes that have what you need at the right price.

C Work in a group. Look at the example from Saud's search and answer the questions.

1. What kind of home does Saud want? an apartment or condo

2. How many bedrooms and bathrooms does he want? three bedrooms and two bathrooms

3. How much can he spend? $3,000 or less

D Read and listen to the conversation. Then practice it with a partner. 🎧

Owner: Hello, this is Mariana.

Saud: Hi, Mariana. This is Saud. I'm interested in the condo you have for rent.

Owner: Ah, yes. Hi, Saud. Thanks for reaching out. As I said in my message, the rent for the condo is $2,500 a month.

Saud: Great! When can I see it?

Owner: How about today at 3:00?

Saud: Perfect! Thank you.

E Listen to the conversations. Take notes and complete the chart. 🎧

	How much is the rent?	What time is the appointment?
1.	$2,500	3:00
2.	$2,800	10:00 a.m.
3.	$3,000	4:30
4.	$2,400	2:00

F Complete the conversation with the information from one of the items in E. Then practice the conversation with a partner. Answers will vary.

Owner: Hello. How can I help you?

Saud: Hi. I'm interested in the apartment for rent. Is it still available?

Owner: Yes, it's still available. We're renting it for _____.

Saud: OK, when can I see it?

Owner: You can stop by at _____.

G Make new conversations using the rest of the information from E.

Presentation 2

20–30 mins. ■■■

D Read and listen to the conversation. Then practice it with a partner. 🎧

Tell students to read as they listen. Play the audio. Then play the audio again, pausing after each line for students to repeat. Put students in pairs to practice.

Workplace Focus

Exercise E: Collect and organize information.

E Listen to the conversations. Take notes and complete the chart. 🎧

Tell students that they are going to listen to Saud talking to the owners of the homes he is interested in. Go over the chart and ask students what information they need to listen for. Play the audio. Pause after the first conversation and ask: *How much is the rent? What time is the appointment?* Point out the answers in the chart. Then play conversations 2–4 twice. Have students compare answers with a partner. Play the audio one or more times and confirm the answers.

Listening Script

1. **Owner:** *Hello, this is Mariana.*
   Saud: *Hi, Mariana. This is Saud. I'm interested in the condo you have for rent.*
   Owner: *Ah, yes. Hi, Saud. Thanks for reaching out. As I said in my message, the rent for the condo is $2,500 a month.*
   Saud: *Great! When can I see it?*
   Owner: *How about today at 3:00?*
   Saud: *Perfect! Thank you.*

2. **Owner:** *Hello. How can I help you?*
   Saud: *Yes, hi. My name is Saud. I'm interested in the apartment for rent. Is it still available?*
   Owner: *Yes, it's still available. We're renting it for $2,800.*
   Saud: *Wow! That's expensive.*
   Owner: *Maybe, but it is a new and beautiful apartment.*
   Saud: *OK, when can I see it?*
   Owner: *You can stop by at 10 a.m.*

3. **Owner:** *Hello.*
   Saud: *Hi. This is Saud. I am calling about the house for rent. I sent you a message yesterday.*
   Owner: *Oh, yes, that's right. So, what would you like to know?*

Saud: *How much is the rent?*
Owner: *It's $3,000 a month. It's a four bedroom.*
Saud: *Hmm. I don't know if I need something that big. When can I see it?*
Owner: *Come by at 4:30.*
Saud: *OK, see you then.*

4. **Saud:** *Hello.*
   Owner: *Hello. Is this Saud?*
   Saud: *Yes, that's me.*
   Owner: *I am returning your call about the three-bedroom apartment.*
   Saud: *Oh, yes. Thank you. How much is the rent?*
   Owner: *It's $2,400 a month.*
   Saud: *Great. Can I come by today?*
   Owner: *Of course. Come by around 2:00.*
   Saud: *Thanks, I will.*

F Complete the conversation with the information from one of the items in E. Then practice the conversation with a partner.

Write the conversation on the board and have students tell you how to complete it. Make sure they give you information from the chart in **E**. Then have two students practice it. Erase the conversation from the board. Put students in pairs and ask them to complete the conversation and then practice it.

Practice 2

10–15 mins. ■■■

G Make new conversations using the rest of the information from E.

Elicit from students what information will change in the new conversations. Monitor as students practice in pairs and help as needed.

Evaluation 2

5–7 mins. ■■■

Ask volunteers to perform the conversations for the class.

BEST PRACTICE

Performing Conversations

Many students are shy about performing conversations in front of the class. When assigning conversations to perform, give students a few minutes to prepare and, if time allows, have students practice with another pair or group before presenting to the entire class.

Presentation 3   15–20 mins. ■■■□

Write and present the following conversation on the board. Use this conversation to help students see when they might use the present continuous.

Ms. Rollings: Hello.
Carmen: Hello. My name is Carmen. I'm calling about the house you have for rent.
Ms. Rollings: Ah, yes. It's still available.
Carmen: Great. When can I see it?
Ms. Rollings: Well, I'm cleaning the house right now, but can you come tomorrow at 3 p.m.?
Carmen: Yes, that works for me! See you tomorrow. Goodbye.
Ms. Rollings: OK, goodbye.

Then say: *I'm talking to you. You are listening.* Write the sentences on the board. Help students understand that these sentences refer to current actions, actions taking place at the moment of speaking.

H Study the chart.

Go over the examples in the chart. Then underline the verb *be* and the verb + *ing* in the conversation and sentences on the board.

BEST PRACTICE

Grammar Presentations

It's important to remember that students will be introduced again and again to the same structures throughout the beginning of their English learning experience. At some point, they will be ready to acquire the structures instead of merely learning them. This means they will be able to produce the structures correctly without thinking about it. Until then, be prepared to repeat each grammar presentation multiple times in new or different contexts.

I Complete the sentences with the present continuous to describe the pictures. Choose the best verbs from the chart in H.

Complete this exercise as a class, eliciting the answers from student volunteers and writing them on the board. Elicit additional sentences to describe the pictures. For example: *He is sitting. He is using his laptop. He is typing. He is smiling.*

Practice 3   5–7 mins. ■□□□

J Complete the sentences with the present continuous.

Have students complete the sentences individually. Refer them back to the chart in **H** as needed.

Evaluation 3   5–7 mins. ■□□□

Check students' work. Ask volunteers to write the sentences on the board.

Workplace Focus

Exercise K: Interact appropriately with team members.

Application   10–15 mins. ■■■□

K RANK Work in a group. Rank the steps from easy (1) to difficult (4).

Make sure students understand the concept of ranking. Then assign them to groups to complete the activity. When they have finished, have groups share their rankings on the board and try to reach a class consensus.

Instructor's Notes

_____

_____

_____

_____

_____

_____

_____

_____

_____

_____

_____

H **Study the chart.**

Present Continuous			
Subject	*Be*	**Verb + *ing***	**Example Sentence**
I	am	talk + ing	I **am talking** on the phone.
You / We / They	are	search + ing make + ing	They **are searching** for a new home. We **are making** an appointment.
He / She / It	is	move + ing	She **is moving** into a new apartment.
Delete the *e* and add *-ing* with verbs that end in *e*.			

I **Complete the sentences with the present continuous to describe the pictures. Choose the best verbs from the chart in H.**

1. Saud _____is searching_____ for a new apartment.

2. He _____is talking_____ to a rental agent.

3. He _____is making_____ an appointment.

J **Complete the sentences with the present continuous.**

look	make	move	~~read~~	talk

1. I _____am reading_____ housing ads.

2. They _____are moving_____ into a new home.

3. We _____are looking_____ at a condominium.

4. Silvia _____is making_____ an appointment.

5. You _____are talking_____ on the phone.

K **RANK** **Work in a group. Rank the steps from easy (1) to difficult (4).** Answers will vary.

_____ He calls and asks questions.   _____ He makes appointments with owners.

_____ He looks at housing ads online.   _____ He looks at homes.

Where Do You Want the Sofa?

GOAL ▶ Identify furniture in a house

A Match the words to the correct part of the house. Share your ideas with a partner.

bathtub   **bed**   **car**   **chair**   **refrigerator**   **sofa**

1. bedroom _____ *bed* _____

2. kitchen _____ refrigerator _____

3. dining room _____ chair _____

4. bathroom _____ bathtub _____

5. garage _____ car _____

6. living room _____ sofa _____

B **CLASSIFY** Work in a group. Write other things you usually see in each place. Use a dictionary or ask your teacher for help. Answers will vary.

Bedroom	Kitchen	Dining Room	Bathroom	Garage	Living Room

C Practice the conversation with a partner. Then make new conversations about the items in B.

Student A: Where do you put the <u>refrigerator</u>?

Student B: We put it in the <u>kitchen</u>.

At-a-Glance Prep

Goal: Identify furniture in a house
Grammar: Prepositions of location
Academic Strategies: Classifying information, focused listening
Vocabulary: Furniture

Agenda

☐ Write a housing ad.
☐ Identify furniture in a house.
☐ Match furniture and rooms.
☐ Use prepositions.
☐ Describe a room.

Resources

Heinle Picture Dictionary: Living Room, pages 73–74

Pacing

■ 1.5 hour classes ■ 2.5 hour classes
■ 3+ hour classes

Standards Correlations

CASAS: 0.1.2, 0.1.5, 1.4.1, 7.4.4, 7.7.3
CCRS: L2, SL1, SL3, W1, W3
ELPS:

S5: Conduct research and evaluate and communicate findings to answer questions or solve problems.

S10: Demonstrate command of the conventions of standard English to communicate in level-appropriate speech and writing.

Warm-up and Review   15–20 mins. ■■■

Ask students to form groups of four or five. Ask each group to choose one student from their group and design a housing ad around that student's home. Ask groups to share their ads with the rest of the class.

Introduction   7–10 mins. ■■■

Ask each group to make a list of furniture without using a dictionary or their books. This will tell you how much students already know. Ask one group to put its list on the board. Then ask the other groups to add to the list. State the goal: *Today, we will identify furniture in a house.*

Presentation 1   7–10 mins. ■■■

Go over the pictures and words in **A**. Help students with pronunciation.

A Match the words to the correct part of the house. Share your ideas with a partner.

Ask students to do this exercise individually and then explain their decisions to a partner.

Workplace Focus

Exercise B: Complete tasks as assigned; Interact appropriately with team members.

Practice 1   15–20 mins. ■■■

B CLASSIFY Work in a group. Write other things you usually see in each place. Use a dictionary or ask your teacher for help.

Copy the chart on the board and elicit an item for each place (different from those presented in **A**). Put students in groups to complete the chart. Then have them add to the chart on the board.

BEST PRACTICE

Limiting Vocabulary

Each student will have a different idea of which vocabulary items are the most important. In a lesson like this one, students may identify so much vocabulary that individual learners become overwhelmed. It is the instructor's job to clarify that it is not necessary to learn all the words. Encourage students to keep a vocabulary notebook (on paper or electronically) where they note vocabulary from each lesson that is useful for them.

C Practice the conversation with a partner. Then make new conversations about the items in B.

Say the question and have students repeat it. Model the conversation with a student. Then have two students model it. Choose a different item and ask a student where you put it. Have students continue in pairs. Monitor and help as needed. Remind students to switch roles.

Evaluation 1   5 mins. ■■■

Ask volunteers to perform one of their conversations for the class.

Presentation 2
10–15 mins. ■■■□

D Study the prepositions.

Go over the prepositions and pictures. Quiz students by asking them where various items are located in the classroom. You can also make sentences about the students. For example: *(Name) is between (name) and (name). (Name) is next to (name).* Elicit further examples from students if you feel they are ready.

On this page, students will see more furniture that they may need help identifying. Ask students to form groups and briefly discuss which room of the house they believe each item belongs in. Discuss their decisions and add the items to the chart in **B** if they're not there already.

Ask students to look at the photo at the bottom of the page. Elicit descriptions using prepositions. Write students' ideas on the board. Make corrections and provide vocabulary as needed.

Practice 2
15–20 mins. ■■□

Workplace Focus
Exercise E: Interpret and communicate information.

E Practice the conversation with a partner. Then make new conversations about the things in D. Ask about the plant, the dog, the armchair, the cat, and the lamp.

Model the conversation with a student. Then ask about a different item and model the conversation again. Encourage the student to ask you about a different item. Put students in pairs to continue practicing. Tell them to take turns asking and answering. Remind them to ask about all the items mentioned.

For further practice, with a partner, have students say and write sentences about the classroom using prepositions.

Evaluation 2
5–7 mins. ■

Observe students as they practice the conversations.

BEST PRACTICE

Prepositions of Place

Teaching prepositions of place is not that difficult. They must simply be practiced, and there are many different ways to give students the practice they need. Start off by presenting the prepositions with easy-to-understand examples. For instance: *The trash can is **next to** the door.* You can check students' understanding of prepositions by asking questions such as: *Where is the trash can?*

Some approaches to practicing prepositions of place include the following:

a. Ask students to write their own example sentences.

b. Have students create their own conversations in pairs asking where something is located.

c. Tell students to move objects in the classroom to different locations using prepositions. For example: *Put your book **on** the desk. Put a piece of paper **under** your book.*

Instructor's Notes

_____

_____

_____

_____

_____

_____

_____

_____

_____

_____

_____

_____

_____

D Study the prepositions.

in   on   next to

between   under   over

E Practice the conversation with a partner. Then make new conversations about the things in **D**. Ask about the plant, the dog, the armchair, the cat, and the lamp.

Student A: Where's the <u>trash</u>?

Student B: It's <u>in the trash can</u>.

Can you describe the people and objects in this living room using prepositions?

F Study the words.

a window   a door   an end table   a coffee table

a plant   a dining room chair   a painting   a lamp

G Listen to the instructions and draw objects in the room below. 🎧

H **APPLY** Show a partner your drawing of the room from **G**. Talk about where the furniture is.

I Find a picture of a room with furniture in a magazine or online. Show the picture to the class and describe it.

Presentation 3   15–20 mins. ■■■□

Take an inventory of the furniture in the classroom. Ask students to help you do this. Ask: *How many chairs are there? How many desks are there?*, etc. For virtual classes, a photo of a classroom could be displayed for students to talk about.

F   Study the words.

Make sure that students understand the meaning of each word. Quiz them on the new vocabulary. For example, ask: *Where is the door?* And have students point to it and / or use a preposition. For example: *It's next to the window.* Or ask: *Where do you put a lamp / painting / plant?*

BEST PRACTICE

Monitoring Student Responses

An easy way to monitor responses is to have students simply respond verbally with a word. Say: *bed*. Students respond: *bedroom*.

With the above method, however, the stronger students sometimes overwhelm the students who need more time to think when asked for a verbal response. You may choose other ways for students to respond where students are less likely to "go along with the crowd." One such response could be to use 3-by-5 index cards with different answers on them. Students hold up the card with their answer on it. Each card could have different rooms. If you choose to use this method, have students create the actual cards themselves so they also get writing practice.

Another way is to number pictures. Students respond by showing the number of fingers that correspond to each picture you describe. They will be listening for target vocabulary words.

Practice 3   10–15 mins. ■□□

G   Listen to the instructions and draw objects in the room below. 🎧

Write *wall* and *middle* on the board and demonstrate their meaning. Say: *Draw a door*, and draw a door on the board. Play the audio and stop after number 1 to check that everyone is drawing in the room in their books. Play the rest of the audio one or two times.

Listening Script

1. *Draw a sofa next to the door.*
2. *Draw a chair under the window.*
3. *Draw an end table between the sofa and the chair.*
4. *Draw a lamp on the end table.*
5. *Draw a painting on the wall over the sofa.*
6. *Draw a coffee table in the middle of the room.*
7. *Draw a plant next to the chair.*

Evaluation 3   10–15 mins. ■■■

Look at the students' drawings to check their understanding of the new vocabulary and prepositions of place.

Application   15–20 mins. ■■■

H   APPLY   Show a partner your drawing of the room from G. Talk about where the furniture is.

Put students in pairs to carry out the activity. Ask: *Are your pictures different?*

To extend this, ask students to draw a diagram of their own living room on a separate sheet of paper. They should identify the location of their furniture using prepositions and describe the furniture's location to a partner.

I   Find a picture of a room with furniture in a magazine or online. Show the picture to the class and describe it.

Ideally, students bring pictures of their own choice, but if necessary, provide a selection. Model the activity by showing one of your pictures and describing it to the class using the vocabulary and prepositions of place from the lesson. Depending on the size of your class, have students carry out the activity as a whole class or in small groups.

At-a-Glance Prep

Goal: Identify employment opportunities in construction

Agenda

☐ Interpret an infographic.

☐ Read about carpenter pay.

☐ Rank the qualities of a carpenter.

☐ Reflect on work preferences.

☐ Search online for openings in construction.

Pacing

■ 1.5 hour classes ■ 2.5 hour classes

■ 3+ hour classes

Standards Correlations

CASAS: 0.1.2, 0.1.5, 4.1.3, 4.1.8, 4.1.9, 4.8.1, 6.1.3, 6.7.3, 7.2.3, 7.4.4, 7.7.3

CCRS: RI1, RI2, RI3, SL1, SL3, W1, W3

ELPS:

S5: Conduct research and evaluate and communicate findings to answer questions or solve problems.

S10: Demonstrate command of the conventions of standard English to communicate in level-appropriate speech and writing.

In this lesson, students are introduced to employment opportunities in the construction field. They will analyze an infographic and compare salaries for different construction jobs. Students will also read about carpenters' hourly pay and overtime rates. They will rank the qualities of a carpenter and reflect on their own work preferences. Finally, students will carry out an online search for openings in construction in their area.

Warm-up and Review   10–15 mins. ■■■

Write *construction* on the board and have students explain what it is. Write *build a house* as an example on the board and elicit the different things involved in building a house. Help students recall the vocabulary from Lesson 5 (*door, window, wall*), and ask who makes these parts of a house to see how much students already know. Write any construction-related jobs students know on the board.

Introduction   5–10 mins. ■■■

Find out if any students work in construction. Remind them that throughout *Stand Out*, they will investigate many job possibilities. Write the goal on the board: *Today we will identify employment opportunities in construction.*

Presentation 1   15–20 mins. ■■■

A INTERPRET Read the infographic. What job do you think is the most difficult?

Go over the infographic together, having students describe what they see in the photos. Read each step in the building process and the people who work in it so students can become familiar with the pronunciation. Encourage students to look up the jobs that they are not familiar with. Then go over the annual pay for each job, asking students to say the amounts to review large numbers. Discuss the question in the direction line as a class.

B Work in a group. Answer the questions.

Write two numbers on the board and elicit which is *more* and which is *less*. Have students complete the sentences individually, then compare with a partner. Go over the answers as a class. Clarify any vocabulary questions students still have from the infographic or questions.

Practice 1   15–20 mins. ■■■

C Study the chart about comparatives and superlatives.

Look at the chart together and help students understand the meaning of each amount. Bear in mind that it may become clearer for students when they do the following activity comparing annual pay.

D Work with a partner. Ask and answer the questions about A.

Say each question and have students repeat them. Connect the questions to the chart in **C** as needed to facilitate understanding. Then put students in pairs to ask and answer the questions. Tell them to alternate so both partners practice asking and answering.

Evaluation 1   5–10 mins. ■■■

Check the answers to **D** as a class and ask students how much the pay is for each job (plumber, tile installer, etc.).

Explore the Workforce

GOAL ▶ Identify employment opportunities in construction

A **INTERPRET** Read the infographic. What job do you think is the most difficult?

STEPS TO BUILDING A HOUSE

Framing
Carpenters
Roofers

Flooring and Walls
Floor Installers
Drywallers

Finishing
Painters
Carpenters
Interior Designers

Foundation
Cement Masons

Utilities
Plumbers, Electricians,
Heater & Air Conditioner
Specialists (HVAC)

Bath and Kitchen
Carpenters
Plumbers
Tile Installers

ANNUAL PAY

Carpenters	$48,000
Cement Masons	$48,000
Electricians	$60,000
Floor, Tile, Drywallers, HVAC	$48,000
Interior Designers	$60,500
Painters	$45,500
Plumbers	$60,000

Source: U.S. Bureau of Labor Statistics

B Work in a group. Answer the questions.

1. Which jobs have an annual pay of $60,000? _electricians and plumbers_

2. Which job pays less, carpenter or plumber? _carpenter_

3. How many steps are there to build a house? _six_

4. Who works on the fifth step? _carpenters, plumbers, and tile installers_

C Study the chart about comparatives and superlatives.

D Work with a partner. Ask and answer the questions about **A**.

1. Which job pays more, cement mason or plumber? _plumber_

2. Which job pays less, electrician or tile installer? _tile installer_

3. Which job pays the least? _painter_

4. Which job pays the most? _interior designer_

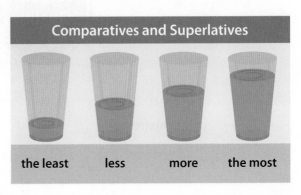

Comparatives and Superlatives

the least   less   more   the most

E Read about carpenter pay. Then complete the chart. 🎧

Carpenters, like many construction workers, work by the hour. They only work when there is a job to do. Sometimes they work *overtime* and make more per hour. Overtime is time worked over 40 hours a week.
How to calculate overtime: Hourly pay x 1.5 = overtime pay
Example: $30.00 x 1.5 = $45.00

Base Pay	Overtime Pay (more than 40 hours)
$25.00 an hour	*$37.50 an hour*
$30.00 an hour	$45.00 an hour
$35.00 an hour	$52.50 an hour
$40.00 an hour	$60.00 an hour
$45.00 an hour	$67.50 an hour
$50.00 an hour	$75.00 an hour

F **RANK** Work in a group. Read about the qualities of good carpenters. Rank the qualities from most important (1) to least important (5). Answers will vary.

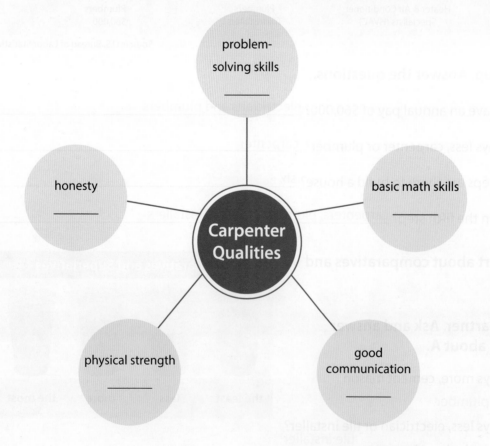

problem-solving skills
_____

honesty
_____

basic math skills
_____

Carpenter Qualities

physical strength
_____

good communication
_____

Presentation 2

15–20 mins. ■■■□

E Read about carpenter pay. Then complete the chart. 🎧

Ask students to read the text. Then ask questions to check students' understanding. For example: *What is overtime? How do you calculate it?* Play the audio as students read the text again. Review any vocabulary questions. Then have students calculate the overtime with a partner and complete the chart. Complete the chart on the board together to confirm the calculations.

Practice 2

15–20 mins. ■■□□

F RANK Work in a group. Read about the qualities of good carpenters. Rank the qualities from most important (1) to least important (5).

Remind students what ranking is. Put students in groups. Tell them to use a dictionary for any of the qualities they are unsure about. Monitor and help as needed.

Evaluation 2

5–10 mins. ■■■□

Have each group share their ranking and explain their reasons. Help as needed. Then try to reach a consensus on the ranking as a class.

BEST PRACTICE

Reflection

When looking for and applying for jobs, students need to be aware of their qualities, strengths, and work preferences to help them find a good match for their profile and to be able to tell a potential employer about their personal qualities. Therefore, the self-evaluation and reflection that is prompted in Lesson 6 is important because it helps students develop both self-awareness and the ability to speak about their personal qualities, strengths, and preferences.

Some students may not be used to this kind of activity, so it may be helpful to tell them that there are no right or wrong answers and that they need to answer based on their own characteristics and preferences.

Instructor's Notes

_____

_____

_____

_____

_____

_____

_____

_____

_____

_____

_____

_____

_____

_____

_____

_____

_____

_____

_____

_____

_____

_____

Presentation 3

Have students look at the photo and read the caption. Discuss the fact that where you work (outside or inside) is an important part of a job and that students should think about their preferences related to work environment. Explain that the following exercises will ask them to think about these preferences.

G REFLECT Answer the questions about you.

Go over each question and clarify any vocabulary doubts. Then have students answer the questions about work preferences individually.

Practice 3   15–20 mins. ■

H Work with a partner. Ask and answer the questions in G.

Model the conversation with a student. Then have two students model the conversation before putting students in pairs. Tell them to take turns asking and answering the questions. Monitor and help as needed.

I Choose a job title from A. Go to a job search site online and see if there are any openings within 25 miles of your school or home. Share what you find with a partner.

Help students get started with their searches by asking which of the jobs in **A** they want to look for. Then share some job search sites that they can use. Monitor as students carry out their searches and help as needed. When they have all found one or two options, put them in pairs to share their information.

Evaluation 3   5–10 mins. ■

Call on different students to share what they found and write the pay on the board for each job. Then have students use *the least, less, more,* and *the most* to compare them.

Instructor's Notes

_____

_____

_____

_____

_____

_____

_____

_____

_____

_____

_____

_____

_____

_____

_____

_____

_____

_____

_____

_____

_____

_____

_____

_____

_____

_____

Carpenters can work outside on construction sites or inside in workshops, factories, or homes.

G **REFLECT Answer the questions about you.** Answers will vary.

1. Do you like to work outside?

   a. yes   b. no   c. maybe

2. Do you like working with your hands?

   a. yes   b. no   c. maybe

3. Do you like to create things?

   a. yes   b. no   c. maybe

4. Do you like to work with others?

   a. yes   b. no   c. maybe

H **Work with a partner. Ask and answer the questions in G.**

EXAMPLE: **Student A:** Do you like to work outside?

                   Student B: Yes, I do. Do you like to work outside?

                   Student A: Sometimes, but not every day.

I **Choose a job title from A. Go to a job search site online and see if there are any openings within 25 miles of your school or home. Share what you find with a partner.**

A Read the housing ads.

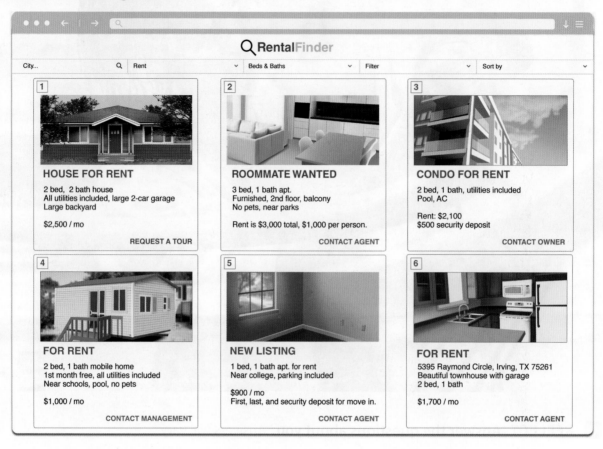

RentalFinder

City... | Rent | Beds & Baths | Filter | Sort by

1

HOUSE FOR RENT

2 bed, 2 bath house
All utilities included, large 2-car garage
Large backyard

$2,500 / mo

REQUEST A TOUR

2

ROOMMATE WANTED

3 bed, 1 bath apt.
Furnished, 2nd floor, balcony
No pets, near parks

Rent is $3,000 total, $1,000 per person.

CONTACT AGENT

3

CONDO FOR RENT

2 bed, 1 bath, utilities included
Pool, AC

Rent: $2,100
$500 security deposit

CONTACT OWNER

4

FOR RENT

2 bed, 1 bath mobile home
1st month free, all utilities included
Near schools, pool, no pets

$1,000 / mo

CONTACT MANAGEMENT

5

NEW LISTING

1 bed, 1 bath apt. for rent
Near college, parking included

$900 / mo
First, last, and security deposit for move in.

CONTACT AGENT

6

FOR RENT

5395 Raymond Circle, Irving, TX 75261
Beautiful townhouse with garage
2 bed, 1 bath

$1,700 / mo

CONTACT AGENT

B Cover the ads in **A** so you can't see them. Ask your partner questions about the first three ads. Then your partner covers the ads and asks about the next three.

Answers will vary.

What type of housing is it?	How many bedrooms are there?	How many bathrooms are there?	Is it near anything?	How much is the rent?

Learner Log

I can identify types of housing.
☐ Yes ☐ No ☐ Maybe

I can interpret housing ads.
☐ Yes ☐ No ☐ Maybe

At-a-Glance Prep

Goal: All unit goals
Grammar: All unit grammar
Academic Strategies: Reviewing, evaluating, developing study skills
Vocabulary: All unit vocabulary

Agenda

☐ Discuss unit goals.
☐ Complete the review.
☐ Evaluate and reflect on progress.

Pacing

■ 1.5 hour classes   ■ 2.5 hour classes
■ 3+ hour classes

Standards Correlations

CASAS: 0.1.2, 0.1.5, 1.4.1, 1.4.2, 7.2.3
CCRS: L1, L2, L3, RI1, RI2, RI3, W3
ELPS:
S9: Create clear and coherent level-appropriate speech and text.

Warm-up and Review   7–10 mins.

Ask students about their homes. Make a list on the board of all the vocabulary students can come up with from the unit.

Introduction   5 mins.

With students' help, write all the goals from Unit 4 on the board. Show students the first page of every lesson so they understand that today will be a review.

Presentation   10–15 mins.

This presentation will cover all three pages of the review. Discuss the goal of each lesson. Ask simple questions to remind students of what they have learned.

Practice 1   15–20 mins.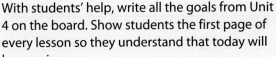

A Read the housing ads.

After students have read the ads, ask general comprehension questions. For example: *Is number 2 near schools? Does number 4 have a pool?*

Workplace Focus

Exercise B: Collect and organize information.

B Cover the ads in A so you can't see them. Ask your partner questions about the first three ads. Then your partner covers the ads and asks about the next three.

Model the activity with a student to make sure students have understood the instructions. Then put students in pairs to carry out the activity. Monitor and help as needed.

Evaluation 1   5–10 mins.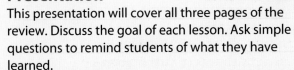

Go around the classroom and check on students' progress. Help individuals as needed. If you see consistent errors among several students, interrupt the class and give a mini lesson or review to help students feel comfortable with the concepts.

Learner Log   5–10 mins.

Have students read the statements and complete the log. If students answer *no* or *maybe*, encourage them to set themselves a goal to practice. Show them where they can find more practice activities.

BEST PRACTICE

Learner Logs

Learner Logs function to help students in many different ways:

1. They serve as part of the review process.
2. They help students to gain confidence and to document what they have learned. Consequently, students see that they are progressing in their learning.
3. They provide students with a tool that they can use over and over to check and recheck their understanding of the target language. In this way, students become independent learners.

Practice 2   15–20 mins. ■■■

C Complete the chart with the words.

Elicit the meaning of *inside* and *outside*. Then have students complete the activity individually.

D Look at the photo and complete the sentences.

Have students tell you what they see in the photo. Encourage them to use the present continuous to talk about the people. For example: *The girl is reading*. Have them complete the sentences individually.

Evaluation 2   5–10 mins. ■■■

Go around the classroom and check on students' progress. Help individuals as needed. If you see consistent errors among several students, interrupt the class and give a mini lesson or review to help students feel comfortable with the concept.

Learner Log   5–10 mins.

Have students read the statement and complete the log. If students answer *no* or *maybe*, encourage them to set themselves a goal to practice. Show them where they can find more practice activities.

BEST PRACTICE

Recycling / Review

The review and the project that follows are part of the recycling / review process. Students at this level often need to be reintroduced to concepts to solidify what they have learned. Many concepts are learned and forgotten while learning other new concepts. This is because students learn but are not necessarily ready to acquire language concepts.

Therefore, it becomes very important to review and to show students how to review on their own. It is also important to recycle the new concepts in different contexts.

Instructor's Notes

C Complete the chart with the words.

| balcony | deck | hall | pool | refrigerator |
| bathtub | driveway | kitchen | porch | sofa |

Inside	Outside
bathtub	balcony
hall	deck
kitchen	driveway
refrigerator	pool
sofa	porch

D Look at the photo and complete the sentences.

1. The dog is _____under_____ the coffee table.

2. The girl is _____in_____ the living room.

3. The black lamp is _____between_____ the sofa and the bookshelf.

4. The book is _____on_____ the _____coffee table_____.

5. The guitar is _____next to_____ the bookshelf.

Learner Log	I can describe parts of a home. Yes No Maybe

Review

E **Describe the pictures with sentences in the present continuous.** Answers will vary.
Example answers included.

Carmen

Simon and Chantal

Marco

1. Carmen is moving into a new home .

2. Simon and Chantal are visiting / looking at an apartment .

3. Marco is talking on the phone / is making an appointment .

F **Write a conversation about making an appointment to see a home for rent.**
Answers will vary.

Owner: _____

You: _____

Owner: _____

You: _____

Owner: _____

You: _____

Owner: _____

You: _____

G **List furniture for each part of the house.** Answers will vary.

Bedroom	Kitchen	Dining Room	Bathroom	Garage	Living Room

Learner Log   I can make appointments.   I can identify furniture in a house.
　　　　　　　　　　□ Yes □ No □ Maybe   □ Yes □ No □ Maybe

Practice 3
20–25 mins. ■■■□

E Describe the pictures with sentences in the present continuous.

Elicit ideas about the pictures. Ask: *Where is she? What are they doing?* Then have students complete the sentences.

F Write a conversation about making an appointment to see a home for rent.

Have students work in pairs to create the conversation. Refer them back to the conversations in Lesson 4 to help them get started. When pairs have finished, have them sit back-to-back to carry out the "phone call." Encourage them to practice several times, switching roles as needed, and then try to do it without looking at their books.

G List furniture for each part of the house.

Give students one minute to do this individually. Then put them in pairs to share and combine their lists.

Evaluation 3
5–10 mins. ■■■□

Go around the room and check on students' progress. Help individuals as needed. If you see consistent errors among several students, interrupt the class and give a mini lesson or review to help students feel comfortable with the concept.

Learner Log
5–10 mins.

Have students read the statements and complete the log. If students answer *no* or *maybe*, encourage them to set themselves a goal to practice. Show them where they can find more practice activities.

Instructor's Notes

Standards Correlations

CASAS: 0.1.2, 0.1.5, 1.4.1, 1.4.2, 4.8.1

CCRS: L1, L3, SL1, SL3, W3

ELPS:

S3: Speak and write about level-appropriate complex literary and informational texts and topics.

S7: Adapt language choices to purpose, task, and audience when speaking and writing.

Workplace Focus

Make decisions and solve problems; Collect and organize information; Combine ideas and information; Exercise leadership roles; Manage time; Complete tasks as assigned; Interact appropriately with team members; Interpret and communicate information.

Soft Skill: Presentation Skills
Prepare and Practice

Direct students to the Soft Skill note. Explain that in the workplace, presentation skills are very important and that preparing and practicing are an important part of that skill set. We need to prepare and practice in order to be able to present effectively. This is especially important when presenting as part of a group. Tell students they will practice these skills in Step 7 of the project.

Warm-up and Review   10 mins.

Go over the review section of the unit and make sure all students have recorded their progress in the learner logs.

Introduction   5 mins.

Let students know that in this project, they will be planning a dream home. Ask students what they think *dream home* means and explain that it is a home they want to have in the future.

Presentation   10–15 mins.

1. Form a team of four or five students. In your team, you need:

Place students in teams of four or five. Then have them choose their positions in the group. To do this, go through each step in the project and explain the role of the person who will lead that step. Make sure students understand that although each person has a specific task, they will work together on each step.

The team leader's job is not associated with a step but has the responsibility of making sure everyone participates and speaks English. The team leader may also have ancillary responsibilities when general information is required.

In **Step 2**, for example, the team leader can manage the discussion of the type of housing the team will choose. Then in **Step 3**, the architect will draw the floor plan based on the other team members' ideas and suggestions. In **Steps 4** and **5**, the decorator will add furniture to the floor plan, but the others will help decide what and where. In **Step 6**, the salespeople will create the ad but all team members will make suggestions and help with the language. Finally, in **Step 7**, the salespeople will organize the presentation, following the steps in the Soft Skill note, and all team members will participate.

Be aware of who volunteers for which position so that through the different units, you can enourage students to try different roles.

Practice / Evaluation / Application   1–2 hours

2. Choose a type of home. Is it an apartment, house, condominium, or mobile home?

3. Make a floor plan of the home.

Refer students to the floor plan in Lesson 2 if necessary. Explain that the floor plan doesn't need to be very detailed; it just needs to show the different rooms in the home as well as doors and windows.

4. Make a list of furniture for your home.

5. Decide where to put the furniture.

Remind students that correct use of prepositions of location is important for describing where furniture should go.

6. Write an ad for your home.

Refer students back to the ads in Lesson 3 for guidance if necessary.

7. Plan a presentation for the class and present your dream home.

Remind students of the steps for preparing and practicing their presentation listed in the Soft Skill note. Have each group practice presenting to another group before presenting to the entire class.

Plan a Dream Home

SOFT SKILL ▶ Presentation Skills

In this project, you will make a floor plan of a dream home, write an ad for the home, and present both to the class.

1. Form a team of four or five students. In your team, you need:

Position	Job Description	Student Name
Student 1: **Team Leader**	Check that everyone speaks English. Check that everyone participates.	
Student 2: **Architect**	With help from the team, draw the floor plan.	
Student 3: **Decorator**	With help from the team, place furniture in your plan.	
Students 4/5: **Salespeople**	With help from the team, write the ad and organize a presentation.	

2. Choose a type of home. Is it an apartment, house, condominium, or mobile home?

3. Make a floor plan of the home.

4. Make a list of furniture for your home.

5. Decide where to put the furniture.

6. Write an ad for your home.

7. Plan a presentation for the class and present your dream home.

PRESENTATION SKILLS:
Prepare and Practice

1. As a group, choose a role for each member of the team.
2. Decide who goes first, second, etc.
3. Prepare notes for your role. Don't write down every word.
4. Practice your presentation as a group many times.
5. Practice speaking loudly and clearly enough for people to hear.

What parts of a home do you see in this photo?

Reading Challenge

About the Photo

The photos here show how houses in disrepair can be fixed up so that they are attractive to home buyers. In the first two photos, we can see how the exterior of a rundown house is transformed into a modern, stylish one. In the second two photos, we see the *before* and *after* of the interior of a house, in this case the kitchen. Again, it has been fixed up to be more modern and attractive to buyers.

- Tell students they are going to read about how people buy houses that have problems, fix the problems, and then sell the houses.
- Read the title out loud and ask students what they think it means. Tell them to look up *risky* in the dictionary. Ask them what the *risky business* could be.

A **Work with a group. Look at the *before* and *after* photos. Make a list of the things that are different about the homes in each photo.**

Put students in groups. Then monitor as they work and provide vocabulary as needed. Ask one group to come to the board and write their list. Then ask the other groups to add anything that is missing.

B **Look at the words and photos. Then complete the sentences.**

Have students read the definitions, look at the photos, and describe what is happening in each one. Provide vocabulary as needed. Then have them complete the sentences. Check the answers as a class.

Reading Challenge

A Work with a group. Look at the *before* and *after* photos. Make a list of the things that are different about the homes in each photo. Answers will vary.

_____ _____

_____ _____ _____ _____

B Look at the words and photos. Then complete the sentences.

Risky means dangerous.

risky

Fix up means to repair or make nice again.

fix up

1. I want to _____fix up_____ my house.

2. It is _____risky_____ to drive too fast.

C Read the text.

D INFER Answer the questions.

1. In line 5, what does *flip* mean?
   - a. buy, fix up, and sell in a few months
   - b. repair a house

2. In line 5, is *flops* something good or bad?
   - a. It is something good.
   - b. It is something bad.

3. In line 6, is *successfully* something good or bad?
   - a. It is something good.
   - b. It is something bad.

E Check (✓) the risks of flipping houses from the text.

- ☑ 1. Fixing up a house can be too expensive.
- ☐ 2. The class on flipping houses is too difficult.
- ☐ 3. There are too many houses to flip.
- ☑ 4. No one wants to buy the house you flipped.

F Work in a group. Look at the photos. Which activity do you think is more risky? Why?

flying riding a horse flipping a house

114 UNIT 4

CASAS FOR READING

0.1.2, 0.1.5, 1.4.1, 4.8.1

CCRS FOR READING

RI1, RI2, SL1, SL3

BEFORE   AFTER

Risky Business

1   Some people use real estate to make money. They buy a house and fix it up. Then they sell it again in a month or two. This is called *flipping*.

Flipping houses can be risky! One risk is that the house can have a lot of problems, and it costs too much to fix. Other times, no one wants to buy it. You can make around
5    $30,000 for every house you flip. You can also lose $30,000 or more if it flops! There are classes to learn how to successfully flip houses. It is a risky business.

BEFORE   AFTER

READING STRATEGIES

Prefixes and Suffixes

Explain to students that when they encounter a new word in a reading, they can sometimes use parts of the word to help understand the meaning. Provide examples of prefixes and suffixes. For example, point out *successfully* in the text and write on the board *successful* and *unsuccessful*. Elicit the difference in meaning. Do the same for a common suffix, such as *-ful* or *-less* (e.g., *useful / useless*).

C Read the text. 🎧

Remind students that they don't need to understand every word. Tell them to try to understand the main ideas and underline words they don't know. When they have finished, ask a few general comprehension questions. For example: *How much money can you make if you fix a house up and sell it? How much can you lose?*

D INFER Answer the questions.

Have students answer the questions individually, then compare with a partner. Have them read the text again if they disagree on an answer. Check the answers as a class.

E Check (✓) the risks of flipping houses from the text.

Tell students to choose their answers and then read the text again to confirm them. Tell them to call out any words they underlined that they still don't understand. Write them on the board and elicit meanings from other students. Explain or have students use a dictionary for any remaining words. Ask students to read the text one more time. Play the audio as they read. Then go over the answers as a class.

F Work in a group. Look at the photos. Which activity do you think is more risky? Why?

Put students in groups to carry out the activity. Have one person from each group share the group's conclusions.

Life
ONLINE

About the Photo

This photo shows a public library in Stuttgart, Germany. There are many shelves of books with people walking around, presumably looking for information. This image is meant to help students draw the comparison between searching for answers in books on shelves and searching for answers by typing questions into a search engine. While the latter is much more efficient, online searches come with their own challenges, as the video explains.

Before You Watch

Have students read the title of the video and look at the photo. Ask students why people go to libraries. If students don't say *to find information*, provide this answer and ask students for other ways they can find information. Read the photo caption to help students understand that a search engine is like a kind of online library.

A Check (✓) the things you look for online. Then share your answers with a partner.

Have students read the items and clarify any vocabulary doubts as a class. Then have them do the exercise individually before sharing with a partner. Take a class poll and see which items are most popular.

B Read the words. Then complete the sentences.

Have students read the words and share any ideas they have

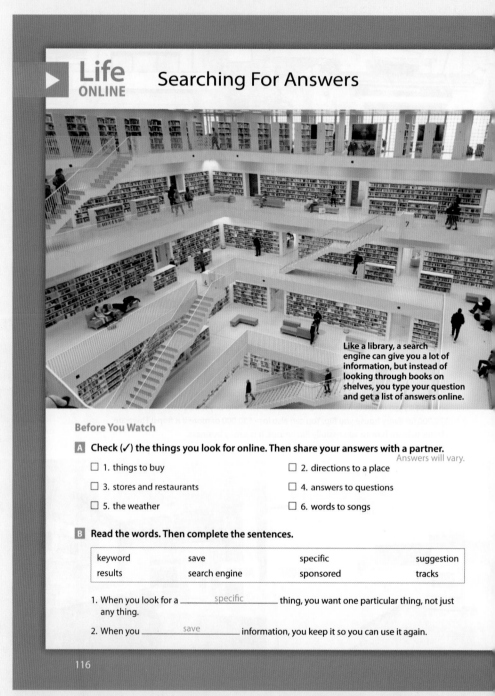

Life
ONLINE
Searching For Answers

Like a library, a search engine can give you a lot of information, but instead of looking through books on shelves, you type your question and get a list of answers online.

Before You Watch

A Check (✓) the things you look for online. Then share your answers with a partner.

Answers will vary.

☐ 1. things to buy   ☐ 2. directions to a place

☐ 3. stores and restaurants   ☐ 4. answers to questions

☐ 5. the weather   ☐ 6. words to songs

B Read the words. Then complete the sentences.

keyword	save	specific	suggestion
results	search engine	sponsored	tracks

1. When you look for a _____specific_____ thing, you want one particular thing, not just any thing.

2. When you _____save_____ information, you keep it so you can use it again.

116

about the meanings. Write their ideas on the board. Then allow students to work in pairs to complete the sentences. Ask them to make guesses first before using a dictionary to check. Go over the answers as a class and provide any additional clarification as needed. Prompt students to add any new words to their vocabulary logs.

3. When a program _____tracks_____ you, it remembers information about you.

4. When someone says, "I think you will like this," they are giving a _____suggestion_____.

5. A program that looks for information online is called a _____search engine_____.

6. When you do an online search, you see _____sponsored_____ websites at the top; companies pay to show you these websites.

7. A _____keyword_____ is an important word that helps you find what you're looking for.

8. When you look for information online, the list of websites you see are called the search _____results_____.

C PREDICT You are going to watch a video about how to search for information online. What tips do you think the video will give? *Answers will vary.*

While You Watch

D Watch the video. Check (✓) the tips you hear.

☐ 1. Write your question in ALL CAPS.   ☑ 2. Be specific in your search.

☑ 3. Use keywords for better searches.   ☐ 4. Do not shop for clothes online.

☑ 5. Look at the search suggestions.   ☐ 6. Always click on ads.

☐ 7. Only look at results in English.   ☑ 8. Try different search engines.

After You Watch

E Read each sentence. Choose *T* if it is true and *F* if it is false.

1. A search engine can help you answer questions. (T)   F

2. Every search engine tracks your information. T   (F)

3. You should use quotation marks when you search for a specific sentence. (T)   F

4. When the search engine shows suggestions, a company pays to show you their website. T   (F)

5. When a search result says *sponsored*, it usually shows you something you can buy. (T)   F

6. Every search engine shows you the same results. T   (F)

F Work with a partner. Write three questions you have on another sheet of paper. Then talk to your partner about how you can find this information online. Which tips will you use? *Answers will vary.*

on how they could search for this information online, referring to the tips from the video. Call on volunteers to share their questions and search solutions with the class.

C PREDICT **You are going to watch a video about how to search for information online. What tips do you think the video will give?**

Have students predict what they think they will see in the video and then share their ideas in pairs.

While You Watch

D **Watch the video. Check (✓) the tips you hear.**

Ask students to read the items. Clarify any doubts. Then ask students to check the items as they watch the video. Have students watch the video a second time to check their answers.

After You Watch

E **Read each sentence. Choose *T* if it is true and *F* if it is false.**

Have students complete the exercise individually. Check answers as a class.

F **Work with a partner. Write three questions you have on another sheet of paper. Then talk to your partner about how you can find this information online. Which tips will you use?**

Have students write their questions individually. Tell them that these should be questions a search engine could help with. Provide an example. Then have them share their questions with a partner and give suggestions

About the Photo

This photo shows the Old Town waterfront in Alexandria, Virginia. It is a park-like promenade along the Potomac River where people come together for events and to socialize. There are restaurants & ice cream shops as well as many boats arriving and leaving from here. People come to listen to live music and watch the sunset or to watch passersby. These kinds of areas that bring people together are essential to forming a sense of community in a town or city.

- Introduce the unit. Ask students to look at the photo. Then discuss what a *community* is.
- Go over the unit outcomes. Then discuss the first two questions about the photo as a class.
- Ask a volunteer to read the photo information out loud. Then have students talk about the remaining four questions in pairs. Ask volunteers to share their answers.

Life Skills Focus

In this unit, students will learn how to identify places in their community as well as find their way and express how to get around these places. Students will also learn how to leave a message by phone and write an email.

5 Our Community

118

UNIT OUTCOMES	GRAMMAR	VOCABULARY	EL CIVICS
• Identify locations and services • Give and follow street directions • Describe locations in an airport • Leave a phone message • Write an email • Identify employment opportunities at the post office	• Imperatives • *In / on* • Prepositions of location • *Yes / no* questions with *can* • Present continuous • Simple present • Adverbs of frequency • *Wh-* questions	• Places in your community • Directions • Places in an airport • Prepositions • Phone messages • Jobs at the post office	The skills students learn in this unit can be applied to the following EL Civics competency area: • Community Resources

▶ Identify locations and services

▶ Give and follow street directions

▶ Describe locations in an airport

▶ Leave a phone message

▶ Write an email

▶ Identify employment opportunities at the post office

Look at the photo and answer the questions.

1. What are the people in the photo doing?

2. Where do you think this is?

People enjoy the sunset at the Old Town Waterfront in Alexandria, Virginia.

1. What kind of transportation do you see in the photo?

2. What do you think the buildings in the photo are?

3. Why do you think people come to this part of the city?

4. What places in your town or city do you like to visit?

119

Workplace Focus

All lessons and units in *Stand Out* include basic communication skills and interpersonal skills important for the workplace. They include *collecting and organizing information, making decisions and solving problems,* and *combining ideas and information.*

- In Unit 5, Lesson 6, *Explore the Workforce,* students will identify jobs at the post office. They will interpret an infographic with different jobs and levels of pay. They will also read and talk about the duties of a mail carrier. They will then reflect on their own job preferences.

- In the Team Project, students practice the soft skill of asking questions, while listening actively to the presentations of their classmates.

- Life Online notes in Lessons 1 and 5 raise awareness about municipal websites and email greetings and closings.

spark Resources

All resources for the unit are centrally located on the Spark platform and include: audio, video, multilevel worksheets, digital literacy worksheets, Online Practice, and Assessment Suite.

STEPS

CASAS COMPETENCIES	ELPS	CCRS
Lesson 1: 0.1.2, 0.1.5, 2.5.1, 3.1.3, 6.7.2, 7.4.4, 7.7.3 Lesson 2: 0.1.2, 0.1.5, 1.9.1, 2.2.1, 2.2.2, 2.2.5, 7.2.3 Lesson 3: 0.1.2, 0.1.5, 2.2.1, 2.2.7 Lesson 4: 0.1.2, 0.1.5, 2.1.7, 2.1.8 Lesson 5: 0.1.2, 0.1.5, 0.2.3, 7.7.4 Lesson 6: 0.1.2, 0.1.5, 4.1.3, 4.1.8, 4.1.9, 4.8.1, 7.4.4, 7.7.3 Review: 0.1.2, 0.1.5, 0.2.1, 0.2.3, 1.9.1, 2.1.7, 2.1.8, 2.2.1, 7.7.4 Team Project: 0.1.2, 0.1.5, 1.9.1, 4.8.1, 7.4.4, 7.7.3 Reading Challenge: 0.1.2, 0.1.5, 2.5.8, 4.8.1, 7.4.4, 7.7.3	**S2:** Participate in level-appropriate oral and written exchanges of information, ideas, and analyses, in various social and academic contexts, responding to peer, audience, or reader comments and questions. **S9:** Create clear and coherent level-appropriate speech and text. **S10:** Demonstrate command of the conventions of standard English to communicate in level-appropriate speech and writing.	L1, L2, L3, RI1, RI2, RI3, SL1, SL3, W1, W3

Places and Services

GOAL ▶ Identify locations and services

A INTERPRET Read the web page. What information does it have?

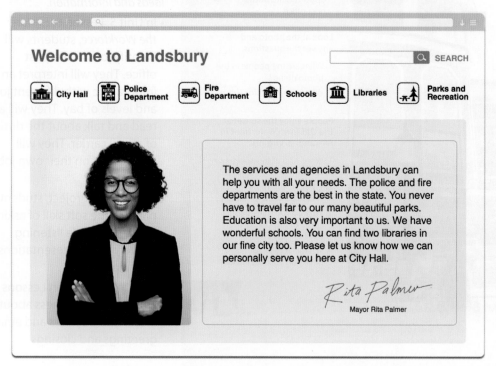

Welcome to Landsbury [Q] SEARCH

City Hall   Police Department   Fire Department   Schools   Libraries   Parks and Recreation

The services and agencies in Landsbury can help you with all your needs. The police and fire departments are the best in the state. You never have to travel far to our many beautiful parks. Education is also very important to us. We have wonderful schools. You can find two libraries in our fine city too. Please let us know how we can personally serve you here at City Hall.

Rita Palmer
Mayor Rita Palmer

B Make a list of public places and services in Landsbury based on the reading.

1. libraries
2. police department
3. fire department
4. parks
5. schools
6. City Hall

Life ONLINE

Municipal Websites
Most cities in the United States have websites where you can find important information, pay city bills, and request services. These websites usually end in *.gov* or *.org*.

At-a-Glance Prep

Goal: Identify locations and services

Academic Strategies: Classifying information, focused listening, doing a survey

Vocabulary: Places in the community, government agencies and services

Agenda

- ☐ Review types of entertainment.
- ☐ Identify locations and services.
- ☐ Read a web page.
- ☐ Identify important community places.
- ☐ Do a survey and make a bar graph.

Resources

Heinle Picture Dictionary: Places Around Town, pages 46–47; City Square, pages 58–59

Pacing

- ■ 1.5 hour classes   ■ 2.5 hour classes
- ■ 3+ hour classes

Standards Correlations

CASAS: 0.1.2, 0.1.5, 2.5.1, 3.1.3, 6.7.2, 7.4.4, 7.7.3

CCRS: RI1, RI2, SL1, SL3, W1, W3

ELPS:

S2: Participate in level-appropriate oral and written exchanges of information, ideas, and analyses, in various social and academic contexts, responding to peer, audience, or reader comments and questions.

S5: Conduct research and evaluate and communicate findings to answer questions or solve problems.

Warm-up and Review   7–10 mins. ■■■

Ask students where they live. Help them use the preposition *in* before the name of the city. Ask students what they like to do in their city. Write *entertainment* on the board and list under it various activities you do for entertainment. Ask students to add to the list. Choose four types of entertainment and do a corners activity. For example, the corners might be *movies, restaurants, sports,* and *shopping.* Ask students to go to the corner that represents the activity they prefer and discuss with their group why they like it. In virtual classes, this can be done in breakout rooms.

Introduction   7–10 mins. ■■■

Ask students to help you brainstorm different places to obtain services in your community. Write them on the board. Start them off with a few, such as *post office* and *hospital.* State the goal: *Today, we will identify locations and services in our community.*

Presentation 1   20–30 mins. ■■■

Take the list that students helped you make on the board about services in the community and see if you can classify each item. Some classifications might include *health, transportation, protection,* etc. Write *neighborhood* on the board and explain to students that a neighborhood is a smaller part of a city or town. Explain how a community can be made up of a few or several neighborhoods.

With books closed, ask students about different aspects of their community. For example, ask: *Where do you keep your money? Where do you go if you are sick? Where can you buy clothes? Where do you mail letters?* Their answers will tell you how much students already know.

A INTERPRET Read the web page. What information does it have?

Ask students to open their books. Give them time to read the information. Then discuss the question as a class. They will probably need examples for some of the categories in the menu at the top of the page.

Workplace Focus

Exercise B: Collect and organize information.

Practice 1   7–10 mins. ■■■

B Make a list of public places and services in Landsbury based on the reading.

Ask students to work in groups to make their lists.

Evaluation 1   7–10 mins. ■■■

Go over students' answers and write them on the board. Review the new vocabulary.

Read the information with the class.
Ask students if they have used this kind of website and have them share experiences.
Find a few examples of local municipal websites and show students the different kinds of information available there.

Life ONLINE

Presentation 2

15–20 mins. ■■■■

Have students close their books. Write the following terms on the board: *lodging, parks and recreation, medical care,* and *residences.* Make sure that students understand each of the phrases. Start with *residences.* Ask students about the kinds of housing they discussed in the previous unit.

C CLASSIFY Work in a group. Match the words to the pictures.

Don't go over the words at first. Allow students to do the activity and try to work out the meanings on their own. Encourage students to discuss in their groups.

After groups have finished completing the activity on their own, review each word in the box with the class by asking questions in a focused-listening fashion. For example: *Where do you go to play with your children?* You can provide more context: *You and your family have a free day and….* Help students listen for clues to determine which words you are targeting. Then, as a class, put all the words in the appropriate categories.

Practice 2

7–10 mins. ■■■

D Listen. Write the number of the correct description for each place. 🎧

Go over the places, having students explain them. Tell them they are going to listen to a description of each place. Play the audio twice, pausing after each item. Then have students compare answers with a partner. Play the audio one or more times as needed.

Listening Script

1. *This is a place where people mail letters and packages, and they buy stamps.*
2. *This is a place with trained workers who help the community when there is an emergency, such as a fire.*
3. *This is a place people go when they are very sick or for medical emergencies or surgeries. They sometimes go by ambulance.*
4. *This is a place where people go to get a driver's license and identification.*
5. *This is a place where people put their money. Sometimes they get a checking account, and sometimes they get credit cards or take out loans.*
6. *This is a place where police officers work. It is the police officers' office.*

Evaluation 2

5–7 mins. ■■

Go over the answers to **D**. Ask students which one was the most difficult.

Then have students look at the photo and say what kind of place it is. Answer the question in the caption as a class.

Instructor's Notes

_____

_____

_____

_____

_____

_____

_____

_____

_____

_____

_____

_____

_____

_____

_____

_____

_____

_____

_____

_____

_____

C **CLASSIFY** Work in a group. Match the words to the pictures.

apartment	hospital	house	park
dentist's office	hostel	mobile home	playground
doctor's office	hotel	motel	tennis court

a. Lodging

hostel

hotel

motel

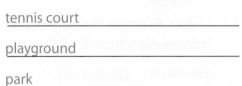

b. Parks and Recreation

tennis court

playground

park

c. Medical Care

hospital

dentist's office

doctor's office

d. Residences

apartment

mobile home

house

D Listen. Write the number of the correct description for each place. 🎧

a. DMV __4__

b. post office __1__

c. hospital __3__

d. bank __5__

e. fire department __2__

f. police department __6__

What do you think the pictures on this sign in Yosemite National Park, California mean?

Lembert Dome
Soda Springs
Dog Lake
Glen Aulin

E PREDICT Look at the picture. Why is Emanuela calling Lisa? Choose a need or problem from the table.

Place	Need or Problem	Location
the hospital	I'm very sick.	First Street
the post office	I need to mail a package.	Grand Street
the DMV	I need a driver's license.	Second Street
the adult school	I want to learn English.	Main Street

F Listen. Practice the conversation with a partner. Then make new conversations with information from E. 🎧

Emanuela: <u>I'm very sick.</u>

Lisa: You need to go to <u>the hospital</u>.

Emanuela: Where is it?

Lisa: It's on <u>First Street</u>.

Emanuela: Thanks!

G SURVEY Make a bar graph of how many students go to each place once a week or more. Answers will vary.

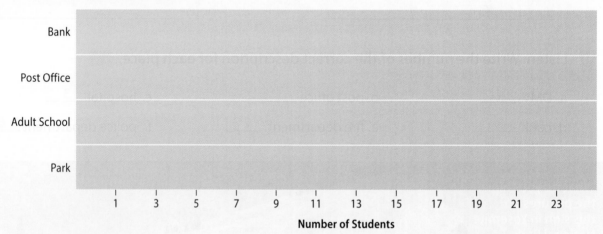

Number of Students

H APPLY Make a list of important places in your community. Then go online and find the locations of these places.

Presentation 3

5–10 mins. ■■■

E PREDICT Look at the picture. Why is Emanuela calling Lisa? Choose a need or problem from the table.

Look at the picture with the class and discuss the question.

Practice 3

10–15 mins. ■■

F Listen. Practice the conversation with a partner. Then make new conversations with information from E. 🎧

Present the conversation. Go over the rhythm by clapping it out. Play the audio to help students hear the rhythm. Then have students carry out the activity with a partner.

Pronunciation   Intonation and Rhythm

Singing or chanting is a good way to teach intonation and rhythm. In this case, students are given the rhythm in the first example, and they will try to fit all the words in the substitutions into the same framework. Keeping the rhythm can be challenging, but it will help students sound more natural in their speech.

I NEED to GO to the HOSpital.

WHY? (pause)

My SISter is VEry SICK.

I NEED to GO to the DMV.

WHY? (pause)

I NEED a DRIver's LIcense.

I NEED to GO to the POST office.

WHY? (pause)

I NEED to SEND a LETter.

Evaluation 3

5–7 mins. ■

Ask volunteers to perform one of their conversations in front of the class.

Workplace Focus

Exercise G: Combine ideas and information.

Application

20–25 mins. ■■■

G SURVEY Make a bar graph of how many students go to each place once a week or more.

Have students work in groups of four or five and ask each other: *Do you go to the* (place) *once a week or more?* They should make notes about how many students go to each place once a week or more. Then come together as a class and ask each group to report their results. Combine the numbers as you write them on the board. Ask groups to discuss the class results before each student fills in the graph in their book. Discuss as a class by asking: *Which place do we go to the most / least?*

H APPLY Make a list of important places in your community. Then go online and find the locations of these places.

Ask some volunteers to share the location of one place they found.

Instructor's Notes

_____

_____

_____

_____

_____

_____

_____

_____

_____

_____

_____

At-a-Glance Prep

Goal: Give and follow street directions
Grammar: Imperatives, *in / on*
Academic Strategies: Focused listening, interpreting maps, analyzing information
Vocabulary: Directions

Agenda

☐ Do a mind map activity.
☐ Listen for directions.
☐ Read directions.
☐ Read a map and give directions.
☐ Ask other students for information.

Resources

Heinle Picture Dictionary: Places Around Town, pages 46–47

Pacing

■ 1.5 hour classes ■ 2.5 hour classes
■ 3+ hour classes

Standards Correlations

CASAS: 0.1.2, 0.1.5, 1.9.1, 2.2.1, 2.2.2, 2.2.5, 7.2.3
CCRS: RI1, RI3, SL1, SL3
ELPS:
S2: Participate in level-appropriate oral and written exchanges of information, ideas, and analyses, in various social and academic contexts, responding to peer, audience, or reader comments and questions.

Warm-up and Review   10–12 mins. ■■■

Use a mind map to review vocabulary from Lesson 1. Draw a circle in the middle of the board. Write *Community* inside the circle. Draw lines out from the circle and make four secondary circles. Label one of them *Lodging*. Make lines from this circle to additional circles. Elicit / provide *Hotels, Motels,* and *Hostels.*

Use *Medical Care, Parks and Recreation,* and *Residences* for the remaining three secondary circles and have students complete the map with the words for each category.

Introduction   7–10 mins. ■■■

Identify well-known places in your community and ask students where they are located. Accept any

answer. They may give you street names or use prepositions to say what they are next to. State the goal: *Today, we will give and follow street directions.*

Presentation 1   25–30 mins. ■■■

Ask students where something is in the classroom; for example, the door. Have students point to the door. Start walking in the opposite direction and ask if what you are doing is right. If students haven't caught on, ask them where the door is again and go through the same process until they do. Encourage students to give a direction such as: *Turn around.* Write it on the board and ask students to repeat.

A PREDICT Look at the picture and read the conversation. Who is Gabriel? Who is Hamed?

Have students look at the picture and say where the men are and what they are doing. Read the conversation together and then answer the questions. Elicit / explain the meaning of *block* as needed.

B Match the phrases to the signs.

Say each phrase. Then ask students to complete the activity individually. Have them compare answers with a partner before going over them as a class.

Practice 1   7–10 mins. ■■■

C Listen and check (✓) the phrases you hear. 🎧

Go over the chart and then tell students they are going to listen to conversations asking for directions to these places. Remind them that there will be words they don't understand. Ask them what they need to focus on (the places and directions). Play the first conversation in the audio and point out the checkmarks in the chart. Play the rest of the audio, pausing after each conversation for students to answer. Have students compare with a partner. Then play the audio one or more additional times as needed.

Note: The listening script for **C** is on page 124a.

Evaluation 1   3–7 mins. ■■■

Go over the answers to **C**. Then call out each phrase and have students move accordingly.

Where Is City Hall?

GOAL ▶ Give and follow street directions

A PREDICT Look at the picture and read the conversation. Who is Gabriel? Who is Hamed?

Hamed: I need to find City Hall. Can you help me?

Gabriel: Of course. Go straight one block and turn right.

B Match the phrases to the signs.

| Go straight. | Turn around. | Turn left. | Turn right. |

1. _Turn left._   2. _Go straight._   3. _Turn right._   4. _Turn around._

C Listen and check (✓) the phrases you hear. 🎧

	Turn right.	Turn left.	Turn around.	Go straight.
1. Directions to the mall	✓		✓	✓
2. Directions to the post office		✓		✓
3. Directions to the movie theater		✓		✓
4. Directions to the museum	✓			✓
5. Directions to the park			✓	✓

D **Look at the picture and study the phrases.**

Go straight one block.

It's on the corner.

It's on the left.

It's on the right.

Turn around.

Turn left.

Turn right.

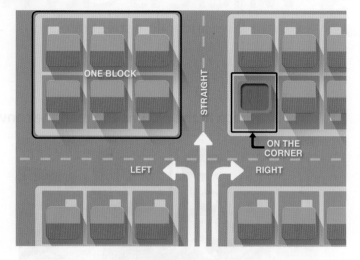

E **Read the directions as a class.**

Place	Directions
1. City Hall	Go straight one block and turn right. It's on the left.
2. the bus station	Go straight one block and turn left. Then go one more block. It's on the corner on the left.
3. Rosco's Restaurant	Go straight two blocks and turn left. It's on the right.
4. the post office	Go straight one block and turn right. Go one more block and turn left. It's on the right.
5. the zoo	Go straight two blocks and turn right. It's on the right.
6. the high school	Go straight two blocks and turn right. Go one more block and turn right. It's on the left.

F **Listen. Practice the conversation with a partner. Then make new conversations with information from E.** 🎧

Hamed: I need to find City Hall. Can you help me?

Gabriel: Of course. Go straight one block and turn right. It's on the left.

Hamed: Can you repeat that slowly for me?

Gabriel: Sure. Go straight one block. Turn right. It's on the left.

Hamed: Thanks!

Gabriel: No problem.

Listening Script

1. **A:** *Can you give me directions, please?*
   B: *Maybe. Where do you want to go?*
   A: *I'm looking for the mall.*
   B: *It's on Broadway. Turn around and go straight for two blocks. Turn right on Hamilton Avenue. You'll see it.*
   A: *Thanks!*

2. **A:** *Excuse me. Do you know the way to the post office?*
   B: *Yes, of course. Go straight ahead two miles. Turn left on Maple.*

3. **A:** *I'm totally confused. Where's the movie theater from here?*
   B: *It's very close.*
   A: *Can you give me directions?*
   B: *Sure. Turn left on First Street. Then go straight ahead three blocks.*
   A: *Thanks so much.*

4. **A:** *Can I help you find something?*
   B: *Yes, I'm looking for the museum. I hear there's a dinosaur exhibit there.*
   A: *Yes, that's right. It's on Main Street.*
   B: *Where's Main Street?*
   A: *Turn right and go straight for three blocks.*
   B: *Thank you.*

5. **A:** *Where is the park?*
   B: *Turn around and go straight for six blocks. You can't miss it.*
   A: *Are you sure?*
   B: *I am absolutely positive.*

Presentation 2   10–15 mins. ■■■

Elicit the phrases for giving directions from page 123 and write them on the board. Ask students for any other related words / phrases they know. For example: *corner*, *block*, etc.

D Look at the picture and study the phrases.

Go over the phrases, pointing to each one in the picture. Have students repeat each phrase after you.

Practice 2   15–20 mins. ■■

E Read the directions as a class.

Read each item together and clarify any doubts about meaning.

F Listen. Practice the conversation with a partner. Then make new conversations with information from E. 🎧

Tell students to listen as they read the conversation. Play the audio. Have two students model the conversation. Then model it with a student but ask about a different place in **E**. Put students in pairs to practice. Remind them to switch roles so they practice both asking for and giving directions.

Evaluation 2   5–7 mins. ■■

Have several pairs perform one of their conversations for the class.

BEST PRACTICE

Performances

Student performances often help you to evaluate what students have learned. They also provide a model for the other students. Take note of any errors related to the lesson goal and go over them with the class after everyone has finished performing their conversation.

Instructor's Notes

_____

_____

_____

_____

_____

_____

_____

_____

_____

_____

Workplace Focus

Exercise G: Make decisions and solve problems.

Presentation 3
10–15 mins. ■■■□

G INTERPRET **Read the directions in E again. Number the places 2–6 on the map.**

Have students look at the map and tell you the street names. Point out the *You are here* sign and make sure they understand that is where they start from for each place. Complete the activity as a class, eliciting as much from students as possible and referring them back to the picture in **D** as needed.

Practice 3
15–20 mins. ■□

H ANALYZE **Work with a partner. Complete the chart.**

Put students in pairs and tell them to use the map in **H** to help them. Check answers as a class.

I **Practice the conversation with a partner. Then make new conversations with information from H.**

Point out the note about the use of *in* and *on*. Model the conversation with a student and then model it again, asking about a different place in **H**. Put students in pairs to practice. Monitor and help with the correct use of *in* and *on* as needed.

Evaluation 3
3–5 mins. ■□

Have volunteers perform one of their conversations. Encourage them to try to do it without using their books.

Workplace Focus

Exercise J: Interact appropriately with team members.

Application
10–15 mins. ■■■□

J **Talk to three classmates and complete the chart.**

Have students carry out the activity. Then call on different students to say where another student lives using *in* and *on*. As they tell you, complete a chart on the board with information about the whole class, including yourself.

BEST PRACTICE

Student Interaction

Students often select people who they know or are comfortable with in activities such as **J**. To encourage students to talk to different classmates, you can set up the activity as an inside / outside circle. You can also divide the class into four parts or quadrants. Then require that students talk to people outside of their own quadrant.

Instructor's Notes

_____

_____

_____

_____

_____

_____

_____

_____

_____

_____

_____

_____

_____

_____

_____

_____

_____

_____

_____

G **INTERPRET** Read the directions in **E** again. Number the places 2–6 on the map.

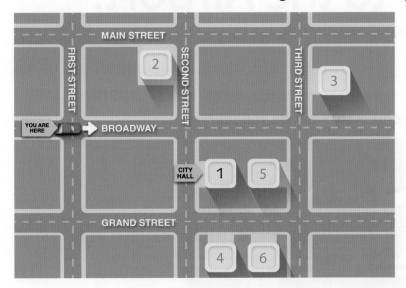

H **ANALYZE** Work with a partner. Complete the chart.

Place	Location
1. City Hall	City Hall is *on Second Street.*
2. the bus station	The bus station is on the corner of Second Street and Main Street.
3. Rosco's Restaurant	Rosco's Restaurant is on Third Street.
4. the post office	The post office is on Grand Street.
5. the zoo	The zoo is on Third Street.
6. the high school	The high school is on Grand Street.

I Practice the conversation with a partner. Then make new conversations with information from **H**.

Student A: Where is <u>City Hall</u>?

Student B: It's on <u>Second Street</u> in <u>Landsbury</u>.

in / on
in the city
on the street
It's **on** Main Street **in** Landsbury.

J Talk to three classmates and complete the chart.
Answers will vary.

Student A: Where do you live?

Student B: I live on <u>Maple Street</u> in <u>Landsbury</u>.

Student Name	Street	City
1. Eshan	Maple Street	Landsbury
2.		
3.		
4.		

Let's Go to the Airport!

GOAL ▶ Describe locations in an airport

A INTERPRET Study the airport map. What do you see?

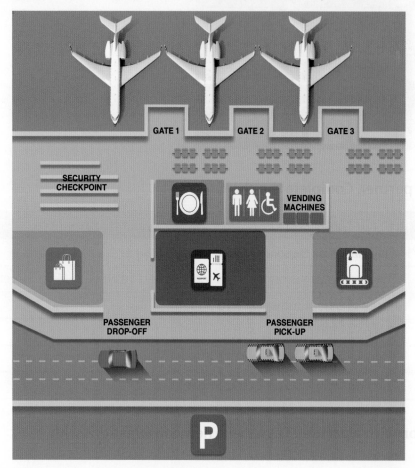

B Match the words with the pictures.

__a__ 1. baggage claim	a.	![baggage claim icon]
__c__ 2. the parking lot	b.	![ticketing icon]
__e__ 3. shops	c.	![P parking icon]
__d__ 4. a restaurant	d.	![restaurant icon]
__f__ 5. restrooms	e.	![shops icon]
__b__ 6. ticketing	f.	![restrooms icon]

At-a-Glance Prep

Goal: Describe locations in an airport
Grammar: Prepositions of location
Academic Strategies: Interpreting information, designing
Vocabulary: Places in an airport, prepositions

Agenda

☐ Review directions.
☐ Talk about places in an airport.
☐ Use prepositions of location.
☐ Ask for and give directions in an airport.
☐ Design an airport.

Resources

Heinle Picture Dictionary: Airport, pages 124–125

Pacing

■ 1.5 hour classes ■ 2.5 hour classes
■ 3+ hour classes

Standards Correlations

CASAS: 0.1.2, 0.1.5, 2.2.1, 2.2.7
CCRS: L1, L2, L3, RI1, RI2, SL1, SL3, W3
ELPS:
S1: Construct meaning from oral presentations and literary and informational text through level-appropriate listening, reading, and viewing.
S8: Determine the meaning of words and phrases in oral presentations and literary and informational text.

Warm-up and Review   10–15 mins. ■■■

Write *directions* on the board and elicit the phrases students have seen in previous lessons. Write them on the board. Write a location that students will know on the board, such as your school, and say: *We are here.* Then ask: *Where is . . .?* (a place nearby) and have the class give you directions. Repeat for other places.

Introduction   5–7 mins. ■■■

Review the prepositions of location students have already learned. They should know *in, on, between,* and *next to.* State the goal: *Today, we will describe locations in an airport.*

Presentation 1   5–10 mins. ■■■

Write the word *airport* on the board and have students share what they know about airports. Remember that at this stage, students don't need to say complete sentences. Words and phrases are sufficient, as the idea is to activate prior knowledge. Write their ideas on the board. For example: *airplanes, tickets, passports, baggage,* etc.

Practice 1   15–20 mins. ■■■

A INTERPRET Study the airport map. What do you see?

Write what students identify on the board. Prompt students to explain what different things are if they can. For example: *You can get food and drinks at vending machines.*

B Match the words with the pictures.

Go over the pronunciation of each item. Then have students complete the activity individually or with a partner. Encourage them to use dictionaries as needed.

BEST PRACTICE

Step-by-Step

At this level, it is important that when there are several tasks to perform, you only ask students to do one at a time. Carefully model the target activity for students. Let students know how much time they have to complete each task as you give it to them, but monitor and provide extra activities for those who finish early so they don't lose interest before the allotted time. For example, depending on the activity, you can ask fast finishers to write a few more sentences, ask more questions, underline the language being focused on (prepositions, verbs, etc.), or switch partners and repeat the conversation. In the case of **B** here, they could ask *Where is . . .?* questions about the places on the map with a partner.

Evaluation 1   3–5 mins. ■■■

Check the answers to **B** as a class. Clarify any other doubts about items on the map, such as *vending machines.*

Presentation 2

C Answer the questions about the airport map in A.

Have students complete this activity without explaining the prepositions first. Allow them to try to work out the meanings by looking at the map. Allow them to work with a partner if they want to.

D Study the prepositions. Then listen to the conversations. 🎧

Go through the prepositions and then check the answers to **C**. Tell students they are going to listen to conversations at the airport, and they need to pay attention to the prepositions. Play the audio and have students point to the prepositions they hear.

Listening Script

1. **Ticket agent:** *Here is your boarding pass, sir. Have a good flight.*
   Passenger: *Thank you. Where is the security checkpoint?*
   Ticket agent: *It's around the corner from here.*
   Passenger: *Thank you.*

2. **Passenger:** *Is there a restaurant after security?*
   Ticket agent: *Yes, of course. It's across from Gate 1.*
   Passenger: *Thanks so much. I'm starving.*

3. **Passenger:** *Excuse me, can you tell me where the restrooms are?*
   Airport staff member: *They're between the restaurant and the vending machines, right over there.*
   Passenger: *Thanks!*

4. **Passenger:** *Where can I get a taxi?*
   Airport staff member: *Directly in front of the passenger pick-up.*
   Passenger: *I appreciate it.*

5. **Passenger:** *Excuse me, can you tell me where the vending machines are?*
   Airport staff member: *They're next to the restrooms.*
   Passenger: *Thanks so much.*

Teach students the difference between *around the corner from* and *on the corner*. Have them look back at the picture on page 124 for reference.

Practice 2
15–20 mins. ■■□□

E Complete the sentences. Then listen and check your answers. 🎧

Point out the note on the use of *is* and *are*. Tell students to use the prepositions from **D** to complete the sentences about the map in **A**. Then play the audio to check the answers.

F Write sentences about the airport map in A.

Go over the example with students so they can see how they need to develop the sentences from the information given. Then have them complete the activity individually.

Evaluation 2
3–5 mins. ■■□□

Ask students to peer-edit each other's sentences. Then call on volunteers to write their sentences on the board. Don't overcorrect, but make sure students spell and use prepositions correctly. Also, make sure they don't omit *from* in the phrases *across from* and *around the corner from*.

BEST PRACTICE

Error Correction

There is sometimes the temptation to overcorrect students. Students will make errors, but too much correcting without explanation can intimidate students so they are afraid to respond or, in this case, write. We suggest that you correct students on the concept you are teaching or have already taught. It is often more desirable to encourage peer-correcting over teacher-correcting because it can be less intimidating. It may also be useful to wait until you hear the error several times and explain the error to the class instead of identifying the students who are making the error.

Finally, be careful to limit correcting in the application stage and team projects. In these activities, students are taking ownership of English and using it to accomplish a goal. Overcorrecting can inhibit this process. As you monitor these activities, take note of common errors and deal with them after the activity or at the start of the next class, again without saying who made the specific errors.

C Answer the questions about the airport map in **A**.

1. What is in front of the security checkpoint? ___shops___

2. What is between the restaurant and the vending machines? ___the restrooms___

3. What is between Gate 1 and Gate 3? ___Gate 2___

4. What is in front of the passenger drop-off? ___a car___

D Study the prepositions. Then listen to the conversations. 🎧

| around the corner from | across from | between | in front of | next to |

E Complete the sentences. Then listen and check your answers. 🎧

1. The security checkpoint is ___around the corner from___ ticketing.

2. The restaurant is ___across from___ Gate 1.

3. The restrooms are ___between___ the restaurant and the vending machines.

4. Taxis are ___in front of___ the passenger pick-up.

5. The vending machines are ___next to___ the restrooms.

is / are
The restaurant **is** ...
The restrooms **are** ...

F Write sentences about the airport map in **A**.

1. the restrooms / the restaurant and the vending machines

   The restrooms are between the restaurant and the vending machines.

2. the baggage claim / the restaurant

   The baggage claim is around the corner from the restaurant.

3. the red car / the passenger drop-off

   The red car is in front of the passenger drop-off.

4. the parking lot / the airport

   The parking lot is across from the airport.

5. the restaurant / the restrooms

   The restaurant is next to the restrooms.

G Work with a partner. Practice the conversations. Then create new ones.
Answers will vary. Sample answer phrases included.

1. You are in ticketing. Find the security checkpoint.

   Student A: Excuse me, where is the security checkpoint?

   Student B: It's around the corner from here.

   Student A: Thank you for your help.

2. You are at the security checkpoint. Find the restrooms.

   Student B: Pardon me, where are the restrooms?

   Student A: They're across from Gate 2.

   Student B: I appreciate it.

3. You are at the restaurant. Find the baggage claim.
   It's around the corner from here.
4. You are at Gate 1. Find the vending machines.
   They're next to the restrooms.
5. You are at the baggage claim. Find the parking lot.
   It's across from the airport.
6. You are at the shops. Find the restrooms.
   They are around the corner, through security.

H DESIGN Work in a group. Create a new airport design. Add popular shops or restaurants. Then ask and answer questions about the places in your airport.

Presentation 3　　　　　　7–10 mins. ■ ■ ■

Go over the airport map in **A** again with students, asking them questions about where places are. First, ask the class as a whole; then call on individuals.

Practice 3　　　　　　7–10 mins. ■

G　Work with a partner. Practice the conversations. Then create new ones.

Carry out choral practice of the first conversation, with the class repeating the lines after you. Then divide the class in half, to be Student A and Student B. Finally, have two students model the conversation. Point out the items below the conversations and make sure students understand they have to create a conversation for each one. Put them in pairs to carry out the activity.

Evaluation 3　　　　　　3–7 mins. ■

Observe students as they practice.

Application　　　　　　10–15 mins. ■ ■ ■

H　DESIGN　Work in a group. Create a new airport design. Add popular shops or restaurants. Then ask and answer questions about the places in your airport.

Encourage students to work together to complete this activity. The group should have one design for the airport, not individual designs for each student. When they decide where places should go, make sure they use prepositions of location. Put groups together to ask and answer questions about the locations of different places. Monitor and help as needed, especially with correct use of *is / are* and prepositions.

Instructor's Notes

_____

_____

_____

_____

_____

_____

_____

_____

_____

_____

_____

_____

_____

_____

_____

_____

_____

_____

_____

_____

_____

_____

_____

Goal: Leave a phone message
Grammar: *Yes / no* questions with *can*
Academic Strategies: Evaluating information, focused listening
Vocabulary: Phone messages
Pronunciation: Intonation of *yes / no* questions

Agenda

☐ Do a mind map activity.
☐ Take a class poll.
☐ Listen to voicemail messages.
☐ Evaluate voicemail messages.
☐ Use *can* to ask questions.
☐ Leave a phone message.

Resources

Heinle Picture Dictionary: The Telephone, pages 16–17

Pacing

■ 1.5 hour classes   ■ 2.5 hour classes
■ 3+ hour classes

Standards Correlations

CASAS: 0.1.2, 0.1.5, 2.1.7, 2.1.8
CCRS: L1, L2, L3, RI1, RI2, SL1, SL3
ELPS:
S10: Demonstrate command of the conventions of standard English to communicate in level-appropriate speech and writing.

Warm-up and Review   15–20 mins. ■■■

In groups, have students create a mind map for *airport* without looking in their books. Have one group draw their map on the board and invite other groups to add to it if anything is missing. Ask them to look at the airport map again on page 126 but to cover page 127 with a piece of paper. Ask each group a *Where is / are . . .?* question. As they say the prepositions of location, write them on the board.

Introduction   3–5 mins. ■■■

Take a class poll. Ask: *Who is nervous when you answer the phone here in the United States? Who likes to call agencies to get information? Who doesn't like to leave voicemail messages? Who has problems understanding voicemail messages?* State the goal: *Today, we will learn how to leave phone messages.*

Presentation 1   15–20 mins. ■■■

Look at the picture together and have students say what they see. Elicit the words *calendar* and *schedule* if they don't come up.

A Look at the calendar on Samira's phone. Do you see a problem?

Discuss the question as a class.

B Read and check your answer to A.

Have students read the text. Tell them to underline any words they don't understand. Confirm the answer to **A.** Clarify any vocabulary doubts as a class. Then ask students to read the text again and listen as they read to help them with pronunciation and rhythm. Play the audio.

Workplace Focus

Exercise C: Interact appropriately with team members.

C EVALUATE What can Samira do? Work in a group. Complete the sentences.

Have students discuss the question in groups before completing the sentences in their books.

Practice 1   10–15 mins. ■■■

D Listen to Samira's message. Choose the correct answers.

Go over the questions and options, then play the audio. Tell students to choose their answers and then play the audio again. Have students compare answers with a partner. Play the audio one or more additional times and check answers as a class.

Listening Script

Voicemail message: *Hello, this is David. I can't come to the phone right now. Please leave a message, and I will get back to you right away.*
Samira: *Hi, David. This is Samira. I texted you this morning. I need to change my doctor's appointment, but I don't know what to say. Can you help me? I hope so. Please call me back today at (253) 555-3765.*

E Read the tips for leaving a voicemail.

After students read, check understanding by asking questions. For example: *Do you speak quickly when you leave a message? Why not?*, etc. Play the audio and have students listen as they read to help them with pronunciation and rhythm.

Call Me Back!

GOAL ▶ Leave a phone message

A Look at the calendar on Samira's phone. Do you see a problem?

B Read and check your answer to A. 🎧

> Samira has a problem. She has two things on her schedule at the same time. This is called a *scheduling conflict*. Both things are very important to her. She decides to change her doctor's appointment. She is nervous. English is not Samira's first language, and she doesn't know what to say on the phone.

C **EVALUATE** What can Samira do? Work in a group. Complete the sentences.
Answers will vary. Sample answers included below.

1. She can ask her teacher _____.

2. She can call her friend _____.

3. She can go to a counselor's office _____.

D Listen to Samira's message. Choose the correct answers. 🎧

1. Who does she talk to?

   a. her doctor   b. David's voicemail   c. her brother David

2. When does she want to talk to David?

   a. today   b. by Monday   c. in a text

E Read the tips for leaving a voicemail. 🎧

> - Speak slowly and clearly.
> - Say your name and your reason for calling.
> - Keep your message short.
> - Say your phone number. Cell phones record your number, but office phones may not.

F There are three important parts of a message. Read the chart.

Your Name	Reason for Calling	Your Phone Number
This is Samira.	I have a question.	My number is (253) 555-3765.
	I want to talk.	You can call me at (253) 555-3765.
It's Samira.	I need some information.	Can you call me back at (253) 555-3765?
	I need to change my doctor's appointment.	Please call me back at (253) 555-3765.

G EVALUATE Work in a group. Read the messages. Choose the good messages.

1. This is Samira. I need to change my doctor's appointment. Please call me at (253) 555-3765. Thanks.

2. Call me. OK?

3. I am Samira. My phone number is 555-3765.

4. This is your friend Samira from school. I have a question for you. You can call me at (253) 555-3765. Thanks.

5. This is Samira. I have a small problem. Can you call me back? My number is (253) 555-3765. Thanks.

H Work in a group. Role-play leaving messages at a doctor's office and taking notes.

Answers will vary.

Student A: Hello, this is Doctor Singh's office. The office is currently closed. Please leave a message.

Student B: Hi, this is Ramon Gonzales. I have a question for Doctor Singh. Can you give me a call back? My number is (717) 555-2125.

Name: _____

Phone number: _____

Reason for calling: _____

_____

_____

Name: _____

Phone number: _____

Reason for calling: _____

_____

_____

Evaluation 1

3–5 mins. ■■■

With their books closed, ask students to explain each tip to you. Call on individuals but encourage the class to help as needed.

Presentation 2

20–30 mins. ■■■

Ask students about Samira's call. Play the audio again to refresh their memories. Write *name, reason for calling,* and *phone number* on the board. Ask students what Samira's phone number is. Have them listen again. Ask why she is calling. Write answers on the board as students give them to you.

BEST PRACTICE

Focused Listening

Most of the listening exercises in *Stand Out* are focused-listening activities. This strategy helps students to listen for important words and to guess at meaning using context clues. Many standardized assessment tests also use focused-listening exercises. **D** is an example of this type of test. Another example at this level is when students look at a series of pictures and listen to a description. Then students choose the picture that the audio best describes.

In focused listening, students always have a task. The task determines what they are listening for. Therefore, on tests, students should learn to prepare to listen by determining what they are listening for. We suggest students read the questions before they listen. If students are choosing from a series of pictures, they should first look at the pictures and try to determine the context and guess at what to listen for.

F There are three important parts of a message. Read the chart.

As you look at the chart with students, number each column *1–3*. Tell them that a good message has all three parts in that order. They should use this information as a reference when they are working on **G**.

G EVALUATE Work in a group. Read the messages. Choose the good messages.

Show students how to do this exercise by doing the first item with them. Write *1–3* above the message where appropriate to highlight the necessary parts of the message. Have students evaluate the remaining items.

This activity is still part of the presentation stage, so it is expected that the teacher help students

if necessary. Go over the answers and make sure students understand how to identify all three important parts of a message.

Practice 2

7–10 mins. ■■

H Work in a group. Role-play leaving messages at a doctor's office and taking notes.

Go over the conversation, having students repeat each line after you. Model the conversation with a student, assigning them the Student A role. Respond with your own details and a different reason for calling than is provided in the example. Then have two students model the conversation. Show them that they need to write the caller's details in their book. Put students in groups of three to carry out the role play. Monitor and help with pronunciation and rhythm. Remind students to switch roles.

Evaluation 2

7–10 mins. ■■

Ask volunteers to role-play the conversation for the class without using their books.

Instructor's Notes

_____

_____

_____

_____

_____

_____

_____

_____

_____

Presentation 3
15–20 mins. ■■■

Ask a few students to help you do some things around the room. For example, ask students to help you move the teacher's desk and move it back again. In virtual classes, ask students to write something in the chat or tell you the time. Ask: *Can you help me?* Write the question on the board and ask students to repeat it.

I Study the chart.

Go over the chart carefully. Show students how word order makes a difference in English. Help them see that a reason for calling (refer them back to **F** if necessary) might be expressed by one of the questions in the chart.

Pronunciation *Yes / No* **Questions**

Point out the note on the intonation of *yes / no* questions. Explain that, like word order, rising intonation is very important to signal questions in English. Play the audio twice. The second time, pause and have students repeat the questions.

Then have students practice further by saying the questions in the chart. Carry out both choral and individual practice.

Listening Script

Yes / no questions have a rising intonation. They go up at the end.
Can I talk to you?
Can you call me?

J Match the questions with the responses.

Have students complete the activity individually. Tell them to read the questions and answer options carefully. Have them compare with a partner by taking turns reading the questions and providing the answers. Remind them to use rising intonation for the questions. Then check answers as a class.

Practice 3
7–10 mins. ■

K Write questions. Put the words in the correct order.

Write the following information on the board: *see / can / I / tomorrow / you.* Ask students to help you unscramble the question. Make sure you add a question mark once the question is complete. Also, briefly explain to students the difference between

me and *I* (object vs. subject). Your explanation doesn't need to be lengthy at this level. Then have students complete the activity individually.

Evaluation 3
7–10 mins. ■

Ask student volunteers to write their questions on the board.

Application
7–10 mins. ■■■

L APPLY Write a message for each situation.

Go over each situation. Explain to students that they are writing what they would say in a voicemail message for each situation. Remind them to include the three parts of a good message from **F**. Monitor and help as needed.

Extension: Have students record the messages they wrote using a voice memo app on their phones. Have them listen back to the messages and record multiple times.

Instructor's Notes

_____

_____

_____

_____

_____

_____

_____

_____

_____

_____

_____

_____

_____

I Study the chart.

Yes / No Questions with *Can*			
Can	**Subject**	**Base Verb**	**Example Question**
Can	I	help ask talk	**Can** I help you? **Can** I ask you a question? **Can** I talk to you?
	you	give call	**Can** you give me the phone number? **Can** you call me back?

Intonation 🎧
***Yes / No* Questions**

Can I talk to you? ↗

Can you call me? ↗

J Match the questions with the responses.

___c___ 1. Can you help me?

___a___ 2. Can I ask you a question?

___b___ 3. Can you call me back?

___e___ 4. Can you give me the phone number?

___d___ 5. Can I talk to you?

a. Of course. What's your question?

b. Sure. I can call you back tomorrow.

c. Sure. How can I help?

d. Yes. What do you want to talk about?

e. Yes. It's (617) 555-3490.

K Write questions. Put the words in the correct order.

1. help / can / I / you

   Can I help you?

2. answer / a question / you / can

   Can you answer a question?

3. I / talk / to you / can / tomorrow

   Can I talk to you tomorrow?

4. I / can / you / see / tomorrow

   Can I see you tomorrow?

L APPLY Write a message for each situation. Answers will vary.

Tell your boss you're sick today:

_____

Tell your friend there is a problem:

_____

Tell your doctor you need to make an appointment:

_____

Let's Meet Up!

GOAL ▶ Write an email

A INTERPRET Read Samira's email to her classmate Paco.

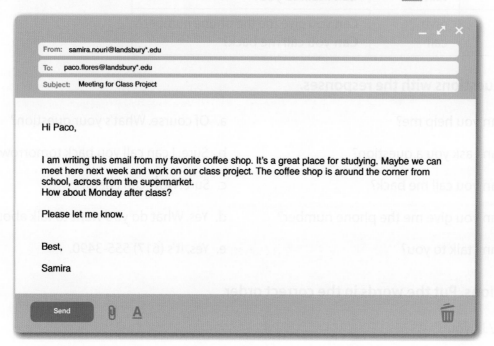

From: samira.nouri@landsbury*.edu

To: paco.flores@landsbury*.edu

Subject: Meeting for Class Project

Hi Paco,

I am writing this email from my favorite coffee shop. It's a great place for studying. Maybe we can meet here next week and work on our class project. The coffee shop is around the corner from school, across from the supermarket.
How about Monday after class?

Please let me know.

Best,

Samira

Send

B Answer the questions about the email.

1. What is Samira's email address?

   samira.nouri@landsbury*.edu

2. What is Paco's email address?

   paco.flores@landsbury*.edu

3. What is the email about? (What is the subject?)

   meeting for a class project

4. Where is the coffee shop?

   around the corner from the school, across from the supermarket

5. When does Samira want to meet?

   Monday after class

6. Where is Samira writing the email from?

   the coffee shop

Life
ONLINE

Email Greetings and Closings

Emails usually begin with a greeting (*Hi, Hello, Good morning*, etc.) and end with a closing (*Best, Thanks, Sincerely*, etc.) before your name. What greeting and closing do you see in the email in **A**?

At-a-Glance Prep

Goal: Write an email
Grammar: Present continuous, simple present, adverbs of frequency
Vocabulary: Email

Agenda

☐ Review family relationships.
☐ Read an email.
☐ Use the present continuous and the simple present.
☐ Ask and answer questions about daily life.
☐ Write an email.

Pacing

■ 1.5 hour classes   ■ 2.5 hour classes
■ 3+ hour classes

Standards Correlations

CASAS: 0.1.2, 0.1.5, 0.2.3, 7.7.4
CCRS: L1, L2, L3, RI1, RI2, SL1, SL3, W1, W3
ELPS:
S9: Create clear and coherent level-appropriate speech and text.
S10: Demonstrate command of the conventions of standard English to communicate in level-appropriate speech and writing.

Warm-up and Review   10–15 mins.

Ask students where their family members live and how they are related. If necessary, review family relationship words. Ask students to list relatives and friends on a separate sheet of paper. See how many they can recall in two minutes.

Introduction   5 mins. ■■■

Ask students to choose one of the people on their list who lives in a different city or country and whom they would like to speak to or write an email to. State the goal: *Today, we will write an email.*

Presentation 1   7–10 mins. ■■■

Before students open their books, ask them if they know how to start and finish an email. Write *Dear...*, on the board and elicit or provide different words they can use to end an email such as *sincerely, best, love,* etc. Tell students that they will read an email by themselves. Explain to them that

reading an email with unfamiliar words is similar to focused listening—they don't have to understand every word.

A INTERPRET Read Samira's email to her classmate Paco.

Have students read through Samira's email without using a dictionary.

Practice 1   7–10 mins. ■■■

B Answer the questions about the email.

Have students answer the questions individually, without using a dictionary. Students should try to answer every question even if they are unsure. This activity is designed for students to do on their own, not with help from other students or the teacher. Walk around the room and make sure students have written something on each line.

BEST PRACTICE

Independent Learners

Some students are intimidated by writing tasks. A few may refuse to write or wait until you or another student gives them the answers. The only way such students will gain confidence is if they try to do activities and discover by so doing that they can do at least part of the activities on their own. Part of the *Stand Out* mission statement is to help students be independent learners. Strongly encourage students to do this activity and to guess when they need to.

Evaluation 1   5–7 mins. ■■

Ask students to check their work in pairs and then go over the answers as a class. You can have students read the email again and listen to the audio as they read if time allows.

> Read through the information with the class. Write *greeting* and *closing* on the board and have students add any other words or phrases they know. For example: *Good afternoon, Regards, See you soon.* Help them decide which greetings and closings are more appropriate when writing to friends and family and which are for doctors, teachers, bosses, work colleagues, etc.

Life ONLINE

Presentation 2

15–20 mins. ■■■

C Study the charts.

Give students examples of the present continuous. Base the examples on classroom actions so students grasp that the present continuous refers to what is happening at the moment. Contrast this with the simple present, which is used for things we do regularly. Since the first sentence of Samira's email in **A** is in the present continuous, point it out and contrast it with the second sentence in the simple present.

In the chart, help students see how the contractions in the present continuous work. Finally, explain that regular activities in the simple present are often associated with adverbs of frequency. There is no need to use metalanguage here to explain it. Ask *yes / no* questions about what students do that will help explain these adverbs. For example: *Do you always drive to school?*

BEST PRACTICE

Metalanguage

Students don't need metalanguage to speak English well or to understand grammar. Some English speakers may never know what the *third-person singular* is. However, sometimes when working with adults, some identification of grammar structures can help them to identify concepts they have learned earlier and to apply them to new structures.

In this case, students have not learned about adverbs yet, and describing what an adverb is may confuse them in this activity. We suggest that you wait to delve into a description of what adverbs are at a more appropriate time.

Practice 2

10–15 mins. ■■□

D Complete the sentences with the present continuous form of the verb in parentheses. Then listen and check your answers. 🎧

Point out the spelling note and explain that for verbs ending in *-e*, we delete the *-e* when we add *-ing*. Have students complete the sentences individually, then compare with a partner. Play the audio to confirm answers.

E Complete the sentences with the simple present form of the verb in parentheses.

Point out the spelling note and explain that for verbs ending in consonant + *-y*, we change the *-y* to *-ies* for the third person singular. Also point out that *go* is an irregular verb, so the third person singular form is *goes* instead of *gos*. Have students complete the sentences individually, then compare with a partner.

Evaluation 2

5–7 mins. ■■□

Ask students to write the answers for **D** and **E** on the board. Help them understand when each verb form is used.

Instructor's Notes

_____

_____

_____

_____

_____

_____

_____

_____

_____

_____

_____

_____

_____

_____

_____

C Study the charts.

Present Continuous				
Subject	***Be***	**Verb + *ing***	**Time**	**Example Sentence**
I	am (I'm)	writing	right now today	**I'm writing** a letter right now.
He / She / It	is (She's)	eating		She**'s eating** a sandwich.
You / We / They	are (They're)	reading		They**'re reading** a book today.

Simple Present			
Subject	**Adverb**	**Verb**	**Example Sentence**
I	always usually sometimes rarely never	write	I always **write** emails in the morning.
He / She / It		goes	He rarely **goes** there.
You / We / They		read	They never **read** the newspaper.

Adverbs of Frequency

0%		50%		100%
never	rarely	sometimes	usually	always

D Complete the sentences with the present continuous form of the verb in parentheses. Then listen and check your answers. 🎧

1. She _____is eating_____ (eat) at a restaurant.

2. They _____are writing_____ (write) emails.

3. We _____are reading_____ (read) a good book in class.

4. I _____am going_____ (go) to the hospital. I am very sick.

5. Samira _____is buying_____ (buy) a book at the bookstore right now.

Spelling
write → writing

E Complete the sentences with the simple present form of the verb in parentheses.

1. She _____lives_____ (live) in Landsbury.

2. I never _____read_____ (read) newspaper ads.

3. We rarely _____study_____ (study) on Saturdays.

4. They usually _____write_____ (write) emails or texts at lunchtime.

5. He _____goes_____ (go) to school at the Orangewood School for Adults.

Spelling
study → studies
go → goes

F Listen and answer the questions. 🎧 Answers will vary.

1. Where do you go to school? <u>I go to</u> _____.

2. Where do you live? <u>I live</u> _____.

3. Where is a restaurant nearby? <u>There is a restaurant</u> _____.

4. What do you sometimes do? <u>Sometimes, I</u> _____.

G Ask a partner the same questions and write his or her answers. Answers will vary.

1. Where do you go to school?

<u>He / She goes to</u> _____.

2. Where do you live?

_____.

3. Where is a restaurant nearby?

_____.

4. What do you sometimes do?

_____.

H COMPOSE Write a message to a friend or family member about your city. Use the information about yourself from F. Answers will vary.

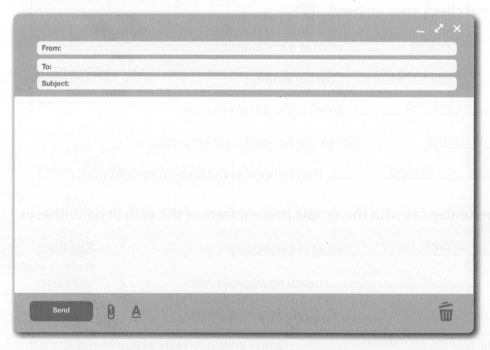

I APPLY Write a real email to a friend or family member. Get an email account if necessary.

Presentation 3   7–10 mins. ■■■

F   Listen and answer the questions. 🎧

Do this activity first orally with the books closed. Play each question in the audio and ask individuals for answers. Play the audio two or three times. Then ask students to open their books and write the answers.

Make sure students understand the meaning of each question and can answer it in a complete sentence. This will help them in **G** as well as in **H**.

Practice 3   7–10 mins. ■

G   Ask a partner the same questions and write his or her answers.

Encourage students to answer in complete sentences. Remind them to use the third person singular *s* when writing about their partner.

Evaluation 3   5–7 mins. ■

Ask students to tell the class about the person they interviewed.

Application   20–30 mins. ■■■

H   COMPOSE   Write a message to a friend or family member about your city. Use the information about yourself from F.

Elicit the greetings and closings that might be appropriate for friends and family. Remind students that images can be sent along with text in an actual email. Encourage them to describe things pictured in the photos, such as the inside of their apartment or a nearby restaurant. Monitor as students write, helping as needed. Remember that some students will find writing uncomfortable and may need more support and suggestions to get started.

Workplace Focus

Exercise I: Apply technology.

I   APPLY   Write a real email to a friend or family member. Get an email account if necessary.

Suggest to students that many local libraries offer the use of computers and internet access at no cost. Have students report who they wrote to in the next class.

Instructor's Notes

_____

_____

_____

_____

_____

_____

_____

_____

_____

_____

_____

_____

_____

_____

_____

_____

_____

_____

_____

_____

_____

_____

_____

_____

At-a-Glance Prep

Goal: Identify employment opportunities at the post office

Agenda

☐ Interpret an infographic.

☐ Ask and answer *wh-* questions about post office jobs.

☐ Read about a mail carrier's duties.

☐ Talk about a mail carrier's duties.

☐ Reflect on interest in post office jobs.

☐ Search online for job openings at the post office.

Pacing

■ 1.5 hour classes   ■ 2.5 hour classes
■ 3+ hour classes

Standards Correlations

CASAS: 0.1.2, 0.1.5, 4.1.3, 4.1.8, 4.1.9, 4.8.1, 7.4.4, 7.7.3

CCRS: L1, RI1, RI3, SL1, SL3, W1, W3

ELPS:

S5: Conduct research and evaluate and communicate findings to answer questions or solve problems.

S10: Demonstrate command of the conventions of standard English to communicate in level-appropriate speech and writing.

In this lesson, students are introduced to employment opportunities at the post office. They will analyze an infographic and compare salaries for different post office jobs and the number of people in each job. Students will also read about a mail carrier's duties and talk about how they feel about those duties. They will reflect on their suitability for a job at the post office. Finally, students will carry out an online search for post office job openings in their area.

Warm-up and Review   10–15 mins. ■■■

Write *post office* on the board and have students explain what services it provides and what we do at the post office. Remember that they don't need to explain in complete sentences. The objective is simply to activate prior knowledge, so accept any words or phrases they come up with and write them on the board. Ask about jobs at the post office. They may already know mail carrier and clerk. Write any they mention on the board.

Introduction   5–10 mins. ■■■

Find out if any of the students work at the post office or know anyone who does. Remind them that throughout *Stand Out*, they will investigate many job possibilities. Write the goal on the board: *Today we will identify employment opportunities at the post office.*

Presentation 1   15–20 mins. ■■■

A INTERPRET **Read the infographic.**

Go over the infographic together, having students describe what they see in the photos and what information is being presented (positions, hourly and annual pay, benefits, and number of people in each job). Explain or have students look up *workforce*, *benefits*, and *health insurance*.

B **Answer the questions.**

Have students answer the questions individually, then compare with a partner. Go over the answers as a class. Clarify any vocabulary questions students still have from the infographic or the questions.

Practice 1   20–25 mins. ■■■

C **Study the chart.**

Look at the chart together and make sure students understand the meaning of each question. Focus their attention on the question words and the verb forms.

D **Work in a group. Ask and answer questions about the infographic in A.**

Put students in pairs to ask and answer the questions. Tell them to alternate so they practice both asking and answering. Encourage them to use all three question words from the chart in **C**. Monitor and help with question formation and intonation as needed.

Evaluation 1   5–10 mins. ■■■

Have a student ask another student a question about the infographic. That student should answer the question and then ask a question of another classmate, and so on.

Explore the Workforce

LESSON 6

GOAL ▶ Identify employment opportunities at the post office

A INTERPRET Read the infographic.

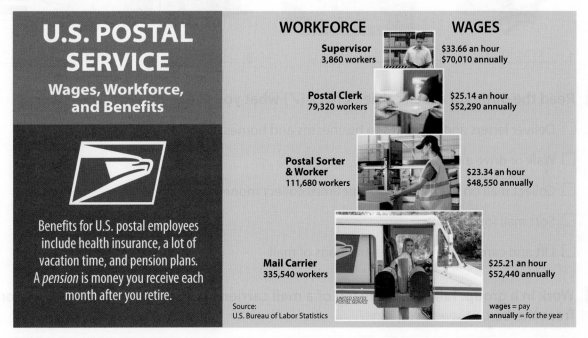

U.S. POSTAL SERVICE
Wages, Workforce, and Benefits

Benefits for U.S. postal employees include health insurance, a lot of vacation time, and pension plans. A *pension* is money you receive each month after you retire.

Source: U.S. Bureau of Labor Statistics

WORKFORCE

Supervisor 3,860 workers

Postal Clerk 79,320 workers

Postal Sorter & Worker 111,680 workers

Mail Carrier 335,540 workers

WAGES

$33.66 an hour / $70,010 annually

$25.14 an hour / $52,290 annually

$23.34 an hour / $48,550 annually

$25.21 an hour / $52,440 annually

wages = pay
annually = for the year

B Answer the questions.

1. What is the average hourly wage for a mail carrier? __$25.21__

2. What is the annual salary for a postal clerk? __$52,290__

3. How many supervisors are in the workforce? __3,860__

4. Who makes $33.66 an hour? __supervisors__

C Study the chart.

Question Words	Verb	
What	is	the annual salary for a mail carrier?
	are	the benefits for a mail carrier?
Who	makes	$33.66 an hour?
How many supervisors	are	in the workforce?

D Work in a group. Ask and answer questions about the infographic in A.

E **Match the words to the pictures.**

envelopes	packages	postage	route

1. envelopes   2. route   3. packages   4. postage

F **Read the duties of a mail carrier. Check (✓) what you like to do.** Answers will vary.

☐ Deliver letters and packages to businesses and homes.

☐ Walk or drive a route.

☐ Collect mail on the route and sometimes collect money for postage.

☐ Sort mail for delivery.

☐ Lift and carry heavy packages and bags of mail.

G **Work in a group. Talk about the job of a mail carrier. Do you like the duties? Use words from the box.** Answers will vary.

bad	boring	difficult	easy	fun	good	interesting

1. How do you feel about delivering mail?

   I think it seems _____.

2. How do you feel about walking all day?

   I think it seems _____.

3. How do you feel about collecting money for postage?

   I think it seems _____.

4. How do you feel about sorting mail?

   I think it seems _____.

5. How do you feel about the pay?

   I think it seems _____.

Presentation 2

E Match the words to the pictures.

Have students do this individually. Tell them to try to do it without a dictionary. Have them compare with a partner, and if they still have doubts, tell them to look the words up. Check answers as a class.

F Read the duties of a mail carrier. Check (✓) what you like to do.

Ask students to read the duties individually. Then ask questions to check students' understanding. For example: *What does a mail carrier take to people? Does a mail carrier always walk?* Review any vocabulary questions. Then have students check the items they like to do and tell a partner.

Practice 2

15–20 mins. ■■■

G Work in a group. Talk about the job of a mail carrier. Do you like the duties? Use words from the box.

Go over the words in the box, eliciting or explaining the meanings. Have students answer the questions with how they feel first and then put them in groups to discuss. Encourage them to provide a reason for their thoughts if they can. Monitor and help as needed.

Evaluation 2

5–10 mins. ■■

Have each group share their opinions with the class. Did they agree on each item? What did most people think about each duty?

Instructor's Notes

_____

_____

_____

_____

_____

_____

_____

_____

_____

_____

_____

_____

_____

_____

_____

_____

_____

_____

_____

_____

_____

_____

_____

_____

Presentation 3   10–15 mins. ■■■

Write *difficult* and *easy* on the board and elicit their meanings. Ask students what kinds of things can make a job difficult.

H **This mail carrier, Paul Canney, is delivering mail after a big snowstorm in Canton, Massachusetts. Look at the photo. What do you think makes Paul's job difficult sometimes? Is this the same for mail carriers in your area? What other difficulties do you think mail carriers have on the job?**

Have students look at the photo and describe what they see. Provide vocabulary as needed (*snow, truck, mailbox,* etc.). Go over the questions and then ask students to discuss them with a partner. Share answers as a class. Write other difficulties students suggest on the board. For example: weather, dogs, traffic.

Practice 3   20–25 mins. ■■□

Ask students in shorter classes to do Practice 3 for homework.

I **REFLECT Answer the questions. Is a job at the post office right for you?**

Read the questions together and clarify any vocabulary doubts. Tell students to answer individually, then share their answers with a partner and decide if a job at the post office is good for them. Call on different students to tell the class about their partner. Encourage them to explain *why* a job at the post office may be right for their partner or not. To help them, write on the board: *She likes to help people. / She doesn't like to help people. She is friendly. / She isn't friendly.* It isn't important that students get these structures correct, but this is an opportunity for them to try to say more.

J **Choose a job title from A. Go to a job search site online and see if there are any openings within 25 miles of your school or home. Share what you find with a partner.**

Help students get started with their searches by helping them decide which of the jobs in **A** they want to look for. Tell them to write down the duties, wages, and benefits for the jobs they find. Elicit what *benefits* are. Write on the board: *health insurance, vacations, pension plans.* Then share specific job search sites that students can use.

Monitor as they carry out their searches and help as needed. When they have all found one or two options, put them in pairs to share their information.

Evaluation 3   5–10 mins. ■■□

Call on different students to share what they found. Ask them questions about the duties, wages, and benefits. Write the details of a few of the jobs on the board and have students compare them.

BEST PRACTICE

Online Job Searches

When looking for jobs online, students need to know first, how to carry out an effective search and second, the parameters for salaries, number of hours, and benefits of the type of position they are interested in, so they can recognize if an opening is within those parameters.

Effective searches require appropriate wording and should be limiting so that students don't get an overwhelming number of options. For example, they should write the specific position they are interested in and the location, as mentioned in **J**.

Students should research typical salaries and benefits for certain types of positions. By looking at several openings for the same position, they can learn what to expect and can compare the different openings they find.

As with searching for housing online, students need to be aware that there may be fake job offers or ones that are not offering the pay and benefits that they should be.

H This mail carrier, Paul Canney, is delivering mail after a big snowstorm in Canton, Massachusetts. Look at the photo. What do you think makes Paul's job difficult sometimes? Is this the same for mail carriers in your area? What other difficulties do you think mail carriers have on the job?

I **REFLECT** Answer the questions. Is a job at the post office right for you?

Answers will vary.

1. Do you like to help people?

   a. Yes, I do. b. No, I don't. c. Sometimes.

2. Are you friendly?

   a. Yes, I am. b. No, I'm not. c. Sometimes.

3. Do you like to work outside?

   a. Yes, I do. b. No, I don't. c. Sometimes.

4. Are you organized?

   a. Yes, I am. b. No, I'm not. c. Sometimes.

5. Do you like to be on your feet (stand up) a lot of the day?

   a. Yes, I do. b. No, I don't. c. Sometimes.

J Choose a job title from A. Go to a job search site online and see if there are any openings within 25 miles of your school or home. Share what you find with a partner.

Review

A **Look at the map. Ask a partner for the location of each place.**

the apartments	the motel	the post office
the hotel	the park	the shoe store
the medical center	the pool	

Student A: Where are the tennis courts?

Student B: They are on the corner of Second Street and Broadway, across from the library.

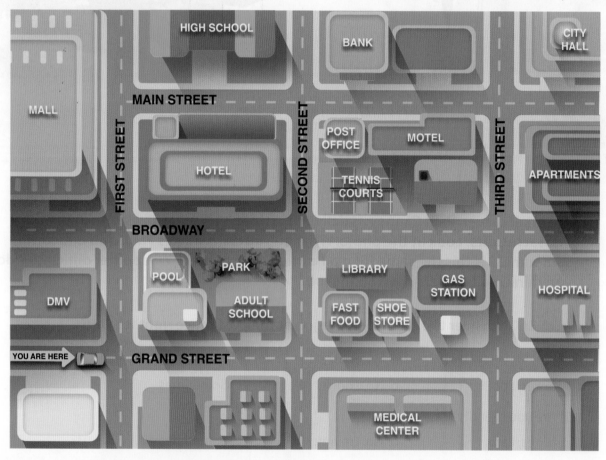

B **Give your partner directions to each location.**

City Hall	the DMV	the library
the adult school	the gas station	the mall
the bank	the high school	

Student A: Can you give me directions to the medical center?

Student B: Yes, go straight on Grand Street for one block. Then turn right. It's on the left.

Learner Log	I can give and follow street directions.	I can describe locations.
	☐ Yes ☐ No ☐ Maybe	☐ Yes ☐ No ☐ Maybe

At-a-Glance Prep

Goal: All unit goals
Grammar: All unit grammar
Academic Strategies: Reviewing, evaluating, developing study skills
Vocabulary: All unit vocabulary

Agenda

☐ Discuss unit goals.
☐ Complete the review.
☐ Evaluate and reflect on progress.

Pacing

■ 1.5 hour classes ■ 2.5 hour classes
■ 3+ hour classes

Standards Correlations

CASAS: 0.1.2, 0.1.5, 0.2.1, 0.2.3, 1.9.1, 2.1.7, 2.1.8, 2.2.1, 7.7.4
CCRS: L1, L3, SL1, SL3, W1, W3
ELPS:
S9: Create clear and coherent level-appropriate speech and text.

Warm-up and Review   7–10 mins. ■■■

With their books closed, ask students to help you make a list on the board of all the vocabulary they can come up with from the unit. Then have a competition where students in groups will look back through the unit and write the first page number for each item on the list. The first group to find the correct page number for each item wins.

Introduction   5 mins. ■■■

Show students the first page of the unit and mention the six goals. Explain that today is review and that students will review the whole unit.

Presentation   10–15 mins. ■■■

This presentation will cover all three pages of the review. Quickly go to the first page of each lesson. Discuss the goal of each. Ask simple questions to remind students of what they have learned.

Practice 1   15–20 mins. ■■■

A Look at the map. Ask a partner for the location of each place.

Tell students to look at the map. Elicit prepositions for location. Read the example conversation together. Then put students in pairs to carry out the activity. Remind them to take turns asking for and giving locations.

B Give your partner directions to each location.

Elicit phrases for giving directions. Then read the example conversation together. Have students carry out the activity in the same pairs as in **A**. Remind them to take turns asking for and giving directions.

Evaluation 1   5–7 mins. ■■■

Go around the classroom and check on students' progress. Help individuals as needed. If you see consistent errors among several students, interrupt the class and give a mini lesson or review to help students feel comfortable with the concept.

Learner Log   5–10 mins.

Have students read the statements and complete the log. If students answer *no* or *maybe*, encourage them to set themselves a goal to practice. Show them where they can find more practice activities.

BEST PRACTICE

Learner Logs

Learner Logs function to help students in many different ways:

1. They serve as part of the review process.
2. They help students to gain confidence and to document what they have learned. Consequently, students see that they are progressing in their learning.
3. They provide students with a tool that they can use over and over to check and recheck their understanding of the target language. In this way, students become independent learners.

Practice 2

C Match the services to the correct places.

As a class, read the phrases describing services in the box. Then have students look at the photos and match the places and phrases individually.

D Listen to the messages. Complete the chart. 🎧

Tell students to look at the chart so they know what information they need to focus on when they listen. Play the audio, pausing after each item for students to write their answers. Play the audio several times as students need to write a lot of information. Have them compare answers with a partner. Then play the audio one or more additional times and check the answers.

Listening Script

1. **Voicemail message:** *This is Herman. I can't come to the phone right now. Please leave a message.*
   Nadia: *Hi, this is Nadia. I have a question for you. Can you give me a call back? My number is (917) 555-2134.*

2. **Voicemail message:** *This is Herman. I can't come to the phone right now. Please leave a message.*
   Vien: *Hey, Herman, it's Vien. I want to talk about this weekend. Can you call me back? My number is (617) 555-7798.*

3. **Voicemail message:** *This is Herman. I can't come to the phone right now. Please leave a message.*
   David: *David here. I need information about the job at City Hall. Please call me back at (786) 555-1234.*

4. **Voicemail message:** *This is Herman. I can't come to the phone right now. Please leave a message.*
   Ricardo: *Hello. This is Ricardo. I need help with something. Can you give me a call? My number is (323) 555-7343.*

E Work in a group. List new airport vocabulary you learned.

Put students in groups to complete the activity. Tell students that they should use this as an opportunity to see what vocabulary they remember from Lesson 3, without looking back at these pages in the book. After they have made a list, they can look back to check their spelling and see which words they forgot.

Evaluation 2

Go around the classroom and check on students' progress. Help individuals as needed. If you see consistent errors among several students, interrupt the class and give a mini lesson or review to help students feel comfortable with the concept.

Learner Log

Have students read the statements and complete the log. If students answer *no* or *maybe*, encourage them to set themselves a goal to practice. Show them where they can find more practice activities.

BEST PRACTICE

Recycling / Review

The review and the project that follows are part of the recycling / review process. Students at this level often need to be reintroduced to concepts to solidify what they have learned. Many concepts are learned and forgotten while learning other new concepts. This is because students learn but are not necessarily ready to acquire language concepts.

Therefore, it becomes very important to review and to show students how to review on their own. It is also important to recycle the new concepts in different contexts.

Instructor's Notes

_____

_____

_____

_____

_____

_____

_____

_____

_____

_____

C **Match the services to the correct places.**

delivers mail	helps sick people	lends books
gives driver's licenses	keeps your money safe	puts out fires

1.
gives driver's licenses

2.
helps sick people

3.
puts out fires

4.
delivers mail

5.
keeps your money safe

6.
lends books

D **Listen to the messages. Complete the chart.** 🎧

Name	Reason for Calling	Phone Number
1. Nadia	I have a question.	(917) 555-2134
2. Vien	I want to talk (about this weekend).	(617) 555-7798
3. Jack	I need information (about the job at City Hall).	(786) 555-1234
4. Ricardo	I need help (with something).	(323) 555-7343

E **Work in a group. List new airport vocabulary you learned.** Answers will vary.

_____   _____

_____   _____

Learner Log	I can identify locations and services. ☐ Yes ☐ No ☐ Maybe	I can leave a phone message. ☐ Yes ☐ No ☐ Maybe

Review

F **Write sentences about yourself.** Answers will vary.

I always _____.

I usually _____.

Sometimes, I _____.

I rarely _____.

I never _____.

G **Write a new email. Use the model email in Lesson 5, Exercise A.** Answers will vary.

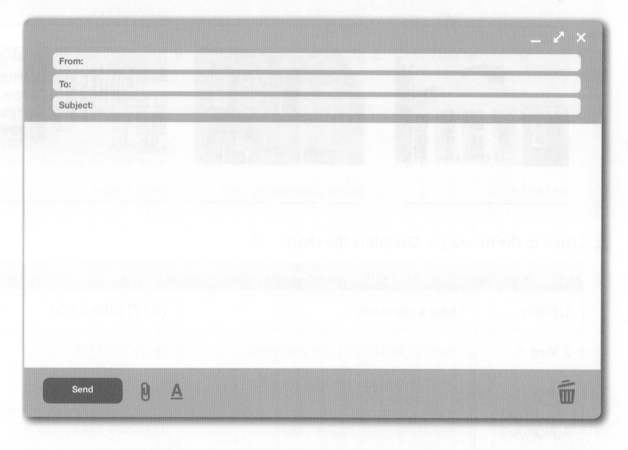

From:	
To:	
Subject:	

Send   🔗   A

Learner Log   I can write an email.

⬜ Yes   ⬜ No   ⬜ Maybe

Practice 3 15–20 mins. ■■■

F Write sentences about yourself.

Ask several students questions about themselves like the ones in Lesson 5 (*What do you sometimes do? What do you never do?*, etc.). Write the questions on the board so they serve as prompts for students to write their sentences. When they have finished, ask them to exchange their sentences with a partner and peer edit each other's work.

G Write a new email. Use the model in Lesson 5, Exercise A.

Elicit greetings and closings and then ask students who they want to write to. Ask them what they can write about in the email. Write their ideas on the board. This will help students who find writing challenging. Have students write their emails individually. Include peer editing again if possible.

Evaluation 3 5–10 mins. ■■■

Go around the room and check on students' progress. Help individuals as needed. If you see consistent errors among several students, interrupt the class and give a mini lesson or review to help students feel comfortable with the concept.

Learner Log 5–10 mins.

Have students read the statement and complete the log. If students answer *no* or *maybe*, encourage them to set themselves a goal to practice. Show them where they can find more practice activities.

Instructor's Notes

_____

_____

_____

_____

_____

_____

_____

_____

_____

_____

_____

_____

_____

_____

_____

_____

_____

_____

_____

_____

_____

_____

_____

_____

_____

Standards Correlations

CASAS: 0.1.2, 0.1.5, 1.9.1, 4.8.1, 7.4.4, 7.7.3

CCRS: SL1, SL3, W3

ELPS:

S3: Speak and write about level-appropriate complex literary and informational texts and topics.

S7: Adapt language choices to purpose, task, and audience when speaking and writing.

Workplace Focus

Make decisions and solve problems; Collect and organize information; Combine ideas and information; Exercise leadership roles; Manage time; Complete tasks as assigned; Interact appropriately with team members; Interpret and communicate information.

Soft Skill: Active Listening
Asking Questions

Direct students to the Soft Skill note. Explain how in the workplace, active listening skills are very important. Active listening means giving your full attention to the speaker. Asking questions to clarify understanding or to encourage the speaker to expand on the topic is part of that skill set. Tell students they will practice this skill in **Step 6** of the project when they listen to other groups' presentations.

Warm-up and Review   10 mins.

Go over the review section of the unit and make sure all students have recorded their progress in the learner logs.

Introduction   2 mins.

Let students know that in this project, they will be designing a new city.

Presentation   10–15 mins.

1. Form a team of four or five students. In your team, you need:

Put students in teams of four or five. Then have them choose their positions in the group. To do this, go through each step in the project and explain the role of the person who will lead that step. Make sure students understand that although each person has a specific task, they will work together on each step.

The team leader's job is not associated with a step but has the responsibility of making sure everyone participates and speaks English. The team leader may also have ancillary responsibilities when general information is required.

In **Steps 2** and **3**, for example, the team leader can manage the discussion of what the team will call their city and what important places they will include. Then in **Step 4**, the city planner will draw the map of the city based on the other team members' ideas and suggestions. In **Step 5**, the artist will create the brochure with input from the other team members for the content. Finally, the organizers will take the lead on the preparation for the presentation in **Step 6** with all members participating. Remind students about the steps for preparing and practicing for a presentation from Unit 4 and refer them there as needed.

Practice / Evaluation / Application   1–2 hours

2. Choose a name for your city.

3. Make a list of important places in your city.

4. Make a map of your city and mark where the important places are.

5. Make a brochure. Include a paragraph about the city, the names of your team members, and a picture that represents the city.

For ideas on the paragraph, refer students back to the web page in Lesson 1 as an example, but make sure they understand they should not just copy this paragraph.

6. Prepare and give a presentation for the class.

Remind students that they need to listen carefully to other teams' presentations to find the answers to the questions in the Soft Skill note. If they don't hear the answers, they should ask the questions at the end of the presentation. To ensure students are doing this, give them a quiz on the questions after each presentation.

Design a New City

SOFT SKILL ▶ Active Listening

In this project, you will design a new city, create a map and brochure for it, and present it to the class.

1. Form a team of four or five students. In your team, you need:

Position	Job Description	Student Name
Student 1: **Team Leader**	Check that everyone speaks English. Check that everyone participates.	
Student 2: **City Planner**	With help from the team, draw a map of your city.	
Student 3: **Artist**	With help from the team, make a brochure to advertise your city.	
Students 4/5: **Organizer(s)**	Organize a presentation to give to the class.	

2. Choose a name for your city.

3. Make a list of important places in your city.

4. Make a map of your city and mark where the important places are.

5. Make a brochure. Include a paragraph about the city, the names of your team members, and a picture that represents the city.

6. Prepare and give a presentation for the class.

ACTIVE LISTENING:
Asking Questions

Listen carefully when other groups present. Listen for answers to the questions below. If you don't hear answers, ask the questions.

What is your favorite place in the city?

Is your city big or small?

Does your city have fun places to go?

Minneapolis, Minnesota has 180 parks with biking and walking paths, tennis and basketball courts, playgrounds, and community gardens.

Reading Challenge

About the Photo

This photo shows the very small town of Whittier, Alaska. The town is so small that the majority of the population lives in the apartment building shown in this photo. Whittier sits at the foot of a mountain and can only be reached by traveling through a tunnel that cuts through the mountain. Both trains and cars use the same tunnel. The town was built and used by the army during World War II, but people stayed on after the war, and it is now a fishing town and a tourist destination. Tourists can take boat trips to see glaciers, kayak, and hike the trails through the beautiful forests and mountains surrounding Whittier.

Have students look at the photo and describe what they see. Provide vocabulary as needed. Read the photo caption and ask students if they would like to live there.

A Work with a partner. Answer the questions.

Put students in pairs to discuss the questions. Call on a few pairs to share their answers. Discuss as a class whether most people live near or far from school, have a grocery store nearby, etc.

B Work in a group. Describe the city or town where you go to school. Answer the questions to help organize your ideas. Research online if you need to.

Go over the questions as a class and clarify any vocabulary doubts. Put students in groups to answer the questions. Monitor

and help as needed. Have each group share one or two answers.

C Read the text. 🎧

Ask students to read the title. Check they understand it by explaining how everyone in the class knows everyone's name.

Reading Challenge

A Work with a partner. Answer the questions.

1. Where is the nearest grocery store? How far is it from your home?
2. Where is the police department in your city or town? How far is it from your home?
3. Where is the post office? How far is it from your home?
4. How far do you travel from home to school?

B Work in a group. Describe the city or town where you go to school. Answer the questions to help organize your ideas. Research online if you need to.

1. What is the population of the city or town?
2. How do you get around? By train, bus, car, bicycle, or another way?
3. What are your favorite places in the city or town?
4. How many floors does a tall building in the city or town have?
5. Do you think there are more houses or apartment buildings in the city or town?

C Read the text.

D INFER Choose the correct answers.

1. What is the population of the city of Whittier?
   - a. more than 300
   - b. almost 300
   - c. exactly 300

2. In line 5, what does *through* mean?
   - a. around
   - b. in one side and out the other
   - c. on top of

3. In line 6, what does *under the same roof* mean?
   - a. in the same building
   - b. in the same town
   - c. in the same job

4. In line 7, what does *views* mean?
   - a. things you can see
   - b. homes
   - c. balconies

E CLASSIFY Work in a group. On a separate sheet of paper, make a list of pros (good things) and cons (bad things) about living in Whittier, Alaska. Use the phrases below and your own ideas.

beautiful views	People live close together under one roof.
cold weather	The school and stores are very close.
not a lot of jobs	You travel to the city through a tunnel.

142   UNIT 5

CASAS FOR READING
0.1.2, 0.1.5, 2.5.8, 4.8.1, 7.4.4, 7.7.3

CCRS FOR READING
RI1, RI2, RI3, SL1, SL3, W1, W3

Where Everyone Knows Your Name

1   How far do you travel to school? How far is the local grocery store? How about the police department? If you live in Whittier, Alaska, your answers to these questions are probably up or down a few floors. That's right; almost everyone in the town of nearly 300 lives in Begich Towers, a 14-story* building that has a post office and a bed-and-
5   breakfast.* You need to take a 2.5-mile tunnel* through a mountain to arrive at this town where most people live under the same roof. The good news is that there are beautiful views from the condominiums in Begich Towers. Do you want to live in a small town where everyone knows your name?

story a level of a building
bed-and-breakfast a small hotel that includes breakfast
tunnel a path underground or through a mountain

The city of Whittier, Alaska and the Begich Towers apartment building

READING CHALLENGE   143

READING STRATEGIES

Classifying

Classifying is a helpful post-reading activity as it helps students process what they have learned from the text. Talking about new knowledge and organizing it in some way, such as classifying it in a Venn diagram, chart, flow diagram, or pros and cons list, are effective strategies to help students demonstrate their understanding of new concepts.

Ask students what they think they will read about in the text. Have them read individually and underline new words but try to continue reading. Remind them to focus on understanding the main ideas. Don't answer vocabulary questions yet as the meanings of words may become clearer after students do **D**.

D INFER Choose the correct answers.

Have students answer the questions individually, then compare with a partner. Check answers as a class. Ask students to read the text again and listen as they read. Play the audio. Ask students if they now understand some of the words they underlined. Write any words that are still unclear on the board and clarify their meaning as a class.

E CLASSIFY Work in a group. On a separate sheet of paper, make a list of pros (good things) and cons (bad things) about living in Whittier, Alaska. Use the phrases below and your own ideas.

If possible, have students use poster paper or slides for this activity so that each group can display their pros and cons list and compare it with other groups.

Go over the items in the box with the class. Put students in groups to carry out the activity. Encourage them to add ideas of their own to the pros and cons list. When they are ready, have groups share their lists. Prompt students to provide reasons for their choices.

About the Photo

This photo shows a roadside sign in Arizona during the COVID-19 pandemic in 2020. Its aim was to remind people entering the Navajo Reservation nearby of the importance of hand washing as a preventative measure in controlling the spread of COVID. Handwashing is one of the most important things we can do to stay healthy, as many viruses and bacteria are killed when we wash our hands with soap for at least 20 seconds.

- Introduce the unit. Read the title out loud and check students' understanding.
- Read the photo information together. Explain that a *reservation* is U.S. land that is kept as a place for Native Americans to live. Have students talk about the questions with a partner.
- Discuss the answers as a class.
- Go over each unit outcome, eliciting any words or phrases students already know related to each one.

Life Skills Focus

In this unit, students will learn how to identify body parts and explain ailments related to them. They will also learn how to give health advice, ask for information, and develop exercise goals.

6 Health and Fitness

144

UNIT OUTCOMES	GRAMMAR	VOCABULARY	EL CIVICS
• Identify parts of the body • Identify illnesses and health problems • Give advice • Ask for information • Develop exercise goals • Identify employment opportunities in health care	• Simple present • Simple present and negative: *Have* • *Should* and *should not* for advice • *Wh-* questions • Prepositions of location • Verb + infinitive	• Body parts • Symptoms and illnesses • Medications • Hospital • *Exercise and health* • Health care jobs	The skills students learn in this unit can be applied to the following EL Civics competency areas: • Health – Pharmacy • Health – Health care

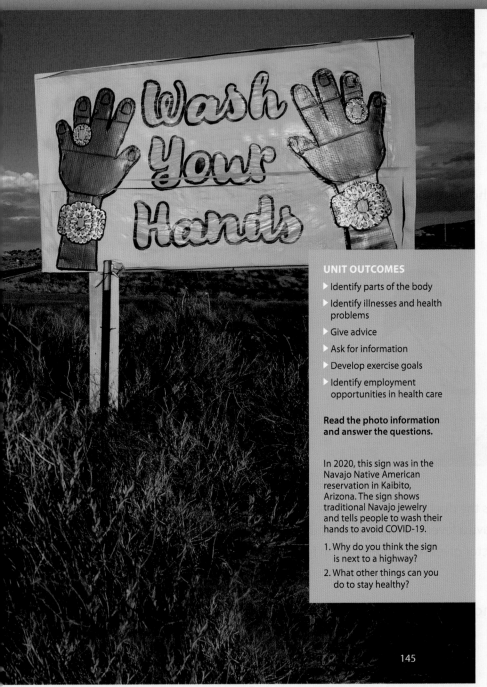

UNIT OUTCOMES

▶ Identify parts of the body
▶ Identify illnesses and health problems
▶ Give advice
▶ Ask for information
▶ Develop exercise goals
▶ Identify employment opportunities in health care

Read the photo information and answer the questions.

In 2020, this sign was in the Navajo Native American reservation in Kaibito, Arizona. The sign shows traditional Navajo jewelry and tells people to wash their hands to avoid COVID-19.

1. Why do you think the sign is next to a highway?
2. What other things can you do to stay healthy?

145

Workplace Focus

All lessons and units in *Stand Out* include basic communication skills and interpersonal skills important for the workplace. They include *collecting and organizing information, making decisions and solving problems,* and *combining ideas and information.*

- In Unit 6, Lesson 6, *Explore the Workforce,* students will identify jobs in health care. They will interpret an infographic with the education requirements and salaries for health care professions, and read and talk about pharmacist jobs.

- In the Team Project, students practice the soft skill of making polite suggestions while collaborating to complete the project.

- Life Online notes in Lessons 1 and 3 raise awareness about the dangers of using the internet for medical advice and the benefits of going online to find the best prices for medicines.

spark Resources

All resources for the unit are centrally located on the Spark platform and include: audio, video, multilevel worksheets, digital literacy worksheets, Online Practice, and Assessment Suite.

— STEPS —

CASAS COMPETENCIES	ELPS	CCRS
Lesson 1: 0.1.2, 0.1.5, 3.6.1, 3.6.4 Lesson 2: 0.1.2, 0.1.5, 3.6.2, 3.6.3, 7.2.3, 7.4.5 Lesson 3: 0.1.2, 0.1.3, 0.1.5, 3.3.1, 3.3.2, 3.3.4 Lesson 4: 0.1.2, 0.1.5, 2.1.2, 2.2.1, 2.5.1, 7.4.4, 7.7.3 Lesson 5: 0.1.2, 0.1.5, 3.5.9, 6.7.4, 7.1.1 Lesson 6: 0.1.2, 0.1.5, 4.1.3, 4.1.8, 4.1.9, 6.7.3, 7.4.4, 7.7.3 Review: 0.1.2, 0.1.5, 2.1.2, 2.5.1, 3.3.1, 3.3.2, 3.5.9, 3.6.1, 3.6.3 Team Project: 0.1.2, 0.1.5, 2.5.1, 3.3.1, 3.3.2, 4.8.1, 7.3.3 Reading Challenge: 0.1.2, 0.1.5, 3.5.9, 7.4.5	S2: Participate in level-appropriate oral and written exchanges of information, ideas, and analyses, in various social and academic contexts, responding to peer, audience, or reader comments and questions. S5: Conduct research and evaluate and communicate findings to answer questions or solve problems. S10: Demonstrate command of the conventions of standard English to communicate in level-appropriate speech and writing.	L1, L2, L3, RI1, RI2, RI3, SL1, SL3, SLK2, W1, W3

Parts of the Body

GOAL ▶ Identify parts of the body

A **PREDICT** Look at the photo. Who is Victor talking to? What is the problem? Then read about Victor. 🎧

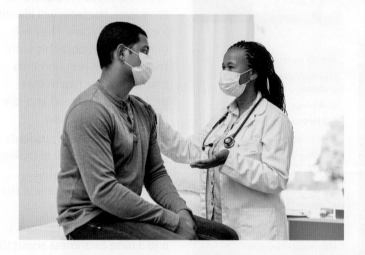

Prescriptions

A prescription is a written message from a doctor that allows you to get the medicine you need from a pharmacy.

Victor is sick. He visits the doctor. The doctor asks, "What is the problem?" Victor answers, "I hurt all over. I think I have a fever. My head hurts and my muscles ache." The doctor checks Victor for the flu. The doctor gives him a prescription for some pain medication.

B Read the statements. Choose *True* or *False*.

1. Victor needs medicine. (True) False

2. Victor's head hurts. (True) False

3. Victor doesn't have a problem. True (False)

C **INFER** Victor says, "I hurt all over." Which body parts does he mean? Make a list.

Answers will vary.

head _____

_____ _____

_____ _____

Life ONLINE **Online Medical Advice** The internet is great for many things, but it is NOT always good at giving medical advice. In fact, it can be dangerous to use the internet to get help instead of going to a doctor. Always talk to your doctor before you change your health habits.

At-a-Glance Prep

Goal: Identify parts of the body
Grammar: Simple present
Academic Strategies: Making predictions, inferring, focused listening
Vocabulary: Parts of the body

Agenda

☐ Discuss visits to the doctor.
☐ Read about Victor's visit to the doctor.
☐ Identify parts of the body.
☐ Practice talking to the doctor.
☐ Use the simple present.
☐ Make a conversation with a doctor.

Resources

Heinle Picture Dictionary: The Human Body, pages 132–133

Pacing

■ 1.5 hour classes   ■ 2.5 hour classes
■ 3+ hour classes

Standards Correlations

CASAS: 0.1.2, 0.1.5, 3.6.1, 3.6.4
CCRS: L1, L2, L3, RI1, RI2, SL1, SL3
ELPS:
S2: Participate in level-appropriate oral and written exchanges of information, ideas, and analyses, in various social and academic contexts, responding to peer, audience, or reader comments and questions.

Warm-up and Review   7–10 mins. ■■■■

Ask students if they like going to the doctor. Ask where they go if they have a medical problem. Write prompts on the board such as: *the emergency room*, *the doctor's office*, and *a clinic*. Ask students why they go to the doctor. They may suggest ailments or illnesses that are generally related to specific body parts. Write the body parts they mention on the board. Then ask them to point to these parts of their bodies as you say them.

Introduction   10–15 mins. ■■■■

Write *body* on the board and explain or elicit the meaning. Then point to different parts of your body and see if students can name them. State the goal: *Today, we will identify parts of the body.*

Presentation 1   15–20 mins. ■■■■

Ask students how often they go to the doctor. Take a class poll. Elicit what a doctor usually says or what questions they ask. Write students' ideas on the board. If question forms are provided incorrectly, write correct forms without drawing attention to errors.

A PREDICT **Look at the photo. Who is Victor talking to? What is the problem? Then read about Victor.** 🎧

Tell students to cover the text in **A** and look at the photo of Victor together. Ask the questions in the direction line and any other questions you consider appropriate. Have students predict what the problem might be or decide if Victor is just there for a checkup. Write their predictions on the board. Then have them read the text and find out if they were right. Clarify any vocabulary doubts. Point out the note on prescriptions. Then play the audio and ask students to follow along as they listen.

Practice 1   7–10 mins. ■■■■

B **Read the statements. Choose *True* or *False*.**

Give students a limited time to do the exercise individually.

BEST PRACTICE

Timed Tasks

Sometimes giving students a limited time to do a task will help them to stay focused and on task. It is good practice to regularly give students a time limit for tasks.

In reading, some students may have the false impression that reading slowly is better than reading quickly. Timed tasks force them to work quickly.

Evaluation 1   3–5 mins. ■■■■

Check the answers to **B**.

Presentation 2   20–25 mins. ■■■■

C INFER **Victor says, "I hurt all over." Which body parts does he mean? Make a list.**

Ask students to make their lists individually. Have volunteers share their answers with the class.

Note: Life Online note will be addressed on page 147a.

Read the information with the class and explain any new vocabulary. Check students' understanding by asking if it is a good idea to look on the internet when you are sick and why it might be dangerous.

Life ONLINE

Workplace Focus
Exercise D: Complete tasks as assigned.

D Label the parts of the body.

Point out the singular and plural forms of the body parts, but only use the singular forms in the presentation. Go over each word and its pronunciation. You may want to give a mini lesson on the *th* sound (/θ/).

Pronunciation   **Final /θ/**

/θ/ is the symbol for voiceless *th*, as in *mouth* and *teeth*. This sound is problematic for many students. Some languages, for example, some dialects of Spanish, have similar sounds that are represented by different letters. Many languages don't have the voiceless *th* sound at all.

To produce this sound properly, it is important to teach two things. First, teach the point of articulation. An easy way to do this is to exaggerate the articulation by asking students to bite the tip of their tongue. Most students won't have trouble with this. The second part is to ask students to attempt to blow air out of their mouths before releasing the tongue. They should build up air pressure and then release the tongue.

Final consonants are very important in English. When speaking words in isolation and at the end of phrases or sentences, the point of articulation is released, and in most cases, the mouth is open. In other languages where the final consonant isn't as important, the final point of articulation is not immediately released and the mouth is closed. Help students see that it is important to release the tongue to finish the /θ/ sound.

E Listen to patients talk to the doctor. What hurts? Complete the sentences. 🎧

Play the audio. If necessary, pause after each conversation and discuss it before you go on to the next one. Have students complete the sentences. Then play the audio again without pausing and check answers as a class.

Listening Script

1. **Cristela:** *Doctor, thank you for seeing me on such short notice.*
   Doctor: *What seems to be the problem?*
   Cristela: *Well, I'm having trouble with my hand.*
   Doctor: *What do you mean, trouble?*
   Cristela: *My hand is very stiff in the morning. I work at a computer, and it is getting very difficult to do my work.*

2. **Doctor:** *How are you today, Roberto?*
   Roberto: *I'm fine except my leg hurts all the time.*
   Doctor: *I see. Let's check it out. Where does it hurt?*
   Roberto: *My leg hurts right here near the knee.*
   Doctor: *We should probably take some X-rays.*

3. **Doctor:** *Well, Jianyu, it seems like you're here every week these days.*
   Jianyu: *I guess so, Doctor. My head is killing me.*
   Doctor: *I know that you were here last week because of your neck. Did the prescription help?*
   Jianyu: *Not at all. It seems to be getting worse.*

Practice 2   7–10 mins.

F Listen. Practice the conversation with a partner. Then make new conversations using the words in D. 🎧

Play the audio and ask students to listen as they read. Note that students are learning clarification skills as well as new vocabulary here. Show them how the intonation rises with the clarification question. Model the conversation with a student, pointing to a different part of the body for the student to say. Put students in pairs to practice. Monitor and help students with their pronunciation and intonation.

Evaluation 2   5–7 mins.
Ask volunteers to perform their conversations in front of the class.

D Label the parts of the body.

arm(s)	chest	eye(s)	hand(s)	leg(s)	neck	stomach
back	ear(s)	foot (feet)	head	mouth	nose	tooth (teeth)

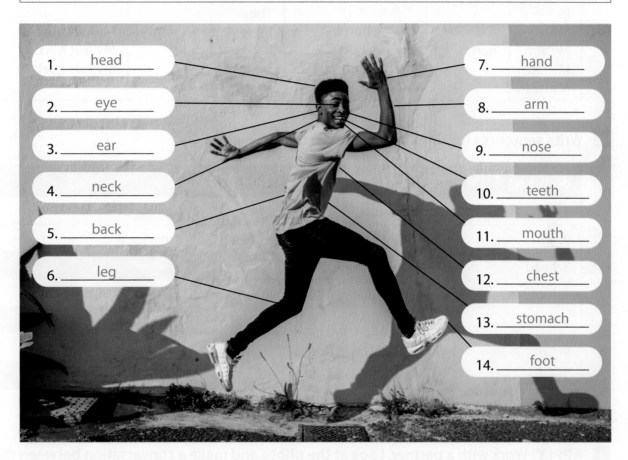

1. ___head___
2. ___eye___
3. ___ear___
4. ___neck___
5. ___back___
6. ___leg___
7. ___hand___
8. ___arm___
9. ___nose___
10. ___teeth___
11. ___mouth___
12. ___chest___
13. ___stomach___
14. ___foot___

E Listen to patients talk to the doctor. What hurts? Complete the sentences. 🎧

1. **Cristela:** Doctor, my ___hand___ hurts.

2. **Roberto:** Doctor, my ___leg___ hurts.

3. **Jianyu:** Doctor, my ___head___ and ___neck___ hurt.

F Listen. Practice the conversation with a partner. Then make new conversations using the words in D. 🎧

Doctor: What is the problem today?

Patient: My leg hurts.

Doctor: Your leg?

Patient: Yes, my leg.

G Study the chart.

Simple Present					
Subject	**Verb**	**Example Sentence**	**Subject**	**Verb**	**Example Sentence**
It My leg My arm My foot My head	hurts	My leg **hurts**. My arm **hurts**. My head **hurts**.	They My legs My arms My feet My ears	hurt	My legs **hurt**. My feet **hurt**. My ears **hurt**.

H Write sentences for singular and plural subjects.

Body Part	Singular	Plural
1. leg	My leg hurts.	My legs hurt.
2. arm	My arm hurts.	My arms hurt.
3. head	My head hurts.	
4. foot	My foot hurts.	My feet hurt.
5. back	My back hurts.	
6. eye	My eye hurts.	My eyes hurt.
7. nose	My nose hurts.	
8. ear	My ear hurts.	My ears hurt.

I **APPLY** Work with a partner. Look at the photo and make a conversation between the man in the photo and his doctor after this accident. What hurts now?

A man falls off his scooter at a skate park.

Presentation 3

10–15 mins. ■■■□

G Study the chart.

Some students might be confused by *my*. Review the possessive adjective and help students to see that the noun is the word that follows.

Ask the class to help you finish sentences you begin with *My leg . . .* or *My feet . . .*

Workplace Focus

Exercise H: Collect and organize information.

Practice 3

7–10 mins. ■□□□

H Write sentences for singular and plural subjects.

Point out that the plural spaces for the words *head*, *back*, and *nose* are shaded in because we don't use those words in the plural with *my*. Have students complete the sentences, then compare with a partner.

BEST PRACTICE

Conversations

Some techniques to add variety to conversations that we have discussed include the following:

- Working with a different partner
- Conversation chaining in a group
- Conversation cards
- Inside / outside circle
- Two lines with students moving one space after each conversation

Evaluation 3

7–10 mins. ■□□□

Invite volunteers to complete the chart on the board with the missing sentences.

Workplace Focus

Exercise I: Interact appropriately with team members.

Application

7–10 mins. ■■■□

I APPLY Work with a partner. Look at the photo and make a conversation between the man in the photo and his doctor after this accident. What hurts now?

Look at the photo together and have students describe what is happening. Write their ideas on the board, providing vocabulary as needed. Remember that at this point they don't need to express their ideas in complete sentences. Pair students with different partners to create their conversations. Monitor and help with vocabulary as needed. Model pronunciation and intonation for them if necessary. Have volunteers perform their conversation for the class.

Instructor's Notes

_____
_____
_____
_____
_____
_____
_____
_____
_____
_____
_____
_____
_____
_____
_____
_____
_____
_____

At-a-Glance Prep

Goal: Identify illnesses and health problems
Grammar: Simple present and negative: *have*
Pronunciation: Intonation: information and clarification questions
Academic Strategies: Focused listening, analyzing information, making comparisons
Vocabulary: Symptoms and illnesses

Agenda
☐ Practice identifying body parts.
☐ Identify illnesses and health problems.
☐ Discuss colds and the flu.
☐ Describe symptoms.
☐ List ailments.

Resources
Heinle Picture Dictionary: Hurting and Healing, pages 136–137; Illnesses, Injuries, Symptoms, and Disabilities, pages 134–135

Pacing
■ 1.5 hour classes   ■ 2.5 hour classes
■ 3+ hour classes

Standards Correlations
CASAS: 0.1.2, 0.1.5, 3.6.2, 3.6.3, 7.2.3, 7.4.5
CCRS: L1, L2, L3, RI1, RI2, SL1, SL3
ELPS:
S10: Demonstrate command of the conventions of standard English to communicate in level-appropriate speech and writing.

Warm-up and Review   7–10 mins. ■■■
Ask students to quiz one another on body parts. In groups, have one person stand up and point to different parts of their body. The other students in the group call out the body part. After a few minutes, ask the person standing to call out a body part and have the other students point to it on themselves.

BEST PRACTICE
Group Drills
Group drills like the one described above can be very effective practice. Have the drill leader stand up so you can easily see that all groups are on task. Ask the leader to do five or six items and sit down. Continue with another student as the leader. Repeat until all students have taken the leader role.

Introduction   5–7 mins. ■■■
Write *cold* and *flu* on the board. Ask individuals how many times a year they catch colds. Ask them why they get colds and what symptoms they get. Write the word *symptoms* on the board. Give some examples, such as *runny nose*. State the goal: *Today, we will identify illnesses and health problems.*

Presentation 1   15–20 mins. ■■■

A Match the health problems to the photos.
Say each word. Pay close attention to how students pronounce *headache*. Some will try to say the *ch* as it is usually pronounced. Before going over the meanings, have students try to do this activity by themselves. Encourage them to use dictionaries as needed. Check answers as a class and clarify any doubts.

> **Intonation Information and Clarification Questions**
> Point out the pronunciation note and play the audio. Have students repeat each question and help them notice the difference in intonation.

Listening Script
Intonation is the rising and falling of our voices as we speak. In information questions that start with words like what, where, *or* when, *the voice rises and then falls at the end.*
What's the matter?
What's the matter?

We ask clarification questions to help us understand something. With these questions, the voice rises at the end.
The flu?
The flu?

B Listen. Practice the conversation with a partner.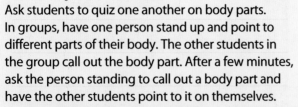
Play the audio. Tell students to read as they listen. Model the conversation with a student using a different symptom. Then ask two students to model the conversation. Have students practice with a partner. Correct students' intonation as needed.

LESSON 2

What's the Problem?

GOAL ▶ Identify illnesses and health problems

A Match the health problems to the photos.

cough	fever	headache	loss of taste / smell	runny nose	sore throat

1.

runny nose

2.

fever

3.

headache

4.

sore throat

5.

cough

6.

loss of taste / smell

B Listen. Practice the conversation with a partner. 🎧

Doctor: What's the matter?

Miguel: I feel very sick. I have a terrible sore throat.

Doctor: It sounds like you might have the flu.

Miguel: The flu?

Doctor: Yes, the flu.

Intonation 🎧

Information Questions

What's the matter?

Clarification Questions

The flu?

C Listen to each conversation. Choose the correct problem. 🎧

1. ~~sore throat~~   runny nose   fever   headache

2. cough   ~~fever~~   headache   loss of taste / smell

3. runny nose   ~~loss of taste / smell~~   fever   headache

4. loss of taste / smell   cough   fever   ~~runny nose~~

D ANALYZE Read about colds and the flu. Then complete the chart. 🎧

Every year people have both colds and the flu. What is the difference? Usually a person with a cold or the flu has a runny nose and a sore throat. A person with a cold sometimes has a low fever, but a person with the flu has a high fever and body aches. Cold symptoms also include sneezing. Flu symptoms can include a dry cough.

Common Cold Symptoms	Common Flu Symptoms
low fever	high fever
sore throat	sore throat
runny nose	runny nose
sneezing	body aches
	dry cough

E COMPARE Complete the diagram using the information in D.

Colds   **Both**   **The Flu**

low fever   sore throat   high fever

sneezing   runny nose   body aches

          dry cough

Practice 1

7–10 mins. ■■■□

C Listen to each conversation. Choose the correct problem. 🎧

Explain to students that they will hear four conversations between doctors and patients. Play the first conversation in the audio and pause to identify the answer together (they are already familiar with this one from **B**). Play the rest of the conversations and have students compare answers with a partner. Remind them that they don't need to understand everything. Play the audio one or more additional times, pausing after each conversation for students to confirm their answers.

Listening Script

1. **Doctor:** *What's the matter?*
   Miguel: *I feel very sick. I have a terrible sore throat.*
   Doctor: *It sounds like you might have the flu.*
   Miguel: *The flu?*
   Doctor: *Yes, the flu.*

2. **Doctor:** *What's the matter?*
   Patient: *I don't know. I'm terribly tired.*
   Doctor: *Do you have any other symptoms?*
   Patient: *Yes, I have a fever.*
   Doctor: *Well, let's examine you. Open up and say, "Aahh."*

3. **Doctor:** *What's the matter?*
   Patient: *I can't smell or taste anything!*
   Doctor: *When did this start?*
   Patient: *About three days ago.*
   Doctor: *You might have COVID-19. We'll give you a test to make sure.*

4. **Doctor:** *What's the matter?*
   Patient: *I have a cold.*
   Doctor: *Maybe I can give you some medicine for that runny nose.*
   Patient: *Yes, I have a terrible runny nose.*

Evaluation 1

3–5 mins. ■■■□

Go over the answers to **C** with the class.

Presentation 2

10–15 mins. ■■■□

Ask students to close their books. Write *cold* and *flu* as headings for two columns on the board. Ask students if they know what the difference is. Talk about some related vocabulary. For example,

remind them what a fever is. Draw a thermometer on the board and ask them what a normal temperature is. Mark it on your thermometer at 98.6˚F. Discuss when students might visit the doctor for a high temperature or take their child to the doctor.

Workplace Focus

Exercises D and E: Collect and organize information.

D ANALYZE Read about colds and the flu. Then complete the chart. 🎧

Go over the chart with students and compare it to what you have on the board. Then have students read the text and complete the chart. Go over any new vocabulary and review the vocabulary students have already learned.

Practice 2

10–15 mins. ■■□□

E COMPARE Complete the diagram using the information in D.

Elicit / remind students what kind of diagram this is and how it works. After students complete the Venn diagram, have them go back to the previous page and practice the conversation in **B** with a partner, inserting the symptoms and diagnosing the problem.

Evaluation 2

5–7 mins. ■■□□

Ask volunteers to perform the conversation in front of the class.

BEST PRACTICE

More Ideas for Using Venn Diagrams

Use Venn diagrams on occasion as an icebreaker or a way to introduce a lesson. Randomly arrange students in small groups and have them make a three-circle Venn diagram.

- Students can talk about themselves and things they like. Then have them write ways they are like other group members and ways they are unique.

- Students can also discuss opinions about the topic at hand. Ask a key topic-related question. Then have group members organize opinions they share and do not share.

Presentation 3 10–15 mins. ■■■

Act out illnesses or symptoms. Start by holding your hands to your head in pain. Write on the board: *What's the matter?* Encourage students to ask you the question. Your response will be: *I have a headache.* Repeat with other symptoms and then ask students to open their books.

F Study the charts.

Go over the simple present again. Review the verb *have.* Concentrate on the negative form. Act out an illness or symptom again. Divide the class in two. One side of the class will ask what your problem is: *What's the matter?* The other side will say what you don't have: *You don't have a stomachache.* Allow other students to act something out. Then extend the practice to the third-person singular.

Practice 3 7–10 mins. ■

G Read the symptoms. Then complete the sentences with the correct form of *have.*

Have students complete the sentences individually.

Evaluation 3 7–10 mins. ■

Ask volunteers to write their completed sentences on the board. Check as a class.

Application 10–15 mins. ■■■

H What other illnesses do you know? Use a dictionary and list illnesses and symptoms in your notebook.

Students can do this in pairs or small groups if they prefer. Set a time limit (7–10 minutes). Then have groups pool their lists and create a chart on the board of illnesses and symptoms.

BEST PRACTICE

Dictionaries

At times, we need to be careful not to introduce too much vocabulary at once. However, studying the language of health and illnesses is not one of those occasions. This vocabulary will be very meaningful for students, and they may need to use it without much notice.

Using dictionaries effectively is a very useful strategy for students both in and out of the classroom, so it is helpful to provide opportunities for them to practice this skill.

Instructor's Notes

_____
_____
_____
_____
_____
_____
_____
_____
_____
_____
_____
_____
_____
_____
_____
_____
_____
_____
_____
_____
_____
_____
_____
_____

F **Study the charts.**

Simple Present: *Have*		
Subject	*Have*	**Example Sentence**
I / You / We / They	have	I **have** a headache. You **have** a sore throat.
He / She	has	She **has** a stomachache. He **has** a fever.

Negative Simple Present: *Have*			
Subject	**Negative**	*Have*	**Example Sentence**
I / You / We / They	do not (don't)	have	I **do not have** a headache. You **don't have** a sore throat.
He / She	does not (doesn't)	have	She **does not have** a stomachache. He **doesn't have** a fever.

G **Read the symptoms. Then complete the sentences with the correct form of *have*.**

Armando
headache,
backache, fever

Yusuf
sore throat,
headache, cough

Tina
backache,
stomachache, sore throat

1. Armando _____has_____ a backache.

2. Armando and Yusuf ____do not / don't have____ stomachaches.

3. Yusuf _____has_____ a cough.

4. Tina ___does not / doesn't have___ a fever.

5. Armando and Tina _____have_____ backaches.

6. Yusuf and Tina _____have_____ sore throats.

H **What other illnesses do you know? Use a dictionary and list illnesses and symptoms in your notebook.**

What Should I Do?

GOAL ▶ Give advice

A Look at the pictures. Study the words and phrases.

pain reliever

cough syrup

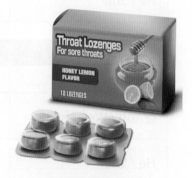
throat lozenges

| go to the doctor | rest | take pain relievers |
| quarantine | take cough syrup | take throat lozenges |

B EVALUATE What do you do when you have these symptoms? Complete the chart.

Answers will vary.

	Take pain relievers.	Rest.	Take cough syrup.	Take throat lozenges.	Go to the doctor.	Quarantine.
fever						
cough						
headache	✓					
sore throat						
stomachache						
backache						
feel tired						

C Practice the conversation. Then use information from **B** to make new conversations.

Patient: I have a headache.

Doctor: Take pain relievers.

Patient: OK, thanks.

At-a-Glance Prep

Goal: Give advice
Grammar: *Should* and *should not* for advice
Academic Strategies: Evaluating, focused listening
Vocabulary: Medications

Agenda

☐ List illnesses and symptoms.
☐ Evaluate remedies.
☐ Read about a doctor's appointment.
☐ Read medicine labels.
☐ Give advice.

Resources

Heinle Picture Dictionary: Pharmacy,
　　pages 142–143

Pacing

■ 1.5 hour classes　■ 2.5 hour classes
■ 3+ hour classes

Standards Correlations

CASAS: 0.1.2, 0.1.3, 0.1.5, 3.3.1, 3.3.2, 3.3.4
CCRS: L1, L2, L3, RI1, RI2, RI3, SL1, SL3, SLK2
ELPS:
S2: Participate in level-appropriate oral and written exchanges of information, ideas, and analyses, in various social and academic contexts, responding to peer, audience, or reader comments and questions.
S10: Demonstrate command of the conventions of standard English to communicate in level-appropriate speech and writing.

Warm-up and Review　10–15 mins. ■■■

To review illnesses and symptoms, elicit what students remember from the lists they came up with in **H** from Lesson 2. Write the words on the board to clarify spelling doubts and practice the pronunciation of each item.

Introduction　5–7 mins. ■■■

Mime different illnesses. Encourage students to ask the question: *What's the matter?* This time, respond with the problem and ask what you should do. Answers will vary, but some students may suggest medicines you should take. State the goal: *Today, we will learn how to give advice.*

Presentation 1　20–25 mins. ■■■■

Ask students to open their books and look at the three medicines closely. See if students know any brand names for the items.

A　Look at the pictures. Study the words and phrases.

Go over the words and phrases in the box. Help students with the pronunciation. Make sure students understand the new vocabulary. Mime ailments or symptoms that go along with the words and phrases. Encourage students to make suggestions using the new words.

BEST PRACTICE

Overcorrection

Be careful not to overcorrect in the presentation stage. We suggested earlier in this book that you should only correct what students are learning at the moment. In this case, you might correct the pronunciation of the new words. A good way to do this is to wait until several students have mispronounced an item. Then discuss with the entire class the pronunciation point at hand.

Workplace Focus

Exercise B: Collect and organize information.

B　EVALUATE　What do you do when you have these symptoms? Complete the chart.

Ask students to complete the chart on their own and then, as a class, go over the answers.

Practice 1　7–10 mins. ■■■

C　Practice the conversation. Then use information from B to make new conversations.

Model the conversation with a student. Repeat the conversation with a different symptom. Have the class provide suggestions if the student struggles. Put students in pairs to practice. Monitor and make sure they are substituting information to use the new vocabulary and that they are taking turns giving advice.

Evaluation 1　5–7 mins. ■■■

Ask volunteers to perform their conversations in front of the class.

Presentation 2   30–40 mins. ■■■

Write *prescription* and *over-the-counter* on the board. Help students understand the meaning of both terms. Ask: *Where can you get a prescription? Where do you get over-the-counter medicine?*

Read the Life Online note with students and help them understand the concepts. Explain the meaning of *comparison shop* by writing three prices on the board and asking which one is the best price. Elicit / Explain *coupons* and *discounts*. Ask students if they have used this kind of website or app and how they choose where to buy their prescription medicines.

Life ONLINE

D   Read about Cristela. 🎧

Have students read the paragraph. Then ask a few comprehension questions. For example: *What is Cristela doing? What's the matter?*, etc. Write *label* on the board and elicit the meaning. Play the audio and have students read the text again as they listen.

E   Read the statements. Choose *True* or *False*.

Have students complete this activity individually to check their understanding. Then check answers as a class. Have students identify which sentence in the text in **D** helped them choose each answer.

F   Read the labels.

Make sure students understand the labels completely. They need to understand every word. Terms that may be new include *tablet*, *ml*, and *as needed*.

Practice 2   7–10 mins. ■■

G   Listen to Cristela reading the medicine labels. Write each medicine from F in the order you hear it. 🎧

Remind students not to worry about understanding everything. Ask them what information they should focus on listening for. Play the audio. Play it again, pausing after each medicine. Play the audio a few additional times if necessary. Allow students to discuss their answers between plays.

Listening Script

Well, let me see. The doctor says that I need to take this medicine for the next few days. Here it says, "Take one lozenge as needed for sore throat pain." I'll probably need that. My throat really hurts. I will especially need it at work when I'm talking to everyone. This one says to take 10 milliliters every four hours. Let me see, that means I should take the first dose when I wake up around 8:00 and then at noon and again at 4:00. I will take the last dose at 8:00 p.m. This last one reads, "Take two tablets every four to six hours." I'll do that until my headache goes away. I hope that is soon. I really don't like to be sick.

Evaluation 2   5–7 mins. ■■

Go over the answers with students and play the audio a few more times to confirm the answers as needed.

BEST PRACTICE
Focused Listening Activities

Before
Explain to students that they should not concentrate on every word they hear. However, go through and identify vocabulary that students may not know. Decide if the vocabulary is important to address before the listening activity and pre-teach if necessary.

During
Play the audio once for understanding and then again so students can complete the activity. Repeat the audio as many times as needed. Pause if necessary. Ask students to write relevant details.

After
Ask students to share and compare their answers. Then have them make a summary of what they heard and make a list of any important vocabulary in their notebooks.

D Read about Cristela. 🎧

Cristela is talking to her doctor. She is sick. She has a bad headache and sore throat. The doctor is giving Cristela a prescription for some medicine. She needs to read the labels on the medicine carefully. The doctor is helping her understand them.

Life ONLINE

Comparison Shop for Medicine

Different pharmacies can have very different prices for prescription medicines. There are websites and apps that can help you find the best prices in your area. Some of these services also give you coupons and discounts on your prescriptions.

E Read the statements. Choose *True* or *False*.

	True	False
1. Cristela has a backache.	True	(False)
2. The doctor gives Cristela a prescription.	(True)	False
3. Cristela should read the medicine labels.	(True)	False

F Read the labels.

DIRECTIONS

Take two tablets every four to six hours.

DIRECTIONS

Take 10 ml every four hours.

DIRECTIONS

Take one lozenge as needed for sore throat pain.

G Listen to Cristela reading the medicine labels. Write each medicine from F in the order you hear it. 🎧

1. ___throat lozenge___   2. ___cough syrup___   3. ___pain reliever___

H **Study the charts.**

Should for Advice			
Subject	**Should**	**Base Verb**	**Example Sentence**
I / You / He / She We / They	should	rest	You **should rest**.
		stay	He **should stay** home.
		see	They **should see** a doctor.
		take	I **should take** a pain reliever.

Should Not for Advice			
Subject	**Should Not**	**Base Verb**	**Example Sentence**
I / You / He / She We / They	should not (shouldn't)	drive	You **shouldn't drive** and take this medicine.
		drink	She **should not drink** alcohol with this medicine.
		go	We **shouldn't go** out.

I **Read each problem and give advice. Use *should* and *shouldn't*.** Answers will vary.

1. Roberto has a cold.

   He should take cold medicine, and he shouldn't go out.

2. Anh and Nam have colds.

   They _____.

3. Michael has a sore throat.

   He _____.

4. Ayumi has a fever.

   She _____.

5. Oscar feels tired.

   He _____.

6. Marina has a stomachache.

   She _____.

J **APPLY** **Work in a group. Make a list of medications you have in your home and what they are good for. Should you buy anything else?**

Presentation 3
10–15 mins. ■■■

Mime a headache, a sore throat, and a cough and prompt students to give you advice.

H Study the charts.

Go over the charts with the class. Help students understand that we use *should* with another verb to express advice and that *should* doesn't change form. In some languages, the equivalent of the modal *should* is a regular verb. This may confuse students. Make sure they understand that the base verb doesn't change either. Help students with the pronunciation of the negative *shouldn't*.

BEST PRACTICE

Grammar Exposure

Students at this level are not always ready to acquire certain grammar points. *Stand Out* is designed to provide a variety of opportunities for students to use key grammar structures throughout their language-learning experience. At this level, students will learn structures, but they will often forget them until the structures are brought up in another context. This recycling process prepares students for the time they are ready to acquire the structures, meaning that they use them correctly in speech and in writing without thinking about the forms themselves.

Practice 3
10–15 mins. ■

I Read each problem and give advice. Use *should* and *shouldn't*.

Read the example as a class to make sure students understand what they need to do. Monitor as students write their advice and help as needed. If students seem to be struggling, have them continue the activity in pairs.

Evaluation 3
5–10 mins. ■

Ask students to write their sentences on the board. Make any necessary corrections as a class.

Application
15–20 mins. ■■■

J APPLY Work in a group. Make a list of medications you have in your home and what they are good for. Should you buy anything else?

Go over the instructions. Model the exercise by writing a few items on the board and asking the class what other medications you should buy. Put students in groups to carry out the activity. Try to ensure that students don't always work with the same people in group activities. Monitor and help as needed. Have groups get together to compare their lists and say what else they should buy and why.

Instructor's Notes

_____

_____

_____

_____

_____

_____

_____

_____

_____

_____

_____

_____

_____

_____

_____

_____

_____

_____

_____

At-a-Glance Prep

Goal: Ask for information
Grammar: *Wh-* questions, prepositions of location
Academic Strategies: Predicting, focused listening, interpreting maps
Vocabulary: Hospital vocabulary

Agenda

☐ Review symptoms and medicines.
☐ Listen to and practice an emergency call.
☐ Interpret a hospital map.
☐ Ask for information at a hospital.
☐ Ask and answer information questions.

Resources

Heinle Picture Dictionary: Hospital, pages 138–139

Pacing

■ 1.5 hour classes   ■ 2.5 hour classes
■ 3+ hour classes

Standards Correlations

CASAS: 0.1.2, 0.1.5, 2.1.2, 2.2.1, 2.5.1, 7.4.4, 7.7.3
CCRS: L1, L2, L3, RI1, RI3, SL1, SL3, W1, W3
ELPS:
S5: Conduct research and evaluate and communicate findings to answer questions or solve problems.
S10: Demonstrate command of the conventions of standard English to communicate in level-appropriate speech and writing.

Warm-up and Review   10–15 mins. ■■◻

Ask students what common illnesses and symptoms they take medicine for. List them on the board. Then ask students to complete the chart below about themselves and four classmates.

Name:	
Symptom	**Medicine**
Headache	
Stomachache	
Backache	
Cold	
Sore throat	
Fever	

Introduction   5 mins. ■■■

Ask students if they have been to a hospital before. Ask if anyone has had to stay overnight and if they liked the food. Ask what questions they might ask in a hospital. State the goal: *Today, we will learn how to ask for information at a hospital.*

Presentation 1   25–30 mins. ■■■

Write *911* on the board. Ask when you should call 911. Give hypothetical situations to elicit discussion; for example:

- You have a cold.
- There is a fire.
- A friend is not breathing.
- You had a car accident.

A PREDICT Look at the photo. What is the problem? Listen and practice the conversation. 🎧

Have students say what they see and what they think the emergency might be. Play the audio. Play it again, pausing after each line for students to repeat. Help students to practice the conversation with appropriate rhythm and intonation.

B Study the chart.

Go over each question and answer and make sure students understand them. Have them practice the questions. Remind them about falling intonation in information questions.

Workplace Focus

Exercise C: Interpret and communicate information.

Practice 1   15–20 mins. ■■■

C Make new conversations with the information in the chart.

Go over the information in the chart and clarify any vocabulary questions. Model the conversation with a student; then have two students model it. Put students in pairs to practice. Have students use the chart as a guide. Students may also substitute their own ideas and addresses.

Evaluation 1   7–10 mins. ■■■

Ask volunteers to perform a conversation in front of the class.

There's an Emergency!

GOAL ▶ Ask for information

A **PREDICT** **Look at the photo. What is the problem? Listen and practice the conversation.** 🎧

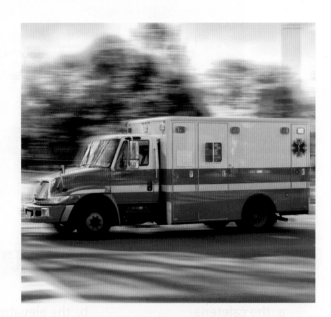

Operator:	What's the emergency?
Victor:	There's a car accident.
Operator:	Where's the accident?
Victor:	It's on Fourth and Bush.
Operator:	What's your name?
Victor:	It's Victor Karaskov.
Operator:	Is anyone hurt?
Victor:	Yes. Please send an ambulance.

B **Study the chart.**

Wh- Questions				
Question Word	**Be**		**Example Question**	**Example Answer**
Who		calling?	Who's calling?	It's Victor Karaskov.
What	is	your name? the emergency?	What's your name? What's the emergency?	It's Victor Karaskov. There's a car accident.
Where		the accident?	Where's the accident?	It's on Fourth and Bush.

C **Make new conversations with the information in the chart.**

Student A: 911. What's the emergency?

Student B: _____.

Student A: Where is it?

Student B: It's _____.

Student A: What's your name?

Student B: It's _____.

Emergency	Location
There's a car accident.	on Fourth and Bush
A tree fell on a car.	at 333 Main Street
A house is on fire.	at 237 Broadway

D **INTERPRET** **Look at the map. Then match the places to the correct symbols.**

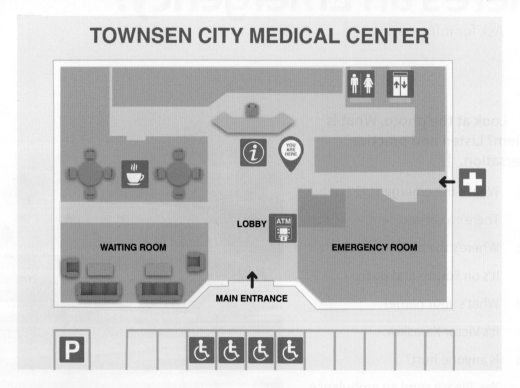

a. the cafeteria

b. the elevators

c. the emergency entrance

d. accessible parking

e. the information desk

f. the restrooms

1. _____f_____

2. _____d_____

3. _____e_____

4. _____c_____

5. _____a_____

6. _____b_____

is / are
Where **is** the information desk?
   It is here.
Where **are** the restrooms?
   They are here.

E **Practice the conversations with a partner. Then ask new questions about the map.**

Student A: Excuse me, where is the information desk?

Student B: It's here. (Student B points to the map.)

Student B: Excuse me, where are the elevators?

Student A: They are here. (Student A points to the map.)

Presentation 2   10–15 mins. ■■■▫

D INTERPRET Look at the map. Then match the places to the correct symbols.

Do this activity as a class. Look at the map of the hospital and discuss any new vocabulary with students, such as *lobby* and *waiting room*. Test their comprehension to find out which words are new for them by asking where specific hospital areas or features are located. Ask students to point to the sites on the map in their books . Then have them match the places to the symbols. Check answers as a class. Review the note on the plural and singular use of the verb *be*.

Workplace Focus
Exercise E: Interpret and communicate information.

Practice 2   7–10 mins. ■■▫

E Practice the conversations with a partner. Then ask new questions about the map.

Model the conversations with a student; then have two students model them. Remind students about intonation in information questions. Put them in pairs to practice.

To make the activity more challenging, ask students to use prepositions of location, such as *next to*, *around the corner from*, and *between*. Refer them to page 127 if necessary.

Evaluation 2   7–10 mins. ■■▫
Observe the pair activity. Ask volunteers who are using prepositions in their responses to perform the conversation in front of the class.

BEST PRACTICE

Mixing Pairs
Pair work is an excellent way for students to practice their English. They benefit from learning from other students. Pair work is also a good approach for large classes. It gives everyone the opportunity to speak. Nevertheless, some students may dominate the exchange. Shy or weak students may talk less and strong students may talk more. Teachers can avoid this potential problem by giving some thought to who students work with and mixing them up. Students shouldn't always work with the same partner.

Instructor's Notes

Presentation 3   10–15 mins. ■■■

Briefly review prepositions of location. Write a few new phrases on the board including *near* and *down the hall*. Go over the map on the previous page using these new words. Then ask students where the waiting room is. This will help prepare them for the listening.

F   Listen to the conversations. Complete the sentences. 🎧

Tell students they are going to listen to conversations about where places are in the hospital. Play the audio. Play it again, pausing after each conversation for students to write their answers. Have students compare with a partner. Then play the audio one or more additional times to check the answers.

Listening Script

1. **Visitor 1:** *Excuse me. Where are the elevators? I can't seem to find them.*
   Staff: *They are down the hall, next to the restrooms.*
   Visitor 1: *Where?*
   Staff: *Go that way, down the hall and the elevators are next to the restrooms.*
   Visitor 1: *Thanks.*

2. **Staff:** *Can I help you?*
   Visitor 2: *Yes. I am looking for the emergency entrance. Is it close by?*
   Staff: *Yes, it is. It's down that hallway, near the emergency room.*
   Visitor 2: *Where? I don't understand.*
   Staff: *Let me walk you there.*
   Visitor 2: *OK, thanks.*

3. **Visitor 3:** *Excuse me, where is the cafeteria?*
   Staff: *It's right over there, across from the waiting room.*
   Visitor 3: *Oh, there it is. Thanks!*

4. **Visitor 4:** *Can you help me?*
   Staff: *What can I do for you?*
   Visitor 4: *I am looking for the ATM.*
   Staff: *It's here in the lobby, near the main entrance.*
   Visitor 4: *Oh, I see it over there. Thank you!*
   Staff: *You're welcome.*

Workplace Focus

Exercises G and H: Interpret and communicate information.

Practice 3   7–10 mins. ■

G   Work with a partner. Take turns asking for information. Ask about the elevators, the emergency entrance, the cafeteria, and the ATM.

Ask two students to model the exchange. Then have students practice in pairs.

Evaluation 3   5–7 mins. ■

Observe the activity and have volunteers perform one of their conversations for the class.

Application   20–30 mins. ■■■

H   CREATE   In groups of four, prepare a role-play that takes place at the hospital information desk.

Put students in groups. Number them 1 through 4 in each group and have them read their roles. Clarify any doubts. Monitor as students work, helping as needed. Encourage them to practice so they can do the role-play without referring to their notes. Call on volunteers to present their role-plays to the class.

Workplace Focus

Exercise I: Apply technology.

I   Find a hospital map online. Share the information you find with the class.

Elicit the names of local hospitals or other hospitals students have heard of and write them on the board. Then have students go online to carry out their search. When they have found a map, have them show it to the class and say where things are using prepositions. Encourage students to ask the presenter questions with *Where is / are . . . ?*

F Listen to the conversations. Complete the sentences. 🎧

1. The elevators are next to the restrooms_____.

2. The emergency entrance is near the emergency room_____.

3. The cafeteria is across from the waiting room_____.

4. The ATM is in the lobby_____.

G Work with a partner. Take turns asking for information. Ask about the elevators, the emergency entrance, the cafeteria, and the ATM.

Student A: Where are the restrooms?

Student B: They are next to the elevators.

H **CREATE** In groups of four, prepare a role-play that takes place at the hospital information desk.

Student 1: You work at the information desk.

Student 2: You are very sick.

Student 3: You are a family member of a patient.

Student 4: You have an emergency.

I Find a hospital map online. Share the information you find with the class.

The Rockefeller University Hospital in New York, New York

Staying Healthy

GOAL ▶ Develop exercise goals

A Look at the photo. Why is exercise important? Read about exercise. 🎧

We need to exercise. It is good for our hearts, muscles, flexibility, and weight. Everyone should exercise. People can run, swim, clean the house, or work in the yard. Doctors say we should exercise every day.

B Match the pictures to the words that describe them.

___d___ 1. muscles ___c___ 2. weight ___b___ 3. flexibility ___a___ 4. heart

a.  b.  c.  d.

At-a-Glance Prep

Goal: Develop exercise goals
Grammar: Verb + infinitive
Academic Strategies: Analyzing a pie chart, focused listening, doing a survey
Vocabulary: Exercise and health vocabulary

Agenda

☐ Write questions with *who, what, where.*
☐ Describe healthy practices.
☐ Talk about exercise.
☐ Read and make a pie chart.
☐ Make goals with *want to.*
☐ Do a survey.

Resources

Heinle Picture Dictionary: Daily Activities, pages 34–35

Pacing

■ 1.5 hour classes ■ 2.5 hour classes
■ 3+ hour classes

Standards Correlations

CASAS: 0.1.2, 0.1.5, 3.5.9, 6.7.4, 7.1.1
CCRS: L1, L2, L3, RI1, SL3, SLK2
ELPS:
S10: Demonstrate command of the conventions of standard English to communicate in level-appropriate speech and writing.

Warm-up and Review   15–20 mins. ■■■

Write *who, what,* and *where* on the board. Ask half the class to write questions about an imaginary accident using the three question words. Tell them to imagine that they are 911 operators. Ask the other half to write sentences about an accident. Have them try to do it without their books at first. After they try for a few minutes, let them open their books and improve their questions and sentences. Then ask volunteers to form pairs and role-play a 911 call. Have them stand back to back or on opposite sides of the room.

Introduction   7–10 mins. ■■■

Write the words *healthy* and *unhealthy* on the board and see if students understand what they mean. Ask students about healthy and unhealthy actions. Make a list on the board. State the goal: *Today, we will talk about developing exercise goals.*

Presentation 1   30–35 mins. ■■■

A Look at the photo. Why is exercise important? Read about exercise. 🎧

Have students look at the photo. Ask what the woman is doing and have students describe where she is. Then ask them why they think exercise is important.

Have students read the paragraph silently and underline any words they don't know. Have them try to figure out the meanings by using the context. Then read the paragraph together with the class or play the audio and have students listen as they read. Discuss the new vocabulary together.

B Match the pictures to the words that describe them.

These are difficult words, but from the discussion of the new vocabulary in **A**, students should be able to do this matching. First, ask them to look carefully at each picture. Second, read each word out loud while students listen. Then ask students to write the letters of the pictures next to the words.

Have students compare their answers with a partner. Then ask volunteers to share their answers with the class. Review and discuss as needed.

Instructor's Notes

_____

_____

_____

_____

_____

_____

_____

_____

_____

Workplace Focus
Exercise C: Perform basic computations.

C ANALYZE Study the pie chart and answer the questions.

Go over the pie chart with students. Help them understand how to read it. Ask questions to confirm that they understand. Then have them answer the questions.

Go over students' answers and make sure they understand how to read the pie chart in preparation for the upcoming practice.

Practice 1   10–15 mins.

Ask students to make a pie chart about favorite types of exercise. Write the information you would like them to include in the chart. For example:

running: 10%

swimming: 10%

working in the yard: 5%

going to the gym: 20%

walking: 25%

no exercise: 30%

Evaluation 1   5–10 mins.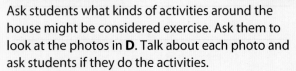

Have a volunteer draw their pie chart on the board and discuss as a class.

Presentation 2   7–10 mins. ■■■

Ask students what kinds of activities around the house might be considered exercise. Ask them to look at the photos in **D**. Talk about each photo and ask students if they do the activities.

BEST PRACTICE

Checking Answers

Many teachers take a traditional approach to going over students' answers. They stand in front of the class, ask students for the answers, and then tell them if they are right or wrong. Although there is nothing wrong with this method, checking answers can be much more interesting and interactive. Here are just a couple of tips:

1. Rather than telling students the correct answers, write them on the board in random order.
2. Allow different groups of students to provide the correct answers.

3. Let the student who answers the question first choose the next person to answer.
4. Have students write all the answers on the board.
5. Ask students to check in pairs first. Then have pairs or individuals give answers to the class.

Practice 2   7–10 mins. ■■■

D Listen. Match the number of the conversation to the correct photo. 🎧

Tell students they will hear four conversations about exercise. Play the audio. Play the audio again, pausing after each conversation for students to write their answers. Have students compare with a partner. Then play the audio a final time for them to confirm.

Listening Script

1. **Woman:** *I'm so tired.*
    Man: *Why?*
    Woman: *I think I need to exercise more. I don't feel very healthy.*
    Man: *I swim every day at the gym. It's great exercise.*
    Woman: *Maybe I'll try that.*

2. **Husband:** *I don't get any exercise.*
    Wife: *Yes, you do.*
    Husband: *What do you mean? I never even leave the house.*
    Wife: *You vacuum every day. That's exercise.*
    Husband: *Oh, I never thought of that.*

3. **Man:** *What do you do for exercise?*
    Woman: *I jog.*
    Man: *What's jogging?*
    Woman: *I run slowly and enjoy nature with my dog.*
    Man: *That sounds great.*

4. **Man:** *I exercise every day.*
    Woman: *Me too.*
    Man: *What do you do?*
    Woman: *I get most of my exercise outside in the yard. Gardening can be good exercise.*
    Man: *Really?*
    Woman: *Sure, why not?*

Evaluation 2   3–5 mins. ■■■

Go over the answers with students. Play the audio one more time to confirm answers if necessary.

C **ANALYZE** Study the pie chart and answer the questions.

How Often Do You Exercise?

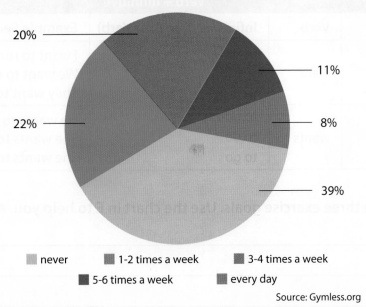

20% —

11%

22% —

8%

39%

■ never   ■ 1-2 times a week   ■ 3-4 times a week
■ 5-6 times a week   ■ every day

Source: Gymless.org

1. What percentage of people don't exercise?

   a. 0%   b. 11%   c. 20%   d. 39%

2. What percentage of people exercise one or two times a week?

   a. 8%   b. 11%   c. 22%   d. 39%

3. What percentage of people exercise every day?

   a. 0%   b. 8%   c. 11%   d. 20%

D Listen. Match the number of the conversation to the correct photo. 🎧

a.

_____3_____

b.

_____1_____

c.

_____2_____

d.

_____4_____

E Study the chart.

Verb + Infinitive			
Subject	**Verb**	**Infinitive (*to* + Base Verb)**	**Example Sentence**
I / You We / They	want	to run to exercise to walk	I **want to run**. We **want to exercise** every day. They **want to walk**.
He / She	wants	to ride to do to go	He **wants to ride** a bicycle. She **wants to do** yard work. She **wants to go** to the gym.

F APPLY **Write three exercise goals. Use the chart in E to help you.** Answers will vary.

1. I want to _____ .

2. _____ .

3. _____ .

G **Ask three classmates about their exercise goals. Write their goals.** Answers will vary.

1. She / He wants to _____ .

2. _____ .

3. _____ .

H SURVEY **Talk to four classmates. Complete the chart.** Answers will vary.

Student A: How much do you exercise every week?

Student B: I exercise about one hour every week.

Hours of Exercise per Week					
Name	**0**	**0–1**	**1–2**	**2–3**	**More Than 3**

Presentation 3
12–15 mins. ■■■

Write the word *goals* on the board. Ask students if they want to make some exercise goals. Ask students what goals might be good to have. Write any interesting comments on the board.

E Study the chart.

Go over the examples in the chart and show students that any verb that follows *want* must be in the infinitive. Write your own exercise goals on the board as an example to help prepare students to do **F** and **G**.

Practice 3
10–15 mins. ■

F APPLY Write three exercise goals. Use the chart in E to help you.

Monitor as students write their goals and check for the correct use of *want* + infinitive. Provide other exercise vocabulary as needed.

G Ask three classmates about their exercise goals. Write their goals.

Elicit the question students can ask. Prompt them by writing *What* on the board. Then write:_____ *your goals?* Have students work in pairs to ask and answer the question and write down each other's goals. Monitor and check their use of the third person singular -*s*.

Evaluation 3
5–10 mins. ■

Ask a few students about their goals and others about their partner's goals. Then have volunteers write their sentences from **F** and **G** on the board.

Workplace Focus

Exercise H: Interpret and communicate information; Interact appropriately with team members.

Application
10–15 mins. ■■■

H SURVEY Talk to four classmates. Complete the chart.

Show students how to do this activity by demonstrating it. Using the example, ask four students and write their answers in your chart. Tell students to use the example conversation as a model. Then have them move around the classroom and carry out their survey. Pool all the results and have students help you create a pie chart on the board to show how many students in the class are in each exercise category.

Instructor's Notes

_____

_____

_____

_____

_____

_____

_____

_____

_____

_____

_____

_____

_____

_____

_____

_____

_____

_____

_____

_____

_____

_____

_____

At-a-Glance Prep

Goal: Identify employment opportunities in health care

Agenda

☐ Interpret an infographic.

☐ Read about pharmacists.

☐ Compare different pharmacist jobs.

☐ Reflect on suitability for health care positions.

☐ Discuss education expectations.

☐ Search online for openings in health care.

Pacing

■ 1.5 hour classes   ■ 2.5 hour classes

■ 3+ hour classes

Standards Correlations

CASAS: 0.1.2, 0.1.5, 4.1.3, 4.1.8, 4.1.9, 6.7.3, 7.4.4, 7.7.3

CCRS: L1, L2, L3, RI1, RI2, RI3, SL1, SL3, W1, W3

ELPS:

S2: Participate in level-appropriate oral and written exchanges of information, ideas, and analyses, in various social and academic contexts, responding to peer, audience, or reader comments and questions.

S5: Conduct research and evaluate and communicate findings to answer questions or solve problems.

In this lesson, students are introduced to employment opportunities in health care. They will analyze an infographic and compare salaries and education requirements for different health care professions. Students will also read about the different kinds of jobs a pharmacist can have. They will reflect on their suitability for a job in health care and their education expectations. Finally, students will carry out an online search for openings in health care in their area.

Warm-up and Review   10–15 mins. ■■■

Write *health care* on the board and have students brainstorm jobs in the field. Write them on the board. Elicit explanations of what each job involves. Remember that students don't need to explain in complete sentences. The objective is simply to activate prior knowledge, so accept any words or phrases they come up with and write them on the board.

Introduction   5–10 mins. ■■■

Find out if any of the students work in health care or know anyone who does. Remind them that throughout *Stand Out*, they will investigate many job possibilities. Write the goal on the board: *Today, we will identify employment opportunities in health care.*

Presentation 1   15–20 mins. ■■■

A INTERPRET Read the infographic on health care professions. Answer the questions.

Go over the infographic together, having students explain what information is being presented (professions, salaries, and education requirements). Explain or have students look up the different professions and review levels of education. Call on different students to say the salaries. Ask: *What is a pharmacy technician's salary?*, etc. Then have them answer the questions and compare with a partner. Go over the answers as a class.

Practice 1   20–25 mins. ■■■

B Study the chart.

Write doctors' and registered nurses' levels of education and salaries on the board and discuss who earns more and who studies for longer. Look at the chart together and make sure students understand the meaning of each sentence.

BEST PRACTICE

Being Informed

When students are looking for a job or career, it is important that they know what information they should be aware of in their research. Knowing about aspects such as salary and education requirements will help them be able to make appropriate decisions regarding study goals, for example. Similarly, being able to compare salaries will be useful in their job searches.

Help students understand that the information they find in each Lesson 6 is directly applicable to their working life and that being informed will help them in their search for a job or career.

LESSON 6

Explore the Workforce

GOAL ▶ Identify employment opportunities in health care

A INTERPRET Read the infographic on health care professions. Answer the questions.

1. What degree does a pharmacist need?

   a. high school only

   b. high school and some college

   c. a bachelor's degree

   d. a doctorate

2. What is the average salary for a nursing assistant?

   a. $36,740

   b. more than a pharmacy technician

   c. less than a pharmacy technician

   d. the same as a pharmacy technician

3. What education does a registered nurse need?

   a. a doctorate

   b. more than a licensed practical nurse (LPN)

   c. less than an LPN

   d. the same as an LPN

Health Care Professions Education & Salaries			
Pharmacy Technician $36,740	Licensed Practical Nurse (LPN) $48,070	Registered Nurse (RN) $77,600	Doctor $208,000
Nursing Assistant $30,310			Pharmacist $128,570
HS Diploma or Equivalent + Certification	HS Diploma + Trade School or Some College	Bachelor's or Master's Degree	Doctorate or Professional Degree

Source: U.S. Bureau of Labor Statistics

B Study the chart.

More Than / Less Than		
Doctors need	**more** education **than**	registered nurses.
Registered nurses need	**less** education **than**	doctors.
Doctors make	**more** money **than**	registered nurses.
Registered nurses make	**less** money **than**	doctors.

LESSON 6   161

C Work with a partner. Practice making true and false statements about A.

> EXAMPLE: **Student A:**   Pharmacy technicians need more education than nursing assistants.
>
> **Student B:**   False.

D Read about pharmacists. 🎧

> Pharmacists can have many different types of jobs. Some work in pharmacies. You see them when you pick up your medications. Other pharmacists work on new medications. They work for companies in laboratories or offices.

E **COMPARE** Read the chart. Which job looks best to you?

Community Pharmacists	• work in a local pharmacy • fill prescriptions • talk to people about their prescriptions
Clinical Pharmacists	• work in hospitals and clinics • work with patients • work on a team with doctors
Industry Pharmacists	• work for companies • research new medicines
Professors	• work in schools • train students in pharmacy technology

F Match the descriptions to the jobs. Write the numbers.

1. I like to help patients and work with a group of people.	5. I work in a store.
2. I like to investigate new ideas.	6. I work in education.
3. I work for a company.	7. I like to work with customers.
4. I work in a hospital.	8. I like to work with students.

Community Pharmacists	Clinical Pharmacists	Industry Pharmacists	Professors
5	1	2	6
7	4	3	8

C **Work with a partner. Practice making true and false statements about A.**

Give students a few minutes to study the infographic again and think about their statements. Put them in pairs to carry out the activity. Tell them to alternate making statements and responding with *true* or *false*.

Evaluation 1   5–10 mins. ■■■

Observe students as they work in pairs. Have volunteers share their statements with the class for everyone to respond to.

Presentation 2   20–25 mins. ■■■

D **Read about pharmacists.** 🎧

Ask students to read the text. Then ask questions to check students' understanding. For example: *Where do pharmacists work? What does a pharmacist in a laboratory do?* Play the audio as students read the text again; then review any vocabulary questions.

E **COMPARE** **Read the chart. Which job looks best to you?**

Say the names of each kind of pharmacist and have students repeat them. Then ask them to read the information about each one. Clarify any vocabulary doubts. Give students time to compare and decide which one looks best. Have them discuss the question in pairs and explain the reasons for their choices. Monitor and help with vocabulary as needed.

Practice 2   10–15 mins. ■■■

F **Match the descriptions to the jobs. Write the numbers.**

Have students carry out this activity individually to check their understanding. Tell them to read the descriptions and use a dictionary if they need to check any vocabulary. Then have them match the descriptions to the pharmacy jobs in the chart. Have them compare answers with a partner.

Evaluation 2   5–10 mins. ■■

Go over the answers to **F** as a class. Survey the class to see which job the majority thinks looks best and why.

Instructor's Notes

_____

_____

_____

_____

_____

_____

_____

_____

_____

_____

_____

_____

_____

_____

_____

_____

_____

_____

_____

_____

_____

_____

Presentation 3
10–15 mins. ■■■

G **Write the statements from F that are true about you.**

Ask students questions about the statements in **F**. For example: *Do you like to work with a group of people? With customers?*, etc. Then tell students to read the statements again, think about how they feel about each one, and write those that are true for them.

Practice 3
35–40 mins. ■■

Ask students in shorter classes to do **H** and **J** for homework.

H REFLECT **Read the sentences. Which sounds most like you? Write *1–3*. 1 is the most like you.**

Read the statements together and clarify any vocabulary doubts. Make sure students understand they need to rank the statements 1–3.

I **Work with a partner. Ask: *What job is best for you: a doctor, a nurse, or a pharmacist?***

Have students share their number 1 ranking from **H** with a partner and explain their choice if they can.

J **How much education do you want? Check (✓) what is true about you.**

Read the statements as a class and clarify any vocabulary questions. Then have students check the statements that are true for them and share with a partner.

K **Choose a job title from A. Go to a job search site online and see if there are any openings within 25 miles of your school or home.**

Help students get started with their searches by helping them decide which of the jobs in **A** they want to look for. Share specific job search sites that they can use. Tell them to write down the salaries and education requirements for the jobs they find. Monitor as they carry out their searches and help as needed. When they have all found one or two options, put them in pairs to share their information.

Evaluation 3
5–10 mins. ■

Call on different students to share what they found. Ask them questions about the salaries. Write the salaries of a few of the jobs on the board and have students compare them using *less than* and *more than*.

Instructor's Notes

_____

_____

_____

_____

_____

_____

_____

_____

_____

_____

_____

_____

_____

_____

_____

_____

_____

_____

G **Write the statements from F that are true about you.** Answers will vary.

_____

_____

_____

_____

H **REFLECT** **Read the sentences. Which sounds most like you? Write _1–3_.**
1 is the most like you. Answers will vary.

_____ Doctors are good at thinking and making decisions.

_____ Nurses are good at helping people and taking care of people.

_____ Pharmacists are good at remembering details and talking to people.

I **Work with a partner. Ask: _What job is best for you: a doctor, a nurse, or a pharmacist?_**

J **How much education do you want? Check (✓) what is true about you.** Answers will vary.

☐ I only want to learn English in school.
☐ I want to learn English and then get a high school diploma.
☐ I want to learn English and then take classes in college.
☐ I want to learn English and then study in college and get a degree.
☐ I want to learn English and then go to a special school for _____.
☐ I can stay in school for only a short time.
☐ I can stay in school for a long time.

K **Choose a job title from A. Go to a job search site online and see if there are any**
openings within 25 miles of your school or home.

A community pharmacist gives information about a medication to a customer.

Review

A **Look at the photo. Write the body parts.**

1. arm
2. nose
3. teeth
4. mouth
5. neck
6. chest
7. stomach
8. foot

9. head
10. eye
11. ear
12. hand
13. back
14. leg

B **Look at the photos and complete the sentences.**

1. My ____feet____ hurt.

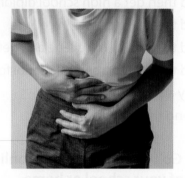

2. I have a ____stomachache____.

3. I have a ____headache____.

4. I have a ____fever____.

5. My ____hand____ hurts.

6. My ____back____ hurts.

Learner Log	I can identify parts of the body.	I can identify illnesses and health problems.
	☐ Yes ☐ No ☐ Maybe	☐ Yes ☐ No ☐ Maybe

At-a-Glance Prep

Goal: All unit goals
Grammar: All unit grammar
Academic Strategies: Reviewing, evaluating, developing study skills
Vocabulary: All unit vocabulary

Agenda

☐ Discuss unit goals.
☐ Complete the review.
☐ Evaluate and reflect on progress.

Pacing

■ 1.5 hour classes   ■ 2.5 hour classes
■ 3+ hour classes

Standards Correlations

CASAS: 0.1.2, 0.1.5, 2.1.2, 2.5.1, 3.3.1, 3.3.2, 3.5.9, 3.6.1, 3.6.3
CCRS: SL1, SL3
ELPS:

S2: Participate in level-appropriate oral and written exchanges of information, ideas, and analyses, in various social and academic contexts, responding to peer, audience, or reader comments and questions.

S10: Demonstrate command of the conventions of standard English to communicate in level-appropriate speech and writing.

Warm-up and Review   7–10 mins. ■■■

With books closed, ask students to help you make a list on the board of all the new vocabulary they can come up with from the unit. Then have a competition where students in groups write a page number for each item on the list. The first group to have a correct page number for each item wins.

Introduction   5 mins. ■■■

Write all the goals from Unit 6 on the board. Explain that today they will review the whole unit.

Presentation   10–15 mins. ■■■

This presentation will cover all three pages of the review. Quickly go to the first page of each lesson. Discuss the goal of each. Ask simple questions to remind students of what they have learned.

Practice 1   15–20 mins. ■■■

A Look at the photo. Write the body parts.

Give students two minutes to complete the activity individually without looking at Lesson 1. Then have them compare with a partner and help each other complete any they are missing.

B Look at the photos and complete the sentences.

Make sure students notice that in some items, they need a body part and in others, a symptom. Have students complete the activity individually.

Evaluation 1   10–15 mins. ■■■

Go around the classroom and check on students' progress. Help individuals as needed. If you see consistent errors among several students, interrupt the class and give a mini lesson or review to help students feel comfortable with the concept.

Learner Log   5–10 mins.

Have students read the statements and complete the log. If students answer *no* or *maybe*, encourage them to set themselves a goal to practice. Show them where they can find more practice activities.

BEST PRACTICE

Learner Logs

Learner Logs function to help students in many different ways:

1. They serve as part of the review process.
2. They help students to gain confidence and to document what they have learned. Consequently, students see that they are progressing in their learning.
3. They provide students with a tool that they can use over and over to check and recheck their understanding of the target language. In this way, students become independent learners.

Practice 2

20–25 mins. ■■□□

C **Match the symptom to the best remedy.**

Have students complete the activity, then compare with a partner.

D **Practice the conversation with a partner. Then make similar conversations with the information from C.**

Elicit how we give advice and write on the board: *should / shouldn't* + verb. Put students in pairs to practice the conversation. Make sure they switch roles and substitute with the items in **C**.

E **Read the medicine bottles and complete the chart.**

Have students complete the chart. Then ask what symptoms each medicine is for.

Evaluation 2

10–15 mins. ■■■□

Go around the classroom and check on students' progress. Help individuals as needed. If you see consistent errors among several students, interrupt the class and give a mini lesson or review to help students feel comfortable with the concept.

Learner Log

5 mins.

Have students read the statement and complete the log. If students answer *no* or *maybe*, encourage them to set themselves a goal to practice. Show them where they can find more practice activities.

BEST PRACTICE

Recycling / Review

The review and the project that follows are part of the recycling / review process. Students at this level often need to be reintroduced to concepts to solidify what they have learned. Many concepts are learned and forgotten while learning other new concepts. This is because students learn but are not necessarily ready to acquire language concepts.

Therefore, it becomes very important to review and to show students how to review on their own. It is also important to recycle the new concepts in different contexts.

C Match the symptom to the best remedy.

_c_ 1. feel tired   a. throat lozenges

_b_ 2. cough   b. cough syrup

_a_ 3. sore throat   c. rest

_d_ 4. fever   d. pain reliever

D Practice the conversation with a partner. Then make similar conversations with the information from C.

Student A: What's the matter?

Student B: I have a headache.

Student A: You should take a pain reliever.

Student B: Thanks. That's a good idea.

E Read the medicine bottles and complete the chart.

1.

2.
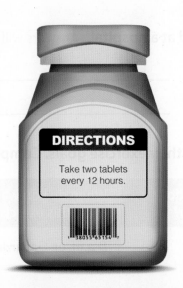

3.

	How Many / Much?	How Often?
1.	10 mL	every four to six hours
2.	two tablets	every 12 hours
3.	one tablet	every four hours

Learner Log   I can give advice.
☐ Yes ☐ No ☐ Maybe

Review

F **Match the questions with the answers.**

_a_ 1. Where is the accessible parking?   a. Across from the main entrance.

_c_ 2. Who is calling?   b. There is a fire.

_b_ 3. What is the emergency?   c. Franco Natali.

_d_ 4. Where is the accident?   d. On Seventh Street and Grand Avenue.

G **Read the conversation and put the sentences in the correct order.**

_2_ **Victor:**   There's a car accident.

_1_ **Operator:**   911, what is the emergency?

_6_ **Victor:**   Yes.

_4_ **Victor:**   It's on Fourth and Bush.

_5_ **Operator:**   OK, Fourth and Bush. Is anyone hurt?

_7_ **Operator:**   OK. The police and ambulance are on the way.

_3_ **Operator:**   Where is the accident?

H **Write six things you can find at a hospital.** Answers will vary.

_____   _____   _____

_____   _____   _____

I **Ask three classmates about their exercise goals. Complete the chart.** Answers will vary.

Name	What exercise do you want to do?	When do you want to do this exercise?	How long do you want to do this exercise?
Nadia	swim	8 a.m. on Saturdays	40 minutes

Practice 3   25–30 mins. ■■☐

F **Match the questions with the answers.**

Elicit *wh-* question words and write them on the board. Ask students when we use each one and / or give an example. Then have students complete the activity.

G **Read the conversation and put the sentences in the correct order.**

Have students complete the exercise individually, then compare answers with a partner. Have students practice the conversation in pairs.

H **Write six things you can find at a hospital.**

Have students write their list individually without looking at Lesson 4, then compare with a partner and add any words they don't have from their partner's list on a separate sheet of paper. Have one pair write their joint list on the board and ask other pairs to add any words that are missing.

I **Ask three classmates about their exercise goals. Complete the chart.**

Briefly review pronunciation of times and days of the week. Write the days of the week on the board if necessary and a few different times (include *a.m.* and *p.m.*) as prompts. Go over the example to make sure students understand the three questions; then have students survey their classmates. When they are ready, call on different students to tell the class about one or two people from their chart. Point out that if two people have the same goal, they can say, *A and B want to . . .* Make sure they are saying *wants* for individuals.

Evaluation 3   15 mins. ■■■

Go around the room and check on students' progress. Help individuals as needed. If you see consistent errors among several students, interrupt the class and give a mini lesson or review to help students feel comfortable with the concept.

Learner Log   5 mins.

Have students read the statements and complete the log. If students answer *no* or *maybe*, encourage them to set themselves a goal to practice. Show them where they can find more practice activities.

Instructor's Notes

Standards Correlations

CASAS: 0.1.2, 0.1.5, 2.5.1, 3.3.1, 3.3.2, 4.8.1, 7.3.3

CCRS: L1, L3, SL1, SL3, W3

ELPS:

S3: Speak and write about level-appropriate complex literary and informational texts and topics.

S7: Adapt language choices to purpose, task, and audience when speaking and writing.

S8: Determine the meaning of words and phrases in oral presentations and literary and informational text.

S9: Create clear and coherent level-appropriate speech and text.

Workplace Focus

Combine ideas and information; Make decisions; Exercise leadership roles; Complete tasks as assigned; Interact appropriately with team members; Interpret and communicate information; Manage time.

Soft Skill: Collaboration
Making Polite Suggestions

Explain that collaboration skills are very important in the workplace and that when collaborating, we often need to make suggestions in order to share our ideas. Explain that it is important to make these suggestions politely and that this can be done with questions. Tell students they will practice this skill in **Step 6** when they are practicing their role-play.

Warm-up and Review   10 mins.

Review items in the review section of the unit and make sure all students have recorded their progress in the learner logs.

Introduction   10 mins.

Let students know that in this lesson, they will be creating a role-play about an emergency. The team members will play the roles of patient, 911 operator, doctor, and family members.

Presentation   10–15 mins.

1. Form a team of four or five students. In your team, you need:

Put students into teams of four or five. To help students choose their positions in the team, go through each step in the project and explain the role of the person who will lead that step.

In **Step 2**, the team leader can manage the discussion of what kind of emergency it is. Then in **Steps 3**, **4**, and **5**, the writer will write the conversations based on the other team members' ideas and suggestions. In **Step 6**, the director will manage the practicing of the role-play. In **Step 7**, the spokespeople will be responsible for preparing an introduction to the role-play for the class. Finally, all members will participate in the performance of the role-play.

As you go through what the different positions are, at this level, it might be easier to ask one volunteer from each team to stand after each description. Be aware of who volunteers for which position so that through the different units, you can encourage students to try different roles.

Practice / Evaluation / Application   1–2 hours

2. Choose an accident or illness. Write down the injured or sick person's symptoms. Who is the patient in your group? What is his or her name in the role-play?

3. Write a conversation between a 911 operator and a family member of the patient.

4. Write a conversation between the patient and a doctor. In the conversation, the doctor gives a prescription to the patient and gives directions for how to take the medicine.

5. Write a conversation between the patient and a family member.

6. Put the conversations together and practice the role-play. The director needs to lead the practice and make suggestions.

Go over the Soft Skill note and read the example question for the director.

7. Perform the role-play for the class.

Create a Role-Play about an Emergency

SOFT SKILL ▶ Collaboration

In this project, you will create a role-play. Members of your group will be a patient, a 911 operator, a doctor, and one or two family members of the patient.

1. Form a team of four or five students. In your team, you need:

Position	Job Description	Student Name
Student 1: **Team Leader**	Check that everyone speaks English. Check that everyone participates.	
Student 2: **Writer**	Write out the role-play with help from the team. Make sure there is a part for everyone.	
Student 3: **Director**	Direct the role-play. Lead the practice.	
Students 4/5: **Spokespeople**	Give a short introduction to the role-play and explain which student is playing each role.	

2. Choose an accident or illness. Write down the injured or sick person's symptoms. Who is the patient in your group? What is his or her name in the role-play?

3. Write a conversation between a 911 operator and a family member of the patient.

4. Write a conversation between the patient and a doctor. In the conversation, the doctor gives a prescription to the patient and gives directions for how to take the medicine.

5. Write a conversation between the patient and a family member.

6. Put the conversations together and practice the role-play. The director needs to lead the practice and make suggestions.

    Director: Can you speak a little louder?
    Can we practice that part again?

7. Perform the role-play for the class.

COLLABORATION:
Making Polite Suggestions

When we work with others, we sometimes want to make suggestions. It is important to be polite and respectful when making suggestions. Using questions is one way to make a suggestion more polite. For example, if the director of the role-play wants to suggest that someone in the group speak louder, they can say:
Can you speak a little louder?

Reading Challenge

About the Photo

This photo shows a woman participating in a roller skating disco event in Central Park, New York City. She is dancing as she skates to the rhythm of the music and flashing lights. Both roller skating and dancing, together or separately, are fun ways of doing exercise. This kind of exercise helps us stay healthy and makes us feel good emotionally, which is also good for our health.

A Take a survey about yourself.

Review the adverbs and expressions to express frequency and clarify any vocabulary doubts. Then have students answer the survey about themselves.

B Use a dictionary. Match the word or phrase with the correct definition.

Read through the words together to help students with the pronunciation. Then have them read the definitions and match them to the words. Allow them to use a dictionary to help them. Students can do this in pairs if preferable. Check the answers and students' understanding of the words as a class so that they are prepared for the text.

C PREDICT Read the title and look at the photo. What do you think the "best medicine" is? Read the text. 🎧

Ask students to read the title and then describe what they see in the photo. Have them answer the question in the direction line. Remind students that they don't need to understand every word of the text. Tell them to try to understand the main ideas and underline words they don't know without looking them up.

Reading Challenge

A Take a survey about yourself. Answers will vary.

1. I sleep well.
   - a. all the time
   - b. usually
   - c. sometimes
   - d. never

2. I think clearly.
   - a. all the time
   - b. usually
   - c. sometimes
   - d. never

3. I'm happy.
   - a. all the time
   - b. usually
   - c. sometimes
   - d. never

4. I'm tired.
   - a. all the time
   - b. usually
   - c. sometimes
   - d. never

B Use a dictionary. Match the word or phrase with the correct definition.

___c___ 1. psychological   a. movement of the body that uses energy

___a___ 2. physical activity   b. a way to show where some information comes from or who said it

___b___ 3. according to   c. relating to the mind and how people think and feel

C PREDICT Read the title and look at the photo. What do you think the "best medicine" is? Read the text.

D Choose the correct answer.

1. What percentage of people in the United States do physical activity?
   - a. 25%–35%
   - b. 65%–75%
   - c. 30%
   - d. 70%

2. What is the "best medicine" according to the text?
   - a. exercise
   - b. medicine
   - c. food
   - d. dancing

E INFER Work in a group. Which statement do you think the author of the text agrees with most?

1. You need to exercise for a long time every day.
2. It is not healthy to sit down all day every day.
3. The most important thing about physical activity is that it makes you stronger.

F Do you think exercise is more important than eating healthily? Talk with a partner.

168   UNIT 6

CASAS FOR READING
0.1.2, 0.1.5, 3.5.9, 7.4.5

CCRS FOR READING
L1, L2, L3, RI1, RI2, RI3, SL1, SL3

The Best Medicine

1   Do you want to sleep better? Do you want to be happier? What can you do about it? The answer isn't medicine, and it isn't something you eat. It is physical activity and exercise! According to the American Psychological Association, 25 to 35% of Americans don't do any physical activity at all. This can cause a lot of health problems,
5 so exercising is very important.

    Even if you can only exercise 10 minutes a day, you will feel better. Make it part of your routine.* Get off the bus early and walk a few extra blocks. Take the stairs instead of the elevator. Go dancing, go roller skating, or do both like the woman in this photo. She is getting some exercise at a disco event in Central Park in New York City. Even
10 housework like vacuuming helps. So, it's time to exercise and to feel better!

routine the activities you usually do

READING CHALLENGE   169

READING STRATEGIES

Checking Comprehension

Students should become accustomed to monitoring their own comprehension. They should also know how to identify what they do not understand. Asking students to underline or circle unfamiliar vocabulary is an effective strategy towards building better comprehension. Once new words have been defined and explained, students can re-read a text to check if their understanding improves.

Point out the glossary below the text. Then have students read the text.

After reading, ask students to share what they have understood. They can share anything they remember, such as a word, a phrase, or an idea.

D Choose the correct answer.

Have students answer the questions individually, then compare with a partner. Check answers as a class. Have students go back to the words they underlined in the text and ask them if they now understand some of them. Write any that they are still unsure about on the board and clarify their meaning as a class.

E INFER Work in a group. Which statement do you think the author of the text agrees with most?

Put students in groups to carry out the activity. Encourage them to go back to the text to check what the author says so they can explain their answer. Check the answer as a class.

F Do you think exercise is more important than eating healthily? Talk with a partner.

Elicit what *eating healthily* means and make two lists on the board with students' ideas for healthy and unhealthy food and drinks. Then have students discuss the question in pairs. Have pairs share their conclusions, and discuss the question as a class.

7 Work

About the Photo

This photo shows the conductor and passengers on a streetcar on the famous St. Charles Line in New Orleans. Beginning its service in 1835, it is the oldest operating streetcar line in the world. The St. Charles Line was the only one to survive the switch to buses in the 1930s. However, since the late 1980s, new streetcar lines have been created, and old ones reopened. Now, streetcars are a very popular form of public transportation in New Orleans.

- Introduce the unit. Read the title out loud.
- Have students look at the photo and describe what they see. Ask them to discuss the questions with a partner. Read the caption and discuss the remaining questions as a class.
- Go over the unit outcomes, eliciting any ideas students have related to each one.

Life Skills Focus

In this unit, students will learn about common occupations. They will also learn what the occupations entail and the steps involved in acquiring them as well as keeping them.

170

UNIT OUTCOMES	GRAMMAR	VOCABULARY	EL CIVICS
• Identify common occupations • Interpret job information • Write your job history • Participate in a job interview • Evaluate work and school performance • Identify employment opportunities in the landscaping industry	• Simple present • Negative simple present • Simple past: Regular verbs, *Be* • *Yes / no* questions with *can* • Simple present and past: *Be* • Adverbs of frequency	• Occupations • Job postings • Job history • Job interviews • Evaluations • Jobs in landscaping	The skills students learn in this unit can be applied to the following EL Civics competency area: • Employment Resources

UNIT OUTCOMES

▸ Identify common occupations

▸ Interpret job information

▸ Write your job history

▸ Participate in a job interview

▸ Evaluate work and school performance

▸ Identify employment opportunities in the landscaping industry

Look at the photo and answer the questions.

1. What is this woman's job?
2. Do you think she likes her job? Why?

A conductor (or driver) of a historic streetcar in New Orleans, Louisiana

1. What do you think are the job duties of a streetcar driver? What does she do at work?
2. What is the woman wearing? Why do you think she wears this at work?
3. Do you think being a streetcar driver is an interesting job? Why or why not?

Workplace Focus

All lessons and units in *Stand Out* include basic communication skills and interpersonal skills important for the workplace. They include *collecting and organizing information*, *making decisions and solving problems*, and *combining ideas and information*.

• In Unit 7, Lesson 6, *Explore the Workforce*, students will identify jobs in the landscaping industry. They will interpret a bar graph with landscaping jobs and their annual salaries. They will also read an infographic about tree trimming safety and analyze a job posting for a tree trimmer.

• In the Team Project, students practice the soft skill of asking for clarification while actively listening.

• Life Online notes in Lessons 3 and 4 raise awareness about online job applications and tips for online job interviews.

spark Resources

All resources for the unit are centrally located on the Spark platform and include: audio, video, multilevel worksheets, digital literacy worksheets, Online Practice, and Assessment Suite.

171

STEPS

CASAS COMPETENCIES	ELPS	CCRS
Lesson 1: 0.1.2, 0.1.5, 4.1.8 Lesson 2: 0.1.2, 0.1.5, 4.1.3, 4.1.6, 4.1.8, 4.8.1, 7.4.4, 7.7.3 Lesson 3: 0.1.2, 0.1.5, 4.1.2, 4.1.8, 7.4.4, 7.7.3 Lesson 4: 0.1.1, 0.1.2, 0.1.5, 0.1.6, 0.2.1, 4.1.5, 4.1.9, 4.6.1 Lesson 5: 4.1.9, 4.4.1, 4.4.4 Lesson 6: 0.1.2, 0.1.5, 3.4.2, 4.1.3, 4.1.8, 4.1.9, 4.3.2, 6.7.2, 7.4.4, 7.7.3 Review: 4.1.2, 4.1.3, 4.1.5, 4.1.6, 4.1.8, 4.4.1, 4.4.4, 4.6.1 Team Project: 0.1.2, 0.1.5, 0.1.6, 4.1.2, 4.1.3, 4.1.5, 4.1.6, 4.1.8, 4.4.1, 4.8.1 Reading Challenge: 0.1.2, 0.1.5, 4.1.9, 6.7.2, 7.4.4, 7.4.5, 7.7.3	S2: Participate in level-appropriate oral and written exchanges of information, ideas, and analyses, in various social and academic contexts, responding to peer, audience, or reader comments and questions. S9: Create clear and coherent level-appropriate speech and text. S10: Demonstrate command of the conventions of standard English to communicate in level-appropriate speech and writing.	L1, L2, L3, RI1, RI2, RI3, SL1, SL3, W1, W3

What's Your Job?

GOAL ▶ Identify common occupations

A IDENTIFY Match the occupations to the photos.

homemaker	mechanic	nurse	office assistant	server	student

Zeynab

1. _____server_____

Lucia

2. _____office assistant_____

Tyra

3. _____mechanic_____

Steven

4. _____student_____

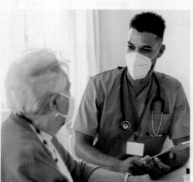

Marcelo

5. _____nurse_____

Jared

6. _____homemaker_____

B Practice the conversations with a partner. Then ask and answer questions about the people in A.

Student A: What is <u>Zeynab</u>'s job?

Student B: <u>She</u> is a <u>server</u>.

Student B: What does <u>Zeynab</u> do?

Student A: <u>She</u>'s a <u>server</u>.

Goal: Identify common occupations

Grammar: Simple present and negative simple present

Pronunciation: Intonation of clarification questions and corrections

Academic Strategies: Identifying, classifying information, focused listening, doing a survey

Vocabulary: Occupations

Agenda
- [ ] Describe your job.
- [ ] Identify occupations.
- [ ] Listen to conversations about different occupations.
- [ ] Discuss occupations.

Resources
Heinle Picture Dictionary: Jobs 1, pages 146–147; Jobs 2, pages 148–149

Pacing
- ■ 1.5 hour classes   ■ 2.5 hour classes
- ■ 3+ hour classes

Standards Correlations
CASAS: 0.1.2, 0.1.5, 4.1.8
CCRS: L1, L2, L3, SL1, SL3
ELPS:

S2: Participate in level-appropriate oral and written exchanges of information, ideas, and analyses, in various social and academic contexts, responding to peer, audience, or reader comments and questions.

S10: Demonstrate command of the conventions of standard English to communicate in level-appropriate speech and writing.

Warm-up and Review   7–10 mins. ■■■
Write on the board: *What do you do?* Ask various students this question. At first, students may describe what they are doing at the moment.

Then ask a few other students to name their jobs or occupations. Explain that the question *What do you do?* usually means *What is your job?*

Make a list on the board of students' jobs. Make sure they know that they can respond *I'm a student / homemaker* to the question *What do you do?* Help with pronunciation as needed.

Introduction   3–7 mins. ■■■
Look at the list you have created with students' input on the board. Ask students if they can think of any other jobs to add to the list. State the goal: *Today, we will identify common occupations.*

Presentation 1   15–20 mins. ■■■
Before students open their books, act out some of the jobs pictured in **A** and ask students to identify the jobs. For job titles that are difficult to act out, give students additional verbal hints. For example, for *mechanic*, tell them that this person works with cars. Write their responses on the board even if they are not exactly accurate. Go over the words you have written on the board several times, correcting inaccuracies as you go.

Ask students to open their books and look at the six occupations.

A IDENTIFY Match the occupations to the photos.
Do this exercise as a class. Then quiz students to test their comprehension.

Practice 1   7–10 mins. ■■■

B Practice the conversations with a partner. Then ask and answer questions about the people in A.
Go over the two exchanges. Make sure students understand that both questions have the same purpose: to find out about a person's job. Tell students that they may try to expand upon the examples given in the book to form longer conversations. Put them in pairs to practice.

Evaluation 1   3–5 mins. ■■■
Observe the activity and ask volunteers to perform their conversations in front of the class.

Presentation 2
10–15 mins. ■■■

Follow the same pattern you did for Presentation 1.
1. With books closed, act out some of the occupations depicted on the page.
2. Write students' responses on the board. This time, if they don't know an answer, don't give it to them yet.

C Look at the photos and read the job titles.

Go over the photos. Say each job title and have students repeat. Then quiz students. Have them use one of the response techniques described in the Best Practice note below.

BEST PRACTICE

Monitoring Student Responses

An easy way to monitor responses is to have students respond verbally with a word.

With the above method, however, stronger students sometimes overwhelm students who need more time to think when asked for a verbal response. You may choose other ways for students to respond in which students are less likely to "go along with the crowd." One such method could be to use 3-by-5 index cards where students choose the card with the correct answer and hold it up. If you choose to use this method, have students create the actual cards themselves so they also get writing practice.

There is another effective technique that doesn't require preparation. Students respond by showing the number of fingers that corresponds to each picture. Start this method by first only saying the target word. Next, embed the word in a sentence, and then embed all the words in a paragraph.

Workplace Focus

Exercise D: Collect and organize information.

D CLASSIFY Write the job titles from C in the correct column.

Do this classifying activity as a class. You might want to draw a Venn diagram on the board. One circle would represent restaurants and the other would represent schools. They might have *custodian* in common.

Practice 2
7–10 mins. ■■

E Listen to each conversation. Choose the correct job title. 🎧

Remind students that they don't need to understand everything. Ask them what they should focus on listening for. Play the audio and tell students to listen without writing anything. Play the audio again, pausing after each conversation for students to choose their answers. Have them compare answers with a partner. Then play the audio one or more additional times as needed to confirm their answers.

Listening Script

1. **Supervisor:** *Hi, Dan. I have something important for you to do today.*
   Dan: *Great. I'm ready.*
   Supervisor: *One of your responsibilities as an administrative assistant is to arrange rooms for meetings and presentations. So, can you arrange a room for our presentation tomorrow morning? There will be around 15 people there.*
   Dan: *Of course! I'll do that right away.*
2. **Woman:** *What do you do?*
   Man: *I am a cook at Market Street Grill.*
   Woman: *Wow, that's great. I hear the food is very good there.*
3. **Woman:** *My job is so great! I love working with people.*
   Man: *Me too. What do you do?*
   Woman: *I have the perfect job.*
   Man: *Well, what is it?*
   Woman: *I am a principal at a high school in Fairmont.*
4. **Woman:** *I'm looking for a job.*
   Manager: *Do you have experience?*
   Woman: *Yes, I do. I worked at a local movie theater for three years.*
   Manager: *What was your job?*
   Woman: *I was a cashier.*
   Manager: *So, you're good at helping customers.*
   Woman: *Yes, I like working in customer service.*
   Manager: *OK, let's get you an application.*

Evaluation 2
7–10 mins. ■■

Play the audio again, pausing when a key word is spoken. After checking the answers, ask students for other information they understood in each conversation.

C Look at the photos and read the job titles.

cook / chef

host

custodian

cashier

administrative assistant

principal

D **CLASSIFY** Write the job titles from **C** in the correct column.

Restaurant Positions	School Positions
cook / chef	*administrative assistant*
host	custodian
cashier	principal

E Listen to each conversation. Choose the correct job title. 🎧

1. ~~administrative assistant~~   principal   custodian
2. cashier   host   ~~cook~~
3. administrative assistant   ~~principal~~   custodian
4. ~~cashier~~   host   cook

F **Study the charts.**

Simple Present		
Subject	**Verb**	**Example Sentence**
I / You / We / They	work	I **work** in an office.
He / She	works	He **works** in a restaurant.

Negative Simple Present			
Subject	**Negative**	**Verb**	**Example Sentence**
I / You / We / They	do not (don't)	work	I **do not work** in an office. You **don't work** in a restaurant.
He / She	does not (doesn't)		He **does not work** in a school. She **doesn't work** in a hospital.

G **Look at the jobs in C. Ask and answer questions about each job.**

Student A: What does <u>he</u> do? (Point to the host.)

Student B: <u>He</u> is a <u>host</u>.

Student A: <u>He</u> works <u>in a school</u>, right?

Student B: No, <u>he</u> doesn't work <u>in a school</u>. <u>He</u> works <u>in a restaurant</u>.

Intonation 🎧

Clarification Questions and Corrections

A: He works in a SCHOOL, right?

B: No, he doesn't work in a SCHOOL. He works in a RESTAURANT.

H **SURVEY** **Talk to three classmates. Complete the chart. Then report to a group.**

Answers will vary.

EXAMPLE: Zeynab is a server. She works in a restaurant.

Steven is a student. He studies at an adult school.

Name	What do you do?	Where do you work?
Zeynab	server	a restaurant
Steven	student	an adult school

Presentation 3   15–20 mins. ■■■

Ask students again: *What do you do?* Also ask: *Where do you work?* Make sure you include students and homemakers. Write what students do in sentences on the board. For example: *Huong is a nurse. She works in a hospital.* After you have written several sentences on the board, point out the third-person singular *-s*. Also, remind them to use *a* or *an* before each occupation. Then have students open their books.

F Study the charts.

Go over the example sentences with the class. Then continue writing examples about students' jobs and where they work / don't work on the board.

BEST PRACTICE

Recycling Grammar

It is important that students learn to transfer the structures they have previously been exposed to to different contexts. The simple present has been introduced many times in this book. Make sure students see the connection of this explanation of the simple present with previous ones. Refer them to the following lessons: Unit 1, Lesson 4; Unit 2, Lesson 1; Unit 4, Lesson 1; Unit 5, Lesson 5; and Unit 6, Lessons 1 and 2. Show students that adding an *s* to the third-person singular verb is a consistent rule. Ask students to help you choose other verbs and show how they are all formed in the same way.

Practice 3   7–10 mins. ■

G Look at the jobs in C. Ask and answer questions about each job.

Read the conversation together. Model the conversation with a student. Take the Student B part and model correction intonation to help students understand.

> **Intonation   Clarification Questions and Corrections 🎧**
>
> Point out the Intonation note and play the audio. Explain to students that clarification is when we check something is correct. Play the audio again and have students repeat the questions.

Students can hear a rising intonation with ease. However, the use of stress to highlight a contrast or to emphasize new information may be new to them. English gives more emphasis to corrections than many other languages, so students may need to be introduced to this concept multiple times to fully grasp it. One way to do this is to have them stand and sit or raise and lower their hand when they say the stressed word or words. In this conversation, have students stand when they say *school* and *restaurant*.

Listening Script

In English, we use a rising intonation for clarification questions. We also stress the information that is important.

A: *He works in a SCHOOL, right?*

When correcting someone, we stress the new information.

B: *No, he doesn't work in a SCHOOL. He works in a RESTAURANT.*

A: *He works in a SCHOOL, right?*

B: *No, he doesn't work in a SCHOOL. He works in a RESTAURANT.*

Practice the conversation again as a class, reminding students of correct pronunciation. Then put them in pairs to carry out the conversations. Remind them to switch roles so they practice both parts. Monitor, and model the intonation and emphasis for them if necessary.

Evaluation 3   2–7 mins. ■

Ask volunteers to perform the conversation in front of the class.

Workplace Focus

Exercise H: Collect and organize information; Interact appropriately with team members.

Application   10–15 mins. ■■■

H SURVEY Talk to three classmates. Complete the chart. Then report to a group.

Go over the information in the chart and the example sentences. Say the questions and have students repeat them. When they have finished surveying their classmates, put students in groups to report their information. Call on different students to report on one of the people they talked to. Make sure they're using the third person singular *-s*.

At-a-Glance Prep

Goal: Interpret job information
Academic Strategies: Interpreting, comparing information, focused listening, evaluating information, making inferences
Vocabulary: Job postings: *benefits, vacation, sick leave, insurance*

Agenda

- ☐ Interview a partner.
- ☐ Read job postings.
- ☐ Listen for benefits.
- ☐ Read about jobs.
- ☐ Choose jobs to match people's skills and schedules.
- ☐ Write a job posting.

Resources

Heinle Picture Dictionary: Jobs 1, pages 146–147; Jobs 2, pages 148–149

Pacing

- ■ 1.5 hour classes
- ■ 2.5 hour classes
- ■ 3+ hour classes

Standards Correlations

CASAS: 0.1.2, 0.1.5, 4.1.3, 4.1.6, 4.1.8, 4.8.1, 7.4.4, 7.7.3
CCRS: L1, L2, L3, RI1, RI3, SL1, SL3, W1, W3
ELPS:
S5: Conduct research and evaluate and communicate findings to answer questions or solve problems.
S7: Adapt language choices to purpose, task, and audience when speaking and writing.
S8: Determine the meaning of words and phrases in oral presentations and literary and informational text.

Warm-up and Review   10–15 mins. ■■■

In pairs, have students ask the questions in Lesson 1, **H**. Make sure they practice with someone different. They should ask: *What do you do?* and *Where do you work?* Then have students introduce their partner to the class. For example: *Oscar is a cook. He works in a restaurant.*

Introduction   5–7 mins. ■■■

Ask the class where they can find out about jobs. List their responses on the board. Ask them if they know about online job postings. Ask how many students read job postings and if they have any trouble understanding them. State the goal: *Today, we will interpret job information.*

Presentation 1   20–30 mins. ■■■

Write the word *benefits* on the board and have students recall what it means. Refer them to Unit 5, Lesson 6 if necessary. Ask for examples. Write *vacation, sick leave,* and *health insurance* on the board and make sure students understand the meaning of each term.

A INTERPRET Read the job postings. Underline any words you don't understand.

Have students open their books and look at the job postings. Ask them to find the job titles, the pay, and the addresses. Then have them read the postings in detail and underline new words. Have students work in pairs or small groups to work out the meaning of the words they have underlined. Encourage them to use dictionaries. When they are ready, go over the words as a class.

Workplace Focus

Exercise B: Collect and organize information.

B COMPARE Write the information in the chart.

Go over the chart with the class. Have students complete it individually before comparing with a partner. Check the answers as a class. Clarify any remaining vocabulary doubts.

Practice 1   7–10 mins. ■■■

C Listen to the conversations. Check (✓) the correct benefits. 🎧

Play the audio and tell students to just listen. Play the audio again, pausing after each conversation. Have students compare with a partner. Then play the audio a final time for students to confirm their answers.

Note: The listening script for **C** is on page 176a.

Evaluation 1   3–5 mins. ■■■

Go over the answers and play the audio again to confirm.

Job Hunting
GOAL ▶ Interpret job information

A INTERPRET Read the job postings. Underline any words you don't understand.

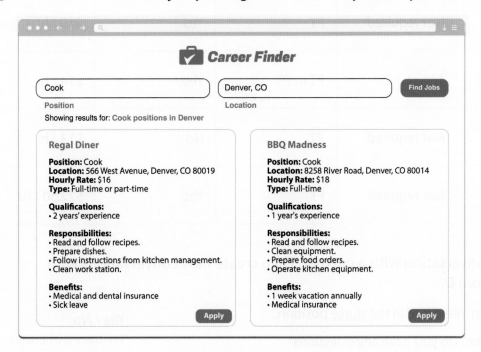

📋 *Career Finder*

| Cook | Denver, CO | **Find Jobs** |

Position   Location

Showing results for: **Cook positions in Denver**

Regal Diner

Position: Cook
Location: 566 West Avenue, Denver, CO 80019
Hourly Rate: $16
Type: Full-time or part-time

Qualifications:
• 2 years' experience

Responsibilities:
• Read and follow recipes.
• Prepare dishes.
• Follow instructions from kitchen management.
• Clean work station.

Benefits:
• Medical and dental insurance
• Sick leave

Apply

BBQ Madness

Position: Cook
Location: 8258 River Road, Denver, CO 80014
Hourly Rate: $18
Type: Full-time

Qualifications:
• 1 year's experience

Responsibilities:
• Read and follow recipes.
• Clean equipment.
• Prepare food orders.
• Operate kitchen equipment.

Benefits:
• 1 week vacation annually
• Medical insurance

Apply

B COMPARE Write the information in the chart.

	Regal Diner	BBQ Madness
Position / Job Title	*cook*	*cook*
Location	566 West Ave., Denver, CO	8258 River Road, Denver, CO
Pay / Wages / Salary	$16 / hour	$18 / hour
Full- or Part-time?	full-time or part-time	full-time
Benefits	medical and dental insurance, sick leave	one week vacation, medical insurance
Experience Required	two years	one year

C Listen to the conversations. Check (✓) the correct benefits. 🎧

1. ☑ vacation   ☐ sick leave   ☐ insurance

2. ☐ vacation   ☐ sick leave   ☑ insurance

3. ☐ vacation   ☑ sick leave   ☐ insurance

D **EVALUATE** **Read the job information. Which position has the best pay?**

The nurse position

Position	Experience	Full-Time / Part-Time	Benefits (Yes / No)	Pay
1. Nurse	2 years	FT	Yes	$37 / hr
2. Server	Not required	PT	Yes	$10 / hr + tips
3. Salesperson	1 year	FT or PT	Yes	$14 / hr
4. Cashier	Not required	PT	No	$13 / hr
5. Mechanic	Not required	FT	Yes	$22.50 / hr

E **Practice the conversation with a partner. Then create new conversations with information from D.**

Applicant: I am interested in the <u>nurse</u> position.

Manager: Great. Do you have any questions?

Applicant: Yes. Is the position full-time or part-time?

Manager: It's <u>full-time</u>. The pay is <u>$37 an hour</u>.

Applicant: Are there any benefits?

Manager: <u>Yes, there are benefits.</u>

Applicant: Thank you for the information. I will apply online.

Yes / No

Yes, there are benefits.

No, there are no benefits.

F **Listen and write the missing words.** 🎧

We need a (1) _____ cook _____ for our restaurant in San Francisco. The salary is (2) _____ $16 _____ an hour. You need (3) _____ two _____ years' experience for this job. This is a full-time position with benefits. We offer (4) _____ sick leave _____ and two weeks of (5) _____ vacation _____ time every year. Apply in person at 3500 West Arbor Place, San Francisco, California.

Listening Script

1. **Manager:** *Sam, you need to take a vacation this month.*
   Sam: *Well, I'm not sure I can. I'm very busy.*
   Manager: *If you don't use your vacation time soon, then you'll lose it. You have five days to make a decision.*
   Sam: *OK, I'll talk to my wife and see what she says.*

2. **Insurance Agent:** *CMM Health Insurance. How can I help you?*
   Anya: *My husband had an accident.*
   Insurance Agent: *An accident? What happened?*
   Anya: *He fell down the stairs and broke his leg.*
   Insurance Agent: *I'm sorry to hear that. How can I help?*
   Anya: *Does my insurance cover hospital care and if so, what is the deductible?*
   Insurance Agent: *I'll check for you. First, I need your member ID.*

3. **Steve:** *I'm sorry. I have to call in sick.*
   Manager: *I'm sorry to hear that.*
   Steve: *Yes, I have a fever. Maybe I have the flu.*
   Manager: *How long will you be out?*
   Steve: *Do you know how much sick leave I have left?*
   Manager: *I'll check on it for you.*

Presentation 2   10–15 mins. ■■■

D EVALUATE Read the job information. Which position has the best pay?

Ask students to read the chart carefully. Point out that there are five positions. Ask students what other information is given and discuss as a class. Ask specific questions about the information shown in the chart. Then have students answer the question in the direction line and check as a class.

Practice 2   10–15 mins. ■■

E Practice the conversation with a partner. Then create new conversations with information from D.

Read the conversation together and point out how the applicant asks about information in the chart in **D**. Model the conversation with a student. Have the student ask about a different position. Point out the note about *yes / no* answers, and ask students whether the cashier position has benefits, eliciting:

No, there are no benefits. Put students in pairs to carry out their conversations. Monitor and make sure they switch roles. Have volunteers perform one of their conversations for the class.

Evaluation 2   10–15 mins. ■■

F Listen and write the missing words. 🎧

Ask students to read the text and suggest what words could go in each space. Then play the audio and have students write the words they hear. Play it again and have students compare answers. Play the audio one more time to confirm answers. After listening, see if students can put the new information in the appropriate places in the chart in **D**.

BEST PRACTICE

Using Text with Audio

There are some listening exercises in *Stand Out* that include the text students will hear on the page. It is good to have students follow along in the text as they listen. Students can benefit from seeing what they hear. This approach also helps them with pronunciation of new vocabulary as well as pronunciation in general.

First, have students listen without reading. Then have them listen while following along in the text. You can repeat this process as many times as you think necessary.

Listening texts can also be used after students have completed the comprehension activity for *noticing* activities. These are activities where we focus students' attention on the vocabulary and grammar they have been working with. To do this, have students highlight the grammar or vocabulary from the lesson in the text. Seeing these elements in context helps students clarify their understanding.

Presentation 3

10–15 mins. ■■■◻

G **Read about Silvia, Anh, and Amal.**

Review the meaning of *retail*. Refer students to Unit 2, Lesson 6 if necessary. Ask students to read the information. Then ask a few comprehension questions. For example: *Does Anh need a full-time job? Who has retail experience?*, etc.

BEST PRACTICE

Group Work

At this level, it is important to model group activities with a few students. In group work, it is good to limit groups to five, with four being ideal for maximum participation.

A variety of grouping strategies are suggested depending on the task. Some considerations might include the following:

- Allow students to self-select groups. Students sometimes perform well with friends or people they feel comfortable with.
- Arrange groups according to similar abilities. Sometimes proficient students in groups with other proficient students can be allowed to excel, while less proficient students don't feel intimidated by more proficient students.
- Arrange diverse-ability groups. More proficient students often enjoy helping the less proficient students, and you'll have several mentors in the class instead of just one teacher.
- Avoid putting students in homogeneous language groups when possible to create an authentic need to communicate in English.

BEST PRACTICE

Random Group Selection

While intentionally choosing student groups has its benefits, it is sometimes desirable to inject some spontaneity into the grouping process and switch up which students work together. To randomly select groups, try the following techniques:

- Count students off by the number of groups needed. For example, all the 1's will be in a group, 2's in another, etc.
- Use playing cards. Count out the number of cards. All students who have 3s, for example, would be in the same group.
- Do a corners activity to form groups. Ask students to go to a corner based on criteria that you set; for

example: homemakers, students, part-time workers, and full-time workers. Then take one student from each corner and form a group, repeating the process until every student has been placed in a group.

Workplace Focus

Exercise H: Interpret and communicate information; Interact appropriately with team members.

Practice 3

10–15 mins. ■◻◻◻

H **INFER** **Work in a group. Look at the information in D. Write the jobs that are good for Silvia, Anh, and Amal. Explain the reasons for your answers.**

Put students in groups using one of the strategies or techniques mentioned in the Best Practice notes. Monitor as they discuss.

Evaluation 3

5–7 mins. ■◻◻◻

Ask groups to report to the class. Do they all agree on the jobs for each person?

Workplace Focus

Exercise I: Combine ideas and information.

Application

15–20 mins. ■■■◻

I **CREATE** **In a group, make a job posting on a separate sheet of paper. Include the information below. See A for an example.**

Students should now be familiar with the items in the box. As a class, go back to the two job postings in **A**. Then put students in new groups to create their posting. Ask students to choose an imaginary job or a job that one of the group members has. Monitor as they work, helping as needed. When they are ready, have groups post their jobs around the classroom for everyone to read. Survey the class to see which jobs people would like to apply for.

Workplace Focus

Exercise J: Apply technology.

J **Search online for a job you are interested in. Tell the class about a job you find.**

Provide suggestions for websites students can use in their searches. Remind them that they won't understand everything but should focus on looking for the information from **I**.

G Read about Silvia, Anh, and Amal.

Silvia

Skills:
She communicates well.
She has retail experience.

Needs:
She needs a part-time job.
She doesn't need benefits.

Anh

Skills:
She communicates well.
She has customer service
experience.

Needs:
She needs a part-time job.
She needs benefits.

Amal

Skills:
He works well with his
hands.
He has hospital experience.

Needs:
He needs a full-time job.
He needs benefits.

H **INFER** Work in a group. Look at the information in D. Write the jobs that are good for Silvia, Anh, and Amal. Explain the reasons for your answers.

Silvia	Anh	Amal
server	server	nurse
salesperson	salesperson	mechanic
cashier		

I **CREATE** In a group, make a job posting on a separate sheet of paper. Include the information below. See **A** for an example.

benefits information	experience needed	hourly pay	location
business name	full- or part-time	job title	

J Search online for a job you are interested in. Tell the class about a job you find.

LESSON 3 What Was Your Job Before?

GOAL ▶ Write your job history

A **PREDICT** Look at the photo. What is Francisco's job? Does he work in an office? Read about Francisco. 🎧

> My name is Francisco. I'm from Mexico. Now, I work in the United States. I'm an auto mechanic. I fix about ten cars a week. I started my job in August of 2019. Before I moved to the United States, I was a cook from March, 2014 to July, 2018. I cooked hamburgers and french fries in a restaurant.

B **SUMMARIZE** Answer the questions. Then tell a summary to a partner.

1. Where is Francisco from? He is from Mexico.

2. What is his job now? He is an auto mechanic.

3. What does he do in his job? He fixes cars.

4. When did he start his job? He started his job in August of 2019.

5. What was his job in Mexico? He was a cook.

6. Where did he work in Mexico? He worked at a restaurant.

C Complete the job history for Francisco.

Job History				
Position	**Company**	**From**	**To**	**Duties (Responsibilities)**
auto mechanic	Fuller Auto Repair	August, 2019	Present	fixes cars
cook	Señor Burger	March, 2014	July, 2018	cooked hamburgers and french fries
server	La Cantina	March, 2011	March, 2014	served customers

At-a-Glance Prep

Goal: Write your job history
Grammar: Simple past: Regular verbs, *Be*
Academic Strategy: Predicting, summarizing information, focused listening
Vocabulary: Job history

Agenda

☐ Do a corners activity about employment status.
☐ Read about Francisco's job history.
☐ Complete a job history for Francisco.
☐ Use the simple past.
☐ Complete a job history form about yourself.

Resources

Heinle Picture Dictionary: Jobs 1, pages 146–147; Jobs 2, pages 148–149

Pacing

■ 1.5 hour classes   ■ 2.5 hour classes
■ 3+ hour classes

Standards Correlations

CASAS: 0.1.2, 0.1.5, 4.1.2, 4.1.8, 7.4.4, 7.7.3
CCRS: L1, L2, L3, RI1, RI2, RI3, SL1, SL3, W1, W3
ELPS:
S2: Participate in level-appropriate oral and written exchanges of information, ideas, and analyses, in various social and academic contexts, responding to peer, audience, or reader comments and questions.
S5: Conduct research and evaluate and communicate findings to answer questions or solve problems.
S10: Demonstrate command of the conventions of standard English to communicate in level-appropriate speech and writing.

Warm-up and Review   7–10 mins. ■■■

Do a corners activity. Send students to corners of the room based on these categories: *employed, unemployed but looking, unemployed and not looking,* and *retired.* If necessary, you can adjust these categories to better suit your class.

Ask students to interview each other in their corners. Give them these questions:

Employed: Where do you work? When do you start work?
Unemployed but looking: What job do you want? Where do you want to work?

Unemployed and not looking: What do you do? Where do you live?

Retired: What do you do? Where do you live?

Introduction   3–5 mins. ■■■

Write your current and previous jobs on the board. Tell students a little about your job history. State the goal: *Today, you will write your job history.*

Presentation 1   15–20 mins. ■■■

Ask students to look at the photo. Ask the questions in **A**. Make sure that students have the paragraph beside the photo covered up so they don't refer to it to answer the questions. With the rest of the page covered, ask students the first four questions in **B**. At this point, they will be guessing, so accept any answer. This method helps students prepare to read. They are predicting what they will read based on the photo.

A   PREDICT   Look at the photo. What is Francisco's job? Does he work in an office? Read about Francisco. 🎧

Ask students to read the paragraph about Francisco by themselves and confirm their answers to the questions in the direction line.

B   SUMMARIZE   Answer the questions. Then tell a summary to a partner.

Have students answer the questions. Then discuss how similar or different the answers are to their predictions. Go over any new words in the text. Then have students use their answers to give a partner a summary of the information about Francisco.

Workplace Focus

Exercise C: Collect and organize information.

Practice 1   12–15 mins. ■■■

C   Complete the job history for Francisco.

Use your job history on the board to show how the most recent job always goes first. Allow students to do this activity on their own.

Evaluation 1   3–7 mins. ■■■

Have students compare with a partner. Then complete the job history together on the board.

Presentation 2   15–20 mins. ■■■

Draw a timeline on the board. Label the center as the present. Put an arrow going to the left and an arrow going to the right. Write *past* and *future* in the appropriate places. Then say some examples about yourself in the past and write them on the board below the timeline. For example: *I lived…* *I worked…*

D Study the charts.

Go over the charts as a class. Have students repeat the sentences. Point out the *-ed* endings for regular verbs and how the verb *be* is different. Have students find examples of the simple past in the paragraph in **A**.

Practice 2   10–15 mins. ■■■

E Complete each sentence with the correct form of the verb in parentheses. Then listen and check your answers. Complete the last item with your information. 🎧

Ask students to work individually to complete this activity. Play the audio so they can confirm their answers.

Evaluation 2   7–10 mins. ■■■

Ask volunteers to write their completed sentences on the board, and go over them as a class.

BEST PRACTICE

Fill-in-the-Blank Activities

Teachers can easily expand fill-in-the-blank activities to give students more practice (particularly when the correct verb form is required). Teachers can write both the correct and incorrect verb forms on the board and ask students which one fits into the sentences. Teachers can ask students to create new sentences using the same verb form. Teachers can also ask students to add more sentences to the example to provide more detail.

Read through the information together. If possible, show students an example of an online application form. Help students understand what they should do before they complete an online form to avoid losing their information. Demonstrate if possible.

Life ONLINE

D Study the charts.

Simple Past: Regular Verbs		
Subject	**Base Verb + *ed***	**Example Sentence**
I / You He / She We / They	cleaned	I **cleaned** tables.
	cooked	You **cooked** hamburgers.
	prepared	He **prepared** breakfast.
	fixed	She **fixed** cars.
	helped	We **helped** other workers.
	moved	They **moved** to the United States.

Simple Past: *Be*		
Subject	***Be***	**Example Sentence**
I / He / She	was	I **was** an auto mechanic.
We / You / They	were	You **were** happy.

E Complete each sentence with the correct form of the verb in parentheses. Then listen and check your answers. Complete the last item with your information. 🎧

1. Anya was an office assistant. She _____answered_____ (answer) the phone.

2. Chioma was a delivery person. She _____delivered_____ (deliver) packages.

3. David was a cashier. He _____helped_____ (help) customers.

4. Ernesto was a nurse. He _____cared_____ (care) for patients.

5. Eva and Soraya were teachers. They _____worked_____ (work) in a school.

6. Anita was a salesperson. She _____talked_____ (talk) to customers.

7. Thu Ya was a mechanic. He _____fixed_____ (fix) cars.

8. Agatha was a manager. She _____supervised_____ (supervise) the other workers.

9. Mary was a cook. She _____prepared_____ (prepare) lunch.

10. I was a ___Answers will vary.___ . I ___Answers will vary.___ .

Online Job Applications

Many companies only accept job applications online. Some applications ask for a lot of information. If you take too long to answer, some websites "time out" and you can lose everything you typed in and need to type it again. It is a good idea to have all your information ready and to save it in a document so you can copy and paste it into the application. This will save you time, and you can make sure it is all correct.

Life ONLINE

F Practice the conversation with a partner. Then make new conversations using the information below.

Saleh: What was your last job?

Anya: I was <u>an office assistant</u>.

Saleh: What did you do as <u>an office assistant</u>?

Anya: I <u>scheduled appointments</u>.

Saleh: What do you do now?

Anya: I am <u>a student</u>. I <u>study English</u>.

-ed Ending 🎧

-ed is pronounced three different ways:

/t/	/d/	/ɪd/
worked	delivered	painted
typed	cleaned	counted

Before

1. office assistant / schedule appointments
2. soccer player / play soccer
3. mechanic / fix cars
4. mail carrier / deliver letters
5. cook / cook hamburgers
6. busser / clean tables

Now

student / study English

teacher / help students

painter / paint buildings

tree trimmer / trim trees

manager / supervise employees

server / serve food

G Listen and complete the job history. Then practice the conversation in F again with the new information. 🎧

Position	Company	From	To	Duties (Responsibilities)
nurse	Arch Memorial Hospital	August, 2021	Present	help doctors and sick people
office manager	Arch Memorial Hospital	May, 2018	January, 2021	supervised three employees
receptionist	Arch Memorial Hospital	January, 2015	May, 2018	answered the phone and greeted people

H **APPLY** Complete the job history for yourself. Answers will vary.

Position	Company	From	To	Duties (Responsibilities)

I Find a job application online. How much can you complete? Can you complete the job history section?

Presentation 3
7–10 mins. ■■■□

Ask students what their last job was. Ask what they did in that job. Help them express themselves, and write new verbs on the board. Write a job history chart, similar to the one in **H**, on the board. Ask a few students for their job history information and complete the chart.

Workplace Focus
Exercise F: Interpret and communicate information.

Practice 3
10–15 mins. ■□□□

F **Practice the conversation with a partner. Then make new conversations using the information below.**

Go over the conversation with students. Show them how the information comes from Item 1 in the *Before* and *Now* columns below. Go over the simple past form of each of the verbs in the *Before* column.

Pronunciation *-ed* Ending

Point out the pronunciation note and play the audio. Play the audio again, pausing for students to repeat each verb.

At this level, students may not be ready to acquire the three different pronunciations of regular simple past verbs, but they should be aware of this difference. It is particularly important for them to recognize and eventually produce the /ɪd/ ending since this adds an additional syllable. When modeling these endings, provide exaggerated versions at first and then have students listen for the endings at a natural pace. They should be able to repeat them after you.

Listening Script
The simple past -ed ending is pronounced three different ways:
/t/ worked, typed
/d/ delivered, cleaned
/ɪd/ painted, counted

Put students in pairs to practice the conversation. Monitor and help them with the pronunciation of the simple past forms. Make sure they take turns asking and answering.

Evaluation 3
15–20 mins. ■□□□

Have students perform their conversations in front of the class.

Workplace Focus
Exercises G and H: Complete tasks as assigned.

G **Listen and complete the job history. Then practice the conversation in F again with the new information.** 🎧

Tell students they are going to listen to someone talking about their work history. Have them read the information in the chart and decide what information they need to listen for. Play the audio. Play the audio again and give students time to write their answers. Have students compare with a partner before playing the audio a final time.

Have students check their work in pairs before they practice the conversation in **F** again.

Listening Script
The first job I ever had was as a receptionist. I worked very hard. I did that job for over three years and learned a lot. I answered the phone and greeted people. I started my second position in 2018. I was an office manager. I supervised three employees. Now I am a nurse. I help doctors and sick people. It is a great job.

Application
15–20 mins. ■■■□

H **APPLY** **Complete the job history for yourself.**

Tell students to make a list of jobs they did in their notebooks first and add dates and duties. When they are ready, have them complete the job history form. Students who don't have a traditional job history can list *student* and / or *homemaker*. Monitor, and help with verbs for different duties as needed.

I **Find a job application online. How much can you complete? Can you complete the job history section?**

Encourage students to find application forms themselves, but have some sites available in case they need them. Depending on internet access during class, print forms if necessary. Have students complete as much of the application as they can. Remind them to use their job history in **H** to help them. Monitor and help as needed.

At-a-Glance Prep

Goal: Participate in a job interview

Grammar: *Yes / no* questions with *can*

Pronunciation: Intonation with clarification questions

Academic Strategies: Classifying information, making predictions, contrasting strengths and weaknesses

Vocabulary: Job interviews

Agenda

☐ Review job histories.

☐ Classify job interview behavior.

☐ Practice interview questions.

☐ Describe strengths and weaknesses.

☐ Practice an interview.

Resources

Heinle Picture Dictionary: Jobs 1, pages 146–147; Jobs 2, pages 148–149

Pacing

■ 1.5 hour classes   ■ 2.5 hour classes
■ 3+ hour classes

Standards Correlations

CASAS: 0.1.1, 0.1.2, 0.1.5, 0.1.6, 0.2.1, 4.1.5, 4.1.9, 4.6.1

CCRS: SL1, SL3

ELPS:

S10: Demonstrate command of the conventions of standard English to communicate in level-appropriate speech and writing.

Warm-up and Review
10–15 mins. ■■■

Ask students to work with a partner. One student should report their job history orally, while the other student takes notes. Then have them switch roles. Tell them to use **H** from the previous lesson to help them.

Introduction
10–15 mins. ■■■

Turn to a student and shake their hand. Remind the class of how to shake hands the American way by curling the fingers around the other person's hand firmly. Write on the board: *I'm looking for a job. Do you have any openings?* Shake hands with a few more students and say the statement and ask the question. Call on volunteers to do the same. Then have all students walk around the room and

practice the exchange. You can also add to the board typical responses such as: *Yes, here is an application.* State the goal: *Today, we will participate in job interviews.*

Presentation 1
15–20 mins. ■■■

Role-play a bad interview with a volunteer. The volunteer will be the person who represents the hiring company. You might include in your presentation sloppy attire, uncombed hair, gum chewing, and texting during the interview.

Ask students what they found wrong with the interview. Make a list on the board. Then ask students to open their books.

A Look at the pictures. What is good at a job interview? What is not good?

Go over each picture carefully with students. Help them understand the new vocabulary. Then decide as a class which ones are good and which ones aren't good.

Practice 1
10–15 mins. ■■■

B CLASSIFY Complete the chart with your answers from A. Then add your own ideas.

After students have added their own ideas, ask them to form groups to compare lists. Send representatives to other groups to compare and add to their lists.

Evaluation 1
10–12 mins. ■■■

Draw the chart on the board and ask group representatives to enter the information. If students disagree, for example, about whether or not bright clothing is good for an interview, discuss how different cultures might view these things differently and how the dress code may be different depending on the job they are applying for.

A Job Interview

GOAL ▶ Participate in a job interview

A **Look at the pictures. What is good at a job interview? What is not good?**

Good: being cheerful, asking questions, dressing professionally

arriving late

checking your phone or watch

being cheerful

Not good: arriving late, checking your phone or watch, being disorganized

asking questions

dressing professionally

being disorganized

B **CLASSIFY** **Complete the chart with your answers from A. Then add your own ideas.**

Answers will vary.

Good at a Job Interview	Not Good at a Job Interview
being cheerful	arriving late
asking questions	checking your phone or watch
dressing professionally	being disorganized

C Study the chart.

Yes / No Questions with Can				
Can	**Subject**	**Base Verb**	**Example Questions**	**Example Answers**
Can	I	ask	**Can** I **ask** you a question?	Yes, of course.
				Absolutely.
	you	work	**Can** you **work** on weekends?	No, I'm sorry. I can't.
		follow	**Can** you **follow** directions?	Yes, I can.
		speak	**Can** you **speak** to customers well in English?	I believe so. I'm studying English in school.

D **PREDICT** Complete each conversation with a question from the chart in **C**. Then listen for the correct answer. 🎧

1. **Applicant:** Can I ask you a question ?

   Interviewer: Yes, please do.

   Applicant: What are the benefits?

2. **Interviewer:** Can you work on weekends ?

   Applicant: Yes, on Saturday but not on Sunday.

   Interviewer: OK, that's good to know.

3. **Interviewer:** Can you speak to customers well in English ?

   Applicant: Yes, I believe so. I'm studying English in school.

   Interviewer: Great, I just wanted to make sure.

E Match each question with a clarification question. Then listen and check your answers. 🎧

__b__ 1. Do you have a resume?   a. Experience for this job?

__e__ 2. What do you do?   b. A resume?

__a__ 3. Do you have experience?   c. You mean full-time?

__c__ 4. Can you work eight hours a day?   d. You mean in the evenings?

__d__ 5. Can you work extra hours?   e. What is my job now?

Intonation 🎧
Clarification Questions

A: Do you have a resume?   **B:** Can you work extra hours?

B: A resume?   **A:** You mean in the evenings?

Presentation 2   15–20 mins. ■■■

C Study the chart.

Ask students to look at the chart. Go over the subjects, base verbs, and the example questions and answers together. Ask students a few questions to help them get familiar with the structure and how it sounds. For example: *Can I ask you a question?* (and then ask a question like: *Do you want to work in a restaurant? Do you have any experience with customers? Can you speak English well? Can you tell me about your job?*).

D PREDICT Complete each conversation with a question from the chart in C. Then listen for the correct answer. 🎧

Ask students to look at the conversations. Go over the responses. Make sure students understand all the responses. Ask them to predict which phrase goes with which conversation. Tell students they are going to listen to the complete conversations. Then play the audio. Play the audio one or more additional times so they can check their answers.

Listening Script

1. **Interviewer:** *Thank you for answering all our questions. We'll contact you soon to let you know about the position.*
   Applicant: *Thank you. I'm very interested. Can I ask you a question?*
   Interviewer: *Yes, please do.*
   Applicant: *What are the benefits?*
   Interviewer: *We offer medical and dental insurance. We also have sick leave and 6 days of vacation every year.*
   Applicant: *Thanks.*

2. **Interviewer:** *Well, I think you look very good for the position. We must speak to many other applicants. We are open every day of the week including Saturdays and Sundays. Can you work on weekends?*
   Applicant: *Yes, on Saturday but not on Sunday.*
   Interviewer: *OK, that's good to know.*
   Applicant: *Is that something that's required?*
   Interviewer: *No. We have many opportunities here.*
   Applicant: *OK, thank you.*

3. **Interviewer:** *In this job, you have to talk to customers all the time. I hear that you speak English a little. Can you speak to customers well in English?*
   Applicant: *Yes, I believe so. I'm studying English in school.*
   Interviewer: *Great. I just wanted to make sure. Where do you study?*
   Applicant: *At the adult school around the corner.*
   Interviewer: *Perfect!*

Practice 2   7–10 mins. ■■

E Match each question with a clarification question. Then listen and check your answers. 🎧

Have students do this activity in pairs. Then play the audio so they can confirm their answers. Focus on the clarification questions in the second column and ask students whether the intonation rises or falls. Tell students to focus on the intonation of those questions and play the audio again.

> **Intonation   Clarification Questions**
> Point out the Intonation note and play the audio. Play the audio again, pausing for students to repeat the clarification questions.

Listening Script

Use rising intonation with clarification questions.

A: *Do you have a resume?*
B: *A resume?*

B: *Can you work extra hours?*
A: *You mean in the evenings?*

Evaluation 2   5–10 mins. ■■

Have students practice the questions and clarification questions in **E** with a partner. Observe and focus on their intonation in the clarification questions.

Presentation 3
10–15 mins. ■■■

F Look at the picture. Who is Shanika talking to? What is she doing?

Ask students to look at the photo and describe the situation.

G CONTRAST Read the sentences describing strengths. Then match the strengths to the weaknesses.

Go over the sentences in the box and clarify any vocabulary doubts. Make sure students understand the concepts of *strengths* and *weaknesses*. Then have students complete the activity individually and compare with a partner. Check the answers as a class.

Practice 3
7–10 mins. ■

H Write your strengths and weaknesses as a student or worker.

Give students time to reflect on their strengths and weaknesses. Provide vocabulary if they want to express an idea that hasn't been mentioned in **G**. Have them complete the chart.

Evaluation 3
5–7 mins. ■
Have students share their lists from **H** with a partner. If they feel comfortable, encourage them to give each other advice about their weaknesses.

Application
10–15 mins. ■■■

I APPLY Work with a partner. Practice asking and answering the interview question: *What are your strengths?*

Pair students with new partners. Tell them they are at an interview. Review the good and not good interview behavior from **A** and **B**. Have pairs practice greeting and handshaking. Then have them carry out their interview, greeting each other and then asking and answering the question in the direction line. Remind them to use clarification questions if they can. Monitor and help as needed. Encourage students to develop the interview further by asking questions from **D** and **E**. Make sure they switch roles so they both have an opportunity to be the interviewee.

Read the title and ask if anyone has had an online interview. Have them share their experience. Read through the tips together and make sure students understand what they should do before an interview online to be better prepared. If possible, demonstrate some of the tips on a video calling platform.

Life ONLINE

Instructor's Notes

_____
_____
_____
_____
_____
_____
_____
_____
_____
_____
_____
_____
_____
_____
_____
_____
_____
_____
_____
_____
_____

F Look at the picture. Who is Shanika talking to? What is she doing?

G CONTRAST Read the sentences describing strengths. Then match the strengths to the weaknesses.

I am a hard worker.	I communicate well.
I am punctual.	I listen and follow directions well.

Strengths	Weaknesses
I am punctual.	I'm sometimes late.
I am a hard worker.	I like to take a lot of breaks.
I listen and follow directions well.	I don't always listen.
I communicate well.	Sometimes, people don't understand me.

H Write your strengths and weaknesses as a student or worker. Answers will vary.

Strengths	Weaknesses

I APPLY Work with a partner. Practice asking and answering the interview question: *What are your strengths?*

Life ONLINE

Online Job Interviews
Things to do before an online interview:
1. Check your camera and microphone and make sure they work.
2. Be sure to use a professional background.
3. Practice looking at the camera and not down at your notes.

He's a Good Worker

GOAL ▶ Evaluate work and school performance

A Read Fernando's employee evaluation. What is good? What is a problem?

EMPLOYEE EVALUATION
FERNANDO GASPAR

Position: Sales Clerk
Supervisor: Leticia García

Heritage
Cakes & Pies

PUNCTUALITY

○ Exceeds Expectations   ○ Meets Expectations   ● Needs Improvement

Comments: Fernando arrives 10-15 minutes late to work about half the time.

TEAMWORK

● Exceeds Expectations   ○ Meets Expectations   ○ Needs Improvement

Comments: He works with other employees very well in a team environment.

COMMUNICATION SKILLS

○ Exceeds Expectations   ● Meets Expectations   ○ Needs Improvement

Comments: He works with customers well and is very helpful.

PRODUCT KNOWLEDGE

○ Exceeds Expectations   ● Meets Expectations   ○ Needs Improvement

Comments: He knows about the products and knows where to find information
when he has a question.

[Submit]   [Clear Form]

B INTERPRET Look at the evaluation and answer the questions.

1. Where does Fernando work? Heritage Cakes and Pies

2. What is his supervisor's name? Leticia Garcia

3. What does Fernando do very well? He works with other employees very well.

4. What does he do well? He works with customers well and is helpful. He knows about the products.

5. What does he need to improve? He needs to improve his punctuality.

At-a-Glance Prep

Goal: Evaluate work and school performance

Grammar: Simple present and past: *Be*, adverbs of frequency

Academic Strategies: Interpreting information, analyzing, focused listening

Vocabulary: *Punctuality, communication skills, teamwork, product knowledge, exceeds / meets expectations, needs improvement*

Agenda

☐ Review and practice interviews.

☐ Read an evaluation form.

☐ Use the verb *be* in the simple past.

☐ Listen to an evaluation.

☐ Read self-evaluations.

☐ Do a self-evaluation.

Resources

Heinle Picture Dictionary: Working, pages 150–151

Pacing

■ 1.5 hour classes ■ 2.5 hour classes
■ 3+ hour classes

Standards Correlations

CASAS: 4.1.9, 4.4.1, 4.4.4

CCRS: L1, L2, L3, RI1, RI2

ELPS:

S9: Create clear and coherent level-appropriate speech and text.

S10: Demonstrate command of the conventions of standard English to communicate in level-appropriate speech and writing.

Warm-up and Review   10–15 mins. ■■■

Ask students to practice their interviews from Lesson 4, **I** and perform them for the class. Remind students about appropriate etiquette when others are performing in front of the class if necessary. Other students should be paying attention and not doing other work or talking.

Introduction   7–10 mins. ■■■

Write *punctuality* on the board. Give a brief definition. Take a class vote to determine which student is the most consistently punctual in the class. State the goal: *Today, we will evaluate work and school performance.*

Presentation 1   15–20 mins. ■■■

Ask students what makes a good worker. Write their ideas on the board. Help them with challenging words. Write new vocabulary next to the ideas students suggest. For example, write *punctuality* next to *comes to work on time.*

A Read Fernando's employee evaluation. What is good? What is a problem?

As a class, go over each area of the evaluation form. Elicit / Explain the meaning of new words as you go through each item.

BEST PRACTICE

Presenting Material

Asking questions is one of the best ways to introduce and present material. Before doing **B**, ask all the questions and several other questions of your own. Make sure students are not completing **B** at this time. You may even ask them to cover it up so they are not tempted.

Ask the easier questions to the class and the more challenging questions to individuals you believe can answer. Keep everyone's attention by asking students to find items and to point to them in their book.

Make it a point to ask easier questions to students who have more trouble communicating and then be ready to guide them if you need to. Another way to include these students is to ask a question to the class and give students time to think before you call on an individual.

Workplace Focus

Exercise B: Collect and organize information; Combine ideas and information.

Practice 1   10–15 mins. ■■■

B INTERPRET Look at the evaluation and answer the questions.

Have students complete the activity individually so they can confirm their understanding. Then have them compare answers with a partner.

Evaluation 1   3–5 mins. ■■■

Go over the answers to **B** as a class.

Presentation 2
15–20 mins. ■■■■

C Study the charts.

Review the simple present of *be*. Read the examples together and elicit further sentences from students. Go over the simple past and remind students about the regular simple past that they studied in this unit. Explain that the verb *be* is an irregular verb.

Review adverbs of frequency. These were last introduced in Unit 5, Lesson 5.

Practice 2
10–15 mins. ■■■

D Complete the sentences with the correct form of *be*.

This activity is more difficult than it looks as it involves both present and past verb forms. Tell students to read each sentence carefully and decide if it is past or present first. Have students work in pairs and then compare answers with another pair.

Evaluation 2
7–10 mins. ■■■

Go over the answers as a class. Refer students back to the charts as needed.

E ANALYZE Read about Alba. Underline the *be* verbs. 🎧

Have students do this activity individually and then discuss with a partner. Tell them to look at the charts in **C** if they need to. Check answers as a class. Have students tell you which ones are present and which are past. Play the audio and have students read as they listen. Tell them to pay attention to the pronunciation of the different forms of the verb *be*.

Instructor's Notes

_____

_____

_____

_____

_____

_____

_____

_____

_____

_____

_____

_____

_____

_____

_____

_____

_____

_____

_____

_____

_____

_____

_____

_____

_____

_____

C Study the charts.

Simple Present: *Be*			
Subject	***Be***		**Example Sentence**
I	am	early late on time punctual	I **am** always early.
He / She / It	is		He **is** sometimes late. She **is** a good worker.
We / You / They	are		We **are** often early. You **are** never on time. They **are** always punctual.

Adverbs of Frequency

0%   50%   100%

never   rarely   sometimes   usually   always

Simple Past: *Be*			
Subject	***Be***		**Example Sentence**
I / He / She / It	was	early late on time punctual	I **was** early yesterday. He **was** often late. She **was** always a good worker.
We / You / They	were		We **were** early on Saturday. You **were** on time today. They **were** never punctual.

D Complete the sentences with the correct form of *be*.

1. Mario and Alberto _____ *were* _____ early for work yesterday.

2. I _____ *was* _____ never on time last year, but now I _____ *am* _____ always on time.

3. She _____ *was* _____ punctual every day last year.

4. We come to work on time every day. We _____ *are* _____ rarely late.

5. You _____ *are* _____ a good worker. You always work well with customers.

E **ANALYZE** Read about Alba. Underline the *be* verbs.

> Alba <u>is</u> a good worker. She works in the evening. She <u>is</u> punctual. The customers love her. Last night, Alba <u>was</u> late for work. She had a problem with her car. Her car <u>is</u> old. She called a tow truck with her cell phone, and the tow truck <u>was</u> late.

F Listen to Amed's evaluation. Choose the correct rating.

1. Communication skills:
   a. Exceeds expectations *(circled)* b. Meets expectations   c. Needs improvement

2. Punctuality:
   a. Exceeds expectations   b. Meets expectations *(circled)*   c. Needs improvement

3. Teamwork:
   a. Exceeds expectations   b. Meets expectations   c. Needs improvement *(circled)*

4. Product knowledge:
   a. Exceeds expectations   b. Meets expectations   c. Needs improvement *(circled)*

G Read Marta's and Neda's self-evaluations. What do they do well? What do they need to improve?

Marta's Self-Evaluation

I am a good employee. I work hard. Sometimes, I'm late. I always listen and follow directions well. I am learning English. Sometimes, people don't understand me. I want to be a great employee. I need to communicate well and come to work on time.

Neda's Self-Evaluation

I don't work. I go to school. I am punctual, but I don't always listen well. I am learning English. Sometimes, people don't understand me. Sometimes, I don't do my homework because I'm very busy. I want to be a great student. I need to communicate well and do my homework every day.

H APPLY Write your own self-evaluation. Use the texts in **G** as examples.

Answers will vary.

Presentation 3　　　　　　　7–10 mins. ■■■

With books closed, elicit what areas are evaluated in a work performance evaluation and the phrases used to evaluate them. Refer students back to **A** as needed.

Practice 3　　　　　　　15–20 mins. ■

F **Listen to Amed's evaluation. Choose the correct rating.** 🎧

Tell students they are going to hear Amed's supervisor giving him his evaluation. Play the audio several times and allow students to discuss their answers between listenings. Check the answers as a class. Play the audio again as needed, pausing after key words.

Listening Script

Supervisor: *Amed, I think in time you will become an excellent worker. You certainly speak well and you are very good with the customers. I gave you* exceeds expectations *for communication skills. This is why I am sure you can be a great employee in time. I did notice that you usually come to work on time. You were late once, but only by a few minutes. For punctuality I have given you a* meets expectations.

I know that you are trying to work hard and make extra money by working more days. But you need to be willing to work with others more. You seem to like working by yourself. Your coworkers can help you learn a lot. When you work better with others, we will feel comfortable giving you more hours. I had to give you a needs improvement *on teamwork for now. You are new, so don't worry too much about this one. You will learn quickly if you apply yourself. I also gave you a* needs improvement *for product knowledge because you are still learning about all of the different items we sell here. I am sure that will change in no time.*

G **Read Marta's and Neda's self-evaluations. What do they do well? What do they need to improve?** 🎧

Have students read the evaluations and underline the answers to the questions in the direction line. If time allows, play the audio and ask students to read as they listen. For some students, it is helpful to hear as well as see the information.

Evaluation 3　　　　　　　3 mins. ■

Discuss the evaluations in **G** together and have students point out the parts that say what each person does well and what they need to improve.

Application　　　　　　　10–15 mins. ■■■

H **APPLY** **Write your own self-evaluation. Use the texts in G as examples.**

Point out that Marta's self-evaluation is about her as an employee and Neda's is about her as a student. Have students decide if they want to evaluate themselves as students or employees. To help prepare them, you can also elicit questions for them to answer. For example: *Are you punctual? Do you listen well?* Encourage students to use adverbs of frequency in their answers.

Instructor's Notes

_____

_____

_____

_____

_____

_____

_____

_____

_____

_____

_____

_____

At-a-Glance Prep

Goal: Identify employment opportunities in the landscaping industry

Agenda

☐ Read about landscaping.
☐ Interpret a bar graph.
☐ Read an infographic.
☐ Interpret a job posting.
☐ Reflect on the characteristics of tree trimmers.
☐ Search online for openings in landscaping.

Pacing

■ 1.5 hour classes ■ 2.5 hour classes
■ 3+ hour classes

Standards Correlations

CASAS: 0.1.2, 0.1.5, 3.4.2, 4.1.3, 4.1.8, 4.1.9, 4.3.2, 6.7.2, 7.4.4, 7.7.3
CCRS: L1, L3, RI1, RI2, RI3, SL1, SL3, W1, W3
ELPS:
S1: Construct meaning from oral presentations and literary and informational text through level-appropriate listening, reading, and viewing.
S5: Conduct research and evaluate and communicate findings to answer questions or solve problems.
S7: Adapt language choices to purpose, task, and audience when speaking and writing.

In this lesson, students are introduced to employment opportunities in the landscaping industry. They will read about landscaping and analyze a bar graph showing jobs in landscaping and their annual salaries. Students will also read an infographic about the job of a tree trimmer and reflect on the characteristics of a tree trimmer and which of these characteristics they have. Finally, students will carry out an online search for job openings in their area related to landscaping.

Warm-up and Review   10–15 mins. ■■■

Write *landscaping* on the board and elicit / have students look up its meaning. Then elicit any jobs they can think of related to landscaping and where people in landscaping might work. Write their ideas on the board.

Introduction   5–10 mins. ■■■

Find out if any of the students work in landscaping or know anyone who does. Remind them that throughout *Stand Out*, they will investigate many job possibilities. Write the goal on the board: *Today we will identify employment opportunities in the landscaping industry.*

Presentation 1   10–15 mins. ■■■

A Read about the landscaping industry. Where do people in this industry work? 🎧

Have students read the text. Then clarify any vocabulary doubts. Discuss the question in the direction line as a class.

Practice 1   20–25 mins. ■■■

B INTERPRET Look at the bar graph and match each word or phrase with the correct meaning.

Go over the graph together, having students explain what it shows (positions and salaries). Review large numbers by asking them to say the salaries in the chart. Have students do the matching activity individually, then compare with a partner. Check answers as a class.

C Work with a partner. Ask and answer questions about the graph.

Remind students of the question: *How much does a…. make?* Point out the example exchange. Then put them in pairs to carry out the activity. Tell them to alternate asking the question.

Evaluation 1   5–10 mins. ■■■
Observe students as they work in pairs.

Explore the Workforce

GOAL ▶ Identify employment opportunities in the landscaping industry

A **Read about the landscaping industry. Where do people in this industry work?** 🎧

> Do you like being outside? Do you like gardening? Do you want to work in a park or a backyard? If you do, you should work in the landscaping industry. Jobs in landscaping help to create and take care of outdoor places like gardens and parks. Landscaping workers keep these places looking nice so people can enjoy them.

B **INTERPRET** **Look at the bar graph and match each word or phrase with the correct meaning.**

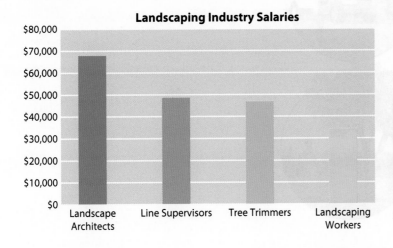

Landscaping Industry Salaries

Legend	
Position	**Annual Salary**
Landscape Architects	$67,950
Line Supervisors	$48,800
Tree Trimmers	$46,970
Landscaping Workers	$34,430

Source: U.S. Bureau of Labor Statistics

___c___ 1. legend

___a___ 2. annual

___b___ 3. a tree trimmer

___e___ 4. a line supervisor

___d___ 5. a landscape architect

a. every year

b. a person who cuts parts of trees

c. a list of information about a graph or map

d. a person who plans and creates outdoor places like parks and gardens

e. a manager of a small landscaping team

C **Work with a partner. Ask and answer questions about the graph.**

EXAMPLE: **Student A:** How much does the average tree trimmer make?

Student B: The average tree trimmer makes $46,970 a year.

D **Read the infographic about tree trimmers. Underline any words you don't know.**

TREE TRIMMING SAFETY TIPS

Tree trimming is a dangerous job. You often have to climb trees and work in high places. Tree trimmers need to follow special safety rules.

1 WEAR PERSONAL PROTECTIVE EQUIPMENT (PPE)

- GLOVES
- HARD HAT
- BOOTS
- SAFETY VEST
- GOGGLES

2 KEEP COWORKERS SAFE

- MARK YOUR WORK AREA.
- KNOW WHERE OTHER WORKERS ARE.
- MAKE PLANS BEFORE YOU START.

3 LOOK AT THE TREE CAREFULLY

- CHECK FOR BROKEN BRANCHES.
- DON'T CLIMB ON BROKEN BRANCHES.

E **Complete the sentences with the words from the infographic.**

climb	branches	goggles	rules	safety	vest

1. People wear _____goggles_____ to keep their eyes safe when doing construction work.

2. My kids love to _____climb_____ trees, but I don't let them. It's very dangerous.

3. One of our classroom _____rules_____ is "No eating in class."

4. Trees have many _____branches_____ that stick out and have leaves on them.

5. A _____vest_____ is a piece of clothing that you wear over your shirt. It doesn't have sleeves.

6. _____Safety_____ means being safe from dangerous things.

Presentation 2

15–20 mins. ◼◼◻

D Read the infographic about tree trimmers. Underline any words you don't know.

Look at the infographic together, having students describe what's happening in each picture. Then have students read it and underline new words. Ask students what the infographic is about. Don't explain vocabulary yet; let them do **E** first.

Practice 2

10–15 mins. ◼◼◻

E Complete the sentences with the words from the infographic.

Have students try to complete the sentences individually first. Tell them to read the infographic again to check the context of each word. Remind them that context can help them understand the meaning of new words. Then let students work in pairs to discuss their choices. Encourage them to use a dictionary as needed.

Evaluation 2

5–10 mins. ◼◻

Go over the answers to **E** as a class. Ask students to go back to the words they underlined and clarify any that are still not clear.

Instructor's Notes

_____
_____
_____
_____
_____
_____
_____
_____
_____
_____
_____
_____
_____
_____
_____
_____
_____
_____
_____
_____
_____
_____
_____

Presentation 3

10–15 mins. ■■■

F **Work in a group. Read the job posting for a tree trimmer and answer the questions.**

Put students in groups using one of the techniques in the Best Practice note. Remind them to refer back to the infographic in **D** and the bar graph in **B** when they discuss the questions. Have a spokesperson from each group share their answers and discuss the job posting as a class.

Practice 3

15–20 mins. ■■

Ask students in shorter classes to do Practice 3 for homework.

G **REFLECT** **The list shows characteristics of tree trimmers. Check (✓) what is true about you. Then talk with a partner about the items you checked.**

Before students look at the list, ask them what characteristics a tree trimmer needs to have. Write their ideas on the board. Read the items together and clarify any vocabulary doubts. Then ask students to check the ones that apply to them. When they are ready, have students share their answers with a partner.

H **Choose a job title from B. Go to a job search site online and see if there are any openings within 25 miles of your school or home.**

Get students started with their searches by helping them decide which of the jobs in **B** they want to look for. Share specific job search sites that they can use. Tell them to write down the salaries, benefits, and training provided for the jobs they find. Monitor as they carry out their searches and help as needed.

Evaluation 3

5–10 mins. ■

Put students into groups of three or four and have them share and discuss what they found. Observe the groups as they discuss.

BEST PRACTICE

More Group Forming Strategies

As previously mentioned, it can sometimes be beneficial to mix up the groups students typically work in. This can sometimes be accomplished best by using a variety of grouping techniques. Here are some additional ways of forming student groups:

- Ask each student to pick a partner. Then combine pairs to make groups.
- Write students' names on small cards. Then randomly pick cards to make groups.
- Give students specific categories for making their own groups. For example, have them choose classmates wearing jeans, a blue shirt, black shoes, etc.
- Have students get into groups of four. Then ask one student from each group to raise their hand. Choose those with raised hands to form a new group. Repeat the process with the remaining students.

Instructor's Notes

_____

_____

_____

_____

_____

_____

_____

_____

_____

_____

_____

_____

A tree trimmer uses a chainsaw to cut branches of a tree in Northern California.

F Work in a group. Read the job posting for a tree trimmer and answer the questions.

NOW HIRING
TREE TRIMMERS

- TOP PAY
- ON-THE-JOB TRAINING
- GOOD BENEFITS:

Paid holidays
Paid vacation time
Health insurance

1. What do you think the pay is for this position?

2. What do you think *on-the-job training* means?

3. Would you like this position? Why or why not?

G **REFLECT** The list shows characteristics of tree trimmers. Check (✓) what is true about you. Then talk with a partner about the items you checked. Answers will vary.

- ☐ I like to work outside.
- ☐ I like to work on a team.
- ☐ I like to work with my hands.
- ☐ I have no problem getting dirty.

- ☐ I like to make things look good.
- ☐ I am not afraid to work in high places.
- ☐ I like to use machines and tools.
- ☐ I am good at following directions.

H Choose a job title from **B**. Go to a job search site online and see if there are any openings within 25 miles of your school or home.

Review

A Write the correct job for each photo.

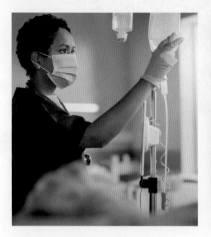  

1. _____nurse_____   2. _____cashier_____   3. _____teacher_____

B Read the job postings and complete the chart below.

Office Assistant
Anaheim, CA 92805
Salary: $17 / hour
Job Type: Full-time
Benefits: Health insurance, paid time off, sick leave
Qualifications: 2 years' experience
Apply Now

Restaurant Manager
Austin, TX 73301
Salary: $28 / hour
Job Type: Part-time
No Benefits
Qualifications: 1 year's experience
Apply Now

Delivery Driver
Providence, RI 02904
Salary: $15 / hour
Job Type: Full-time
Benefits: Health insurance, paid time off
Qualifications: No experience required, need current driver's license
Apply Now

Position	Experience	FT or PT	Benefits	Pay
1. office assistant	2 years' experience	full-time	health insurance, paid time off, sick leave	$17 / hour
2. restaurant manager	1 year's experience	part-time	no benefits	$28 / hour
3. delivery driver	no experience required	full-time	health insurance, paid time off	$15 / hour

Learner Log   I can identify common occupations.
☐ Yes ☐ No ☐ Maybe

I can interpret job information.
☐ Yes ☐ No ☐ Maybe

At-a-Glance Prep

Goal: All unit goals
Grammar: All unit grammar
Academic Strategies: Focused listening, reviewing, evaluating, developing study skills
Vocabulary: All unit vocabulary

Agenda
☐ Discuss unit goals.
☐ Complete the review.
☐ Evaluate and reflect on progress.

Pacing
■ 1.5 hour classes   ■ 2.5 hour classes
■ 3+ hour classes

Standards Correlations
CASAS: 4.1.2, 4.1.3, 4.1.5, 4.1.6, 4.1.8, 4.4.1, 4.4.4, 4.6.1
CCRS: RI1, RI2, W3
ELPS:
S9: Create clear and coherent level-appropriate speech and text.
S10: Demonstrate command of the conventions of standard English to communicate in level-appropriate speech and writing.

Warm-up and Review   10–15 mins. ■ ■ ■
With books closed, ask students to help you make a list on the board of all the vocabulary they can come up with from the unit. Then have a competition where students in groups will write a page number for each item on the list. The first group to have a correct page number for each item wins.

Introduction   3 mins. ■ ■ ■
Write all the goals from Unit 7 on the board. Explain that today will be a review.

Presentation   10–15 mins. ■ ■ ■
This presentation will cover all three pages of the review. Quickly go to the first page of each lesson. Discuss the goal of each. Ask simple questions to remind students of what they have learned.

Practice 1   15–20 mins. ■ ■ ■

A Write the correct job for each photo.
Before they open their books, have students brainstorm jobs. Then have them complete the activity.

Workplace Focus
Exercise B: Collect and organize information.

B Read the job postings and complete the chart below.
Have students read the information about each job, then complete the chart. When they are ready, have them compare with a partner.

Evaluation 1   5–10 mins. ■ ■ ■
Go around the classroom and check on students' progress. Help individuals as needed. If you see consistent errors among several students, interrupt the class and give a mini lesson or review to help students feel comfortable with the concept.

Learner Log   5–10 mins.
Have students read the statements and complete the log. If students answer *no* or *maybe*, encourage them to set themselves a goal to practice. Show them where they can find more practice activities.

BEST PRACTICE
Learner Logs
Learner Logs function to help students in many different ways:

1. They serve as part of the review process.
2. They help students to gain confidence and to document what they have learned. Consequently, students see that they are progressing in their learning.
3. They provide students with a tool that they can use over and over to check and recheck their understanding of the target language. In this way, students become independent learners.

Practice 2

25–30 mins. ■■■

C **Write a job posting for a receptionist.**

Give students sufficient time to think about a job and its details before they complete the posting. Have them share their job postings in groups of three or four and decide which job each person would like to apply for and why.

If time allows, extend this activity and have students carry out interviews.

D **Complete the paragraph with the simple past form of the verbs in parentheses. Then listen and check your answers.** 🎧

Have students read the paragraph first without writing anything so they understand the context. Then have them write the simple past verb forms. Play the audio to check answers. Play the audio again and tell students to pay attention to the pronunciation of each simple past verb. Pause after each one for students to repeat.

E **Complete the job history for Jinhua.**

Elicit what information a job history gives. Then have students carry out the activity. Remind students that their most recent occupation goes first in a job history.

F **Match the interview questions with the answers.**

Have students complete the activity, then compare answers with a partner. Give them time to practice the interview if possible.

Evaluation 2

5–10 mins. ■■■

Go around the classroom and check on students' progress. Help individuals as needed. If you see consistent errors among several students, interrupt the class and give a mini lesson or review to help students feel comfortable with the concept.

Learner Log

5–10 mins.

Have students read the statements and complete the log. If students answer *no* or *maybe*, encourage them to set themselves a goal to practice. Show them where they can find more practice activities.

BEST PRACTICE

Recycling / Review

The review and the project that follows are part of the recycling / review process. Students at this level often need to be reintroduced to concepts to solidify what they have learned. Many concepts are learned and forgotten while learning other new concepts. This is because students learn but are not necessarily ready to acquire language concepts.

Therefore, it becomes very important to review and to show students how to review on their own. It is also important to recycle the new concepts in different contexts.

Instructor's Notes

_____

_____

_____

_____

_____

_____

_____

_____

_____

_____

_____

_____

_____

_____

_____

_____

C **Write a job posting for a receptionist.** Answers will vary.

Company: _____

Position: _____

Location: _____

Hourly Rate: _____ ☐ **Full-Time** ☐ **Part-Time**

Benefits: _____

D **Complete the paragraph with the simple past form of the verbs in parentheses. Then listen and check your answers.** 🎧

> In 2013, Jinhua was a carpenter. He (1) _____constructed_____ (construct) homes for a company called Builders Plus. In 2016, Jinhua was a custodian. He (2) _____cleaned_____ (clean) offices and (3) _____fixed_____ (fix) things for Clean Sweep, Inc. In 2019, Jinhua was a student. He (4) _____learned_____ (learn) about education at Willington Community College. Now Jinhua is a teacher. He (5) _____started_____ (start) in 2021. He helps students at Jefferson Adult School.

E **Complete the job history for Jinhua.**

Position	Company / School	From	To	Duties (Responsibilities)
teacher	Jefferson Adult School	2021	Present	helps students
student	Willington Community College	2019	2021	learned about education
custodian	Clean Sweep, Inc.	2016	2019	cleaned offices and fixed things
carpenter	Builders Plus	2013	2016	constructed homes

F **Match the interview questions with the answers.**

__c__ 1. What are your strengths?   a. I can work both Saturday and Sunday.

__d__ 2. Do you have experience?   b. Yes, I can work 40 hours a week.

__a__ 3. Can you work on weekends?   c. I have very good communication skills.

__b__ 4. Can you work full-time?   d. Yes, I worked as a nurse in Texas for two years.

Learner Log	I can write my job history. ☐ Yes ☐ No ☐ Maybe	I can participate in a job interview. ☐ Yes ☐ No ☐ Maybe

G Look at the pictures. Choose which are good or bad for a job interview.

1.

good / ~~bad~~

2.

good / ~~bad~~

3.

~~good~~ / bad

4.

~~good~~ / bad

H Complete the employee evaluation with the simple present or simple past form of the verbs. You will use one of the verbs three times.

be	come	help	need

Stella (1) _____is_____ a good worker. She always (2) _____comes_____ to work on time. She is often early. Last week, she (3) _____helped_____ a customer make a very big purchase. Her communication skills exceed expectations. Stella (4) _____was_____ a salesperson in her last job, so her product knowledge (5) _____is_____ good. She (6) _____needs_____ to get better at working with others.

I Choose the best answers for Stella's employee evaluation. Use the text in **H.**

1. Punctuality: **Exceeds expectations** / Meets expectations / Needs improvement

2. Communication: **Exceeds expectations** / Meets expectations / Needs improvement

3. Product Knowledge: Exceeds expectations / **Meets expectations** / Needs improvement

4. Teamwork: Exceeds expectations / Meets expectations / **Needs improvement**

Learner Log	I can evaluate work and school performance.
	☐ Yes ☐ No ☐ Maybe

Practice 3

15–20 mins. ■■■

G Look at the pictures. Choose which are good or bad for a job interview.

When students have completed the activity, ask them to explain each situation.

H Complete the employee evaluation with the simple present or simple past form of the verbs. You will use one of the verbs three times.

Have students read the paragraph and write the verbs in the correct form. Remind them to pay attention to the time, past or present. Have them check answers with a partner. Then review the pronunciation of simple past forms.

I Choose the best answers for Stella's employee evaluation. Use the text in H.

Elicit the meaning of each evaluation phrase. Then have students complete the evaluation. Remind them to go back to Stella's evaluation in **H** and read it again as needed. Have students compare answers with a partner. Then discuss Stella's strengths and weaknesses.

Evaluation 3

5–10 mins. ■■■

Go around the room and check on students' progress. Help individuals as needed. If you see consistent errors among several students, interrupt the class and give a mini lesson or review to help students feel comfortable with the concept.

Learner Log

5 mins.

Have students read the statement and complete the log. If students answer *no* or *maybe*, encourage them to set themselves a goal to practice. Show them where they can find more practice activities.

Instructor's Notes

Standards Correlations

CASAS: 0.1.2, 0.1.5, 0.1.6, 4.1.2, 4.1.3, 4.1.5, 4.1.6, 4.1.8, 4.4.1, 4.8.1

CCRS: L1, L3, SL1, SL3

ELPS:

S7: Adapt language choices to purpose, task, and audience when speaking and writing.

S8: Determine the meaning of words and phrases in oral presentations and literary and informational text.

Workplace Focus

Make decisions and solve problems; Collect and organize information; Combine ideas and information; Make decisions; Exercise leadership roles; Manage time; Complete tasks as assigned; Interact appropriately with team members; Interpret and communicate information.

Soft Skill: Active Listening
Asking for Clarification

Explain that in the workplace, active listening skills are very important. When colleagues are talking, we need to focus our attention on what they are saying and make sure that we have understood correctly; therefore, asking for clarification is part of the active listening skill set. Tell students they will practice this skill throughout the steps of the project.

Warm-up and Review   10 mins.

Review items in the review section of the unit and make sure all students have recorded their progress in the learner logs.

Introduction   5 mins.

Let students know that in this project, they will prepare one member of their team to complete the process for getting a job.

Presentation   10–15 mins.

1. Form a team of four or five students. In your team, you need:

Put students in groups of four or five. Once students are in groups, ask them to choose their positions in the team. To do this, go through each step in the project and explain the role of the person who will lead that step. Make sure students understand that they will complete one step before going on to the next and that although each person has a specific task, they will work together on each step.

The team leader's job is not associated with a step but has the responsibility of making sure everyone participates and speaks English. The team leader may also have ancillary responsibilities when general information is required.

In **Step 2**, for example, the team leader can manage the discussion around choosing who will be the person looking for a job and what job they're interested in. Then in **Steps 3** and **4**, the writer will write the job posting and job history based on the other team members' ideas and suggestions. In **Step 5**, the director will write and manage the practicing of the role play with the help of the team. The whole team will choose who will be the interviewer. For **Step 6**, the organizers will be responsible for planning a presentation of the job posting and job history with ideas and suggestions from the other team members. Point out the Soft Skill note and go over the example clarification questions. As you monitor while groups are working, prompt them to use these questions as needed.

Be aware of who volunteers for which position so that through the different units, you can encourage students to try different roles.

Practice / Evaluation / Application   1–2 hours

2. Choose one member of your team to look for a new job. Decide on a position they are interested in.

3. Write a job posting describing the position.

Refer students back to the job postings in the unit to use as examples if necessary.

4. Write a real or imaginary job history for the person looking for a job.

Refer students back to the examples job histories found in Lesson 3 as needed.

5. Write a job interview role play. Then choose who will be the interviewer and practice the role play.

6. As a team, give a presentation about the job posting and job history. Then perform the role play.

Get a New Job

SOFT SKILL ▶ Active Listening

In this project, you will prepare one member of your team to complete the process for getting a job.

1. Form a team of four or five students. In your team, you need:

Position	Job Description	Student Name
Student 1: **Team Leader**	Check that everyone speaks English. Check that everyone participates.	
Student 2: **Writer**	With help from the team, write a job posting and a job history.	
Student 3: **Director**	With help from the team, write and direct a job interview role play.	
Students 4/5: **Organizer(s)**	With help from the team, organize a presentation to give to the class.	

2. Choose one member of your team to look for a new job. Decide on a position they are interested in.

3. Write a job posting describing the position.

4. Write a real or imaginary job history for the person looking for a job.

5. Write a job interview role play. Then choose who will be the interviewer and practice the role play.

6. As a team, give a presentation about the job posting and job history. Then perform the role play.

ACTIVE LISTENING:
Asking for Clarification

Any time you work with others, there can be misunderstandings. It's a good idea to ask people to repeat any information you don't understand. The polite way to do this is by using phrases or questions such as:

I'm not sure I understand. Can you explain that again?
I don't know that word. What does it mean?
I'm sorry. Can you repeat that, please?

You can also check what you heard by repeating it back. For example:

So, you want to look for a job as a cook, right?
You said you want to look for a job as a cook. Is that right?

Reading Challenge

About the Photo

This photo shows a young man working as a server in a cafe. It is likely that he will do this job for a short period of time, maybe only a few months or a year or two. In the past, people often stayed in one job or one career for a long time, but now it is more common for people to change jobs more often, and even to retrain and change careers.

- Have students look at the photo and describe what they see. Prompt with questions if necessary. For example: *Where is the man? What is he doing? What does he do?* Find out if anyone in the class works in food service.

A SURVEY Ask your classmates how many jobs they think they will have in their life. Make a bar graph.

Go over the bar graph together to make sure students understand how to complete it. Draw the graph on the board. Then elicit or provide the question students need to ask: *How many jobs will you have in you life? Will* is new for them but you don't need to explain it in detail, just that it refers to the future. Use a timeline as needed. Tell the class about different jobs you have had and how many in total. Model the activity by asking one or two students and completing the bars on the graph. Then have students carry out the activity. When they are ready, complete the bar graph on the board together.

Reading Challenge

A **SURVEY** Ask your classmates how many jobs they think they will have in their life. Make a bar graph. Answers will vary.

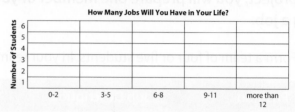

How Many Jobs Will You Have in Your Life?

B Match each word or phrase with its meaning. Use a dictionary if you need to.

- __c__ 1. career
- __a__ 2. social media
- __d__ 3. networking
- __b__ 4. lifetime

a. websites or apps where you share information and connect with others

b. your entire life

c. a job that someone has for a long time

d. building relationships with people to learn about a career or to find a new job

C Read the text and answer the questions.

1. Why do workers today need to be good at interviews and networking?

  a. because it is a good way to learn English   b. because they will probably have many jobs in their lifetime   c. because jobs are important

2. How do we know that the average American has 12 jobs in a lifetime?

  a. The Bureau of Labor Statistics (BLS) has this information.   b. We learned this from the news.   c. We don't know this.

D Work in a group. Look at the reasons for changing jobs. Check (✓) the top five reasons you think people change jobs. Answers will vary.

- ☐ better pay
- ☐ better benefits
- ☐ less stress
- ☐ moving somewhere new
- ☐ for a better position
- ☐ for a better work schedule
- ☐ don't like where they work
- ☐ getting fired or laid off
- ☐ changing careers

E **INVESTIGATE** As a class, investigate social media sites and apps for networking. Do you think they are useful? Why or why not?

B Match each word or phrase with its meaning. Use a dictionary if you need to.

Go over the words and phrases together, saying each one. Then ask students to carry out the activity. Have them compare answers with a partner. Then check as a class.

CASAS FOR READING
0.1.2, 0.1.5, 4.1.9, 6.7.2, 7.4.4, 7.4.5, 7.7.3

CCRS FOR READING
L1, L2, L3, RI1, RI2, RI3, SL1, SL3

How Many Jobs?

1   100 years ago, many Americans had a goal of working one or two jobs for life. Today, according to the Bureau of Labor Statistics (BLS), Americans have around 12 jobs in a lifetime. On average, they work about four or five years per job. Changing jobs more often means workers need to be good at interviews and networking.

5   Networking is a way for workers to talk to other workers and leaders in their field.* Networking is done in many ways. One of the most popular ways is through social media. There are websites and apps where you can connect with people in your workplace and from other companies. Do you have a social media account for networking? It is never too early to start one.

field   area of work or study

One third of all Americans had their first job in a restaurant.

READING CHALLENGE   195

READING STRATEGIES

Question-Answer Relationship

This is a reading strategy that requires students to analyze types of questions asked and where to find answers in a reading. The strategy is used after students have read. Question types are usually those that:

- require students to use background knowledge to answer.
- have answers from different parts of the reading.
- are literal and have answers using the same words.
- ask students to relate the question to their own personal experience.

8 Lifelong Learning

About the Photo

In this photo, students are doing a step dance on their graduation day. Step dancing, or *stepping*, is a fast and exciting form of dance in which the body is used as an instrument. Dancers step, clap, and slap, as well as use their voices to create dynamic rhythms. Stepping was developed by students in African-American fraternities and sororities at several universities in the U.S. One of those is Howard University in Washington, D.C., where the students in this photo have graduated from. They belong to the Phi Beta Sigma fraternity.

- Introduce the unit by reading the title. Then go over the unit outcomes.
- Have students look at the photo and discuss the first two questions in pairs. Have volunteers share their answers with the class.
- Read the information about the photo out loud. Discuss the following four questions as a class. Provide vocabulary support for *achieved*, *goal*, *graduating*, and *celebrate* as needed.

Life Skills Focus

In this unit, students will review what they have learned throughout *Stand Out 1*. They will also learn how to develop future goals pertaining to academia and the workplace.

196

UNIT OUTCOMES	GRAMMAR	VOCABULARY	EL CIVICS
• Evaluate study habits • Make a study guide • Identify learning opportunities • Identify vocational preferences • Develop goals • Identify employment opportunities in education	• Simple past: Regular and irregular verbs • *Should* • Verb + infinitive • Verb + noun • Future with *be going to* and *will*	• Study words • Skills • Education in the U.S. • Goals • Jobs in education	The skills students learn in this unit can be applied to the following EL Civics competency areas: • Employment Resources • Employment Soft Skills

UNIT OUTCOMES

▸ Evaluate study habits
▸ Make a study guide
▸ Identify learning opportunities
▸ Identify vocational preferences
▸ Develop goals
▸ Identify employment opportunities in education

Look at the photo and answer the questions.

1. What are the men wearing?
2. What are they doing?

Members of the Phi Beta Sigma fraternity do a step dance after graduating from Howard University in Washington, D.C.

1. Why do you think the men are dancing?
2. How do you think they feel?
3. These men achieved the goal of graduating from college. What goals do you have for the future?
4. When you achieve a goal, how do you celebrate?

Workplace Focus

All lessons and units in *Stand Out* include basic communication skills and interpersonal skills important for the workplace. They include *collecting and organizing information*, *making decisions and solving problems*, and *combining ideas and information*.

- In Unit 8, Lesson 6, *Explore the Workforce*, students will identify jobs in education. They will interpret an infographic about teaching positions and salaries in education and read about the job of an ESL tutor. They will also reflect on their suitability for a teaching job and discuss the characteristics of a good teacher.

- In the Team Project, students practice the soft skill of engaging the audience while giving a presentation.

- Life Online notes in Lesson 5 raise awareness about study apps and spell checkers.

spark Resources

All resources for the unit are centrally located on the Spark platform and include: audio, video, multilevel worksheets, digital literacy worksheets, Online Practice, and Assessment Suite.

197

— STEPS —

CASAS COMPETENCIES	ELPS	CCRS
Lesson 1: 6.1.1, 6.1.3, 7.2.3, 7.4.1, 7.4.3, 7.4.9 Lesson 2: 0.1.2, 0.1.5, 7.1.1, 7.1.4, 7.4.1, 7.4.3 Lesson 3: 0.1.2, 0.1.5, 2.8.2, 7.1.1, 7.2.3, 7.4.4 Lesson 4: 0.1.2, 0.1.5, 4.1.9, 7.1.1, 7.5.1 Lesson 5: 2.3.1, 4.1.9, 7.1.1, 7.1.2, 7.4.1, 7.4.4, 7.7.3 Lesson 6: 0.1.2, 0.1.5, 4.1.3, 4.1.8, 4.1.9, 6.7.4, 7.4.4, 7.7.3 Review: 0.1.2, 0.1.5, 7.1.1, 7.1.4, 7.4.1, 7.4.9, 7.5.1 Team Project: 0.1.2, 0.1.5, 4.8.1, 7.1.2, 7.1.4, 7.4.1, 7.4.3, 7.5.6 Reading Challenge: 0.1.2, 0.1.5, 7.4.1, 7.4.3, 7.4.4, 7.4.5, 7.5.1	S2: Participate in level-appropriate oral and written exchanges of information, ideas, and analyses, in various social and academic contexts, responding to peer, audience, or reader comments and questions. S9: Create clear and coherent level-appropriate speech and text. S10: Demonstrate command of the conventions of standard English to communicate in level-appropriate speech and writing.	L1, L2, L3, RI1, RI2, RI3, SL1, SL3, W1, W3

How Are Your Study Habits?

GOAL ▸ Evaluate study habits

A PREDICT Look at the photo. What is Nubar doing? Why? Read about Nubar. 🎧

Nubar is an ESL student at Franklin Adult School. He has good study habits. He has class three days a week, two days in person and one day online. He speaks English with his classmates. Nubar practices English at work and with his family. He also watches TV and listens to podcasts in English.

B CLASSIFY In a group, write different ways to study or practice English. Answers will vary.

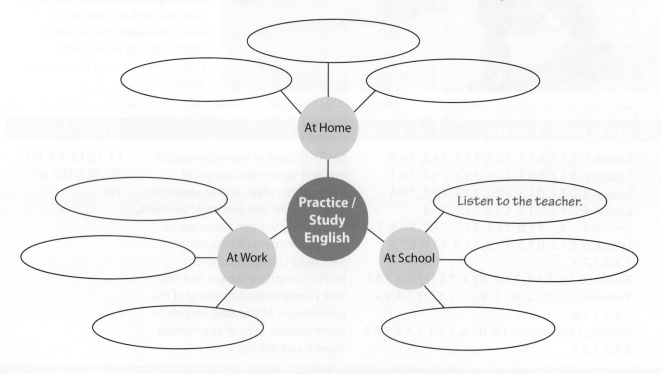

At-a-Glance Prep

Goal: Evaluate study habits

Grammar: Simple past: Regular and irregular verbs

Academic Strategies: Predicting, classifying information, focused listening, evaluating

Vocabulary: Study words

Agenda

☐ List activities you do outside of school.

☐ Classify ways to study.

☐ Use simple past verbs.

☐ Listen for good habits.

☐ Evaluate your study habits.

Resources

Heinle Picture Dictionary: Classroom, pages 18–19

Pacing

■ 1.5 hour classes ■ 2.5 hour classes

■ 3+ hour classes

Standards Correlations

CASAS: 6.1.1, 6.1.3, 7.2.3, 7.4.1, 7.4.3, 7.4.9

CCRS: L1, L2, L3, RI1, RI2, RI3

ELPS:

S10: Demonstrate command of the conventions of standard English to communicate in level-appropriate speech and writing.

Warm-up and Review   7–10 mins. ■■■

Ask students what they do when they are not in school. Make a list on the board. Provide vocabulary as needed. The list may or may not include *study*. Ask students if they study at home.

Introduction   3 mins. ■■■

Write *habit* on the board. Ask students if they know what the word means. Tell them that it is when they do things over and over again. Explain that there are good and bad habits. Ask for examples of both. State the goal: *Today, we will learn to evaluate study habits.*

Presentation 1   10–15 mins. ■■■

Prepare students for the reading by asking them for ideas on how to study English at home. List their ideas on the board.

A PREDICT Look at the photo. What is Nubar doing? Why? Read about Nubar. 🎧

Have students look at the photo. Tell them to cover up the reading and the activity that follows. Discuss the questions in the direction line.

Then ask students to read the paragraph silently. Only give them one minute before having them close their books, whether they have finished or not. Ask comprehension questions to see how much students retained from the paragraph. Then have them open their books, play the audio, and ask them to read along.

BEST PRACTICE

Reading

As mentioned earlier, some students read slowly because they think it is better than reading fast. Some students will read and vocalize what they are reading. Teach students that this is not a productive way to read. Some students will want to stop and check words in the dictionary. Ask them instead to underline words they don't know and not stop reading. Teach students that reading is like focused listening in that they may not understand every word, but they can still understand the important information.

Practice 1   10–15 mins. ■■■

Workplace Focus

Exercise B: Collect and organize information.

B CLASSIFY In a group, write different ways to study or practice English.

Remind students about mind maps and how they help us to brainstorm ideas and to learn vocabulary by grouping related words together. Groups can use ideas from the paragraph and add any other ideas they may have.

Evaluation 1   3–5 mins. ■■■

Ask groups to report to the class. Create a mind map on the board with students' ideas.

Presentation 2
10–15 mins. ■■■

C Study the charts.

Reintroduce the simple past. Explain to students that there are many irregular forms that they will need to memorize. However, this is merely an introduction, so don't expect students to memorize the verbs at this point. Go over the regular forms and have students say each one to practice the pronunciation of the *-ed* endings. Practice the pronunciation of the irregular forms as well. Make sure students understand the meaning of all the verbs. Say a few examples about yourself and write them on the board. For example: *I spoke to my mom yesterday. I helped my students.* etc. If students seem confident, elicit examples from them.

Practice 2
15–20 mins. ■■

D Rewrite the sentences in the past. Then use the sentences to write a paragraph in your notebook.

Have students complete the sentences individually. Check the answers as a class. Then have them put the sentences together in paragraph form. Tell them to use the paragraph in **A** as a model.

Evaluation 2
7–10 mins. ■■

Ask a volunteer to write their paragraph on the board. Make corrections as a class if necessary.

Presentation 3
3–5 mins. ■■■

Prepare students for listening by eliciting students' study habits. Ask them to look at the mind map in **B** again and ask: *What do you do?* After a few responses, say: *Yesterday?* Encourage students to use the simple past forms to talk about their study habits.

Practice 3
7–10 mins. ■

E Listen to Angela describe her study habits. Check (✓) the things she talks about. 🎧

Go over the list of study habits. Play the audio several times and allow students to discuss the answers between listenings.

Listening Script

My name is Angela Sheldon. I am in college now. I studied English in school so I could go to college here in the United States. I took advantage of every opportunity so I could learn quickly. For example, I never missed class, and I always came to class on time. I wrote down new words in my notebook every day. At home, I watched TV in English. It was really good for me. I watched the news and other programs. I also helped and taught other students. I think this was the best thing I did. Now I'm in college and I'm happy to be here.

Evaluation 3
3–5 mins. ■

Check the answers to **E** as a class. Play the audio one more time to confirm that students heard all of the information. Pause the audio after key words as needed.

Instructor's Notes

_____

_____

_____

_____

_____

_____

_____

_____

_____

_____

_____

_____

_____

C Study the charts.

Regular Past Verbs	
Base	Simple Past
study	studied
participate	participated
help	helped
listen	listened
watch	watched
practice	practiced
learn	learned
Spelling Note: When the base verb ends in *-y*, remove the *-y* and add *-ied*. study → studied	

Irregular Past Verbs	
Base	Simple Past
come	came
have	had
write	wrote
speak	spoke
read	read
teach	taught
go	went
do	did
make	made

D Rewrite the sentences in the past. Then use the sentences to write a paragraph in your notebook.

1. Nubar practices English in many different ways.

   Nubar practiced English in many different ways.

2. He speaks English with his classmates.

   He spoke English with his classmates.

3. Nubar practices English at work and with his family.

   Nubar practiced English at work and with his family.

4. He watches TV in English.

   He watched TV in English.

5. Nubar also listens to podcasts.

   Nubar also listened to podcasts.

E Listen to Angela describe her study habits. Check (✓) the things she talks about.

☑ came to class every school day

☑ came to class on time

☑ helped other students

☐ listened to music in English

☐ participated in class

☐ practiced at work

☐ studied at home

☑ taught other students

☑ watched TV in English

☑ wrote down new words

F **EVALUATE** **Answer the questions about your study habits in this course. Then calculate your score.** Answers will vary.

Study Habits Questionnaire

1. How often did you come to class?

    a. most of the time   b. around 50%   c. less than 50%

2. How often did you come to class <u>on time</u>?

    a. most of the time   b. around 50%   c. less than 50%

3. How much did you study outside of class each week?

    a. more than 6 hours   b. 4–6 hours   c. 3 hours or less

4. How often did you speak English in class and participate?

    a. most of the time   b. around 50%   c. less than 50%

5. How often did you teach and help other students in class?

    a. a lot   b. a little   c. never

6. How often did you listen to music in English?

    a. a lot   b. a little   c. never

7. How often did you watch TV in English?

    a. a lot   b. a little   c. never

8. How often did you ask the teacher or other students questions when you didn't understand?

    a. a lot   b. a little   c. never

How many *a* answers, *b* answers, and *c* answers do you have?

# of *a* answers _____	# of *b* answers _____	# of *c* answers _____

Do the math below.

of *a* answers x 3 = _____
of *b* answers x 2 = _____
of *c* answers x 1 = _____
        Total = _____

Score: **20–24** Super – You have great study habits!

Score: **16–19** Good – You have good study habits.

Score: **Under 16** – You need to change your study habits.

Workplace Focus
Exercise F: Complete tasks as assigned.

Application
10–15 mins. ■■□

F EVALUATE **Answer the questions about your study habits in this course. Then calculate your score.**

Go through the questions and clarify any doubts. Then have students fill out the questionnaire. Ask students to calculate their score using the instructions at the bottom. If students are comfortable, have them compare and discuss their study habits in pairs or groups. You may decide that it would be interesting if students interviewed one another instead of evaluating themselves. See the Best Practice note below for suggestions on carrying this out.

BEST PRACTICE

Student-to-Student Interviews

Having students conduct their own interviews is an excellent way for them to practice their English and the lesson goals. Treating the interview as a real-life experience will also be a fun and engaging activity for students. With this goal in mind, teachers should provide students with a few effective tips on conducting interviews.

1. Ask students to review the interview questions beforehand. This allows them to sound less stilted when asking their questions and makes the interview go along more smoothly. Tell them that it is very important that the interviewer know the information that he or she is looking for.
2. Help students pick a pre-determined location to conduct their interviews. It can be in different locations around the classroom, for example. This gives students as much privacy as possible with a minimum chance of interference from classmates.
3. Ask students to open their interview with small talk (*How are you doing today? What country are you from? Where do you live?*). Small talk is a good warm-up and helps students feel more comfortable with each other before they participate in the interview process.
4. Discourage students from interrupting each other. Instruct them to ask the question and let the interviewee respond with his or her own answers, whatever they may be. Explain that this provides them with more reliable data and it also gives each student the chance to speak his or her own mind without interruption.

Instructor's Notes

_____

_____

_____

_____

_____

_____

_____

_____

_____

_____

_____

_____

_____

_____

_____

_____

_____

_____

_____

_____

_____

_____

_____

At-a-Glance Prep

Goal: Make a study guide
Academic Strategies: Collaborating, summarizing information
Vocabulary: Skills

Agenda
☐ Talk about learning in English class.
☐ Identify strengths and areas to work on.
☐ Organize a study guide.
☐ Complete a study guide.

Resources
Heinle Picture Dictionary: Classroom, pages 18–19

Pacing
■ 1.5 hour classes   ■ 2.5 hour classes
■ 3+ hour classes

Standards Correlations
CASAS: 0.1.2, 0.1.5, 7.1.1, 7.1.4, 7.4.1, 7.4.3
CCRS: SL1, SL3
ELPS:
S2: Participate in level-appropriate oral and written exchanges of information, ideas, and analyses, in various social and academic contexts, responding to peer, audience, or reader comments and questions.

Warm-up and Review   10–15 mins. ■■■
Write the word *study* on the board. Ask students what they should study if they want to learn English. Help them get started by writing *vocabulary* on the board. They may need additional help, so lead them through aspects of classroom study, such as *grammar, vocabulary,* and *teamwork.*

Introduction   5–7 mins. ■■■
Ask students which of the items they mentioned in the warm-up are most important to them. Take a class poll. State the goal: *Today, we will learn how to make a study guide.*

Presentation 1   20–25 mins. ■■■

A Talk about the pictures with your classmates and teacher.
Ask students to cover up **B**. Talk about each photo and see how many photos they can identify without the word box.

B What do you learn in English class? Match the words and phrases to the pictures in A.
Do this activity as a class.

Workplace Focus
Exercise C: Interact appropriately with team members.

C COLLABORATE In a group, write other things you learn in English class.
Have students work in small groups of three or four to complete this activity. Have a spokesperson from each group call out the group's list and make a class list on the board.

Practice 1   10–15 mins. ■■■

D APPLY Complete the chart about yourself. Use ideas from B and C.
Write the chart headings on the board. Make sure students understand them. Share with the class something that you personally do well and something that you don't do so well. As another example, point out a student who speaks very well and another who writes very well.

After students have had five or ten minutes to complete the chart, do a corners activity. Designate the corners of the room as *reading, writing, listening,* and *speaking.* Then ask students to go to the corner that represents the skill they do best. While in their corners, have students ask one another which skill they do second best.

Evaluation 1   5–7 mins. ■■■
Observe the activity. Discuss what students discovered from the activity. For example, discuss whether there is a consensus on what students do well or whether students have different strengths.

Staying Organized

GOAL ▶ Make a study guide

A Talk about the pictures with your classmates and teacher.

1. ___listening___

2. ___writing___

Simple Present
I **like** . . .
He / She **likes** . . .
We / They **like** . . .

3. ___grammar___

4. ___teamwork___

5. ___speaking___

6. ___career options___

7. ___reading___

8. ___vocabulary___

B What do you learn in English class? Match the words and phrases to the pictures in A.

career options	listening	speaking	vocabulary
grammar	reading	teamwork	writing

C COLLABORATE In a group, write other things you learn in English class. Answers will vary.

_____   _____

_____   _____

D APPLY Complete the chart about yourself. Use ideas from B and C. Answers will vary.

Things I Do Well	Things I Need Help With

E Read about study guides. 🎧

> A good way to prepare for your next English course is to review and study what you learned in *Stand Out*, Level 1. One way to do this is to organize what you learned in a clear way so you can look at it when you want to remember something. We call this a *study guide*. You can also add to this study guide in each class you take in the future.

F Your study guide will have five different sections: *Unit Goals*, *Vocabulary*, *Grammar*, *Writing Practice*, and *Career Options*. These can be sections of a notebook, dividers in a binder, or folders on a computer. Write the name of each section.

EXAMPLE:

G **SUMMARIZE** In your *Unit Goals* section, write the goal for each lesson of Unit 1. Then write two important things you learned in Unit 1. Follow the example.

EXAMPLE:

> <u>Unit Goals</u>
>
> Unit 1
> Lesson 1: Ask for and give personal information
> Lesson 2: Describe people
> Lesson 3: Describe family relationships
> Lesson 4: Express preferences
> Lesson 5: Plan a schedule
> Lesson 6: Reflect on career options
>
> Two important things I learned in Unit 1:
>   1. I learned how to describe people.
>   For example: He has black hair.
>   2. I learned how to talk about schedules.
>   For example: I have English class from 9 a.m. to 11 a.m.
> Unit 2

Presentation 2   15–20 mins. ■■◻

Show students a notebook or binder and dividers before they see this page. Tell them that notebooks and binders are good ways to organize their work.

E Read about study guides. 🎧

Have students read the text. Then ask them what they understood from it. Clarify any vocabulary doubts and write the key ideas from the text on the board: *review*, *study*, *organize*.

Workplace Focus

Exercise F: Combine ideas and information.

F Your study guide will have five different sections: *Unit Goals, Vocabulary, Grammar, Writing Practice*, and *Career Options*. These can be sections of a notebook, dividers in a binder, or folders on a computer. Write the name of each section.

Discuss the study guide sections with the class and show them an example in a notebook if possible. Have students decide how they want to do their guide (notebook, binder, computer) and write down the sections it will have. Ideally, have students bring a notebook or binder to class specifically for this activity, or have them do this activity in their regular notebook and do their study guide for homework.

Practice 2   10–15 mins. ■■

G SUMMARIZE In your *Unit Goals* section, write the goal for each lesson of Unit 1. Then write two important things you learned in Unit 1. Follow the example.

Elicit what *Unit Goals* are and have students identify the goals for Unit 8. Then go over the example. Have students copy the unit goals for Unit 1 and write the important things they learned in their study guide.

Evaluation 2   3–5 mins. ■■

Ask students to share with the class the two things that were important to them from Unit 1.

Instructor's Notes

Presentation 3　　　10–15 mins. ■■■

Go through Unit 1 in the book with students. Ask them which words they think are most important. Write them on the board.

H In the *Vocabulary* section, write 15 words you want to remember from Unit 1. Follow the example:

Have students choose their words and write them in their study guide (or regular notebook to transfer to their guide later). Encourage students to share and discuss their choices with a partner.

Practice 3　　　20–30 mins. ■

I In the *Grammar* section, write the important grammar points you learned in Unit 1 and the page numbers where the grammar charts are. Follow the example:

Have students carry out the same steps as they did in **H**. Having students discuss their choices with each other helps them both clarify their understanding of the vocabulary / grammar and reflect on their learning processes.

J Find any writing you did for Unit 1 and put it in the *Writing Practice* section.

Have students go through their notebooks for any writing activities; for example, the paragraph in **D** in Lesson 1 of this unit.

K In the *Career Options* section, write about the career options you studied in Unit 1. Follow the example:

Without looking at the example, have the class brainstorm employment opportunities they have seen earlier in *Stand Out 1*. Write them on the board. Then have them look at Unit 1 and write the career options in their study guide.

Evaluation 3　　　5 mins. ■

Observe as students are reviewing Unit 1 vocabulary, grammar, writing, and career options. Ask them questions to check their understanding and have them explain to you their reasons for what they want to put in their study guide.

Workplace Focus

Exercise L: Complete tasks as assigned.

Application　　　1–2 hours ■

L APPLY Go through all the sections again and add information for each unit.

Explain to students that what they have done to help them review Unit 1, they now need to do for Units 2 through 7 so their study guide will be complete for this English class. Remind them that they can use their study guide to review items when they are in their next English class and that they can add new vocabulary, grammar, etc.

Instructor's Notes

_____

_____

_____

_____

_____

_____

_____

_____

_____

_____

_____

_____

_____

_____

_____

_____

_____

_____

H In the *Vocabulary* section, write 15 words you want to remember from Unit 1. Follow the example:

> ## Vocabulary
>
> Unit 1
> | | | |
> |---|---|---|
> | 1. divorced | 2. weight | 3. inches |
> | 4. | 5. | 6. |
> | 7. | 8. | 9. |
> | 10. | 11. | 12. |
> | 13. | 14. | 15. |
>
> Unit 2
> | | | |
> |---|---|---|
> | 1. | 2. | 3. |

I In the *Grammar* section, write the important grammar points you learned in Unit 1 and the page numbers where the grammar charts are. Follow the example:

> ## Grammar
>
> Unit 1
> Simple Present
> be: I am 43 years old. He is single. They are from Iran. (page 16)
> have: They have white hair. She has blue eyes. (page 18)
> like: We like music. She likes restaurants. (page 24)
>
> Unit 2

J Find any writing you did for Unit 1 and put it in the *Writing Practice* section.

K In the *Career Options* section, write about the career options you studied in Unit 1. Follow the example:

> ## Career Options
>
> Unit 1
> Career Fields
> Health: pharmacist, dentist
> Art and Communication: photographer, actor
> Human Services: chef, tutor
> Natural Resources: pest control worker, fisher
> Business: customer service representative, accountant
> Industry: carpenter, auto mechanic
>
> Careers that interest me:
>   1. I like careers in industry.
> Why I like these careers:
>   1. I like to work with my hands.
>   2. I like to make new things.
>   3. I don't like to work at a desk.

L APPLY Go through all the sections again and add information for each unit.

LESSON 3 Schools in the United States

GOAL ▶ Identify learning opportunities

A INTERPRET Read the diagram with your classmates and teacher.

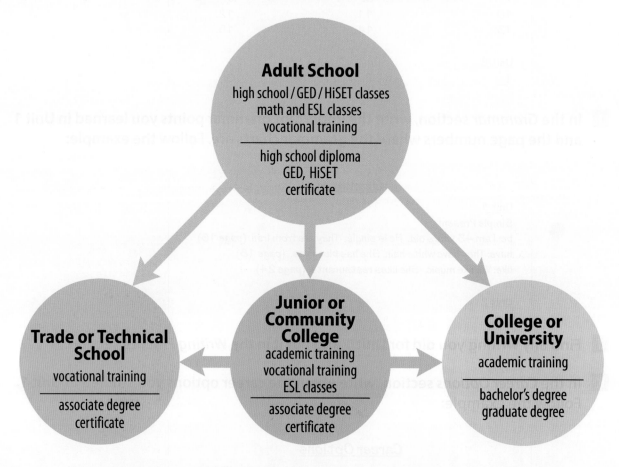

B ANALYZE Complete the chart about learning opportunities.

School	Degree or Diploma
adult school	high school diploma, GED, HiSET, certificate
trade or technical school	associate degree, certificate
junior or community college	associate degree, certificate
college or university	bachelor's degree, graduate degree

At-a-Glance Prep

Goal: Identify learning opportunities
Grammar: *Should*
Academic Strategies: Interpreting charts, analyzing, making predictions, focused listening
Vocabulary: Educational choices, learning opportunities

Agenda

☐ Review vocabulary, grammar, and career options from Units 1–7.
☐ Analyze learning opportunities.
☐ Listen to advice from counselors.
☐ Think about your future plans.

Resources

Heinle Picture Dictionary: Life Events, pages 30–31

Pacing

■ 1.5 hour classes   ■ 2.5 hour classes
■ 3+ hour classes

Standards Correlations

CASAS: 0.1.2, 0.1.5, 2.8.2, 7.1.1, 7.2.3, 7.4.4
CCRS: RI1, RI2, RI3, SL1, SL3
ELPS:

S2: Participate in level-appropriate oral and written exchanges of information, ideas, and analyses, in various social and academic contexts, responding to peer, audience, or reader comments and questions.

S10: Demonstrate command of the conventions of standard English to communicate in level-appropriate speech and writing.

Warm-up and Review   10–15 mins. ■■□

Ask students to share the vocabulary, grammar, and career options they came up with from each unit in **L** in Lesson 2. Have them create a mind map on the board with the three categories. Have everyone participate in completing it. Remind them to pay attention to what others are writing to avoid repetition. Elicit example sentences / explanations using the grammar and vocabulary from the map.

Introduction   5–7 mins. ■■□

Ask students if they have any future plans for their education. Have a short discussion about possible educational paths. State the goal: *Today, we will learn about educational opportunities.*

Presentation 1   15–20 mins. ■■■

A INTERPRET **Read the diagram with your classmates and teacher.**

Discuss the different possible paths students can take. Briefly explain each one and the number of years a full-time student might go to school. Ask students if this system is similar to or different from the educational system they are familiar with in their native countries.

Tell them your own educational path as an example.

BEST PRACTICE

Student-Centered Instruction

When there is a lot of information for students to learn, it is tempting to simply lecture without much interaction. However, it is important to connect the content to students' lives and make the class interactive and communicative even though students have minimal English language skills at this point.

Try asking questions such as: *Do you have a high school diploma from your country? Who wants to go to college? Who likes math? Do you have trade schools in your country? Does anyone have vocational training? What kind of vocational training do you have?*

Practice 1   10–15 mins. ■■■

Workplace Focus

Exercise B: Collect and organize information.

B ANALYZE **Complete the chart about learning opportunities.**

Have students complete this activity individually to check their understanding of the information in **A**.

Evaluation 1   5 mins. ■■□

Check students' answers in their books as they are working.

Presentation 2

15–20 mins. ■■■□

C PREDICT Read the information about the students. What kind of education do you think they need?

Do this activity as a class. Discuss each person and have students predict what education they need.

D Listen to the conversations and choose the information from C that you hear. 🎧

Elicit / Explain what a counselor does. Tell students they are going to listen to a counselor giving advice to the people in **C**. Play the audio, pausing after conversation 1 to check the answers together. Play the remaining conversations. Have students discuss with a partner. Then play the audio again and check as a class.

Listening Script

1. **Yusuf:** *I want to be a legal assistant, but first I need to learn more English.*
   Counselor: *That's very important. Do you have a high school diploma?*
   Yusuf: *No, I don't.*
   Counselor: *Well, that is always a good place to start. Maybe you can get work without it, but it's very important.*
   Yusuf: *Yes, I know. That's one of my plans.*
   Counselor: *Great! Then you need an associate degree or certificate from a community college.*
   Yusuf: *OK, and what should I study there?*
   Counselor: *Most legal assistants get a degree or certificate in paralegal studies.*

2. **Counselor:** *That's great you want to be a teacher.*
   Minh: *Yes, but I need to learn a lot more first.*
   Counselor: *Well, you are taking classes at the adult school now, so I'm sure you are learning a lot. Do you have a high school diploma?*
   Minh: *Not yet. I'll get it at the end of the year.*
   Counselor: *That's good! Then you will need a bachelor's degree. You can start at a two-year college and then go to a university, or you can go right to the university.*
   Minh: *Hmm. Which is better for me?*
   Counselor: *They are both good, but community college is cheaper.*

3. **Counselor:** *Being a nurse is a good job. If you want to be a registered nurse, you'll need a bachelor's degree from a university.*
   Sarah: *Yes, I already have plans to go to a four-year college here in town. Do I need to be a citizen?*

Counselor: *No, but you do need to be a state resident, or it will cost you a lot more money.*
Sarah: *Good. I am a state resident.*

4. **Carolina:** *I want to get a job as a web developer so I can design beautiful websites that are easy to use.*
   Counselor: *That sounds great! So, you are taking English classes at the adult school now. What are your plans after you finish studying here?*
   Carolina: *I'm not sure. Do I need a degree to be a web developer?*
   Counselor: *Some web developer jobs require a bachelor's degree, but others just require experience. Maybe you can take some classes at a community college and work on your design skills on your own. You can take more English classes too. Then you can decide if you want to go to a four-year college and get your bachelor's degree.*
   Carolina: *That sounds like a good plan.*

5. **Counselor:** *So, Alan, you want to be a cook, right?*
   Alan: *That's right.*
   Counselor: *Do you want to be a chef in an expensive restaurant where you can make special food?*
   Alan: *That sounds interesting, but I'm not sure. Is it hard to be a chef?*
   Counselor: *Most jobs require a high school diploma and for some you need an associate degree or certificate.*
   Alan: *That sounds like a lot of work, but I'll think about it.*

6. **Javi:** *I just want to learn a little more English before I get a job as a mechanic. I already have my GED.*
   Counselor: *That's great! Do you also have a certificate in automotive technology?*
   Javi: *No. Do I really need one?*
   Counselor: *It's not always required, but it will help prepare you for work as a mechanic. It might also help you find a job faster. You should think about going to trade school.*
   Javi: *Thanks. I'm going to think about it.*

Practice 2

7–10 mins. ■■□

E Practice the conversation with a partner. Then make new conversations about the students in C.

Model the conversation with a student. Go over the grammar note as a class before students practice.

Evaluation 2

5 mins. ■■□

Observe students as they practice the conversation. Make sure they use *should* correctly.

C **PREDICT** Read the information about the students. What kind of education do you think they need?

1.

Yusuf wants to be a legal assistant.

- ☑ high school diploma
- ☑ certificate
- ☑ associate degree
- ☐ bachelor's degree

2.

Minh wants to be a high school teacher.

- ☑ high school diploma
- ☐ certificate
- ☐ associate degree
- ☑ bachelor's degree

3.

Sarah wants to be a nurse.

- ☐ high school diploma
- ☐ certificate
- ☐ associate degree
- ☑ bachelor's degree

4.

Carolina wants to be a web developer.

- ☐ high school diploma
- ☐ certificate
- ☐ associate degree
- ☑ bachelor's degree

5.

Alan wants to be a cook.

- ☑ high school diploma
- ☑ certificate
- ☑ associate degree
- ☐ bachelor's degree

6.

Javi wants to be a mechanic.

- ☑ high school diploma / GED
- ☑ certificate
- ☐ associate degree
- ☐ bachelor's degree

D Listen to the conversations and choose the information from **C** that you hear. 🎧

E Practice the conversation with a partner. Then make new conversations about the students in **C**.

Student A: What should Yusuf do after finishing adult school?

Student B: He should get an associate degree or a certificate.

Should

I **should** go to college.
You **should** go …
He / She **should** go …
We **should** go …
They **should** go …

F Look at the photos. What are the people doing? In a group, make a list of three or four places you can go for advice about learning opportunities. Answers will vary.

_____

_____

_____

_____

G APPLY What do you want to do after adult school? Fill in the boxes and talk to a partner. Answers will vary.

| Adult School | → | _____ | → | _____ |

H What websites or other resources can help you with your educational choices? Talk about them as a class.

Presentation 3

5–7 mins. ■■■

Look at the photos with the class. Ask questions about what the people might be doing, where they might be, and other questions that seem relevant.

Workplace Focus

Exercise F: Interact appropriately with team members.

Practice 3

10–15 mins. ■

F **Look at the photos. What are the people doing? In a group, make a list of three or four places you can go for advice about learning opportunities.**

Discuss the photos as a class. Then put students in groups to carry out the activity.

Evaluation 3

5 mins. ■

Ask groups to report to the class and write their ideas on the board.

Application

10–15 mins. ■■■

G **APPLY** **What do you want to do after adult school? Fill in the boxes and talk to a partner.**

Give students time to think about their plans and complete the boxes before putting them in pairs to share.

H **What websites or other resources can help you with your educational choices? Talk about them as a class.**

Have students think about the question with a partner first, then discuss resources as a class. Create a list together on the board. Be prepared to provide some examples. If time allows, have students take a look at some of the websites and resources that were suggested, or have them do this for homework and report back to the class.

BEST PRACTICE

Student Research

Often exercises call for students to conduct research on their own. This may be via the internet or finding information in books or other print resources. This is nothing new to most students. However, they may be at a loss about where to begin, particularly when conducting research in their non-native language.

Teachers should always help students start their online research by providing them with a list of useful websites. It is beneficial if the list contains the website names, brief one-line descriptions of content, and the URL. Teachers may print these lists and distribute them to the class or simply email them to students. If choosing the latter, they may consider authoring the list with hyperlinks so that students only need to click on the link to reach the target source.

The same advice applies to having students use books and other print resources. Teachers should provide students with directions on where to look. Students may not be familiar with the local library or even how it works. If students take along a suggested bibliography, it will be easier for them to start looking on their own or ask for assistance from library personnel.

Exhaustive or long bibliographies are not necessary, but teachers should give students enough to get them off to a good start. Research activities should be enjoyable and a beneficial addition to the lesson. If well-planned, students will learn more and start to look forward to conducting research. Teachers will also gain valuable insight into students' grasp of lesson goals.

At-a-Glance Prep

Goal: Identify vocational preferences

Grammar: Verb + infinitive, verb + noun

Academic Strategies: Making predictions, focused listening, evaluating preferences

Vocabulary: Goals

Agenda

☐ Identify work preferences.

☐ Predict jobs.

☐ Discuss your preferences.

☐ Take a personal inventory survey.

Resources

Heinle Picture Dictionary: Jobs, pages 146–149

Pacing

■ 1.5 hour classes ■ 2.5 hour classes

■ 3+ hour classes

Standards Correlations

CASAS: 0.1.2, 0.1.5, 4.1.9, 7.1.1, 7.5.1

CCRS: L1, L2, L3, SL1, SL3, W3

ELPS:

S9: Create clear and coherent level-appropriate speech and text.

S10: Demonstrate command of the conventions of standard English to communicate in level-appropriate speech and writing.

Warm-up and Review   10–15 mins. ■■■

Write the word *counselor* on the board. Ask students if they have spoken to either a school counselor or a job counselor before. Ask students if they have any job goals for the future. Talk to students with goals and ask them what kind of education they would need for these jobs.

Introduction   5–7 mins. ■■■

State the goal: *Today, we will identify vocational preferences.* Explain that *vocational* means related to work.

Presentation 1   15–20 mins. ■■■

A PREDICT **Read the information about the students. Choose the job that you think is the best for each one.**

Look at the photos and the information together. Ask students to predict what would be the best job for each person.

B Listen. Check your answers in A.

Tell students they are going to listen to each person in **A** talk about themselves. Ask them what information they need to focus on when they listen. Play the audio several times. Check to see if their predictions were correct.

Listening Script

1.

My name is Erendira. I am a student at Pine Adult School. I like to study and go to school. I think I would like to be a student for my whole life, but I know I'll have to get a job someday. I love history, so maybe I should look into being a teacher. I think that would be a great profession for me.

2.

I'm Ruth and I love people. Every chance I get, I talk to people. They're so interesting. I like to help people too. For that reason, I am going to choose a career that will allow me to be around people who I can help. I think being a nurse would be very interesting and rewarding. My mother's a nurse too.

3.

My name is Changming. I have a lot of experience working with my hands. I like to fix things too. I love to make things work. That's why I think being a mechanic might be a good job for me. Also, I like cars, so I think that this is a good choice.

Workplace Focus

Exercise C: Interpret and communicate information.

Practice 1   10–15 mins. ■■■

C Talk to a partner. Ask: *What do you like to do?* **Write three things.**

Give students time to think about what they like to do. Encourage them to use the information from **A** to come up with ideas of their own.

Evaluation 1   3–5 mins. ■■■

Ask students to report to the class about their partners. Check for correct use of third person singular -s.

Choosing the Right Job

GOAL ▶ Identify vocational preferences

A PREDICT Read the information about the students. Choose the job that you think is the best for each one.

Student	Job
1. Erendira likes to study. She likes school. She likes history.	(a.) teacher b. mechanic c. doctor
2. Ruth likes to help people. She likes to talk to people. She likes to learn about health.	a. gardener (b.) nurse c. receptionist
3. Changming likes to work with his hands. He likes to fix things. He likes cars.	(a.) mechanic b. carpenter c. salesperson

B Listen. Check your answers in A. 🎧

C Talk to a partner. Ask: *What do you like to do?* Write three things. Answers will vary.

_____   _____   _____

D Study the charts.

Verb + Infinitive			
Subject	**Verb**	**Infinitive**	**Example Sentence**
I / You We / They	like want need	to read to travel to work to talk to learn to study	I **like to read**. You **want to travel**. We **need to work** alone. They **like to talk** on the phone.
He / She	likes wants needs		He **needs to learn** English. She **wants to study**.

Verb + Noun			
Subject	**Verb**	**Noun**	**Example Sentence**
I / You We / They	like want need	cars a computer books school food	I **like cars**. You **want a computer**. We **need books** for class. They **like school** this year.
He / She	likes wants needs		He **likes computers**. She **wants food** soon.

E Complete each sentence with the correct form of the verb in parentheses. Then listen and check your answers. 🎧

1. They like _____to work_____ (work) outside.

2. He _____wants_____ (want) a car for his job.

3. She needs _____to make_____ (make) money right now.

4. They _____want_____ (want) to study at school every day.

5. I want _____to learn_____ (learn) English.

6. You _____need_____ (need) a new cell phone right away.

7. They _____like_____ (like) their jobs.

8. She _____wants_____ (want) to find a new job.

F Work with a partner. Ask: *What do you want to do in the future?* List three things.

Answers will vary.

_____   _____   _____

Presentation 2 10–15 mins. ■■■

D Study the charts.

Go over the charts carefully. Help students see that they can use these forms to write their goals and what they like to do more clearly. Focus their attention on the infinitive form of the verb after *like*, *want*, and *need*. Say some examples about your goals. Then elicit examples from students if they feel ready.

Practice 2 7–10 mins. ■■

E Complete each sentence with the correct form of the verb in parentheses. Then listen and check your answers. 🎧

Ask students to complete the sentences individually. Then play the audio. After students have checked their answers, ask them if any of the sentences are true for them.

Workplace Focus

Exercise F: Interpret and communicate information.

Evaluation 2 7–10 mins. ■■

F Work with a partner. Ask: *What do you want to do in the future?* List three things.

Give students time to think about what they want to do. Then put them in pairs to ask and answer the question. Have them report to the class about their partner.

BEST PRACTICE

Example Sentences in Grammar Charts

Studying grammar is an integral part of language learning. There is no escape; it has to be learned. Although most adult students understand this, they are not all motivated to complete grammar exercises or review grammar charts.

Teachers should point out that a grammar chart in itself is a straightforward and valuable tool, much like a dictionary. They should also mention that it is useful for grasping often complex grammar rules and that the example sentences in the chart are of equal importance.

Because most students prefer to learn grammar in a social context, teachers can take advantage of this inclination by calling attention to these example sentences. Teachers should let students know that

the examples usually mimic lifelike social interactions. Teachers can further exemplify this by asking students to create a short and natural conversation in pairs using the featured grammar item. Students will see that the forms of some statements and responses in their conversations will match the example sentences already provided.

Instructor's Notes

_____

_____

_____

_____

_____

_____

_____

_____

_____

_____

_____

_____

_____

_____

_____

_____

_____

Presentation 3

15–20 mins. ■■■

Review how to form questions with students. Write on the board: *Do you like to work outside?* Go around the room and ask students about some of the items in **E**. For example: *Do you want to study at school every day? Do you want to learn English?*

G REFLECT A counselor is going to ask you questions to help you with your future plans. Answer the questions about yourself. Check (✓) *Yes* or *No*.

Have students read the items without responding. Discuss any vocabulary questions that come up and provide examples or additional explanation as needed. Then have students complete the inventory individually. Give them time to think about their answers.

Practice 3

7–10 mins. ■

H Write three sentences about the things in G you like and don't like.

Monitor as students write, helping as needed.

Evaluation 3

5–7 mins. ■

Ask volunteers to write their sentences on the board.

Application

10–15 mins. ■■■

I Work in a group. Read your sentences to the group. Give advice about jobs that are good for each person.

Put students in groups using one of the grouping techniques previously described. Remind students to put into practice their active listening skills when their classmates share their sentences. Tell them to explain why they suggest each job. Monitor and prompt with questions as needed to keep the conversation going.

BEST PRACTICE

Asking Questions

Students have plenty of opportunities to answer questions, but seldom have as many chances to ask them. When presenting lessons that teach the correct forms for asking questions, it is important that teachers give students as much practice as possible. This can go beyond exercises in the book. See the following game that can help practice question formation after the model forms have been presented:

Guess the Question

Divide the class into two groups. Ask students to make a list of a set number of answers to commonly asked questions they might hear (in school, at home, at work, etc.). Then ask each group member to take a turn giving an answer and waiting for an opposing group member to come up with a possible correct question. There may be many possible correct questions, so accept any question that is grammatically correct and makes sense with the answer provided. Tell students that they only have one guess per answer. Have students play the game until all the answers have been used. The team with the highest number of correct questions wins the game.

Instructor's Notes

_____

_____

_____

_____

_____

_____

_____

_____

_____

_____

_____

_____

_____

_____

_____

_____

_____

_____

G **REFLECT** A counselor is going to ask you questions to help you with your future plans. Answer the questions about yourself. Check (✓) *Yes* or *No.* Answers will vary.

Personal Inventory

		Yes	No
1.	Do you have a high school diploma?	☐	☐
2.	Do you have good study skills?	☐	☐
3.	Do you have work experience?	☐	☐
4.	Do you like technology (computers, machines)?	☐	☐
5.	Do you like to do the same thing every day?	☐	☐
6.	Do you like to handle money?	☐	☐
7.	Do you like to read?	☐	☐
8.	Do you like to study and to learn new things?	☐	☐
9.	Do you like to listen to people?	☐	☐
10.	Do you like to talk on the phone?	☐	☐
11.	Do you like to travel?	☐	☐
12.	Do you like to work with other people?	☐	☐
13.	Do you like to work alone?	☐	☐
14.	Do you like to work at night?	☐	☐
15.	Do you like to work in the daytime?	☐	☐
16.	Do you like to work with your hands?	☐	☐
17.	Do you work now?	☐	☐
18.	If you have a job, do you like it?	☐	☐
19.	Do you have goals for the future?	☐	☐

H Write three sentences about the things in **G** you like and don't like. Answers will vary.

_____

_____

_____

I Work in a group. Read your sentences to the group. Give advice about jobs that are good for each person.

Making Goals

GOAL ▶ Develop goals

A Read Nubar's journal entry. Answer the questions about his study goals. 🎧

> May 5
> I have many study goals for the next month. I am going to
> read the news online, listen to podcasts, and talk to people in
> English every day. I am also going to study a lesson from my
> textbook every night for 30 minutes in my bedroom.

1. How often is Nubar going to study? <u>every day / night</u>

2. How long is Nubar going to study for? <u>30 minutes</u>

3. What is he going to study? <u>a lesson from his textbook</u>

4. Where is he going to study? <u>in his bedroom</u>

B Look at the clocks. Then listen to Nubar talk about his plans. Write the correct activity for each time. 🎧

| listen to a podcast | read the news online | study the textbook | write in a journal |

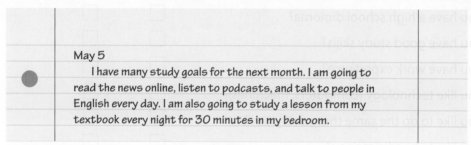

1. From ⏰ to ⏰ <u>read the news online</u>

2. From ⏰ to ⏰ <u>study the textbook</u>

3. From ⏰ to ⏰ <u>listen to a podcast</u>

4. From ⏰ to ⏰ <u>write in a journal</u>

At-a-Glance Prep

Goal: Develop goals
Grammar: Future with *be going to* and *will*
Academic Strategies: Focused listening, classifying information
Vocabulary: Study plans, goals

Agenda

☐ Review work preferences.
☐ Read and listen to Nubar's study goals.
☐ Use the future with *be going to* and *will*.
☐ Read about Nubar's long-term goals.
☐ Make personal, educational, and work goals.

Resources

Heinle Picture Dictionary: Life Events, pages 30–31

Pacing

■ 1.5 hour classes ■ 2.5 hour classes
■ 3+ hour classes

Standards Correlations

CASAS: 2.3.1, 4.1.9, 7.1.1, 7.1.2, 7.4.1, 7.4.4, 7.7.3
CCRS: L1, L2, L3, RI1, RI2, RI3, SL2, SL3, W3
ELPS:
S9: Create clear and coherent level-appropriate speech and text.
S10: Demonstrate command of the conventions of standard English to communicate in level-appropriate speech and writing.

Warm-up and Review   10–15 mins. ■■■

Write *teacher* on the board and ask: *What does a teacher like to do?* Write sentences on the board that students come up with. Do the same for other jobs.

Introduction   10–15 mins. ■■■

Write *goal* on the board. Ask students for work, education, and family goals. State the goal: *Today, we will develop goals.*

Presentation 1   10–15 mins. ■■■

Write on the board *long-term goals* and *short-term goals*. Explain that a short-term goal is one that helps you reach long-term goals. Ask students if they have made any study goals for the next month.

A **Read Nubar's journal entry. Answer the questions about his study goals.** 🎧

Give students a time limit to read the paragraph. Then ask them to answer the questions on their own.

Play the audio and tell students to listen as they read and check their answers.

Workplace Focus

Exercise B: Collect and organize information.

Practice 1   10–15 mins. ■■■

B **Look at the clocks. Then listen to Nubar talk about his plans. Write the correct activity for each time.** 🎧

Review the times with the class. Then play the audio. Play the audio again and give students time to write their answers. Remind them to write notes, not complete answers at this point (see Best Practice: Taking Notes below). Have students compare with a partner. Then play the audio again.

Listening Script

I think that if I plan, I will be able to learn English well even when there is no school. I am going to read the news online, listen to podcasts, and talk to people in English every day. Well, let's see. If I am going to do all this, I need to schedule these things. I will get home at 6:00, and then from 6:30 to 6:45, I will read the news online. I need to find time to study the textbook. I know—I will do that from 7:00 to 7:30. I will listen to a podcast from 8:00 to 8:45. That should be good practice. Then from 9:00 to 9:15, I will write in my journal. I am going to do this for a full month. Then I will make new goals.

Evaluation 1   3–5 mins. ■■■

Go over the answers as a class.

BEST PRACTICE

Taking Notes

B is a good opportunity to teach students how to take notes. Some will want to write the entire phrase next to the clock and by so doing will miss all the other items. Tell students that you will not stop the audio after each item and that they will hear the audio only three times.

Show students how to write a word or two as a reminder to go back and add details later. They might write the first letter of the phrase or write the item number next to the phrase in the word bank when they hear it.

Presentation 2 15–20 mins. ■■□

C Study the chart.

Go over examples in the chart. Focus students' attention on the use of *be* with *going to* and then the main verb. Practice the new sentence structure with them. Go back to **A** so students can see how it is used in context. Prepare some example sentences and ask students to complete them on the board in the context of this lesson. The sentences might be the following:

I _____ (study) 30 minutes every day.
We _____ (listen) to a podcast from 7:00 to 7:30.
They _____ (write) sentences every day.
She _____ (speak) English at work.
You _____ (learn) three new words a day.

Practice 2 10–15 mins. ■■□

D Write sentences about Nubar's plans. Use the information from B.

Have students complete the activity individually to check their understanding. Ask volunteers to write each sentence on the board. Check them as a class and make corrections if necessary.

Workplace Focus

Exercise E: Interact appropriately with team members.

Evaluation 2 10 mins. ■■□

E PLAN What are your study plans? Write sentences and share them in a group.

Monitor as students work and help as needed. Make sure they are using *be going to* correctly. When they are ready, put them in groups to share and discuss their study plans.

BEST PRACTICE

Sharing Work

Students may be initially reluctant to share their written work with classmates. They may be sensitive about possible errors and not want to feel inferior to others. Teachers should point out that mistakes are part of the learning process and that classmates can give valuable feedback from a student's perspective. Teachers should explain that checking someone else's work is also a good way to test their own understanding of the lesson. Encourage students to be respectful when giving feedback. Have students share work as much as possible. They will eventually become more comfortable with the practice.

Read the information together and clarify new vocabulary as needed. Ask if anyone uses a study app. If so, have them share their experience. Show examples of study apps if possible. Ask about using their cell phones to help them study. Have students share if they use the calendar, alerts, or alarms. **Life ONLINE**

Instructor's Notes

_____
_____
_____
_____
_____
_____
_____
_____
_____
_____
_____
_____
_____
_____
_____
_____
_____
_____

C Study the chart.

Future with *Be Going to*			
Subject	*Be Going to*	**Base Verb**	**Example Sentence**
I	am going to (I'm going to)	learn listen practice read speak study write	I **am going to learn** English. I'**m going to read** the news.
You / We / They	are going to (you're / we're / they're going to)		We **are going to practice** English. They'**re going to study** every day.
He / She	is going to (he's / she's going to)		She **is going to speak** English. He'**s going to write** in a journal.

Use *be going to* for future plans and predictions.

D Write sentences about Nubar's plans. Use the information from B.

1. He is going to read the news online from 6:30 to 6:45.

2. He is going to study the textbook from 7:00 to 7:30.

3. He is going to listen to a podcast from 8:00 to 8:45.

4. He is going to write in his journal from 9:00 to 9:15.

E **PLAN** What are your study plans? Write sentences and share them in a group.

Answers will vary.

1. I

2.

3.

4.

Life ONLINE

Study Habits

There are many study apps that you can use to help you be more organized. Search "study apps" to find them. You can also use your smartphone to schedule study time in your calendar and set alerts to remind you to study. Another helpful hint is to turn off your email and text notifications when you are studying so you are not interrupted.

F **Study the chart.**

Future with *Will*			
Subject	***Will***	**Base Verb**	**Example Sentence**
I / You He / She We / They	will	study work get married	I **will study** every day.
			She **will work** hard.
			They **will get** married.

Use *will* for statements and predictions about the future. *Will* is more formal than *be going to*.
When speaking, people often use the contraction form: *I'll, You'll, He'll, She'll, We'll, They'll*.

G **Read about Nubar's long-term goals.** 🎧

I have many goals for the future. Some of my goals will take a long time. I will study every day and get a high school diploma. After that, I will start college. I want to start in about three years. I also want to get married and have children sometime in the future. I will be a web developer one day.

Life
ONLINE

Spell Checkers
Many online writing programs use a spell checker to tell you if there is a spelling mistake in your writing. These programs can be helpful, but they aren't perfect. Always check the spelling suggestion first and see if it makes sense before you correct it.

H **CLASSIFY** **Write Nubar's goals in the chart.**

Personal Goals	Educational Goals	Work Goals
get married	get a high school diploma	be a web developer
have children	start college in three years	

I **APPLY** **Write your personal, educational, and work goals. Use *will*.** Answers will vary.

Personal: _____

Educational: _____

_____

Work: _____

_____

Presentation 3
10–15 mins. ■■■

F Study the chart.

Go over the examples. Point out that *will* never changes and the main verb is always in the base form. Go over the note about when we use *will* and contractions. Play the audio from **B** and ask students to listen for this structure.

Write *Personal Goals, Educational Goals,* and *Work Goals* on the board and elicit what each one refers to. Have students give examples for each one.

Practice 3
10–15 mins. ■

G Read about Nubar's long-term goals. 🎧

Ask students to read the text. Then ask a few general questions. For example: *What will Nubar do first?* Clarify any vocabulary questions.

Read the information together and clarify new vocabulary as needed. If possible, demonstrate use of a spell checker and perhaps even an instance where a spell checker doesn't get something right. Encourage students to use spell checkers, but make sure they understand the need to check what it is suggesting before making the correction.

Life ONLINE

Workplace Focus
Exercise H: Collect and organize information.

H CLASSIFY Write Nubar's goals in the chart.

Allow students to do this activity in pairs or in groups.

Evaluation 3
5–7 mins. ■

Have groups or pairs report to the class and complete the chart on the board.

Application
20–30 mins. ■■■

I APPLY Write your personal, educational, and work goals. Use *will*.

Give students sufficient time so they can focus on expressing themselves accurately, using *will* correctly. Provide vocabulary if necessary.

If time allows, have students exchange books with a partner and peer edit each other's sentences. Encourage them to also talk about each other's goals and give advice and / or encouragement.

Instructor's Notes

_____

_____

_____

_____

_____

_____

_____

_____

_____

_____

_____

_____

_____

_____

_____

_____

_____

At-a-Glance Prep

Goal: Identify employment opportunities in education

Agenda

☐ Interpret an infographic.

☐ Read a job description.

☐ Infer information from the job description.

☐ Reflect on the job of a teacher.

☐ Discuss the characteristics of a good teacher.

☐ Search online for openings in education.

Pacing

■ 1.5 hour classes ■ 2.5 hour classes

■ 3+ hour classes

Standards Correlations

CASAS: 0.1.2, 0.1.5, 4.1.3, 4.1.8, 4.1.9, 6.7.4, 7.4.4, 7.7.3

CCRS: L1, L2, L3, RI1, RI2, RI3, SL1, SL3

ELPS:

S1: Construct meaning from oral presentations and literary and informational text through level-appropriate listening, reading, and viewing.

S5: Conduct research and evaluate and communicate findings to answer questions or solve problems.

S7: Adapt language choices to purpose, task, and audience when speaking and writing.

Warm-up and Review 10–15 mins. ■■■

Write *education* on the board and elicit jobs students can think of related to education and places where people in education work. This will help them review the different levels of education they saw in this unit. Write their ideas on the board.

Introduction 5–10 mins. ■■■

Find out if any of the students have worked in education or know anyone who does. Write the goal on the board: *Today we will identify employment opportunities in education.*

Presentation 1 15–20 mins. ■■■

A INTERPRET Read the infographic and talk about it with your classmates and teacher.

Go over the infographic together, having students explain what it shows (positions, salaries, and advantages of teaching positions). Review large numbers by asking students to say the salaries in the infographic. Ask where the information comes from and point out the source at the bottom right. Tell students that it is always important to check where information in graphs, charts, and infographics comes from to ensure that it is reliable.

Practice 1 20–25 mins. ■■■

B Answer the questions about the infographic.

Remind students of the meaning of *the most* and *the least*. Have them answer the questions individually, then compare and discuss their answers with a partner. Check as a class.

C Work in a group. Ask questions about the infographic in A.

Point out the Comparative Questions and Answers note and model the example exchange with a student. Then put students in pairs to carry out the activity. Tell them to alternate asking and answering.

Evaluation 1 5–10 mins. ■■■

Observe students as they work in pairs.

Explore the Workforce

GOAL ▶ Identify employment opportunities in education

A **INTERPRET** Read the infographic and talk about it with your classmates and teacher.

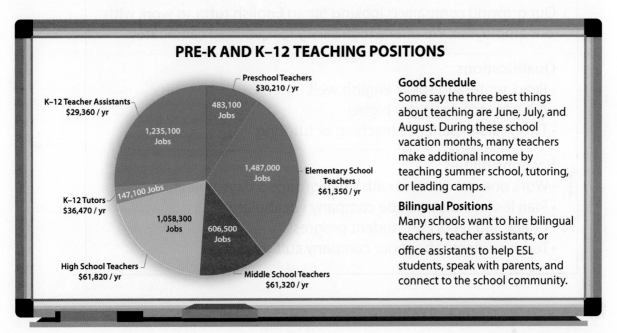

PRE-K AND K–12 TEACHING POSITIONS

Preschool Teachers
$30,210 / yr

K–12 Teacher Assistants
$29,360 / yr

483,100
Jobs

1,235,100
Jobs

1,487,000
Jobs

Elementary School
Teachers
$61,350 / yr

K–12 Tutors
$36,470 / yr

147,100 Jobs

1,058,300
Jobs

606,500
Jobs

High School Teachers
$61,820 / yr

Middle School Teachers
$61,320 / yr

Good Schedule
Some say the three best things about teaching are June, July, and August. During these school vacation months, many teachers make additional income by teaching summer school, tutoring, or leading camps.

Bilingual Positions
Many schools want to hire bilingual teachers, teacher assistants, or office assistants to help ESL students, speak with parents, and connect to the school community.

Source: U.S. Bureau of Labor Statistics

B **Answer the questions about the infographic.**

1. Which position has the most jobs? ___elementary school teacher___

2. Which position has the fewest jobs? ___K–12 tutor___

3. Which position pays the most? ___high school teacher___

4. Which position pays the least? ___K–12 teacher assistant___

C **Work in a group. Ask questions about the infographic in A.**

EXAMPLES: **Student A:** Are there more elementary school teachers than middle school teachers?

Student B: Yes, there are.

Student B: Are there fewer high school teachers than preschool teachers?

Student A: No, there aren't.

Comparative Questions and Answers

Are there **more** teacher assistants **than** K–12 tutors?
  Yes, there are.

Are there **fewer** teacher assistants **than** K–12 tutors?
  No, there aren't.

D Read the job description. Underline words you don't know.

ESL TUTOR

Rowen Technical
2500 W. Pederson Ave.
Los Angeles, CA 90004

1 Our growing company is looking for an English tutor to work with
our employees. We offer a high salary for qualified candidates.

Qualifications
- Read, write, and speak English well.
5 • A bachelor's degree or higher
- Two years' experience teaching or tutoring

Responsibilities
- Work one-on-one and with small groups 5 days a week.
- Plan lessons that include company vocabulary.
10 • Check and report on student progress.
- Teach students about our company culture.

E Choose the correct answers.

1. What do you think *growing company* means in line 1?

   a. The company is small.
   b. The company is getting bigger.
   c. The company is big.

2. What do you think *qualified candidates* means in line 2?

   a. workers at the company
   b. students
   c. people who are good for the job

3. What do you think *one-on-one* means in line 8?

   a. with small groups of students
   b. with two students at a time
   c. with one student at a time

F INFER Work in a group. Give your opinion about the questions. Answers will vary.

1. What days do you think are included in *5 days a week*?

2. How much do you think the *high salary* is for this job?

3. What do you think *company culture* means in the ad?

Presentation 2   10–15 mins. ■■▨

D   Read the job description. Underline words you don't know.

Ask students to look at the job description quickly and tell you what basic information it has about the job. Tell them not to worry about the details. Then have students read it in detail and underline new words. Don't explain vocabulary yet; let them do **E** and **F** first.

Practice 2   20–25 mins. ■■■

E   Choose the correct answers.

Have students read the questions and answers individually first. Point out the line numbers and make sure students understand how to use them. Encourage them to read the job description again to check the context of each phrase. Remind them that context can help them understand the meaning of new words. Then have students work in pairs to discuss their choices. Suggest they use a dictionary if necessary.

F   INFER   Work in a group. Give your opinion about the questions.

Put students in groups using one of the techniques that has been presented previously. Remind them to refer to the job description in **D** when they discuss the questions. Have a spokesperson from each group share their answers and discuss the job description as a class. Find out if there is an ESL tutor where any of the students work.

Evaluation 2   5–10 mins. ■■■

Go over the answers to **E** and **F** as a class. Ask students to go back to the words they underlined in **D** and clarify any that are still not clear.

Instructor's Notes

_____

_____

_____

_____

_____

_____

_____

_____

_____

_____

_____

_____

_____

_____

_____

_____

_____

_____

_____

_____

_____

_____

_____

_____

_____

_____

Presentation 3

5–10 mins. ■■■

Ask students what activities a teacher does and who they work with. Write their ideas on the board. Elicit or provide qualities that teachers have. If students are struggling to come up with anything, ask *yes / no* questions. For example: *Are teachers organized? Do they like to work with students?*

Practice 3

15–20 mins. ■

Ask students in shorter classes to do Practice 3 for homework.

G REFLECT Answer the questions about you for a job as a teacher.

Read the questions together and clarify any vocabulary doubts. Then ask students to choose the answers that apply to them. When they are ready, have students share their answers with a partner. Call on different students to report on whether their partner should be a teacher or not.

H Look at the photo. Kurt Russell is a high school history teacher in Oberlin, Ohio. In 2022, he won the teacher of the year award for his state. What do you think makes Kurt a great teacher? Discuss in a group.

Look at the photo together and have students describe what they see. Ask how Kurt feels and how the students feel. Then put students in groups to discuss the question. Ask each group to write a list. Monitor as they discuss and provide vocabulary as needed. Have one group write their list on the board and ask other groups to add to it if they have anything different on their list. Ask if there are any other characteristics of good teachers in general that they want to add.

I Choose a job title from A. Go to a job search site online and see if there are any openings within 25 miles of your school or home.

Help students get started with their searches by helping them decide which of the jobs in **A** they want to look for. Share specific job search sites that they can use. Tell them to write down the salaries, benefits, training provided, and any other relevant information for the jobs they find. Monitor as they carry out their searches and help as needed.

Evaluation 3

5–10 mins. ■

Put students into pairs or new groups to share and discuss what they found. Observe as they discuss.

BEST PRACTICE

Visual Data

Being able to both interpret and create graphs, charts, and infographics is important in many workplace situations, so it is important that students spend time analyzing this kind of visual data that *Stand Out* provides throughout the book. It is also helpful to provide students with opportunities to create their own visual data. For example, as an extension of **I**, in groups, students can create an infographic that combines and presents the information about the different jobs they found, or a bar graph that compares the different salaries. Have them share their visual data with the class. Encourage them to give each other feedback if the information is not clear.

Instructor's Notes

_____

_____

_____

_____

_____

_____

_____

_____

_____

_____

_____

_____

G **REFLECT** Answer the questions about you for a job as a teacher. Answers will vary.

1. Do you like to teach people new things?

   a. yes   b. no   c. sometimes

2. Do you like working with children or teenagers?

   a. yes   b. no   c. sometimes

3. Do you like to plan?

   a. yes   b. no   c. sometimes

4. Are you organized?

   a. yes   b. no   c. sometimes

5. Do you like to be on your feet (standing up) a lot of the day?

   a. yes   b. no   c. sometimes

H Look at the photo. Kurt Russell is a high school history teacher in Oberlin, Ohio. In 2022, he won the teacher of the year award for his state. What do you think makes Kurt a great teacher? Discuss in a group.

I Choose a job title from **A**. Go to a job search site online and see if there are any openings within 25 miles of your school or home.

Kurt Russell teaches U.S. History and African American History at Oberlin High School in Ohio.

Review

A **What are six things you did in this course to help you study English? Use the verbs to write sentences in the simple past.** Answers will vary.

ask	~~come~~	help	listen	participate	read	speak

1. I came to class on time. _____

2. _____

3. _____

4. _____

5. _____

6. _____

7. _____

B **Check (✓) the study skills.**

☐ learn English   ☐ get a high school diploma   ☑ read the news online

☐ go to college   ☑ listen carefully   ☑ write down new words

☐ go to the supermarket   ☑ ask questions   ☐ eat a good breakfast

C **Write the things you can do well in class.** Answers will vary.

1. I can _____

2. _____

3. _____

D **Ask a partner:** *What can you do well in class?* Answers will vary.

1. Ming can listen well. _____

2. _____

3. _____

4. _____

Learner Log	I can evaluate my study habits.	I can make a study guide.
	☐ Yes ☐ No ☐ Maybe	☐ Yes ☐ No ☐ Maybe

At-a-Glance Prep

Goal: All unit goals
Grammar: All unit grammar
Academic Strategies: Reviewing, evaluating, developing study skills
Vocabulary: All unit vocabulary

Agenda
☐ Discuss unit goals.
☐ Complete the review.
☐ Evaluate and reflect on progress.

Pacing
■ 1.5 hour classes   ■ 2.5 hour classes
■ 3+ hour classes

Standards Correlations
CASAS: 0.1.2, 0.1.5, 7.1.1, 7.1.4, 7.4.1, 7.4.9, 7.5.1
CCRS: L1, L2, L3, SL1, SL3, W3
ELPS:
S2: Participate in level-appropriate oral and written exchanges of information, ideas, and analyses, in various social and academic contexts, responding to peer, audience, or reader comments and questions.
S9: Create clear and coherent level-appropriate speech and text.

Warm-up and Review   7–10 mins. ■■■□
With books closed, ask students to help you make a list on the board of all the vocabulary they can come up with from the unit. Then have a competition where students in groups write the first page numbers where they can find each item on the list. The first group to have a correct page number for each item wins.

Introduction   5 mins. ■■■□
Write all the goals from Unit 8 on the board. Show students the first page of every lesson so they understand that today will be a review.

Presentation   10–15 mins. ■■■□
This presentation will cover all three pages of the review. Quickly go to the first page of each lesson. Discuss the goal of each. Ask simple questions to remind students of what they have learned.

Practice 1   20–25 mins. ■■■□

A **What are six things you did in this course to help you study English? Use the verbs to write sentences in the simple past.**
Say the verbs in the box and elicit the simple past forms. Have students write their sentences, then compare with a partner.

B **Check (✓) the study skills.**
Have students complete the activity and discuss with a partner which of the study skills they do.

C **Write the things you can do well in class.**
Elicit some class activities. For example: *listening, reading, discussing with a partner,* etc. Then have students write their sentences.

D **Ask a partner:** *What can you do well in class?*
Put students in pairs to ask and answer the question. Then have them write what their partner can do well.

Evaluation 1   5–10 mins. ■■■■
Go around the classroom and check on students' progress. Help individuals as needed. If you see consistent errors among several students, interrupt the class and give a mini lesson or review to help students feel comfortable with the concept.

Learner Log   5–10 mins.
Have students read the statements and complete the log. If students answer *no* or *maybe*, encourage them to set themselves a goal to practice. Show them where they can find more practice activities.

BEST PRACTICE
Learner Logs
Learner Logs function to help students in many different ways:

1. They serve as part of the review process.
2. They help students to gain confidence and to document what they have learned. Consequently, students see that they are progressing in their learning.
3. They provide students with a tool that they can use over and over to check and recheck their understanding of the target language. In this way, students become independent learners.

Practice 2 20–25 mins. ■■■□

E **Complete the paragraph with the words from the box.**

Have students complete the paragraph individually, then discuss their answers with a partner.

F **Complete the sentences with the correct form of the verb in parentheses.**

Tell students to read each sentence completely before deciding the form of the verb. Have them compare answers with a partner.

G **Read the sentences and write the best job for each person.**

Brainstorm a few jobs as a class and then ask what people who do those jobs like to do. Provide an example about yourself. For example: *I'm a teacher. I like to help people learn.* Then have students carry out the activity.

Evaluation 2 5–10 mins. ■■■□

Go around the classroom and check on students' progress. Help individuals as needed. If you see consistent errors among several students, interrupt the class and give a mini lesson or review to help students feel comfortable with the concept.

Learner Log 5–10 mins.

Have students read the statements and complete the log. If students answer *no* or *maybe*, encourage them to set themselves a goal to practice. Show them where they can find more practice activities.

BEST PRACTICE

Recycling / Review

The review and the project that follows are part of the recycling / review process. Students at this level often need to be reintroduced to concepts to solidify what they have learned. Many concepts are learned and forgotten while learning other new concepts. This is because students learn but are not necessarily ready to acquire language concepts.

Therefore, it becomes very important to review and to show students how to review on their own. It is also important to recycle the new concepts in different contexts.

Instructor's Notes

E Complete the paragraph with the words from the box.

adult	certificate	college	degree	diploma	GED	trade

In the United States, adults can go to school in many different places. They can go to an
(1) _____ adult _____ school to learn English or to get a high school
(2) _____ diploma _____ or (3) _____ GED _____. After adult
school, students can study at a (4) _____ college _____ or a
(5) _____ trade _____ school. Students who go to a trade school usually get a
(6) _____ certificate _____ when they complete the courses. Some students get a
(7) _____ degree _____ from a university after adult school.

F Complete the sentences with the correct form of the verb in parentheses.

1. Javier likes _____ to study _____ (study) in the afternoon.

2. The students _____ want _____ (want) to learn English.

3. I _____ like _____ (like) books.

4. She _____ likes _____ (like) to read books.

5. We want _____ to go _____ (go) to college.

6. You need _____ to speak _____ (speak) to a teacher.

7. Eva _____ wants _____ (want) to do her homework.

8. He likes _____ to work _____ (work) at night.

G Read the sentences and write the best job for each person.

Answers may vary. Sample answers are given.

1. Hamed likes to take care of people. _____ nurse _____

2. Carlos likes to fix things. _____ mechanic _____

3. Canab likes to sell things. _____ salesperson _____

4. Gaspar likes to teach children. _____ teacher _____

5. Mei likes to take care of her family. _____ homemaker _____

6. Lina likes to prepare food. _____ cook / chef _____

Learner Log   I can identify learning opportunities.   I can identify vocational preferences.
☐ Yes ☐ No ☐ Maybe   ☐ Yes ☐ No ☐ Maybe

Review

H **Write sentences about Nam's future goals. Use *be going to*.** Answers will vary. Sample answers are given.

Nam

Now: Alton Adult School
Educational Goals: learn English, go to a community college
Work Goal: become a chef
Personal Goal: buy a house

1. Nam is going to learn English.

2. He is going to go to a community college.

3. He is going to become a chef.

4. He is going to buy a house.

I **Write sentences about Debora's future goals. Use *will*.** Answers will vary. Sample answers are given.

Debora

Now: Alton Adult School
Educational Goals: get a high school diploma, go to a trade school
Work Goal: become an electrician
Personal Goal: get married

1. Debora will get a high school diploma.

2. She will go to a trade school.

3. She will become an electrician.

4. She will get married.

Learner Log   I can develop goals.
 Yes No Maybe

Practice 3

10–15 mins. ■■■

H **Write sentences about Nam's future goals. Use *be going to*.**

Review *be going to* by asking a few students: *What are you going to do after this English course?* Then ask another student about the previous student's plans: *What is . . . going to do after this English course?* Point out the use of *are* and *is*. Tell students to read the information about Nam carefully, then write his goals. Remind them to use *be going to*. Have them compare answers with a partner.

I **Write sentences about Debora's future goals. Use *will*.**

First say something about yourself. For example: *I will study French next year.* Then elicit a few sentences with *will*. Ask another student about the previous student's plans: *What will . . . do?* Point out that there is no change in the structure. Tell students to read the information about Debora carefully, then write her goals. Remind them to use *will*. Have them compare answers with a partner.

Evaluation 3

10–15 mins. ■■■

Go around the room and check on students' progress. Help individuals as needed. If you see consistent errors among several students, interrupt the class and give a mini lesson or review to help students feel comfortable with the concept.

Ask students what their favorite lesson or page in the unit was and why.

Learner Log

5 mins.

Have students read the statement and complete the log. If students answer *no* or *maybe*, encourage them to set themselves a goal to practice. Show them where they can find more practice activities.

Instructor's Notes

_____

_____

_____

_____

_____

_____

_____

_____

_____

_____

_____

_____

_____

_____

_____

_____

_____

_____

_____

_____

_____

_____

_____

Standards Correlations

CASAS: 0.1.2, 0.1.5, 4.8.1, 7.1.2, 7.1.4, 7.4.1, 7.4.3, 7.5.6

CCRS: L1, L3, SL1, SL3, W1, W3

ELPS:

S3: Speak and write about level-appropriate complex literary and informational texts and topics.

S7: Adapt language choices to purpose, task, and audience when speaking and writing.

S8: Determine the meaning of words and phrases in oral presentations and literary and informational text.

Soft Skill: Presentation Skills
Engaging the Audience

Explain that in the workplace, presentation skills are very important. Giving an effective presentation involves keeping the audience interested and interacting with them so they feel more invested in the presentation. Tell students they will practice this skill during the preparation and practicing of their presentation, and when they give the presentation.

Warm-up and Review   10 mins.

Review items in the review section of the unit and make sure all have recorded their progress in the learner logs.

Introduction   10 mins.

Let students know that in this project, they will prepare a study plan for an imaginary student and present it to the class.

Presentation   10–15 mins.

1. Form a team of four or five students. In your team, you need:

Put students in teams of four or five. Once students are in groups, ask them to choose their positions in the group. To do this, go through each step in the project and explain the role of the person who will lead that step. Make sure they understand that they will complete one step before going on to the next and that although each person has a specific task, they will work together on each step.

The team leader's job is to make sure everyone participates and speaks English. The team leader may also have ancillary responsibilities when general information is required.

For example, in **Step 2**, the team leader can manage the discussion around defining a list of study habits the imaginary student will develop. Then in **Step 3**,

the scheduler will create the calendar and schedule days and times for each activity with the help of the team. In **Step 4**, the goal setter will create the student's study goals based on the other team members' ideas and suggestions and write the paragraph with the team's help. In **Step 5**, the organizers will be responsible for preparing the presentation of the study plan and determining how they will teach the class the best ways to learn; however, all team members will contribute suggestions. All team members will also participate in practicing and giving the presentation. Point out the Soft Skill note and go over the examples of how to involve the audience in the presentation.

Practice / Evaluation / Application   1–2 hours

2. Make a list of study habits your imaginary student will develop. Is this student going to come to school every day, arrive on time, etc.?

3. Complete a calendar for one week. Write what days and times your imaginary student will do the following activities:

Show students an example of a weekly calendar if necessary.

4. Write a paragraph about the imaginary student's study goals on another piece of paper. Start your paragraph like this:

Remind students that they should use *be going to* and *will* to talk about future plans.

5. Present your ideas to the class. Teach the class what your team thinks are the best ways to learn.

As you monitor while groups are working, prompt them to use the questions in the Soft Skill note when they are practicing the presentation so they are comfortable with them when they give the presentation. While they are planning, refer them back to the Unit 4 Team Project for tips on preparing and practicing their presentation.

Set Study Goals

SOFT SKILL ▶ Presentation Skills

In this project, you will prepare a study plan for an imaginary student.

1. Form a team of four or five students. In your team, you need:

Position	Job Description	Student Name
Student 1: **Team Leader**	Check that everyone speaks English. Check that everyone participates.	
Student 2: **Scheduler**	With help from the team, create a calendar and schedule study times.	
Student 3: **Goal Setter**	With help from the team, write a paragraph about study goals.	
Students 4 / 5: **Organizer(s)**	With help from the team, organize a presentation to give to the class.	

2. Make a list of study habits your imaginary student will develop. Is this student going to come to school every day, arrive on time, etc.?

3. Complete a calendar for one week. Write what days and times your imaginary student will do the following activities:

   - study a textbook
   - listen to a podcast
   - read the news online
   - watch TV in English
   - review flashcards
   - write in a journal

4. Write a paragraph about the imaginary student's study goals on another piece of paper. Start your paragraph like this:

   > Juan has many goals for learning English. He is going to speak and listen to English every day. First, he . . .

5. Present your ideas to the class. Teach the class what your team thinks are the best ways to learn.

PRESENTATION SKILLS:
Engaging the Audience

1. Involve your audience in your presentation. Ask questions or teach them something.
   For example, ask:
   How many of you listen to podcasts to practice your English?
   What other study activities do you do?

2. Use visuals like slides or posters to help people understand your ideas.

3. Stop and ask if everyone understands before moving on to the next section.
   For example, say:
   Do you have any questions so far?
   Raise your hand if you understand.

Reading Challenge

About the Photo

The photo shows three students who are representing their school at the world's largest pre-college international science and engineering fair. They are presenting their robotic arms project. These three students collaborated to develop their project and create the final product we see here. Working as a team on this kind of project is generally very beneficial as collaboration leads to more ideas, deeper discussion, and consequently, a better outcome.

Look at the photo together and have students describe what they see. Provide vocabulary as needed.

A REFLECT Choose the correct answers for you and share with a partner.

Tell students to think about how they learn best. Ask them to read each item carefully before answering. Take a class survey of preferences. Point out how we all learn in different ways.

B Look up the words in a dictionary. Then complete the sentences.

Provide dictionaries in the classroom or have students use online dictionaries. Encourage students to discuss their answers with a partner. Check answers as a class before they read the text.

C Read the text. Underline any words you don't know. 🎧

Read the title together and ask students what they think the text is going to be about. Then have them read and underline words they don't understand. Ask a few comprehension questions. For example: *Does everybody like to be alone when they study? What are study groups?* etc. Then have students share the words they underlined and try to explain them as a class. Remind students to look at the whole sentence and try to work out the

---

Reading Challenge

A REFLECT Choose the correct answers for you and share with a partner. Answers will vary.

1. Where do you learn best?

   a. at home   b. at school   c. somewhere else

2. I learn better _____.

   a. in silence   b. with music   c. in a noisy place

3. When do you learn better?

   a. in the morning   b. in the afternoon   c. in the evening

4. I learn better when I study _____.

   a. alone   b. with a partner   c. in a group

B Look up the words in a dictionary. Then complete the sentences.

collaboration	connections	distractions	solution

1. She doesn't want any _____distractions_____. She can't think when there is too much noise.

2. It is a difficult problem. I hope we find a _____solution_____ soon.

3. _____Collaboration_____ is when people work together to fix a problem.

4. Our teacher helps us make _____connections_____ between what we learn in class and our daily lives.

C Read the text. Underline any words you don't know.

D List four benefits of collaboration according to the text.

Collaboration can help you . . .

remember more.   make connections with the information.

have positive feelings.   want to learn more.

E Read the conversation. With a partner, add to the conversation with information from D.

Student A: How does collaboration help us learn better?

Student B: According to the article, it helps us remember more.

Student A: What else?

F EXPRESS Do you agree that collaboration is good for learning? Why or why not? Talk about your ideas in a group.

220   UNIT 8

CASAS FOR READING

0.1.2, 0.1.5, 7.4.1, 7.4.3, 7.4.4, 7.4.5, 7.5.1

CCRS FOR READING

L1, L2, L3, RI1, RI2, RI3

Learning Together 🎧

1   There are many different ways of learning. Some people like to study alone. They want to stay away from distractions. Other people make study groups and talk together about problems and solutions. But which way of studying is better for learning?

5   Research shows that collaboration is key.* When students work with others and help each other, they remember more. Explaining something in your own words and hearing your classmates' ideas can help you make better connections with the information. Also, studying with others can create positive* feelings. For example, the girls in the photo worked together on a project for an international science and

10   engineering fair. Here, they are sharing what they learned, and they are having fun while doing it. If you enjoy learning, you will want to learn more, and when you want to learn, you learn better!

key very important
positive good

Participants in the International Science and Engineering Fair (ISEF), the largest pre-college science competition in the world, discuss their project.

READING STRATEGIES

Pre-Reading Vocabulary

It is important to pre-teach key vocabulary in a text when it will be difficult for students to work out the meaning from context. One way of doing this is to have students look up the words or phrases themselves. They can then use them to complete sentences, as they do in **B**. Another way is to give students the definitions and have them match them to the words / phrases. Students are more likely to remember the meanings of words if they are actively involved in working out the meanings.

meaning from the context. Play the audio and ask students to read as they listen so they can hear the pronunciation of the new vocabulary.

D List four benefits of collaboration according to the text.

Elicit the meaning of *benefits*. Then tell students to read the text again carefully to find the benefits and complete the activity. Check answers as a class and have students point out where the information is in the text.

E Read the conversation. With a partner, add to the conversation with information from D.

Read the conversation with the class. Help them with the intonation of the questions. Then model the conversation with a student. Prompt the student to add another item from **D** to the conversation. Put students in pairs. Remind them to switch roles so they practice asking and answering.

F EXPRESS Do you agree that collaboration is good for learning? Why or why not? Talk about your ideas in a group.

Tell students to use their answers in **D** and the conversations they had in **E** to help them. Put students in groups to discuss the questions. Monitor and help as needed. Prompt them with questions to help keep the discussion going.

Life
ONLINE

About the Photo

This photo shows a very messy desk covered in sticky notes with various messages and reminders on them. This is meant to illustrate what *not* to do since this organizational system is not likely to be effective. Many of the notes are vague, difficult to read, and don't appear to be in any particular order.

Before You Watch

Have students read the title of the video and look at the photo. Provide or elicit the meaning of *organized*. Then have students read the photo caption and discuss the questions as a class.

A Check (✓) the things you keep on your phone or computer. Share with a partner.

Have students read the items and clarify any vocabulary doubts as a class. Then have them do the exercise individually before sharing with a partner. If there are students without phones or computers, have them choose things they think are good to have on a phone or computer.

B Study the words and expressions. Then complete the sentences.

Have students read the words and share any ideas they have about the meanings. Write their ideas on the board. Then allow students to work in pairs to complete the sentences. Ask them to make guesses first before using a dictionary to check. Go over the answers as a

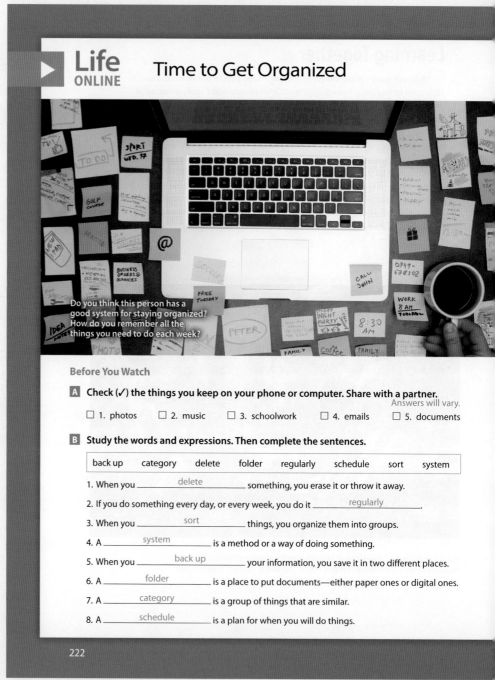

Life ONLINE   Time to Get Organized

Do you think this person has a good system for staying organized? How do you remember all the things you need to do each week?

Before You Watch

A Check (✓) the things you keep on your phone or computer. Share with a partner.

Answers will vary.

☐ 1. photos   ☐ 2. music   ☐ 3. schoolwork   ☐ 4. emails   ☐ 5. documents

B Study the words and expressions. Then complete the sentences.

back up	category	delete	folder	regularly	schedule	sort	system

1. When you _____delete_____ something, you erase it or throw it away.

2. If you do something every day, or every week, you do it _____regularly_____.

3. When you _____sort_____ things, you organize them into groups.

4. A _____system_____ is a method or a way of doing something.

5. When you _____back up_____ your information, you save it in two different places.

6. A _____folder_____ is a place to put documents—either paper ones or digital ones.

7. A _____category_____ is a group of things that are similar.

8. A _____schedule_____ is a plan for when you will do things.

222

class and provide any additional clarification as needed. Prompt students to add any new words to their vocabulary logs.

C PREDICT You are going to watch a video about how to organize files on your phone or computer. What tips do you think the video will give? Answers will vary.

While You Watch

D Watch the video. Check (✓) the categories the video mentions.

☑ 1. pets ☐ 2. cars ☐ 3. musicians ☑ 4. friends ☑ 5. food

☑ 6. travel ☐ 7. movies ☑ 8. selfies ☐ 9. books ☐ 10. sports

E Watch the video again. Choose the ideas you hear.

a. Don't delete anything—you might need it!

(b.) When you are organized, you save time.

(c.) Using folders makes it easier to find the files you're looking for.

d. Everyone needs to use the same organization system.

After You Watch

F Match the advice (1–6) to the examples (a–f).

_b_ 1. Create a system for answering important emails.

_d_ 2. Delete items you don't need any more.

_e_ 3. Use a schedule to sort through your files regularly.

_a_ 4. Look at your files and create categories to organize them.

_f_ 5. Create a folder for each important category.

_c_ 6. Come up with a system for getting organized and use it!

a. Marta looks at her files and sees she has essays, presentations, and group projects.

b. Sergei puts the emails he needs to answer in a folder called *follow-up*.

c. Musa always names his school assignments in the same way so it is easy to find them.

d. When a project is over, Joann saves the final project and deletes her drafts and notes.

e. Every Sunday night, Luca sorts his files into folders and looks at his homework for the week.

f. Fatima has folders called *schoolwork*, *photos*, and *personal projects*.

G Work with a partner. On a separate piece of paper, write three tips from the video that you will use to organize your schoolwork. Do you use other systems as well? Discuss your ideas. Answers will vary.

C PREDICT You are going to watch a video about how to organize files on your phone or computer. What tips do you think the video will give?

Have students predict what they think the video will say and then share their ideas in pairs.

While You Watch

D Watch the video. Check (✓) the categories the video mentions.

Ask students to read the items. Clarify any doubts. Then ask students to check the items as they watch the video. Have students watch the video a second time to check their answers.

E Watch the video again. Choose the ideas you hear.

Have students read the items. Clarify any doubts. Then ask students to say which ideas they think are in the video. Watch the video again and have students circle the ideas they hear. Check answers as a class.

After You Watch

F Match the advice (1–6) to the examples (a–f).

Have students read the items. Clarify any doubts and make sure students understand that the numbered items are the tips from the video and the lettered items are examples of people following the tips. Have students complete the exercise individually before checking answers as a class.

G Work with a partner. On a separate piece of paper, write three tips from the video that you will use to organize your schoolwork. Do you use other systems as well? Discuss your ideas.

Have students write the tips they want to use individually and think about other things they do to stay organized. After sharing with a partner, have students report to the class what their partner said.

Life Skills Video Practice

Where Are You From?

A BEFORE Ask and answer the questions with a partner.

1. How many people are in your family?

2. Is anyone in your family married? Who?

3. Does anyone in your family have kids? Who and how many?

B WHILE Watch the video. Complete the conversation.

Naomi: Hector was showing me some of the (1) _____family_____ photos.

Mrs. Sanchez: Oh, was he? Well, this is my (2) _____sister_____. She's (3) _____married_____, and she has two kids.

Naomi: So, these are your (4) _____cousins_____?

C AFTER Read the statements. Write *T* for True and *F* for False.

1. Hector's mother is from Mexico. __F__

2. Hector's father is 50 years old. __F__

3. Mrs. Sanchez's sister is married. __T__

4. Hector has two cousins named Aidan and Marta. __T__

5. Naomi is from Japan. __F__

UNIT 2 Can I Help You?

A BEFORE Ask and answer the questions with a partner.

1. What are you wearing now?

2. Do you need to buy any new clothes? If yes, what?

3. Where do you like to buy clothes?

B WHILE Watch the video. Check (✓) the things you see.

☑ A customer comes to the store.

☐ The customer asks for a dress.

☐ The customer sees three pairs of jeans.

☐ The customer chooses the green sweater.

☑ The customer is happy.

☑ Hector helps the customer find the boys' section.

C AFTER Number the sentences in order to make a new conversation.

a. __5__ **Sales Clerk:** Please follow me to the men's department.

b. __2__ **Customer:** I'm looking for a sweater.

c. __1__ **Sales Clerk:** Can I help you?

d. __4__ **Customer:** No, it's for my brother.

e. __3__ **Sales Clerk:** Is the sweater for you?

f. __6__ **Customer:** Thank you.

g. __7__ **Sales Clerk:** You're welcome.

UNIT 1 Where Are You From?

BEFORE

A Ask and answer the questions with a partner.

Read the questions and have students repeat them. Put students in pairs. Call on several students to report to the class about their partner.

WHILE

B Watch the video. Complete the conversation.

Have students read the conversation and predict the missing words. Then play the video and ask students to complete the conversation. Have them compare answers with a partner. Play the video again. Ask if their predictions were correct.

AFTER

C Read the statements. Write T for True and F for False.

Ask students to read the sentences and write T for ones that are true or F for ones that are false. Have them compare with a partner. Then play the video again and check the answers as a class.

UNIT 2 Can I Help You?

BEFORE

Ask students to read the title of the video and guess what it will be about. Discuss as a class.

A Ask and answer the questions with a partner.

Read the questions and have students repeat them. Put students in pairs. Call on several students to report to the class about their partner.

WHILE

B Watch the video. Check (✓) the things you see.

Have students read each item and clarify any doubts. Play the video. Tell students to complete their answers. Have them compare with a partner. Play the video again. Then check answers as a class.

AFTER

C Number the sentences in order to make a new conversation.

Point out the first line of the conversation. Tell students to read each line carefully and put them in order. Have them compare with a partner. Then check answers as a class. Have students practice the conversation in pairs.

UNIT 3 Nobody Has Pizza for Breakfast

A **BEFORE** Ask and answer the questions with a partner.

1. What do you eat for breakfast?

2. What food do you have in your refrigerator right now?

3. What is your favorite meal? Why?

B **WHILE** Watch the video. Check (✓) the foods you hear.

☑ eggs   ☑ pizza   ☑ potato chips

☑ toast   ☐ chicken   ☐ oranges

☐ soda   ☐ pasta   ☑ cheese

C **AFTER** Read the statements. Write *T* for true or *F* for false.

1. Hector eats pizza for breakfast.   F

2. Mr. Sanchez wants cake for breakfast.   F

3. Mrs. Sanchez helps Hector make an omelet.   T

4. Hector puts sugar on his omelet.   F

UNIT 4 Are Utilities Included?

A **BEFORE** Ask and answer the questions with a partner.

1. Where do you live?   2. Who do you live with?   3. What utilities do you pay for?

B **WHILE** Watch the video. Use the words to complete the parts of the conversation.

garbage	parking	rent	utilities

Apartment Manager: Some (1) _____utilities_____ are included. Water and (2) _____garbage_____ are included, but you have to pay for the electricity.

Naomi: How much is the (3) _____rent_____?

Apartment Manager: It's only $900 a month—plus electricity. But the (4) _____parking_____ is free!

C **AFTER** Match the questions and answers.

1. __d__ How much is the rent?   a. Water is included, but not electricity.

2. __a__ Are the utilities included?   b. Cats are allowed, but dogs aren't.

3. __b__ Do you allow any pets?   c. No, you have to park on the street.

4. __c__ Does the building have a garage?   d. The rent is $900 a month.

UNIT 3   Nobody Has Pizza for Breakfast

BEFORE

Have students read the title of the video and guess what it will be about. Ask if they ever have pizza for breakfast. Discuss as a class.

A   **Ask and answer the questions with a partner.**

Read the questions and have students repeat them. Put students in pairs. Call on several students to report to the class about their partner.

WHILE

B   **Watch the video. Check (✓) the foods you hear.**

Have students read each item. Clarify any pronunciation doubts. Tell students to check their answers as they watch. Play the video. Have them compare with a partner. Play the video again. Then check answers as class.

AFTER

C   **Read the statements. Write *T* for true and *F* for false.**

Ask students to read the sentences and write *T* for ones that are true or *F* for ones that are false. Have them compare with a partner. Then play the video again and check answers as a class.

UNIT 4   Are Utilities Included?

BEFORE

Have students read the title of the video and guess what it will be about. Make sure students understand *utilities* and *included*. Discuss as a class.

A   **Ask and answer the questions with a partner.**

Read the questions and have students repeat them. Put students in pairs. Call on several students to report to the class about their partner.

WHILE

B   **Watch the video. Use the words to complete the parts of the conversation.**

Go over the words in the box. Say them for students to repeat. Have them predict the missing words. Play the video. Then ask students to complete the conversation. Have them compare answers with a partner. Play the video again. Ask if their predictions were correct.

AFTER

C   **Match the questions and answers.**

Tell students to read each question and then the answer options carefully and match them. Have them compare with a partner. Then check answers as a class. Have students practice the conversation in pairs.

UNIT 5 How Do I Get There?

A **BEFORE** Ask your partner how to get from your school to a nearby restaurant. Write down the directions and check with your partner that they are correct.

B **WHILE** Watch the video. Use the words to complete the conversation.

on	on the corner of	signs	straight

Naomi: Ask him what street he's (1) _____on_____.

Hector: Do you see any street (2) _____signs_____?

Mateo: I'm (3) _____on the corner of_____ Atlantic and Broadway.

Naomi: Tell him to walk (4) _____straight_____ for two blocks.

C **AFTER** Number the sentences to put the directions in order.

a. __3__ Then turn right.

b. __2__ Go toward City Hall.

c. __5__ The diner is on the left.

d. __4__ Walk one block.

e. __1__ Walk down Atlantic for two blocks.

UNIT 6 You'd Better Call the Doctor

A **BEFORE** Describe the symptoms of an illness or medical problem to a partner. See if your partner can guess the problem. Take turns.

EXAMPLE: **Student A:** My head hurts.   **Student B:** Do you have a headache?

B **WHILE** Watch the video. Check (✓) Mr. Sanchez's symptoms.

☑ headache   ☐ runny nose   ☑ shoulder ache

☑ dizziness   ☐ sore throat   ☑ cough

☑ fever   ☑ backache   ☐ stomachache

C **AFTER** Match the statements and responses.

1. __a__ My back aches.   a. Take a pain reliever.

2. __d__ I have a sore throat.   b. You need to get more rest.

3. __b__ I'm tired all the time.   c. You should take some cough syrup.

4. __c__ I have a bad cough.   d. You should take some throat lozenges.

UNIT 5 How Do I Get There?

BEFORE

A Ask your partner how to get from your school to a nearby restaurant. Write down the directions and check with your partner that they are correct.

Ask students: *How do I get to (somewhere in the school or nearby)?* Elicit other direction words and phrases. Write them on the board together with the question prompt. Put students in pairs to carry out the activity.

WHILE

B Watch the video. Use the words to complete the conversation.

Go over the words in the box. Tell students to read the parts of the conversation. Make sure they understand that this isn't the complete conversation. Play the video. Have students write their answers. Then play the video again for them to finish writing if necessary. Have them compare with a partner. Play the video a third time and check answers as a class.

AFTER

C Number the sentences to put the directions in order.

Point out the first direction. Tell students to read each one carefully and put them in order. Have them compare with a partner. Then check answers as a class. Have students practice giving the directions in pairs.

UNIT 6 You'd Better Call the Doctor

BEFORE

Have students read the title of the video and explain or elicit that *you'd better* is used when giving strong advice and is similar to *should*.

A Describe the symptoms of an illness or medical problem to a partner. See if your partner can guess the problem. Take turns.

Go over the example. Elicit an illness and then ask students for the symptoms. Put students in pairs to carry out the activity. Call on different pairs to perform their conversations for the class.

WHILE

B Watch the video. Check (✓) Mr. Sanchez's symptoms.

Have students read each item. Clarify any pronunciation or vocabulary doubts. Tell students to check the symptoms as they watch. Play the video. Have them compare with a partner. Play the video again. Then check answers as class.

AFTER

C Match the statements and responses.

Tell students to read each statement and then the answer options carefully and match them. Have them compare with a partner. Then check answers as a class. Have students practice making the statements and responding in pairs.

UNIT 7 — How Did You Hear About This Job?

A **BEFORE** Discuss the questions with a partner.

1. What is a resume?
2. Where can you find job postings?
3. What are the best clothes for a job interview?

B **WHILE** Watch the video. Use the words to complete the conversation.

answered	assistant	did	experience	history

Hector: I know I don't have very much (1) _____experience_____.

Mr. Patel: Tell me about your work (2) _____history_____.

Hector: I was an . . . (3) _____assistant_____.

Mr. Patel: And what was it that you (4) _____did_____ as an "assistant"?

Hector: I (5) _____answered_____ the phones and took messages.

C **AFTER** Read the statements. Write *T* for true or *F* for false.

1. Hector does not have an appointment for an interview. _____F_____
2. Mr. Patel is the store manager. _____T_____
3. Hector saw the job posting online. _____F_____
4. Hector can work in the mornings and evenings. _____F_____

UNIT 8 — I Have Lots of Different Interests

A **BEFORE** Discuss the questions with a partner.

1. What job did you want when you were a child?
2. What job do you want now? Why?
3. What are you going to do after you finish this class?

B **WHILE** Watch the video. Use the words to complete the conversation.

gave	like	take	took

Mrs. Smith: Tell me, which classes did you (1) _____take_____ last semester?

Hector: I (2) _____took_____ a class in public speaking. That was fun.

Mrs. Smith: Oh, really? You (3) _____like_____ to speak in public?

Hector: Let's just say I'm not shy. I (4) _____gave_____ a speech at least twice a week.

C **AFTER** Read the statements. Write *T* for true or *F* for false.

1. Hector needs to choose his classes for the new semester. _____T_____
2. He's not sure what classes he's going to take. _____T_____
3. Last semester he took a class in journalism. _____F_____
4. Hector likes to watch and listen to news programs. _____T_____

227   **LIFE SKILLS VIDEO PRACTICE**

How Did You Hear About This Job?

BEFORE

Have students read the title of the video and guess what it will be about. Ask students for possible answers to the title question (an online ad, through a friend, etc.). Discuss as a class.

A **Discuss the questions with a partner.**

Read the questions together. Put students in pairs to discuss them. Call on different pairs to explain each one.

WHILE

B **Watch the video. Use the words to complete the conversation.**

Go over the words in the box. Tell students to read the conversation. Encourage them to predict where each word goes. Play the video. Have students write their answers. Play the video again for them to finish writing if necessary. Have them compare with a partner. Play the video again and check answers as a class.

AFTER

C **Read the statements. Write *T* for true or *F* for false.**

Ask students to read the sentences and write *T* for ones that are true and *F* for ones that are false. Have them compare with a partner. Then play the video again and check answers as a class.

UNIT 8 # I Have Lots of Different Interests

BEFORE

Have students read the title of the video and guess what it will be about. Clarify the meaning of *interests* if necessary.

A **Discuss the questions with a partner.**

Read the questions together. Put students in pairs to discuss them. Call on different students to report to the class about their partner.

WHILE

B **Watch the video. Use the words to complete the conversation.**

Go over the words in the box. Tell students to read the conversation. Encourage them to predict where each word goes. Play the video. Have students write their answers. Play the video again for them to complete them if necessary. Have them compare with a partner. Play the video a third time and check answers as a class.

AFTER

C **Read the statements. Write *T* for true or *F* for false.**

Ask students to read the sentences and write *T* for ones that are true and *F* for ones that are false. Have them compare with a partner. Then play the video again and check answers as a class.

Stand Out Vocabulary List

dining room
driveway
drywaller
electrician
electricity
end table
floor plan
floor / tile installer
front porch
front yard
garage
gas
hall
interior designer
kitchen
lamp
living room
mobile home
overtime
painter
painting
parking
plumber
refrigerator
rent
security deposit
sofa
stairs
swimming pool
trash can
utilities
yard

UNIT 5 pp. 118–143

across from
airport
around the corner from
baggage claim
bank
between
block
bus station
city hall
dentist's office
DMV (Department of
    Motor Vehicles)

doctor's office
envelopes
fire department
high school
hospital
hostel
hotel
in front of
library
mail carrier
mall
motel
museum
next to
on the corner
on the right / left
packages
park
parking lot
pension
playground
police station
post office
postal clerk
postal sorter / worker
restrooms
route
salary
security checkpoint
stamps
straight
tennis court
ticketing
turn around
turn left
turn right
vending machines
wages
zoo

UNIT 6 pp. 144–169

ambulance
arm
back
backache
chest

cold
cough
cough syrup
ear(s)
emergency
eye(s)
fever
flu
foot (feet)
hand(s)
head
headache
leg(s)
licensed practical nurse
    (LPN)
loss of taste / smell
medicine
mouth
muscle ache
neck
nose
nursing assistant
pain reliever
pharmacy technician
prescription
registered nurse (RN)
runny nose
sneezing
sore throat
stomach
stomachache
throat lozenges
tooth (teeth)

UNIT 7 pp. 170–195

administrative assistant
application
auto mechanic
benefits
branches
cashier
climb
communicate
custodian
evaluation
exceed expectations

experience
full-time
goggles
homemaker
improve(ment)
insurance
interview
landscape architect
landscaping worker
line supervisor
meet expectations
office assistant
part-time
principal
rules
safety
sick leave
tree trimmer
vacation

UNIT 8 pp. 196–221

adult school
associate degree
bachelor's degree
certificate
college
community college
degree
diploma
elementary school
GED (General Education
    Development)
goal
graduate degree
high school
HiSET (High School
    Equivalency Test)
junior college
middle school
teacher assistant
technical school
trade school
tutor
university
vocational training

Stand Out Grammar Reference

UNIT 1

Simple Present: *Be*			
Subject	**Be**		**Example Sentence**
I	am	43 years old	I **am** 43 years old.
He / She	is	single from Venezuela	He **is** single. (Cumar **is** single.) She **is** from Venezuela. (Gabriela **is** from Venezuela.)
We / You / They	are	married 30 years old from Iran	We **are** married. (Sara and I are married.) You **are** 30 years old. They **are** from Iran. (Sara and Arash are from Iran.)

Simple Present: *Have* and *Like*		
Subject	**Verb**	**Noun**
I / You We / They	**have**	black hair.
	like	social media.
He / She	**has**	brown eyes.
	likes	gaming.

UNIT 2

Be Verb (Questions)			
Question Words	**Be**	**Singular or Plural Noun**	**Example Question**
How much (money)	is	the dress	How much **is** the dress?
How much (money)	are	the socks	How much **are** the socks?

Be Verb (Answers)		
Singular or Plural Noun or Pronoun	**Be**	**Example Answer**
It	is	It **is** $48. It's $48. (The dress **is** $48.)
They	are	They **are** $12. They're $12. (The socks **are** $12.)

Possessive Adjectives

Pronoun	Possessive Adjective	Example Sentence
I	my	**My** shirt is blue.
you	your	**Your** shorts are brown.
he	his	**His** belt is black.
she	her	**Her** dress is yellow.
we	our	**Our** shirts are white.
they	their	**Their** shoes are red.

UNIT 3

Comparative Adjectives

Cheaper

	Question	Answer
Singular	Where is pasta **cheaper**?	It's **cheaper** at Puente Market.
Plural	Where are carrots **cheaper**?	They're **cheaper** at Food City.

More Expensive

	Question	Answer
Singular	Where is pasta **more expensive**?	It's **more expensive** at Food City.
Plural	Where are carrots **more expensive**?	They're **more expensive** at Puente Market.

Yes / No Questions and Answers

Question	Yes	No
Do you want a hamburger?	Yes, I do.	No, I don't.
Do they want sandwiches?	Yes, they do.	No, they don't.
Does he want a sandwich?	Yes, he does.	No, he doesn't.
Does she want a hot dog?	Yes, she does.	No, she doesn't.

UNIT 4

Yes / No Questions

Question	Answer
Does it have three bedrooms?	Yes, it does. No, it doesn't.
Does it have air-conditioning?	Yes, it does. No, it doesn't.

Present Continuous

Subject	*Be* Verb	Base Verb + *ing*	Example Sentence
I	am	talk + ing	I **am talking** on the phone.
You / We / They	are	search + ing	They **are searching** for a new home.
He / She / It	is	make + ing	We **are making** an appointment.
		plan + ing	She **is planning** to buy a new house.

Spelling note: If the base verb ends in *e*, remove the *e* before adding -*ing*. make → making

UNIT 5

Yes / No Questions with *Can*

Can	Subject	Base Verb	Example Question
Can	I	help	**Can** I help you?
		ask	**Can** I ask you a question?
		talk	**Can** I talk to you?
	you	give	**Can** you give me the phone number?
		call	**Can** you call me back?

Present Continuous

Subject	*Be*	Verb + *ing*	Time	Example Sentence
I	am (I'm)	writing	right now today	I'**m writing** a letter right now.
He / She / It	is (she's)	eating		She**'s eating** a sandwich.
You / We / They	are (they're)	reading		They**'re reading** a book today.

Simple Present

Subject	Adverb	Verb	Example Sentence
I	always usually sometimes rarely never	write	I always **write** emails in the morning.
He / She / It		eats	He rarely **eats** here.
You / We / They		read	They never **read** the newspaper.

Adverbs of Frequency

0%		50%		100%
never	rarely	sometimes	usually	always

UNIT 6

Simple Present: *Have*		
Subject	***Have***	**Example Sentence**
I / You / We / They	have	I **have** a headache. You **have** a sore throat.
He / She	has	She **has** a stomachache. He **has** a fever.

Negative Simple Present: *Have*			
Subject	**Negative**	***Have***	**Example Sentence**
I / You / We / They	do not (don't)	have	I **don't have** a headache. You **don't have** a sore throat.
He / She	does not (doesn't)	have	She **doesn't have** a stomachache. He **doesn't have** a fever.

Should for Advice			
Subject	***Should***	**Base Verb**	**Example Sentence**
I / You / He / She We / They	should	rest	You **should** rest.
		stay	He **should** stay home.
		see	They **should** see a doctor.
		take	I **should** take a pain reliever.

Should Not for Advice			
Subject	***Should Not***	**Base Verb**	**Example Sentence**
I / You / He / She We / They	should not (shouldn't)	drive	You **shouldn't** drive and take this medicine.
		drink	He **shouldn't** drink alcohol with this medicine.
		go	We **shouldn't** go out.

Wh- Questions				
Question Word	***Be***		**Example Question**	**Example Answer**
Who		calling?	Who's calling?	It's Victor Karaskov.
What	is	the emergency?	What's the emergency?	There's a car accident.
Where		the accident?	Where's the accident?	It's on Fourth and Bush.

Verb + Infinitive			
Subject	**Verb**	**Infinitive (*to* + Base Verb)**	**Example Sentence**
I / You / We / They	want	to run to exercise to walk	I **want to run**. We **want to exercise** every day. They **want to walk.**
He / She / It	wants	to ride to go	He **wants to ride** a bicycle. She **wants to go** to the gym.

UNIT 7

Simple Past: Regular Verbs		
Subject	**Base Verb + *ed***	**Example Sentence**
I / You He / She We / They	cleaned	I **cleaned** tables.
	cooked	You **cooked** hamburgers.
	prepared	He **prepared** breakfast.
	fixed	She **fixed** cars.
	helped	We **helped** other workers.
	moved	They **moved** to the United States.
Spelling note: If the base verb ends in *e*, just add *d*. move → moved		

Simple Past: *Be*		
Subject	***Be***	**Example Sentence**
I / He / She	was	I **was** an auto mechanic.
We / You / They	were	You **were** late yesterday.

UNIT 8

Regular Past Verbs	
Base Verb	**Simple Past**
study	studied
participate	participated
help	helped
listen	listened
watch	watched
practice	practiced
learn	learned
plan	planned

Spelling notes: When the base verb ends in *y*, remove the *y*, and add *-ied*.
study → studied
When the base verb is one syllable and ends in a vowel and a consonant, double the last consonant and add *-ed*.
plan → planned

Irregular Past Verbs	
Base Verb	**Simple Past**
come	came
have	had
write	wrote
speak	spoke
read	read
teach	taught
go	went
do	did
make	made

Future with *Be Going to*			
Subject	***Be Going to***	**Base Verb**	**Example Sentence**
I	am going to (I'm going to)	learn practice speak	I **am going to learn** English.
You / We They	are going to (you're / we're / they're going to)		We **are going to practice** English.
He / She	is going to (he's / she's going to)		She **is going to speak** English.
Use *be going to* for future plans and predictions.			

Future with *Will*			
Subject	***Will***	**Base Verb**	**Example Sentence**
I / You He / She We / They	will	study work get married	I **will study** every day.
			She **will work** hard.
			They **will get** married.
Use *will* for statements and predictions about the future. *Will* is more formal than *be going to*. When speaking, people often use the contraction: *I'll, You'll, He'll, She'll, We'll, They'll*			

ILLUSTRATIONS: Illustrations created by Oscar Hernandez. All illustrations and graphics are owned by © Cengage Learning, Inc.

PHOTOS: v (tl) © Charlie Zevon, (tr) © Priscilla Caraveo; **xii** (tl) Shapecharge/E+/Getty Images, (tc) (tr) © Christopher Payne/Esto, (cl1) (cr2) © Chris Crisman Photography, (cl2) (cr1) © Brian Doben Photography; **2** (tr) (br) © Chris Crisman Photography, (cl) Shapecharge/E+/Getty Images, (c) (bl) © Brian Doben Photography, (cr) (bc) © Christopher Payne/Esto; **3** SDI Productions/E+/Getty Images; **4** (bl) Morsa Images/DigitalVision/Getty Images, (br) Kilito Chan/Moment/Getty Images; **6** As-artmedia/Shutterstock.com; **7** Yun Han Xu/EyeEm/Getty Images; **8** (tl) Morsa Images/DigitalVision/Getty Images, (tc) Ground Picture/Shutterstock.com; **9** (tl1) Yuri Arcurs/Alamy Stock Photo, (tl2) AsiaVision/E+/Getty Images, (tr1) FreshSplash/E+/Getty Images, (tr2) Klaus Vedfelt/DigitalVision/Getty Images; **10** (tl) Dean Drobot/Shutterstock.com, (tr) Nipitphon Na Chiangmai/EyeEm/Getty Images, (cl1) FreshSplash/E+/Getty Images, (cl2) Yuri Arcurs/Alamy Stock Photo, (cr1) Hill Street Studios/The Image Bank/Getty Images, (cr2) SDI Productions/E+/Getty Images, (bl) Image Source/Getty Images, (br) Dean Drobot/Shutterstock.com; **11** HBRH/Shutterstock.com; **12–13** (spread) © Corey Arnold/National Geographic Image Collection; **15** (tl1) Andresr/Shutterstock.com, (tl2) Charday Penn/E+/Getty Images, (tr) Dasha Petrenko/Shutterstock.com, (bl) MoMo Productions/DigitalVision/Getty Images, (bc) JohnnyGreig/E+/Getty Images, (br) Miodrag Ignjatovic/E+/Getty Images; **16** (cl) (c) (cr) Morsa Images/DigitalVision/Getty Images; **17** (tl) 123ducu/E+/Getty Images, (bl) (br) Morsa Images/DigitalVision/Getty Images; **18** NDAB Creativity/Shutterstock.com; **23** (tl) Heath Korvola/DigitalVision/Getty Images, (tc) Michael Blann/Stone/Getty Images, (tr) Ferenc Cegledi/Shutterstock.com, (cl1) Alistair Berg/DigitalVision/Getty Images, (cl2) Africa Studio/Shutterstock.com, (c1) Teera Konakan/Moment/Getty Images, (c2) Monkey Business Images/Shutterstock.com, (cr1) Gpetric/iStock/Getty Images, (cr2) Prasit photo/Moment/Getty Images; **26** Canoneer/Shutterstock.com; **27** Canoneer/Shutterstock.com; **29** (tl) Andy Krisbianto Herlambang/EyeEm/Getty Images, (tc) Oksana Shufrych/EyeEm/Getty Images, (tr) Jose Luis Pelaez Inc/DigitalVision/Getty Images, (cl) Klaus Vedfelt/DigitalVision/Getty Images, (c) Luis Alvarez/DigitalVision/Getty Images, (cr) New Africa/Shutterstock.com; **31** Triff/Shutterstock.com; **32** (tl) (tc) (tr) Morsa Images/DigitalVision/Getty Images; **34** Canoneer/Shutterstock.com; **35** Klaus Vedfelt/DigitalVision/Getty Images; **37** RF Pictures/The Image Bank/Getty Images; **38–39** (spread) Jackie Molloy/The New York Times/Redux; **40** (cl1) Fcafotodigital/E+/Getty Images, (cl2) Mirage_studio/Shutterstock.com, (bl1) Ifong/Shutterstock.com, (bl2) Crystal01/Shutterstock.com, (bl3) Melinda Fawver/Shutterstock.com; **41** Ifong/Shutterstock.com; **44** (tl1) (tl2) United States Government, (tr1) United States Mint/United States Government, (tr2) United States coin image from the United States Mint, (cl1) (cr1) United States government, (cl2) Petra Wallner/Alamy Stock Photo, (cr2) Tewin Kijthamrongworakul/Alamy Stock Photo, (bl) Mirage_studio/Shutterstock.com, (bc) Yevgen Romanenko/Moment/Getty Images, (br) Fcafotodigital/E+/Getty Images; **45** Ifong/Shutterstock.com; **48** SolStock/E+/Getty Images; **52** (cl1) Ifong/Shutterstock.com, (cl2) Kateryna998/Shutterstock.com, (tr1) Thanate Rooprasert/Shutterstock.com, (tr2) Mint Images/Getty Images, (cl1) Lalocracio/E+/Getty Images, (cl2) Konstantinos Moraitis/Alamy Stock Photo, (cr1) Goir/Shutterstock.com, (cr2) Olga Pink/Shutterstock.com, (bl1) Kavaliova Iryna/Shutterstock.com, (bl2) MstudioG/Shutterstock.com, (br1) (br2) Crystal01/Shutterstock.com; **54** Silwen Randebrock/Alamy Stock Photo; **57** Gorodenkoff/Shutterstock.com; **58** (tl1) Ifong/Shutterstock.com, (tl2) Tale/Shutterstock.com, (tl3) Mega Pixel/Shutterstock.com, (cl1) Mivr/Shutterstock.com, (cl2) Chakrapong Worathat/EyeEm/Getty Images, (cl3) Karkas/Shutterstock.com, (bl1) Ruslan Kudrin/Shutterstock.com, (bl2) Goir/Shutterstock.com; **59** (bl) Elenovsky/Shutterstock.com, (bc) Gowithstock/Shutterstock.com, (br) Magdalena Wielobob/Shutterstock.com; **62** (cl) TuktaBaby/Shutterstock.com, (c) Natalia van D/Shutterstock.com, (cr) Dennisvdw/iStock/Getty Images; **63** Mel Melcon/Los Angeles Times/Getty Images; **64–65** (spread) Mediterranean/E+/Getty Images; **68** (tl1) Elena Shashkina/Shutterstock.com, (tl2) Anna Shepulova/Shutterstock.com, (tr1) Igor Dutina/Shutterstock.com, (tr2) PhotoStock-Israel/Photodisc/Getty Images; **72** Alvarez/E+/Getty Images; **73** (tl1) Bahadir Yeniceri/Shutterstock.com, (tl2) Danilaleo/Shutterstock.com, (tc1) Tatiana Popova/Shutterstock.com, (tc2) Donatas1205/Shutterstock.com, (tr1) Macondo/Shutterstock.com, (tr2) Jiri Hera/Shutterstock.com; **76** Ken Penn/EyeEm/Getty Images; **79** Roberto Westbrook/Blend Images/Getty Images; **80** (cl) (c) (cr) Morsa Images/DigitalVision/Getty Images; **82** Studiocasper/E+/Getty Images; **83** Monkeybusinessimages/iStock/Getty Images; **88** (tl1) Fevziie/Shutterstock.com, (tl2) Olga Leschenko/Shutterstock.com, (tr1) Ground Picture/Shutterstock.com, (tr2) DWImages/Alamy Stock Photo; **90–91** (spread) Undefined/iStock/Getty Images, **92** (tr) Rob Marmion/Shutterstock.com, (cl) Atlaspix/Shutterstock.com, (cr) LesPalenik/Shutterstock.com, (bl) Eky Studio/Shutterstock.com, (br) RichLegg/E+/Getty Images; **105** Sura Nualpradid/Shutterstock.com; **107** (tl1) Sakoat Contributor/Shutterstock.com, (tl2) James R. Martin/Shutterstock.com, (tc1) Ungvar/Shutterstock.com, (tc2) DUO Studio/Shutterstock.com, (tr1) Viki2win/Shutterstock.com, (tr2) JodiJacobson/E+/Getty Images; **109** Alistair Berg/DigitalVision/Getty Images; **111** Mixetto/E+/Getty Images; **112** (tl) Kali9/E+/Getty Images, (tc) Roberto Westbrook/Tetra images/Getty Images, (tr) Cavan Images/Getty Images; **113** Neil Podoll/Shutterstock.com; **114** (tl) Daniel Milchev/The Image Bank/Getty Images, (tr) Hill Street Studios/DigitalVision/Getty Images, (bl) Mo_Ses Premium/Shutterstock.com, (bc) Osetrik/Shutterstock.com, (br) Powerofforever/iStockGetty Images; **115** (t) CapturePB/Shutterstock.com, (b) Powerofforever/iStock/Getty Images; **116** Elpaqu/Shutterstock.com; **118–119** (spread) Edwin Remsberg/Alamy Stock Photo; **120** Morsa Images/DigitalVision/Getty Images; **121** Allard Schager/Moment/Getty Images; **135** (tr1) M-Production/Shutterstock.com, (tr2) Prapass Pulsub/Moment/Getty Images, (cr1) Gorodenkoff/Shutterstock.com, (cr2) Steve Bly/Alamy Stock Photo; **137** Boston Globe/Getty Images; **139** (tl) 7713 Photography/Shutterstock.com, (tc) Spiroview Inc/Shutterstock.com, (tr) Stockbyte/Getty Images, (cl) Patrick Donovan/Moment/Getty Images, (c) Sshepard/E+/Getty Images, (cr) Baona/E+/Getty Images; **141** Davel5957/E+/Getty Images; **143** Design Pics Inc/Alamy Stock Photo; **144–145** (spread) Brian van der Brug/Los Angeles Times/Getty Images; **146** PeopleImages/iStock/Getty Images; **147** MStudioImages/E+/Getty Images; **148** Hans Neleman/Stone/Getty Images; **149** (cl1) Jelena Stanojkovic/iStock/Getty Images, (cl2) Thianchai sitthikongsak/Moment/Getty Images, (c1) Ljubaphoto/E+/Getty Images, (c2) Klebercordeiro/iStock/Getty Images, (cr1) Svetikd/E+/Getty Images, (cr2) DimaBerlin/Shutterstock.com; **151** (cl) Moyo Studio/E+/Getty Images, (c) MixMedia/E+/Getty Images, (cr) Kate Kultsevych/Shutterstock.com; **155** Wsfurlan/E+/Getty Images; **157** Florentina Georgescu Photography/Moment/Getty Images; **158** Jenner Images/Moment/Getty Images; **159** (bl1) Gorillaimages/Shutterstock.com, (bl2) Bambu Productions/DigitalVision/Getty Images, (bc1) Kali9/E+/Getty Images, (bc2) MGP/DigitalVision/Getty Images; **163** Terry Vine/DigitalVision/Getty Images; **164** (t) Xavier Lorenzo/Moment/Getty Images, (cl) Fizkes/Shutterstock.com, (c) Athima Tongloom/Moment/Getty Images, (cr) Svetikd/E+/Getty Images, (bl) Ljubaphoto/E+/Getty Images, (bc) Champion studio/Shutterstock.com, (br) Ponchai Soda/EyeEm/Getty Images; **169** Taylor Hill/Getty Images Entertainment/Getty Images; **170–171** (spread) Meinzahn/iStock Editorial/Getty Images, **172** (tl) DGLimages/iStock/Getty Images, (tc) Jetta Productions Inc/DigitalVision/Getty Images, (tr) FG Trade/E+/Getty Images, (bl) Pormezz/Shutterstock.com, (bc) Halfpoint Images/Moment/Getty Images, (br) Ariel Skelley/DigitalVision/Getty Images; **173** (tl) Klaus Vedfelt/DigitalVision/Getty Images, (tc) Comeback Images/Shutterstock.com, (tr) LifestyleVisuals/E+/Getty Images, (cl) Alvarez/E+/Getty Images, (c) Morsa Images/DigitalVision/Getty Images, (cr) Sean Locke Photography/Shutterstock.com; **177** (tl) FG Trade/iStock/Getty Images, (tc) Yellow Dog Productions Inc./The Image Bank/Getty Images, (tr) Ems-Forster-Productions/DigitalVision/Getty Images; **178** Ferrantraite/E+/Getty Images; **183** Sturti/E+/Getty Images; **189** Bill Oxford/E+/Getty Images; **190** (tl) Gorodenkoff/iStock/Getty Images, (tc) Alvarez/E+/Getty Images, (tr) Ariel Skelley/DigitalVision/Getty Images; **195** Hinterhaus Productions/DigitalVision/Getty Images; **196–197** (spread) © Jared Soares; **198** Dotshock/Shutterstock.com; **201** (tl1) AsiaVision/E+/Getty Images, (tl2) Jeremy Frechette/The Image Bank/Getty Images, (tr) Fizkes/Shutterstock.com, (cl1) Klaus Vedfelt/DigitalVision/Getty Images, (cl2) Kali9/E+/Getty Images, (cr1) Wavebreakmedia/Shutterstock.com, (cr2) Wakila/E+/Getty Images; **205** (tl) Burak Karademir/Moment/Getty Images, (tc) Layland Masuda/Moment/Getty Images, (tr) Guenterguni/E+/Getty Images, (cl) Andresr/E+/Getty Images, (c) Andresr/E+/Getty Images, (cr) Rachel Kolokoff Hopper/Alamy Stock Photo; **206** (tl) MoMo Productions/DigitalVision/Getty Images, (tr) Tetra Images, LLC/Alamy Stock Photo, (c) SDI Productions/E+/Getty Images; **207** (c1) Alejandra de la Fuente/Moment/Getty Images, (c2) Pixelheadphoto Digitalskillet/Shutterstock.com, (bc) XiXinXing/Getty Images; **215** © Cody York Photography; **218** (tl) Amos Morgan/Photodisc/Getty Images, (bl) Morsa Images/DigitalVision/Getty Images; **221** Dina Litovsky/Redux; **222** Kreus/Adobe Stock Photos; **240** © NG Maps/National Geographic Image Collection.

Stand Out Skills Index

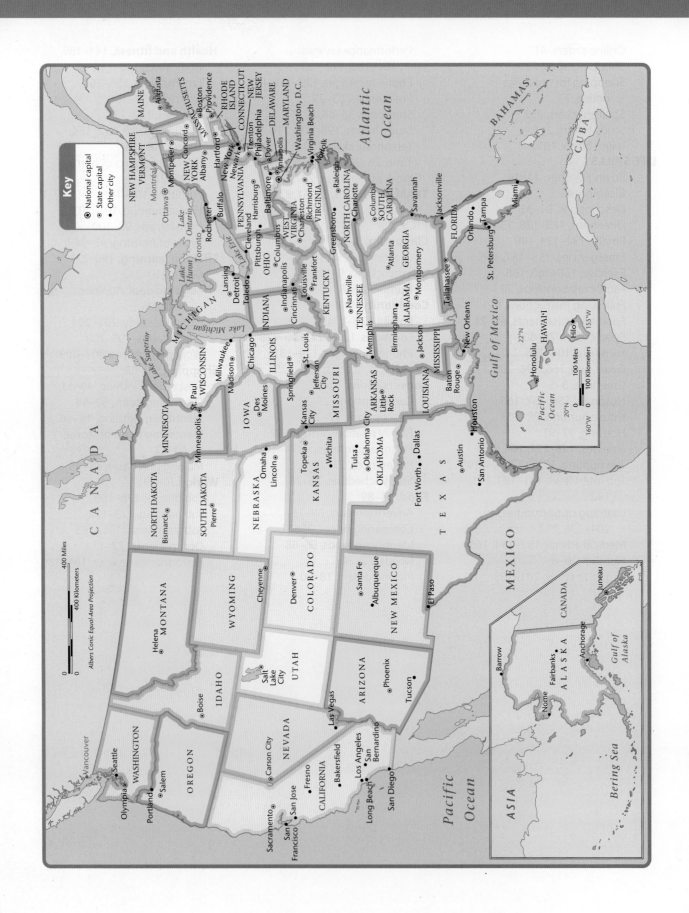

Life Online Video Scripts

LIFE ONLINE VIDEO 1: Searching for Answers

What is the capital of Morocco? What time does Gina's Restaurant open? Where can you shop for a new sofa? Is it raining in Dallas? You have questions every day. And where do you find answers? The internet, of course! Use a search engine to find information online. On your smartphone or a computer, a search engine looks for answers.

Some search engines use information about you. Maybe the search engine knows the city you live in, so it shows you stores or restaurants in your city. Maybe it knows that you speak Spanish, so it shows you websites in Spanish. Maybe you bought brown sandals before, so it shows you ads for brown sandals.

Sometimes, this is helpful, but sometimes you don't want the search engine to track you. You can change the search engine's settings to keep more of your information private. You can also use a different search engine that does not save your information.

Here are some tips to help you find what you are looking for online:

1. Be specific. Don't just search "clothes"—that will show you a billion web pages! Do you want sneakers? A baseball cap? Some shorts? To find what you want, give more information. Men's shorts or women's shorts? What color? This way, you'll find what you want fast.

2. Use keywords. Maybe you are shopping for a green sweater for your mother. Don't write "I would like a green sweater for my mother." Instead, write "green sweater." Or "women's green sweater."

3. Use quotation marks when you are looking for two or more words in a specific order, like the name of a book or song, or words from someone famous. For example, if you're looking for a children's book called "The Little White Dog," use quotation marks around the words. This way, you can find the book you are looking for and not just pictures of small white dogs!

4. Read the suggestions from the search engine. When you type "refrigerator," what does the search engine say? Maybe it suggests "refrigerator sale" or "refrigerator repair" or "refrigerator pickles." The suggestions can give you new ideas.

5. Watch out for ads. Sometimes the first results are advertisements for things you can buy. If you see the word *sponsored*, that means a company pays the search engine to show you their website. Look below the sponsored results to see results that are not ads.

6. Not finding your answer? Try a different search engine! Different search engines find different results. Maybe another one will be better.

Happy searching!

Time to Get Organized

Oh, hi! I'm just taking a selfie to show off my new haircut. What do you think? And now I'll save that photo to . . . Selfies.

Do you take a lot of photos? I sure do. I probably have ten thousand of them! And I love to send them to friends and show them to people. But with so many photos on my phone, it's really important to stay organized. Otherwise, I can't find what I'm looking for!

Here's how I keep my photos organized:

First, I look at all of the photos I take and I choose categories. I have a very cute cat, so Pets is an important category for me. And I take lots of photos of my friends, so Friends is another one. You see how it goes.

Then I create a folder for each category: Pets, Friends, Food, Travel, Selfies. And each time I take a photo, I put it in the right folder. That way, when I'm at a party and I want to share a photo of my cat, Fluffernutter, it's easy to find all of the photos of her!

Of course, some days I take so many photos that I don't have time to sort every single one right away. So, I sit down one evening each week, and I sort through all of my new photos. I ask myself: *Should I keep it or throw it away? If I keep it, what folder does it go in? Do I need to add a new folder?* Then I delete everything I don't need, and I put all the new photos in their folders.

The other thing I do once a month is back up my photos. I save them to an online account with a strong password. That way, I know that if I lose my phone, I won't lose all of my information.

But you know, this works for more than just photos. You can do the same thing with emails. First, look at the types of emails you get and choose categories. Then make folders for each category. Then make a schedule—maybe every day, maybe every week—and sort through your emails. Throw away the ones you don't need, and put the ones you want to keep in the right folders. Use a system to remember which emails you need to respond to. Maybe you use folders, or maybe you use different colored labels. Either way, it's important to have a schedule to sort and respond to those emails regularly.

You can do the same thing with documents and files from school or work. Think of a system that works for you. There are lots of ways to organize your files, but the important thing is to create a system and use it! That way you'll save space on your phone or computer, you won't lose important information, and you'll save time . . . you know, so you can take more selfies.

Life Skills Video Scripts

UNIT 1 Where Are You From?

Hector: I'll get it!

Naomi: I hope you're not busy.

Hector: Not at all. I was framing pictures. Let me introduce you to my family. This is the Sanchez family. That's my dad's side of the family.

Naomi: Which one is your dad?

Hector: Here he is. Dad, meet my friend Naomi. Naomi, meet my dad.

Naomi: Your father is very young.

Hector: I'm sure he would love you for saying that. Actually, this photo was taken a long time ago. My dad's 45 years old.

Naomi: Where is your father from?

Hector: He's from Sinaloa. It's in Mexico.

Naomi: When did your father come to the U.S.?

Hector: When he was about 20. First he moved to San Diego, then he moved to L.A. He met my mom, and the rest is history.

Naomi: What is your mother's maiden name?

Hector: Yilmaz.

Naomi: That sounds like a Middle Eastern name.

Hector: You're right. It's Turkish. She was born in Istanbul. She moved to New York, and then to L.A.

Naomi: How interesting. Is this your mom?

Hector: How did you guess?

Naomi: You look just like her.

Hector: You think so? I think I look like my father. I have his eyes.

Naomi: Yes, but you have your mother's smile.

Mrs. Sanchez: Oh, how sweet.

Hector: Mom, this is my friend Naomi.

Mrs. Sanchez: How nice to meet you, Naomi.

Naomi: Nice to meet you too, Mrs. Sanchez. Hector was showing me some of the family photos.

Mrs. Sanchez: Oh, was he? Well, this is my sister. She's married and she has two kids.

Naomi: So, these are your cousins?

Hector: Yes, Aidan and Marta.

Mrs. Sanchez: Aidan is 10 and Marta is 8. Aren't they cute? Oh, and this is my brother, and these are my parents. They all live in New York. Oh, and over here we have my parents at their . . .

Hector: Ma, take it easy! Naomi doesn't need to know our whole family history.

Mrs. Sanchez: I was only saying . . . Oh, honey. Come meet Hector's friend. Her name is Naomi.

Mr. Sanchez: Hello, Naomi. Nice to meet you.

Naomi: Nice to meet you too, Mr. Sanchez.

Mrs. Sanchez: Naomi is from . . . Where are you from, dear?

Naomi: I'm from Pasadena. I was born in Washington. My father's from Japan, and my mother's from L.A.

Mrs. Sanchez: Do you have any brothers or sisters?

Naomi: No, I'm an only child, like Hector.

Mrs. Sanchez: Honey, where are the rest of the pictures?

Mr. Sanchez: There are a lot more in the photo album. I think it's right here. Here it is. Ahh. Here's a photo of Hector when he was two.

Mrs. Sanchez: Wasn't he cute? Here's another picture of Hector. He's 10 years old in that picture. Oh, look at him!

Hector: Here we go!

UNIT 2 Can I Help You?

Mr. Patel: Good morning, Mateo.

Mateo: Good morning.

Mr. Patel: Did you put that sign in the window?

Mateo: The one that says "Help Wanted"? Yes, I did. I put it in the window yesterday.

Mr. Patel: Good. Now I have something else for you. Here is a dress, a blouse, and a sweater. Can you put them away for me, please?

Mateo: Yeah. OK, sure.

Mr. Patel: Thank you. I'll be in my office.

Hector: Hey, Mateo!

Mateo: Hey Hector. What are you doing here?

Hector: I saw the sign in the window. It says "Help Wanted." Are you looking for sales clerks?

Mateo: Yeah, we are. But do you think you have what it takes to be a sales clerk?

Hector: Well you never know unless you try, right?

Customer: Excuse me.

Mateo: Yes? Can I help you?

Customer: I'm looking for a sweater. Do you have any blue sweaters?

Mateo: Well, is the sweater for you or for someone else?

Customer: It's for me.

Hector: Well, what about this sweater right here? I think this would look great on you.

Customer: I like it. It might be a bit big. What size is it?

Mateo: That is a large. Here is a small.

Customer: Yes, I think this is the right size. How much is it?

Mateo: It's $48.

Customer: Oh, no. I only have $40.

Hector: What about this green sweater? It's only $34.

Customer: I love it! And I really love the price. I'll take it.

Mateo: Are you sure? Because this red sweater is even less expensive. It's only $27.

Customer: It's perfect. And I'll still have extra money. Thank you so much.

Hector: Well, is there anything else we can help you with?

Customer: Well, my little brother wants a pair of blue jeans. Can you show me the way to the boy's section?

Hector: I would be happy to show you the way. Please follow me.

Mr. Patel: Who was that?

Mateo: That is my friend, Hector. He's a bit of a show-off.

Mr. Patel: He might make a good sales clerk. Why don't you ask him to come in for an interview?

UNIT 3 Nobody Has Pizza for Breakfast

Mrs. Sanchez: What was that?

Mr. Sanchez: Was that the refrigerator?

Hector: Probably.

Mrs. Sanchez: Hector! That was your stomach!

Hector: Sorry, Ma. I didn't eat breakfast.

Mrs. Sanchez: Why not? Breakfast is the most important meal of the day, you know.

Hector: It's OK. I can wait until lunch.

Mr. Sanchez: Hector, please eat something.

Hector: Like what?

Mr. Sanchez: We have fruit. Why don't you have an apple?

Mrs. Sanchez: Or I can make you some bacon and eggs with toast. Would you like that?

Hector: It's OK, Ma. Don't bother. There's some cold pizza. That's good enough.

Mrs. Sanchez: Pizza for breakfast? That is not a good way to start the day.

Mr. Sanchez: I agree with your mother. Nobody ever has pizza for breakfast.

Hector: Well, why not? People have toast for breakfast, and toast is bread, right? Well, so is pizza, basically. Now all I need is some potato chips.

Mr. Sanchez: Really, now. This is too much.

Hector: OK, OK.

Mrs. Sanchez: You should have real food for breakfast: eggs, milk, fruit. Please, let me make something for you.

Hector: How about some cake? Cake has eggs and milk and fruit!

Mrs. Sanchez: It also has sugar in it. Lots and lots of sugar. Isn't there anything else in the refrigerator besides pizza and cake?

Hector: Let's see. Well, there's vegetables, cheese, and eggs.

Mr. Sanchez: Why don't you make an omelet?

Mrs. Sanchez: That's a wonderful idea. Give me a hand, will you, dear? It will only take about 15 minutes.

Hector: What should I do?

Mrs. Sanchez: First, you take a few eggs and you beat them in a bowl. Then you pour some milk into the bowl. Then you can add some grated cheese if you like . . .

Mrs. Sanchez: Now isn't this better than having pizza and cake for breakfast?

Hector: It sure is. Thanks, Ma.

Mr. Sanchez: Can you pass the pepper?

Hector: Sure, here you go, Dad. Can you pass me that sugar?

Mr. Sanchez: Sugar? What do you want sugar for?

Hector: I like to put sugar on my omelet.

Mr. Sanchez: What?

Hector: I was only kidding!

UNIT 4 Are Utilities Included?

Apartment Manager: Hello?

Naomi: Uh, hello. I'm calling about the apartments for rent.

Apartment Manager: Hello. Yes, we have several apartments available. What kind of apartment are you looking for?

Naomi: I'm looking for a one-bedroom apartment with a pool and near a bus stop. Do you have any one-bedroom apartments?

Apartment Manager: Uh, no, but we do have a studio apartment available. It's small, but it does have a kitchen area with a microwave, a refrigerator, and a very nice view of the city.

Naomi: Oh. Well, does it have a swimming pool?

Apartment Manager: No. It doesn't have a swimming pool, but it does have a parking area for your car.

Naomi: Oh. Well, I don't have a car. I'm looking for something near a bus stop. Is there a bus stop near the apartment building?

Apartment Manager: Uh, the building is about six blocks from a bus stop, but the highway is very near.

Naomi: The highway is very near?

Apartment Manager: It goes right by the back of the building! It's very useful.

Naomi: But I don't have a car.

Apartment Manager: Do you have any pets?

Naomi: No.

Apartment Manager: Good, because we don't accept pets. Do you smoke?

Naomi: No.

Apartment Manager: Good. This is a non-smoking apartment building.

Naomi: That's good. What about electricity and water? Are the utilities included in the rent?

Apartment Manager: Yes, some utilities are included. Water and garbage are included, but you have to pay for the electricity. Do you want to make an appointment to come look at the apartment? It has a very nice view. I'm sure you'll like it.

Naomi: Well, how much is the rent?

Apartment Manager: It's only $900 a month—plus electricity. But the parking is free!

Naomi: Um, I don't have a car. Well, let's see: $900 a month, plus electricity . . .

Apartment Manager: Don't forget, it's close to the highway. It has a nice view!

Naomi: Okay . . . near the highway, has a nice view. But it's six blocks to the nearest bus stop, and it doesn't have a swimming pool. Wait . . . Oh, I'm sorry. Can I think about it? Thank you, bye! Wait!

Apartment Manager: Good-bye?

UNIT 5 How Do I Get There?

Naomi: Wow. Mateo is really late. Where is he?

Hector: You know Mateo. He's probably lost again. He has a terrible sense of direction. That's probably him now. Hello?

Mateo: Yo, Hector. This is Mateo.

Hector: I know who you are. The question is where you are.

Mateo: I'm not sure. I'm in front of the bookstore. The bookstore is next to a coffee shop.

Naomi: Ask him what street he's on.

Hector: What street are you on? Do you see any street signs?

Mateo: Yeah, I'm on the corner of Atlantic and Broadway.

Hector: He's on the corner of Atlantic and Broadway.

Naomi: Tell him to walk straight for two blocks.

Hector: Walk straight for two blocks.

Mateo: On Atlantic or Broadway?

Hector: On Atlantic or Broadway?

Naomi: On Atlantic. Go towards City Hall.

Hector: Walk down Atlantic towards City Hall.

Mateo: OK. Then what?

Hector: Then what? Here, you talk to him.

Naomi: Did you hear that? Walk down Atlantic two blocks.

Mateo: Then what?

Naomi: Then turn right and walk one block. The diner is on the left.

Mateo: Turn right, walk down one block, the diner's on your left, right?

Naomi: Right, I mean correct.

Mateo: OK, see you in a few minutes.

Hector: See, I told you Mateo isn't good with directions.

Naomi: I wouldn't be surprised if he calls us again.

Hector: Hello.

Mateo: Hector, I'm here at the diner, but I still can't find you guys. Where are you?

Hector: It's complicated. I'll try to explain this to you. Take two steps back.

Mateo: Two steps back? Well, OK then.

Hector: Now, turn around.

Mateo: Very funny!

Naomi: Come sit down and have some coffee. I think you need it!

UNIT 6 You'd Better Call the Doctor

Mrs. Sanchez: Victor? Are you feeling alright?

Mr. Sanchez: Not really. My head hurts . . . I feel dizzy . . . I'm too warm.

Mrs. Sanchez: Here, sit down on the couch. You don't look well. And you have a fever. You are not going to work. You need to see the doctor.

Mr. Sanchez: No, no, I'm fine. I need to go to work . . .

Mrs. Sanchez: I don't think so. Sit!

Mr. Sanchez: Really, I'm okay.

Hector: Morning, Mom. Morning, Dad. What's the matter with Dad?

Mrs. Sanchez: He's sick. Can you get the thermometer?

Mr. Sanchez: And some water? With ice?

Mrs. Sanchez: Hello? Dr. Badaoui? This is Miriam Sanchez. My husband, Victor Sanchez, seems to be very sick.

Dr. Badaoui: What are his symptoms?

Mrs. Sanchez: He has a headache. He's dizzy. And he feels warm.

Dr. Badaoui: Any aches and pains?

Mrs. Sanchez: Do you have any aches and pains?

Mr. Sanchez: My knees ache . . .

Hector: His back aches. His shoulders ache too. His elbow aches?

Mrs. Sanchez: Yes, he has aches and pains.

Dr. Badaoui: Does he have a fever?

Mrs. Sanchez: Does he have a fever?

Hector: Yes, he does have a fever. 101.2.

Mrs. Sanchez: He does have a fever. 101.2. And now he has a cough.

Dr. Badaoui: He needs to rest. Give him lots of water, and keep him warm. Give him lots of vitamin C. And give him some ibuprofen or acetaminophen for the fever and aches.

Mrs. Sanchez: Vitamin C, ibuprofen, and acetaminophen. Okay, Dr. Badaoui. Thank you very much.

Dr. Badaoui: No problem.

Mr. Sanchez: I need to get to work.

Mrs. Sanchez: Your only job today is to rest and get well. Nurse?

Hector: Yes, doctor.

Mrs. Sanchez: Get ready. Acetaminophen?

Hector: Check.

Mrs. Sanchez: Ibuprofen?

Hector: Check.

Mrs. Sanchez: Don't worry, Mr. Sanchez. You're in good hands.

UNIT 7 How Did You Hear About This Job?

Hector: Excuse me . . . I have an appointment for 3 o'clock.

Mr. Patel: Oh, yes. Mr. Sanchez is it?

Hector: Yes, Hector Sanchez. But you can just call me Hector.

Mr. Patel: Nice to meet you, Hector. You can call me Mr. Patel. I'm the store owner and manager. I supervise all the employees and make sure everything is going smoothly. What brings you here?

Hector: Well, I'd like to apply for the sales position.

Mr. Patel: Please have a seat. Tell me, how did you find out about this job?

Hector: I saw your ad, and I have a friend who works here.

Mr. Patel: Who is that?

Hector: Mateo Trujillo.

Mr. Patel: Oh yes, Mateo . . .

Hector: He said that you are looking for a part-time sales clerk, which is perfect for me, because I'm a student.

Mr. Patel: Let's take it one step at a time . . . Did you bring an application?

Hector: Yes. Here it is. I know I don't have very much experience.

Mr. Patel: Never mind that. Tell me about your work history. What was your last job?

Hector: I was an . . . assistant.

Mr. Patel: And what was it that you did as an "assistant"?

Hector: I answered the phones and took messages.

Mr. Patel: I see. And what do you do now?

Hector: I'm a student at Glendale Community College. I'm majoring in business and taking classes in accounting, and some day I would like to be a store manager like yourself, Mr. Patel.

Mr. Patel: Can you work the cash register?

Hector: Not exactly, but I learn very quickly.

Mr. Patel: Well, Hector, let's be honest. You really don't have much work experience. But I like your attitude, and I'd like to give you a chance. What hours can you work?

Hector: I can work the afternoons and the evenings and on the weekends. But I can't work in the mornings because I have class.

Mr. Patel: That sounds fine. Now we have a few rules around here, Hector. Rule number one: Never be late. Rule number two: Have the right attitude. Rule number three: Always be on time.

Hector: Wait a second. Isn't rule number three the same as rule number one?

Mr. Patel: I was only testing you, Hector. I can tell you'll make a very good employee. Welcome to the staff.

UNIT 8 **I Have Lots of Different Interests**

Mrs. Smith: Hello, Hector. How nice to see you. What can I do for you today?

Hector: Well, we're starting a new semester in a few weeks.

Mrs. Smith: I know!

Hector: And we need to choose our classes.

Mrs. Smith: The sooner the better. Which classes are you going to take?

Hector: I'm not sure yet. That's why I came to see you. Do you have any suggestions?

Mrs. Smith: That depends. Have a seat. What's your goal? What do you want to study?

Hector: That's hard. I'm interested in lots of things. First, I wanted to be an actor. Then I wanted to be a teacher. Now I'm not sure. I'm taking lots of different classes.

Mrs. Smith: Tell me, which classes did you take last semester?

Hector: I took a class in public speaking. That was fun.

Mrs. Smith: Oh, really? You like to speak in public?

Hector: Let's just say I'm not shy. I gave a speech at least twice a week. And I took a class in world events too.

Mrs. Smith: World events. Very interesting. And what classes are you taking now?

Hector: This semester? I'm taking English, Social Studies, and Business.

Mrs. Smith: And which class do you like the most?

Hector: English. I like to read, and I really like to write reports. Last month I wrote an investigative report.

Mrs. Smith: What was it about?

Hector: Local politics, the upcoming election.

Mrs. Smith: I see. What else do you like to do?

Hector: After class, I usually go to the gym. Sometimes I play soccer. When I get home, I like to watch TV or listen to the radio.

Mrs. Smith: What kinds of programs do you like?

Hector: Oh, definitely the news. I watch the local news report every night. After dinner I watch another news program, and I listen to the BBC on the radio at least three times a week.

Mrs. Smith: I think I see a pattern. You like taking English, and you like watching the news. Last semester you took a class in public speaking. You liked that too. You seem to be interested in the media and communications. Did you ever think about studying journalism?

Hector: Journalism? I never thought about it. But I should think about it. I like to watch the news. I like to listen to the radio. Plus I like English. It makes perfect sense. "This is Hector Sanchez, reporting from Los Angeles." Yeah, I can imagine that.

Mrs. Smith: Mr. Hopkins is going to teach a class in journalism next semester. Why don't you take it?

Hector: I think I will take Mr. Hopkins's class. I think I'm going to take another English class too.

Mrs. Smith: That's an excellent idea. Sign up for the journalism class soon, though. I think it's going to fill up.

Hector: OK, I'll sign up today. Thanks for talking to me, Mrs. Smith. I really appreciate it.

Mrs. Smith: It was my pleasure, Hector. I'm glad I could help you. Let me know if you have any other questions.

Hector: I will. See you soon.

Mrs. Smith: Take care. See you in class.

Stand Out Audio Script

PRE-UNIT

LESSON 1

B pg 3

Teacher: Hi! Welcome to our class!
Student: Hello. Thank you!
Teacher: How are you?
Student: Fine! How are you?

E pg 4

Jian: Good morning! I'm Jian. What's your name?
Gabriela: Hello. My name is Gabriela.
Jian: Nice to meet you, Gabriela. How are you today?
Gabriela: I'm fine, thanks! How are you?
Jian: I'm doing well. Welcome to our class!

LESSON 1, PRONUNCIATION 1 pg 4

Contractions

A contraction is a short way of saying a group of words.
Instead of saying *I am*, we often say *I'm*.
/m/ I'm

F pg 4

Gabriela: Hi! I'm Gabriela. G-A-B-R-I-E-L-A.
Jian: Hello. I'm Jian. J-I-A-N.

G pg 4

A B C D E F G H I J K L M N O P Q R S T U V W X Y Z

H pg 5

1. Hi! I'm Ellen. E-L-L-E-N
2. Hello! My name is Cyrus. C-Y-R-U-S
3. How are you? I'm Ana. A-N-A
4. Hi! My name is Duong. D-U-O-N-G

LESSON 1, PRONUNCIATION 2 pg 5

Yes / No Questions

We use a rising intonation with *yes / no* questions. They go up at the end.
Can you spell that?
Can you speak slower, please?
Can you repeat that?

LESSON 2

B pg 6

Welcome to Ms. Smith's class. There are 12 students in the class. The students study for six hours every week. The school address is 19 Lincoln Street, Chicago, Illinois 60127.

D pg 7

0 zero / oh
1 one
2 two
3 three
4 four
5 five
6 six
7 seven
8 eight
9 nine
10 ten
11 eleven
12 twelve
13 thirteen
14 fourteen
15 fifteen
16 sixteen
17 seventeen
18 eighteen
19 nineteen
20 twenty

E pg 7

a. five
b. eight
c.
Student A: How many students are in your class?
Student B: I think there are nine.
d.
Student A: My class is bigger.
Student B: Really? How many?
Student A: We have 19 students.
e.
Student B: How long is your class?
Student A: It's two hours a day.

F pg 7

My name is Gabriela. My address is 14 Main Street. The zip code is 06119. My phone number is 401-555-7248. There are nine students in my class.

LESSON 3

B pg 9

1. I am very busy and have many things to do. I write everything I need to do in a notebook. It helps me stay organized.

2. I want to learn English quickly. I speak to my friends and my family in English for practice every day.

3. I like to listen to music. When I listen to music in English, I learn a lot.

4. I enjoy reading. I often read in my free time.

5. Here is the test paper. Write your answers in pencil, please.

6. I will find the information. I can look it up online.

F pg 10

Please stand up.

Please sit down.

Please read page one in your book.

Please listen carefully.

Please take out a sheet of paper.

Please write your name on the sheet of paper.

G pg 11

Teacher: Please open your books to page 15.
Student: What page?
Teacher: Page 15. That's one, five.
Student: Thank you.

UNIT 1

LESSON 1

B pg 14

My name is Roberto Garcia. I'm a new student in this school. I'm from Guatemala City, Guatemala. I'm 43 years old and I'm married. I'm very happy in my new class.

G pg 15

1. Yan Wu is happy to be in the United States. She wants to learn English. She learned some English in her hometown of Shanghai, China. China is spelled: C-H-I-N-A. She wants to help other people in her family learn English. She is divorced, and she is 60 years old.

2. Maha Khan is 28. She wants to learn English quickly. She watches TV and reads the news in English every day. She is single and is from Riyadh, Saudi Arabia. Saudi Arabia is two words. It is spelled: S-A-U-D-I space A-R-A-B-I-A.

3. Andre Paul is a student, and he is a salesperson. He works hard during the day and goes to school at night. He is 33 years old. He is married with three

kids. Some of Andre's family live in his home country of Haiti. He talks to them on the phone once a week. Haiti is spelled: H-A-I-T-I.

LESSON 2, PRONUNCIATION pg 18

Pronunciation of /v/

To make the /v/ sound, touch your teeth to your bottom lip and push air out.

/v/ /v/ /v/ have

In English, the /v/ sound is different from the /b/ sound.

He is very tall.

Berries are my favorite fruit.

/v/ very, /b/ berry

D pg 18

1.

Antonio: Excuse me. I am looking for my son, Roberto Garcia.
Mary: I don't think I know him. What does he look like?
Antonio: He has brown hair and brown eyes.
Mary: And his height . . . how tall is he?
Antonio: He is five foot eleven. And he is 43 years old.
Mary: Oh, I think he's in Room 114.
Antonio: Thanks!

2.

Ana: Do you see my friend Fabiana over there?
Brad: No, I don't see her.
Ana: She has black hair and brown eyes. She's about five-one.
Brad: Oh, I see her now. Is she around 30 years old?
Ana: She is actually 32.

3.

Mary: Excuse me. I am looking for Maha Khan. She is tall, maybe five-eight. She has brown hair and brown eyes. She is 28 years old. Have you seen her?
Brad: No, sorry. I haven't seen her.

4.

Alan: My name is Alan.
Mary: Please describe yourself.
Alan: I am five foot nine. I have red hair and green eyes. I am 55 years old.

E pg 18

A: What does Roberto look like?
B: He has brown hair and brown eyes.
A: How tall is he?
B: He is five foot eleven.
A: Thank you.

LESSON 3

B pg 20

Roberto: Jie, this is my mother, my father, and my sister.
Rebecca: Nice to meet you, Jie. Where are you from?
Jie: Nice to meet you too! I'm from China.
Rebecca: Do your parents live here in the United States?
Jie: No. Right now they live in China.

E pg 21

My name is Roberto Garcia. I am very happily married. My wife's name is Silvia. This is a picture of my family. The older man and woman in the picture are my parents. My mother's name is Rebecca, and my father's name is Antonio. I have one sister, Lidia, and one brother, Julio. The girl and the boy are my children, Carla and Juan.

LESSON 4

A pg 23

Roberto and Silvia are happily married. Roberto likes movies, gaming, and books. Silvia likes parks, restaurants, and music. They both like sports, social media, and TV.

D pg 24

1. Antonio likes social media.
2. Rebecca likes parks.
3. Antonio and Rebecca like movies.
4. We like gaming.
5. The students like books.
6. I like music.
7. My mother likes restaurants.
8. My brother likes sports.

LESSON 5

B pg 26

Online calendars can help you stay organized and remember the things you need to do. You can use online calendars to see activities in different parts of your life. Tuan has three different calendars: Personal, School, and Work.

F pg 27

Aisha is a good student. She wants to learn English so she can get a better job. She has a regular schedule and follows it every day. She eats breakfast every morning from 6:00 to 6:30. She usually eats cereal, but sometimes she has eggs. Directly after she eats, she does her homework from 6:30 to 7:00. Then she usually reads in English from 7:00 to 7:15. After that, she writes in her journal from 7:15 to 7:45. She practices English in class from 8:30 to 10:30 a.m. Monday through Friday.

LESSON 6

A pg 29

a. photographer: A photographer takes pictures.
b. carpenter: A carpenter makes things out of wood.
c. pharmacist: A pharmacist prepares medications.
d. chef: A chef prepares meals at a restaurant.
e. customer service representative: A customer service representative helps customers.
f. pest control worker: A pest control worker sprays insecticide.

REVIEW

E pg 33

Agus and Sri are married. They have three children. Dewi is 15, Endang is 17, and Haji is 22. Haji is married. His wife's name is Dian. They have a baby named Siti.

READING CHALLENGE pg 37

Does My Dog Look Like Me?

Look at the man and his dog. Do you see anything interesting? The dog has short hair. The man has no hair. The man has a black and gray beard. The dog does too! They both have round faces. They even have the same expression. Some people say that dogs often look like their owners. Maybe people find pets that look like them. But what about personality? Research shows that dogs and their owners can have the same personalities too. A calm, happy owner usually has a calm, happy dog. Do you agree? Do you know any dogs and owners that look the same?

UNIT 2

LESSON 1

E pg 41

Caller: Hello, I'd like to speak to Noor Hassan.
Noor: This is she. How can I help you?
Caller: I am with Harrington Consumer Reports. We are doing a survey to see where people shop. Do you have a few minutes?
Noor: Sure.
Caller: Thank you. My first question is, do you shop for groceries online, at your local market, or at a big-box store?
Noor: Well, that is hard to say. If I only have food to buy, I usually go to the market. My market has very fresh produce.
Caller: Very good. What about shoes? Do you go to a big-box store for those?
Noor: No, they don't have many choices. I shop at a shoe store so I can try the shoes on.

Caller: Have you bought a laptop in the past few years?
Noor: I have. I buy all my electronics online. Then I can find exactly what I need.
Caller: And clothing? Do you buy clothing online?
Noor: Most of the time, I shop for clothing at big-box stores. It's so much cheaper.
Caller: And finally, do you get your medicine at a pharmacy?
Noor: I do. I go to a small pharmacy on my street.
Caller: Thanks for all this information. Have a good day.

H pg 42

1. Noor shops for electronics online.
2. They shop for food at a market.
3. We shop for sneakers at a shoe store.
4. He shops for soda at a big-box store.
5. I shop for books online.

LESSON 2

C pg 43

EXAMPLE: How much is it? It's $22.50.
1. That's $34.15.
2. Here's $33.00.
3. That comes to $15.70.
4. The total cost is $77.95.

D pg 43

1.

Customer: Excuse me. How much is the vacuum?
Salesperson: It's $89.99 on sale.
Customer: Thanks, I'll take it.

2.

Customer: Excuse me, can you help me? I'm looking for a washing machine.
Salesperson: This is a good brand.
Customer: Is that right? OK, how much is it?
Salesperson: It's four hundred and fifty dollars.
Customer: Four hundred and fifty dollars? That much?
Salesperson: I'm afraid so.

3.

Customer: I just want these candy bars.
Salesperson: That will be $2.50, please.
Customer: Here you go—two dollars and fifty cents.

4.

Customer: I want to buy a ream of white paper.
Salesperson: The paper is over there. It's $6.50.
Customer: Thank you.

5.

Customer: Every time I buy a cell phone, I get a bad one. Maybe I should buy an expensive one.
Salesperson: How about this one for $999.99?

K pg 45

Here are some online credit card safety tips:

- Look for the lock symbol next to the website address. This means the website is safe for typing your credit card information.
- Never save your credit card information on a phone or computer that isn't yours.
- If you do save your card on your phone or computer, make sure it has a good password.
- Never send your credit card information over email.

LESSON 3

A pg 46

We have many good deals at Dress for Less. Be sure to come in. Socks are $12, ties are $22, and suits are $285. Our dresses are $48, and our skirts are $35! We have great deals on sweaters at $36, and women's hats are $38. Don't miss our great deals!

F pg 48

Nilda shops at Dress for Less. It is a clothing store on Main Street. The prices are good, but she only has $75. She needs clothes for a party. She needs a new blouse, a skirt, and a hat. She has a problem.

LESSON 4

A pg 49

Musa: Nilda, what are you wearing on the first day of classes?
Nilda: I think I'll wear a white top. How about you?
Musa: I'll wear my red T-shirt. And I think I will go casual and wear shorts.
Nilda: Nice. I'm wearing my blue pants with a black belt.
Musa: Sounds great! You won't miss me. I'll be wearing a blue baseball cap and brown sandals.

LESSON 5

D pg 53

Liping: Excuse me. I want a TV.
Salesperson: A *big* TV or a *small* TV?
Liping: I want a *small* TV.
Salesperson: OK, how about this one?
Liping: Yes, that's good. How much is it?
Salesperson: It's $135.
Liping: I'll take it!

LESSON 5, PRONUNCIATION pg 53

Stress

In English, we use stress to show the difference between two choices. When you stress a word, you say it louder and longer than usual.

A: Do you want a *big* TV or a *small* TV?

B: I want a *small* TV.

H pg 54

1.

Liping: Excuse me. I want a TV.

Salesperson: A *big* TV or a *small* TV?

Liping: I want a *small* TV.

Salesperson: OK, how about this one?

Liping: Yes, that's good. How much is it?

Salesperson: It's $135.

Liping: I'll take it!

2.

Emily: We need to move.

Steve: I know. What do you want? Do you want a new house or an old house?

Emily: Well, I'm not sure. They both have benefits. I guess I want an old one.

Steve: OK, we want an old house, right?

Emily: Right.

3.

Nancy: I am here to buy a shirt for my friend Gabriela.

Salesperson: OK, do you know her size?

Nancy: She needs a medium, I think.

Salesperson: All right. Step over here, and we'll see what we can find in a medium.

4.

Ivan: I want a new car.

Natasha: I want a new car too.

Ivan: They're expensive.

Natasha: How can we afford it?

Ivan: I guess we want a new car, but we'll have to wait to buy one.

LESSON 6

I pg 57

- Good salespeople are sociable. *Sociable* means they like to talk and work with customers.
- Good salespeople are compassionate. *Compassionate* means they understand how people feel.
- Good salespeople are supportive. *Supportive* means they like to help others.

REVIEW

A pg 58

The TV is $459.99.

The shoes are $58.98.

The laptop is $899.

The dictionary is $18.95.

The shirt is $34.50.

The sweater is $33.99.

The vacuum is $168.

The shorts are $17.

READING CHALLENGE pg 63

Business Is Good!

Starting your own business is not easy, but millions of immigrants do it and many are successful. One in five business owners in the United States is an immigrant; that is a big number! With these businesses come a lot of jobs: Around eight million people in the U.S. work at immigrant-owned businesses.

Maria Lopez is an immigrant. She came with her kids to the U.S. from Mexico in 1987. Maria owns a nursery in a busy part of Los Angeles, California that she opened more than 35 years ago. She has a lot of plants. Her family calls the nursery "the jungle." Maria's family often helps out at the nursery. Her daughter-in-law, Wendy Lopez, whom you can see in the photo, makes colorful holiday wreaths to sell. Maria's business is very successful. Visiting L.A.? Go to Avalon Nursery and Ceramics. Say hello!

UNIT 3

LESSON 1

A pg 66

I'm Dave Chen. I'm an English teacher in Florida. I like to eat! I eat a big breakfast in the morning at around seven, a small lunch at noon, and a big dinner at about six o'clock.

F pg 67

Hello, my name is Dave. I am a teacher at Alexander Community College. I eat lunch here. They have a cafeteria. I teach all day, so I can eat here for all three meals. For breakfast before class, I eat eggs, cereal, and toast. For lunch after my first class, I eat a hamburger and french fries. Sometimes, I eat a sandwich for lunch instead of a hamburger. For dinner, I either have pasta, roast beef, or fried chicken. Pasta is my favorite.

H pg 68

Student A: What do you like for lunch?

Student B: I like hamburgers.

Student C: He likes hamburgers, and I like sandwiches.

Student D: He likes hamburgers, she likes sandwiches, and I like soup.

LESSON 2

B pg 69

Mario: We need to go shopping. We're out of a few things.

Lucy: I'll open my shopping app and make a list.

Mario: Good idea. Well, I know we need ground beef. We really need carrots and tomatoes too.

Lucy: OK, I'll add those to the list … ground beef, carrots … and tomatoes.

Mario: Let's buy some soda too.

Lucy: OK. Oh, look. Avocados are on sale. Let's buy three.

Mario: That sounds good!

Lucy: Can you think of anything else?

Mario: No, I think that's it.

Lucy: OK. I have ground beef, carrots, tomatoes, soda, and avocados on the list.

LESSON 3

B pg 72

My name is Abdul. I study at North Creek Adult School. It is very expensive to eat out every day, so I bring my lunch to school. My wife and I go to the store every Saturday. We buy bread and meat for sandwiches.

D pg 72

Abdul: It is too expensive to buy food at school every day. I have the same sandwiches every week. Maybe we should buy something different, but I need something healthy.

Laila: OK. What do you have in mind?

Abdul: Well, I thought I might try tuna fish. It is delicious.

Laila: Yes, they say fish is good for you too. What about chicken?

Abdul: Chicken is OK, but I don't have time to prepare it.

Laila: We can buy it in slices. You don't need to prepare it.

Abdul: Great. I also need peanut butter and jelly.

Laila: Yes, we do need both. We are completely out.

LESSON 3, PRONUNCIATION pg 73

Plural -s

The plural -s makes three different sounds.

/z/ jars bags cans

/s/ chips snacks

/ɪz/ packages boxes

J pg 74

1. Abdul needs one jar of jelly.
2. They like soup for dinner.

3. Abdul eats sandwiches at school.

4. Laila makes sandwiches for lunch.

5. They want three packages of cheese.

LESSON 4, PRONUNCIATION pg 76

Stress

Stress the words that give meaning to the sentence.

Where are *carrots cheaper*?

They're *cheaper* at *Food City*.

E pg 76

1. Soda is $2.14 at Food City and $2.99 at Puente Market. Soda is more expensive at Puente Market.

2. Avocados are $1.50 at Food City and $1.25 at Puente Market. Avocados are cheaper at Puente Market.

3. Tomatoes are $1.75 at Food City and $1.50 at Puente Market. Tomatoes are cheaper at Puente Market.

4. Pasta is $2.20 at Food City and $1.98 at Puente Market. Pasta is more expensive at Food City.

G pg 77

I shop at Food City. They have a lot of different fruits and vegetables there. The fruit is cheaper at Puente Market, but there aren't many choices. Food City has good specials too. It is also near my home.

I pg 77

Sonia: Excuse me. Does this store do price matching? If I find a cheaper price at a different store, can you give me the same price here?

Salesperson: Yes, we do. Do you have an ad?

Sonia: Yes. It says right here that at Puente Market, bananas are ninety-two cents a pound.

Here at Food City, they are ninety-eight cents.

Salesperson: That looks right. We can give you that price.

Sonia: Here are more examples. Puente Market is always cheaper.

Salesperson: Let's see. You're right. Oranges at Puente Market are $2.20 a pound and at Food City, they cost $2.39 a pound. Pears at Puente Market are $1.29 a pound. Here at Food City, they are $1.59.

Sonia: Look at this! Apples are $1.49 at Food City and only $1.31 at Puente Market.

Salesperson: Wow. It looks like we need to change a lot of prices!

LESSON 5

B pg 78

Sebastian: Hi! I want a turkey sandwich, please.

Server: Do you want a side order?

Sebastian: Yes, a green salad.

Server: Great! Do you want a drink?

Sebastian: A bottle of water, thanks.

Server: Great, that's a turkey sandwich for $4.00, a green salad for $3.25, and a bottle of water for $3.00. Is that right?

Sebastian: Perfect.

Server: That will be $10.89 with tax.

Sebastian: Here you go!

E pg 79

1.

Manny: I want a cheeseburger, a green salad, and an orange juice please.

Server: No orange juice today. Would you like milk or soda?

Manny: A soda, please.

Server: OK, two minutes. Next.

2.

Tran: I'll have a grilled cheese sandwich, please.

Server: OK. Anything else?

Tran: And a fruit cup, too.

Server: Of course. What about a drink?

Tran: No, thanks.

Server: OK. That's a grilled cheese sandwich and fruit cup, right?

Tran: That's right. Thanks.

3.

Delia: I want some milk, please, and a hotdog.

Server: Do you want mustard?

Delia: No, thanks. Just french fries.

Server: OK. A hot dog, no mustard, french fries, and a milk coming up.

LESSON 6

E pg 82

There are many different restaurant jobs. For these jobs, you don't always need to know a lot of English and there are opportunities to move up. For example, people often start working in restaurants as bussers. A busser cleans tables, gives customers water, and sets the tables. Many bussers work hard and become servers or cooks. Over time, servers and hosts can become supervisors and managers. Many cooks work hard to become chefs. In restaurants, there are a lot of opportunities to learn and grow.

F pg 82

A tip is money a customer pays for good service. You can give a tip in cash or with a credit card. In the U.S., servers' salaries are sometimes low because they also get tips. A tip is usually 20–25% of the check.

To calculate a 20% tip, multiply the check amount by .20. For example: $25.00 x .20 = $5.00 (20% of 25). Then add the tip to the check amount to get the total: $25.00 + $5.00 = $30.00.

READING CHALLENGE pg 89

How to Stop Food Waste at Home

Food waste is food that is wasted, or not used. Restaurants, stores, and families throw away food every day. At the same time, some people go hungry. What can we do?

1. Only buy what you need. Check your refrigerator and cabinets before you shop.
2. Plan your meals every week.
3. Choose ugly fruits and vegetables.
4. Donate extra food that you have at home.
5. Learn how to store food safely.
6. Learn about expiration dates.
7. Give extra food to pets.
8. Use old food in your garden.

UNIT 4

LESSON 1

B pg 92

Irving, Texas, is a thriving community near Dallas. There is a lot to do and friendly people to meet. Irving has many different housing options. There are approximately thirty-six thousand houses in the city, and even more apartments and condos—around fifty-two thousand. There are also about three thousand five hundred townhouses in Irving. Finally, there are nearly one thousand six hundred mobile homes in the area. Irving is a wonderful place to live.

LESSON 1, PRONUNCIATION pg 93

Pronunciation of /v/

/v/ /v/ live, live

We live in an apartment.

F pg 94

Saud and his family are from Iraq. Saud lives in an apartment in Irving, Texas. His sister also lives in Irving. She lives in a townhouse. Saud's brothers live in a small house in Los Angeles, California. Their parents live in a condominium in Iraq.

LESSON 2

B pg 95

1.

Angela: Hello, this is Irving Properties. How can I help you?

Saud: Hello, I'm looking for an apartment to rent for my family. I checked online, but I'm not sure what is still available.

Angela: OK. How many bedrooms do you need?

Saud: I need three bedrooms and two bathrooms.

Angela: I think we can help you. We have a three-bedroom, two-bath available now.

2.

Angela: Hello, how can I help you?

Silvia: Hi, we're interested in the small house on Market Street.

Angela: The one with two bedrooms and one bathroom, right?

Silvia: Yes, that's right. Is it still available?

Angela: Yes, it is.

Silvia: Great! How much is the rent?

Angela: It's only $1,800 a month.

Silvia: $1,800 a month? This is going to be more difficult than I thought.

3.

Angela: Hello, what can I do for you?

Wei: Hello, I don't see any large properties on your website. Do you have any properties for a big family?

Angela: Well, let's see . . .

Wei: I think I need a house with four bedrooms.

Angela: OK. We have one on Foley Lane with four bedrooms and two bathrooms.

Wei: That's perfect! How much is the rent?

Angela: $3,000 a month.

Wei: Can we come and look at it?

Angela: Yes, of course.

4.

Angela: Hello, this is Irving Properties. How can I help you?

Felipe: What do you have in terms of one-bedroom apartments?

Angela: We have a one-bedroom apartment on Sycamore Street.

Felipe: OK. How much is the rent?

Angela: It's $1,400 a month, plus utilities.

Felipe: Is it one-bathroom too?

Angela: Yes, that's right. One bathroom and one bedroom.

LESSON 3

E pg 99

1. This is a large three-bedroom townhouse with a lot of good features. There is a pool. All utilities are included, and it's near elementary and middle schools. Come and see it. You won't be sorry.

2. This apartment is the best out there. It has three bedrooms, and it's only $2,500 a month. It's on the second floor, so you can enjoy a beautiful balcony. First and last month's rent are required for move-in.

3. This great apartment is far from city traffic. Hot summers are no problem. We have air-conditioning, and we pay the electric bill. Request a tour today.

4. This is a bargain! One thousand dollars a month to lease this one-bedroom, one-bath apartment. No pets please! Available September 1st.

LESSON 3, PRONUNCIATION pg 100

Yes / no questions have a rising intonation. They go up at the end.

Does it have three bedrooms?

Does it have air-conditioning?

LESSON 4

A pg 101

1. Decide where I want to live.

2. Decide how many bedrooms and bathrooms I need.

3. Look online.

4. Talk to an agent, the manager, or the owner.

5. Make an appointment.

6. See the apartment.

B pg 101

Many real estate apps or websites have filters to make your online search easier. With filters, you can choose the type of home you want, the number of bedrooms and bathrooms, and the rent amount. This way you only see homes that have what you need at the right price.

D pg 102

Owner: Hello, this is Mariana.
Saud: Hi, Mariana. This is Saud. I'm interested in the condo you have for rent.
Owner: Ah, yes. Hi, Saud. Thanks for reaching out. As I said in my message, the rent for the condo is $2,500 a month.
Saud: Great! When can I see it?
Owner: How about today at 3:00?
Saud: Perfect! Thank you.

E pg 102

1.

Owner 1: Hello, this is Mariana.
Saud: Hi, Mariana. This is Saud. I'm interested in the condo you have for rent.
Owner 1: Ah, yes. Hi, Saud. Thanks for reaching out. As I said in my message, the rent for the condo is $2,500 a month.
Saud: Great! When can I see it?
Owner 1: How about today at 3:00?
Saud: Perfect! Thank you.

2.

Owner 2: Hello. How can I help you?
Saud: Yes, hi. My name is Saud. I'm interested in the apartment for rent. Is it still available?
Owner 2: Yes, it's still available. We're renting it for $2,800.
Saud: Wow! That's expensive.
Owner 2: Maybe, but it is a new and beautiful apartment.
Saud: OK, when can I see it?
Owner 2: You can stop by at 10 a.m.

3.

Owner 3: Hello.
Saud: Hi. This is Saud. I am calling about the house for rent. I sent you a message yesterday.
Owner 3: Oh, yes, that's right. So, what would you like to know?
Saud: How much is the rent?
Owner 3: It's $3,000 a month. It's a four-bedroom.
Saud: Hmm. I don't know if I need something that big. When can I see it?
Owner 3: Come by at 4:30.
Saud: OK, see you then.

4.

Saud: Hello.
Owner 4: Hello. Is this Saud?
Saud: Yes, that's me.

Owner 4: I am returning your call about the three-bedroom apartment.
Saud: Oh, yes. Thank you. How much is the rent?
Owner 4: It's $2,400 a month.
Saud: Great. Can I come by today?
Owner 4: Of course. Come by around 2:00.
Saud: Thanks, I will.

LESSON 5
G pg 106

1. Draw a sofa next to the door.
2. Draw a chair under the window.
3. Draw an end table between the sofa and the chair.
4. Draw a lamp on the end table.
5. Draw a painting on the wall over the sofa.
6. Draw a coffee table in the middle of the room.
7. Draw a plant next to the chair.

LESSON 6
E pg 108

Carpenters, like many construction workers, work by the hour. They only work when there is a job to do. Sometimes they work overtime and make more per hour. Overtime is time worked over 40 hours a week.

To calculate overtime, multiply the hourly pay by 1.5. Hourly pay times 1.5 equals overtime pay.

For example: $30.00 x 1.5 = $45.00

READING CHALLENGE pg 115
Risky Business

Some people use real estate to make money. They buy a house and fix it up. Then they sell it again in a month or two. This is called *flipping*.

Flipping houses can be risky! One risk is that the house can have a lot of problems, and it costs too much to fix. Other times, no one wants to buy it. You can make around $30,000 for every house you flip. You can also lose $30,000 or more if it flops! There are classes to learn how to successfully flip houses. It is a risky business.

UNIT 5
LESSON 1
D pg 121

1. This is a place where people mail letters and packages, and they buy stamps.
2. This is a place with trained workers who help the community when there is an emergency, such as a fire.

3. This is a place people go when they are very sick or for medical emergencies or surgeries. They sometimes go by ambulance.

4. This is a place where people go to get a driver's license and identification.

5. This is a place where people put their money. Sometimes they get a checking account, and sometimes they get credit cards or take out loans.

6. This is a place where police officers work. It is the police officers' office.

F pg 122

Emanuela: I'm very sick.
Lisa: You need to go to the hospital.
Emanuela: Where is it?
Lisa: It's on First Street.
Emanuela: Thanks!

LESSON 2

C pg 123

1.
A: Can you give me directions, please?
B: Maybe. Where do you want to go?
A: I'm looking for the mall.
B: It's on Broadway. Turn around and go straight for two blocks. Turn right on Hamilton Avenue. You'll see it.
A: Thanks!

2.
A: Excuse me. Do you know the way to the post office?
B: Yes, of course. Go straight ahead two miles. Turn left on Maple.

3.
A: I'm totally confused. Where's the movie theater from here?
B: It's very close.
A: Can you give me directions?
B: Sure. Turn left on First Street. Then go straight ahead three blocks.
A: Thanks so much.

4.
A: Can I help you find something?
B: Yes, I'm looking for the museum. I hear there's a dinosaur exhibit there.
A: Yes, that's right. It's on Main Street.
B: Where's Main Street?
A: Turn right and go straight for three blocks.
B: Thank you.

5.
A: Where is the park?
B: Turn around and go straight for six blocks. You can't miss it.
A: Are you sure?
B: I am absolutely positive.

F pg 124

Hamed: I need to find City Hall. Can you help me?
Gabriel: Of course. Go straight one block and turn right. It's on the left.
Hamed: Can you repeat that slowly for me?
Gabriel: Sure. Go straight one block … Turn right … It's on the left.
Hamed: Thanks!
Gabriel: No problem.

LESSON 3

D pg 127

1.
Ticket agent: Here is your boarding pass, sir. Have a good flight.
Male passenger: Thank you. Where is the security checkpoint?
Ticket agent: It's around the corner from here.
Male passenger: Thank you.

2.
Male passenger: Is there a restaurant after security?
Ticket agent: Yes, of course. It's across from Gate 1.
Male passenger: Thanks so much. I'm starving.

3.
Female passenger: Excuse me, can you tell me where the restrooms are?
Airport staff member: They're between the restaurant and the vending machines, right over there.
Female passenger: Thanks!

4.
Female passenger: Where can I get a taxi?
Airport staff member: Directly in front of the passenger pick-up.
Female passenger: I appreciate it.

5.
Female passenger: Excuse me, can you tell me where the vending machines are?
Airport staff member: They're next to the restrooms.
Female passenger: Thanks so much.

E pg 127

1. The security checkpoint is around the corner from ticketing.
2. The restaurant is across from Gate 1.
3. The restrooms are between the restaurant and the vending machines.
4. Taxis are in front of the passenger pick-up.
5. The vending machines are next to the restrooms.

LESSON 4

B pg 129

Samira has a problem. She has two things on her schedule at the same time. This is called a *scheduling conflict*. Both things are very important to her. She decides to change her doctor's appointment. She is nervous. English is not Samira's first language, and she doesn't know what to say on the phone.

D pg 129

Voicemail message: Hello, this is David. I can't come to the phone right now. Please leave a message, and I will get back to you right away.
Samira: Hi, David. This is Samira. I texted you this morning. I need to change my doctor's appointment, but I don't know what to say. Can you help me? I hope so. Please call me back today at (253) 555-3765.

E pg 129

Speak slowly and clearly.
- Say your name and your reason for calling.
- Keep your message short.
- Say your phone number. Cell phones record your number, but office phones may not.

LESSON 4, PRONUNCIATION pg 131

Yes / No Questions

Yes / no questions have a rising intonation. They go up at the end.
Can I talk to you?
Can you call me?

LESSON 5

A pg 132

Hi Paco,

I am writing this email from my favorite coffee shop. It's a great place for studying. Maybe we can meet here next week and work on our class project. The coffee shop is around the corner from school, across from the supermarket. How about Monday after class?

Please let me know.
Best,
Samira

D pg 133

1. She is eating at a restaurant.
2. They are writing emails.
3. We are reading a good book in class.
4. I am going to the hospital. I am very sick.
5. Samira is buying a book at the bookstore right now.

F pg 134

1. Where do you go to school?
2. Where do you live?
3. Where is a restaurant nearby?
4. What do you sometimes do?

REVIEW

D pg 139

1.
Voicemail message: This is Herman. I can't come to the phone right now. Please leave a message.
Nadia: Hi, this is Nadia. I have a question for you. Can you give me a call back? My number is (917) 555-2134.

2.
Voicemail message: This is Herman. I can't come to the phone right now. Please leave a message.
Vien: Hey Herman, it's Vien. I want to talk about this weekend. Can you call me back? My number is (617) 555-7798.

3.
Voicemail message: This is Herman. I can't come to the phone right now. Please leave a message.
David: David here. I need information about the job at City Hall. Please call me back at (786) 555-1234.

4.
Voicemail message: This is Herman. I can't come to the phone right now. Please leave a message.
Ricardo: Hello. This is Ricardo. I need help with something. Can you give me a call? My number is (323) 555-7343.

READING CHALLENGE pg 143

Where Everyone Knows Your Name

How far do you travel to school? How far is the local grocery store? How about the police department? If you live in Whittier, Alaska, your answers to these questions are probably up or down a few floors. That's right; almost everyone in the town of nearly 300 lives in Begich Towers, a 14-story building that has a post office and a bed-and-breakfast. You need to take a 2.5-mile tunnel through a mountain to arrive at this town where most people live under the same roof. The good news is that there are beautiful views from the condominiums in Begich Towers. Do you want to live in a small town where everyone knows your name?

UNIT 6

LESSON 1

A pg 146

Victor is sick. He visits the doctor. The doctor asks, "What is the problem?" Victor answers, "I hurt all over. I think I have a fever. My head hurts and my muscles ache." The doctor checks Victor for the flu. The doctor gives him a prescription for some pain medication.

E pg 147

1.

Cristela: Doctor, thank you for seeing me on such short notice.
Doctor: What seems to be the problem?
Cristela: Well, I'm having trouble with my hand.
Doctor: What do you mean, trouble?
Cristela: My hand is very stiff in the morning. I work at a computer, and it is getting very difficult to do my work.

2.

Doctor: How are you today, Roberto?
Roberto: I'm fine except my leg hurts all the time.
Doctor: I see. Let's check it out. Where does it hurt?
Roberto: My leg hurts right here near the knee.
Doctor: We should probably take some X-rays.

3.

Doctor: Well, Jianyu, it seems like you're here every week these days.
Jianyu: I guess so, Doctor. My head is killing me.
Doctor: I know that you were here last week because of your neck. Did the prescription help?
Jianyu: Not at all. It seems to be getting worse.

F pg 147

Doctor: What is the problem today?
Patient: My leg hurts.
Doctor: Your leg?
Patient: Yes, my leg.

LESSON 2

B pg 149

Doctor: What's the matter?
Miguel: I feel very sick. I have a terrible sore throat.

Doctor: It sounds like you might have the flu.
Miguel: The flu?
Doctor: Yes, the flu.

LESSON 2, PRONUNCIATION pg 149

Intonation of Information and Clarification Questions

Intonation is the rising and falling of our voices as we speak. In information questions that start with words like *what*, *where*, or *when*, the voice rises and then falls at the end.
What's the matter?
What's the matter?

We ask clarification questions to help us understand something. With these questions, the voice rises at the end.
The flu?
The flu?

C pg 150

1.

Doctor: What's the matter?
Miguel: I feel very sick. I have a terrible sore throat.
Doctor: It sounds like you might have the flu.
Miguel: The flu?
Doctor: Yes, the flu.

2.

Doctor: What's the matter?
Patient: I don't know. I'm terribly tired.
Doctor: Do you have any other symptoms?
Patient: Yes, I have a fever.
Doctor: Well, let's examine you. Open up and say, "Aahh."

3.

Doctor: What's the matter?
Patient: I can't smell or taste anything!
Doctor: When did this start?
Patient: About three days ago.
Doctor: You might have COVID-19. We'll give you a test to make sure.

4.

Doctor: What's the matter?
Patient: I have a cold.
Doctor: Maybe I can give you some medicine for that runny nose.
Patient: Yes, I have a terrible runny nose.

D pg 150

Every year people have both colds and the flu. What is the difference? Usually a person with a cold or the flu has a runny nose and a sore throat. A person with a cold sometimes has a low fever, but a person with the flu has a high fever and body aches. Cold symptoms also include sneezing. Flu symptoms can include a dry cough.

LESSON 3

D pg 153

Cristela is talking to her doctor. She is sick. She has a bad headache and sore throat. The doctor is giving Cristela a prescription for some medicine. She needs to read the labels on the medicine carefully. The doctor is helping her understand them.

G pg 153

Well, let me see. The doctor says that I need to take this medicine for the next few days. Here it says, "Take one lozenge as needed for sore throat pain." I'll probably need that. My throat really hurts. I will especially need it at work when I'm talking to everyone. This one says to take 10 milliliters every four hours. Let me see, that means I should take the first dose when I wake up around 8:00 and then at noon and again at 4:00. I will take the last dose at 8:00 p.m. This last one reads, "Take two tablets every four to six hours." I'll do that until my headache goes away. I hope that is soon. I really don't like to be sick.

LESSON 4

A pg 155

Operator: What's the emergency?
Victor: There's a car accident.
Operator: Where's the accident?
Victor: It's on Fourth and Bush.
Operator: What's your name?
Victor: It's Victor Karaskov.
Operator: Is anyone hurt?
Victor: Yes. Please send an ambulance.

F pg 157

1.

Visitor 1: Excuse me. Where are the elevators? I can't seem to find them.
Staff: They are down the hall, next to the restrooms.
Visitor 1: Where?
Staff: Go that way, down the hall and the elevators are next to the restrooms.
Visitor 1: Thanks.

2.

Staff: Can I help you?
Visitor 2: Yes. I am looking for the emergency entrance. Is it close by?
Staff: Yes, it is. It's down that hallway, near the emergency room.
Visitor 2: Where? I don't understand.
Staff: Let me walk you there.
Visitor 2: OK, thanks.

3.

Visitor 3: Excuse me, where is the cafeteria?
Staff: It's right over there, across from the waiting room.
Visitor 3: Oh, there it is. Thanks!

4.

Visitor 4: Can you help me?
Staff: What can I do for you?
Visitor 4: I am looking for the ATM.
Staff: It's here in the lobby, near the main entrance.
Visitor 4: Oh, I see it over there. Thank you!
Staff: You're welcome.

LESSON 5

A pg 158

We need to exercise. It is good for our hearts, muscles, flexibility, and weight. Everyone should exercise. People can run, swim, clean the house, or work in the yard. Doctors say we should exercise every day.

D pg 159

1.

Woman: I'm so tired.
Man: Why?
Woman: I think I need to exercise more. I don't feel very healthy.
Man: I swim every day at the gym. It's great exercise.
Woman: Maybe I'll try that.

2.

Husband: I don't get any exercise.
Wife: Yes, you do.
Husband: What do you mean? I never even leave the house.
Wife: You vacuum every day. That's exercise.
Husband: Oh, I never thought of that.

3.

Man: What do you do for exercise?
Woman: I jog.
Man: What's jogging?

Woman: I run slowly and enjoy nature with my dog.
Man: That sounds great.

4.

Man: I exercise every day.
Woman: Me too.
Man: What do you do?
Woman: I get most of my exercise outside in the yard. Gardening can be good exercise.
Man: Really?
Woman: Sure, why not?

LESSON 6

D pg 162

Pharmacists can have many different types of jobs. Some work in pharmacies. You see them when you pick up your medications. Other pharmacists work on new medications. They work for companies in laboratories or offices.

READING CHALLENGE pg 169

The Best Medicine

Do you want to sleep better? Do you want to be happier? What can you do about it? The answer isn't medicine, and it isn't something you eat. It is physical activity and exercise! According to the American Psychological Association, 25–35% of Americans don't do any physical activity at all. This can cause a lot of health problems, so exercising is very important.

Even if you can only exercise 10 minutes a day, you will feel better. Make it part of your routine. Get off the bus early and walk a few extra blocks. Take the stairs instead of the elevator. Go dancing, go roller skating, or do both like the woman in this photo. She is getting some exercise at a disco event in Central Park in New York City. Even housework like vacuuming helps. So, it's time to exercise and to feel better!

UNIT 7

LESSON 1

E pg 173

1.

Supervisor: Hi, Dan. I have something important for you to do today.
Dan: Great. I'm ready.
Supervisor: One of your responsibilities as an administrative assistant is to arrange rooms for meetings and presentations. So, can you arrange a room for our presentation tomorrow morning? There will be around 15 people there.
Dan: Of course! I'll do that right away.

2.

Woman: What do you do?
Man: I'm a cook at Market Street Grill.
Woman: Wow, that's great. I hear the food is very good there.

3.

Woman: My job is so great! I love working with people.
Man: Me too. What do you do?
Woman: I have the perfect job.
Man: Well, what is it?
Woman: I'm a principal at a high school in Fairmont.

4.

Woman: I'm looking for a job.
Manager: Do you have experience?
Woman: Yes, I do. I worked at a local movie theater for three years.
Manager: What was your job?
Woman: I was a cashier.
Manager: So, you're good at helping customers.
Woman: Yes, I like working in customer service.
Manager: OK, let's get you an application.

LESSON 1, PRONUNCIATION pg 174

Intonation of Clarification Questions and Corrections

In English, we use a rising intonation for clarification questions. We also stress the information that is important.
A: He works in a SCHOOL, right?

When correcting someone, we stress the new information.
B: No, he doesn't work in a SCHOOL. He works in a RESTAURANT.

A: He works in a SCHOOL, right?
B: No, he doesn't work in a SCHOOL. He works in a RESTAURANT.

LESSON 2

C pg 175

1.

Manager: Sam, you need to take a vacation this month.
Sam: Well, I'm not sure I can. I'm very busy.
Manager: If you don't use your vacation time soon, then you'll lose it. You have five days to make a decision.
Sam: OK, I'll talk to my wife and see what she says.

2.

Insurance Agent: CMM Health Insurance. How can I help you?

Anya: My husband had an accident.

Insurance Agent: An accident? What happened?

Anya: He fell down the stairs and broke his leg.

Insurance Agent: I'm sorry to hear that. How can I help?

Anya: Does my insurance cover hospital care and if so, what is the deductible?

Insurance Agent: I'll check for you. First, I need your member ID.

3.

Steve: I'm sorry. I have to call in sick.

Manager: I'm sorry to hear that.

Steve: Yes, I have a fever. Maybe I have the flu.

Manager: How long will you be out?

Steve: Do you know how much sick leave I have left?

Manager: I'll check on it for you.

F pg 176

We need a cook for our restaurant in San Francisco. The salary is $16 an hour. You need two years' experience for this job. This is a full-time position with benefits. We offer sick leave and two weeks of vacation time every year. Apply in person at 3500 West Arbor Place, San Francisco, California.

LESSON 3

A pg 178

My name is Francisco. I'm from Mexico. Now I work in the United States. I'm an auto mechanic. I fix about ten cars a week. I started my job in August of 2019. Before I moved to the United States, I was a cook from March, 2014 to July, 2018. I cooked hamburgers and french fries in a restaurant.

E pg 179

1. Anya was an office assistant. She answered the phone.

2. Chioma was a delivery person. She delivered packages.

3. David was a cashier. He helped customers.

4. Ernesto was a nurse. He cared for patients.

5. Eva and Soraya were teachers. They worked in a school.

6. Anita was a salesperson. She talked to customers.

7. Thu Ya was a mechanic. He fixed cars.

8. Agatha was a manager. She supervised the other workers.

9. Mary was a cook. She prepared lunch.

LESSON 3, PRONUNCIATION pg 180

-ed Ending

The simple past -ed ending is pronounced three different ways:

/t/ worked, typed

/d/ delivered, cleaned

/ɪd/ painted, counted

G pg 180

The first job I ever had was as a receptionist. I worked very hard. I did that job for over three years and learned a lot. I answered the phone and greeted people. I started my second position in 2018. I was an office manager. I supervised three employees. Now I am a nurse. I help doctors and sick people. It is a great job.

LESSON 4

D pg 182

1.

Interviewer: Thank you for answering all our questions. We'll contact you soon to let you know about the position.

Applicant: Thank you. I'm very interested. Can I ask you a question?

Interviewer: Yes, please do.

Applicant: What are the benefits?

Interviewer: We offer medical and dental insurance. We also have sick leave and six days of vacation every year.

Applicant: Thanks.

2.

Interviewer: Well, I think you look very good for the position. We must speak to many other applicants. We are open every day of the week including Saturdays and Sundays. Can you work on weekends?

Applicant: Yes, on Saturday but not on Sunday.

Interviewer: OK, that's good to know.

Applicant: Is that something that's required?

Interviewer: No. We have many opportunities here.

Applicant: OK, thank you.

3.

Interviewer: In this job, you have to talk to customers all the time. I hear that you speak English a little. Can you speak to customers well in English?

Applicant: Yes, I believe so. I'm studying English in school.

Interviewer: Great. I just wanted to make sure. Where do you study?

Applicant: At the adult school around the corner.

Interviewer: Perfect!

E pg 182

1.
A: Do you have a resume?
B: A resume?

2.
A: What do you do?
B: What is my job now?

3.
A: Do you have experience?
B: Experience for this job?

4.
A: Can you work eight hours a day?
B: You mean full-time?

5.
A: Can you work extra hours?
B: You mean in the evenings?

LESSON 4, PRONUNCIATION pg 182

Clarification Questions
Use rising intonation with clarification questions.
A: Do you have a resume?
B: A resume?

B: Can you work extra hours?
A: You mean in the evenings?

LESSON 5

E pg 185

Alba is a good worker. She works in the evening. She is punctual. The customers love her. Last night, Alba was late for work. She had a problem with her car. Her car is old. She called a tow truck with her cell phone, and the tow truck was late.

F pg 186

Supervisor: Amed, I think in time you will become an excellent worker. You certainly speak well and you are very good with the customers. I gave you *exceeds expectations* for communication skills. This is why I am sure you can be a great employee in time. I did notice that you usually come to work on time. You were late once, but only by a few minutes. For punctuality I have given you a *meets expectations*.

I know that you are trying to work hard and make extra money by working more days. But you need to be willing to work with others more. You seem to like working by yourself. Your coworkers can help you learn a lot. When you work better with others, we will feel comfortable giving you more hours. I had to give you a

needs improvement on teamwork for now. You are new, so don't worry too much about this one. You will learn quickly if you apply yourself. I also gave you a *needs improvement* for product knowledge because you are still learning about all of the different items we sell here. I am sure that will change in no time.

G pg 186

Marta's Self-Evaluation

I am a good employee. I work hard. Sometimes, I'm late. I always listen and follow directions well. I am learning English. Sometimes, people don't understand me. I want to be a great employee. I need to communicate well and come to work on time.

Neda's Self-Evaluation

I don't work. I go to school. I am punctual, but I don't always listen well. I am learning English. Sometimes, people don't understand me. Sometimes, I don't do my homework because I'm very busy. I want to be a great student. I need to communicate well and do my homework every day.

LESSON 6

A pg 187

Do you like being outside? Do you like gardening? Do you want to work in a park or a backyard? If you do, you should work in the landscaping industry. Jobs in landscaping help to create and take care of outdoor places like gardens and parks. Landscaping workers keep these places looking nice so people can enjoy them.

REVIEW

D pg 191

In 2013, Jinhua was a carpenter. He constructed homes for a company called Builders Plus. In 2016, Jinhua was a custodian. He cleaned the offices and fixed things at Clean Sweep, Inc. In 2019, Jinhua was a student. He learned about education at Willington Community College. Now Jinhua is a teacher. He started in 2021. He helps students at Jefferson Adult School.

READING CHALLENGE pg 195

How Many Jobs?

100 years ago, many Americans had a goal of working one or two jobs for life. Today, according to the Bureau of Labor Statistics (BLS), Americans have around 12 jobs in a lifetime. On average, they work about four or five years per job. Changing jobs more often means workers need to be good at interviews and networking.

Networking is a way for workers to talk to other workers and leaders in their field. Networking is done in many ways. One of the most popular ways is through social media. There are websites and apps where you can connect with people in your workplace and from other companies. Do you have a social media account for networking? It is never too early to start one.

UNIT 8

LESSON 1

A pg 198

Nubar is an ESL student at Franklin Adult School. He has good study habits. He has class three days a week, two days in person and one day online. He speaks English with his classmates. Nubar practices English at work and with his family. He also watches TV and listens to podcasts in English.

E pg 199

My name is Angela Sheldon. I am in college now. I studied English in school so I could go to college here in the United States. I took advantage of every opportunity so I could learn quickly. For example, I never missed class, and I always came to class on time. I wrote down new words in my notebook every day. At home, I watched TV in English. It was really good for me. I watched the news and other programs. I also helped and taught other students. I think this was the best thing I did. Now I'm in college and I'm happy to be here.

LESSON 2

E pg 202

A good way to prepare for your next English course is to review and study what you learned in *Stand Out*, Level 1. One way to do this is to organize what you learned in a clear way so you can look at it when you want to remember something. We call this a *study guide*. You can also add to this study guide in each class you take in the future.

LESSON 3

D pg 205

1.

Yusuf: I want to be a legal assistant, but first I need to learn more English.

Counselor: That's very important. Do you have a high school diploma?

Yusuf: No, I don't.

Counselor: Well, that is always a good place to start. Maybe you can get work without it, but it's very important.

Yusuf: Yes, I know. That's one of my plans.

Counselor: Great! Then you need an associate degree or certificate from a community college.

Yusuf: OK, and what should I study there?

Counselor: Most legal assistants get a degree or certificate in paralegal studies.

2.

Counselor: That's great you want to be a teacher.

Minh: Yes, but I need to learn a lot more first.

Counselor: Well, you are taking classes at the adult school now, so I'm sure you are learning a lot. Do you have a high school diploma?

Minh: Not yet. I'll get it at the end of the year.

Counselor: That's good! Then you will need a bachelor's degree. You can start at a two-year college and then go to a university, or you can go right to the university.

Minh: Hmm. Which is better for me?

Counselor: They are both good, but community college is cheaper.

3.

Counselor: Being a nurse is a good job. If you want to be a registered nurse, you'll need a bachelor's degree from a university.

Sarah: Yes, I already have plans to go to a four-year college here in town. Do I need to be a citizen?

Counselor: No, but you do need to be a state resident, or it will cost you a lot more money.

Sarah: Good. I am a state resident.

4.

Carolina: I want to get a job as a web developer so I can design beautiful websites that are easy to use.

Counselor: That sounds great! So, you are taking English classes at the adult school now. What are your plans after you finish studying here?

Carolina: I'm not sure. Do I need a degree to be a web developer?

Counselor: Some web developer jobs require a bachelor's degree, but others just require experience. Maybe you can take some classes at a community college and work on your design skills on your own. You can take more English classes too. Then you can decide if you want to go to a four-year college and get your bachelor's degree.

Carolina: That sounds like a good plan.

5.

Counselor: So, Alan, you want to be a cook, right?

Alan: That's right.

Counselor: Do you want to be a chef in an expensive restaurant where you can make special food?

Alan: That sounds interesting, but I'm not sure. Is it hard to be a chef?

Counselor: Most jobs require a high school diploma and for some you need an associate degree or certificate.

Alan: That sounds like a lot of work, but I'll think about it.

6.

Javi: I just want to learn a little more English before I get a job as a mechanic. I already have my GED.

Counselor: That's great! Do you also have a certificate in automotive technology?

Javi: No. Do I really need one?

Counselor: It's not always required, but it will help prepare you for work as a mechanic. It might also help you find a job faster. You should think about going to trade school.

Javi: Thanks. I'm going to think about it.

LESSON 4

B pg 207

1.

My name is Erendira. I am a student at Pine Adult School. I like to study and go to school. I think I would like to be a student for my whole life, but I know I'll have to get a job someday. I love history, so maybe I should look into being a teacher. I think that would be a great profession for me.

2.

I'm Ruth and I love people. Every chance I get, I talk to people. They're so interesting. I like to help people too. For that reason, I am going to choose a career that will allow me to be around people who I can help. I think being a nurse would be very interesting and rewarding. My mother's a nurse too.

3.

My name is Changming. I have a lot of experience working with my hands. I like to fix things too. I love to make things work. That's why I think being a mechanic might be a good job for me. Also, I like cars, so I think that this is a good choice.

E pg 208

1. They like to work outside.
2. He wants a car for his job.
3. She needs to make money right now.
4. They want to study at school every day.
5. I want to learn English.
6. You need a new cell phone right away.
7. They like their jobs.
8. She wants to find a new job.

LESSON 5

A pg 210

May 5

I have many study goals for the next month. I am going to read the news online, listen to podcasts, and talk to people in English every day. I am also going to study a lesson from my textbook every night for 30 minutes in my bedroom.

B pg 210

I think that if I plan, I will be able to learn English well even when there is no school. I am going to read the news online, listen to podcasts, and talk to people in English every day. Well, let's see. If I am going to do all this, I need to schedule these things. I will get home at 6:00, and then from 6:30 to 6:45, I will read the news online. I need to find time to study the textbook. I know—I will do that from 7:00 to 7:30. I will listen to a podcast from 8:00 to 8:45. That should be good practice. Then from 9:00 to 9:15, I will write in my journal. I am going to do this for a full month. Then I will make new goals.

G pg 212

I have many goals for the future. Some of my goals will take a long time. I will study every day and get a high school diploma. After that, I will start college. I want to start in about three years. I also want to get married and have children sometime in the future. I will be a web developer one day.

READING CHALLENGE pg 221

Learning Together

There are many different ways of learning. Some people like to study alone. They want to stay away from distractions. Other people make study groups and talk together about problems and solutions. But which way of studying is better for learning?

Research shows that collaboration is key. When students work with others and help each other, they remember more. Explaining something in your own words and hearing your classmates' ideas can help you make better connections with the information. Also, studying with others can create positive feelings. For example, the girls in the photo worked together on a project for an international science and engineering fair. Here, they are sharing what they learned, and they are having fun while doing it. If you enjoy learning, you will want to learn more, and when you want to learn, you learn better!

Video Viewing Strategies

Video Repeats

The first viewing introduces students to content. The second and subsequent viewings allow students to watch objectively and focus on specific content.

Comprehension While Viewing

There are several strategies that teachers can use while viewing to help students better understand videos. These involve manipulation of the video to suit your needs:

1. **Stop or pause** the video while watching.
2. **Rewind the video** to clarify meaning and understanding.
3. **Watch the video** again with different objectives or purposes in mind.
4. **Adjust the viewing speed** (if possible) to focus on specific visuals.

True / False Statements

Explain to students that there are strategies for correctly answering true / false statements.

1. Look for extreme *modifiers* that might make the question or statement false, such as *all*, *always*, *never*, *only*, *none*, and *nobody*.
2. Look for a qualifying word that might make the question or statement true, such as *usually*, *probably*, *often*, *most*, and *sometimes*.
3. Look for negative words and prefixes, such as *not* and *un-*.

Multitasking

Tell students that it is possible to engage in another activity while watching a video. Ask students to think about a time when they were watching TV, for example, and doing something else simultaneously. Explain that this is called multitasking. Point out that in a previous exercise students looked at pictures, read job titles, and matched jobs to the correct pictures while watching and listening to the video. This is another example of multitasking.

Matching Quotes

Explain to students that a video still or picture from the video will often give them clues on matching quotes. Ask students to look at the number of people in the picture, the setting or scene, whether the person is male or female, age and / or physical characteristics.

Best Practices

There are many ways to use video in the classroom. Students should rarely watch a video without some kind of task. You might introduce comprehension questions before they watch so they know what they are looking for. Following are some techniques that you may try for variety beyond the comprehension checks and other ideas already presented.

Freeze Frame: Pause the video during viewing and use it like a picture dictionary, identifying and expanding on the vocabulary.

Silent Viewing: Show the video in segments without sound so students can guess at the story line. This helps them to understand that listening is more than just the words people say.

Prediction Techniques: Show portions of the video and ask students to predict what will come next.

Listening without Viewing: This helps students create their own image of what is happening. After a discussion, allow students to watch the video and the sound together.

Back-to-Back: In pairs, one student faces the video and the other faces away. Play the video without sound and ask the student viewing to report to the student who is facing away what is happening.

Summary Strips: Create strips of sentences that describe the events. Have students watch the video and then put the strips in the correct order, or ask students to predict the story line before watching and then check their answers.

Visual Memory

When students complete an exercise that requires them to match pictures from a video with the correct descriptions, it is important for them to be able to recall what they saw. Visual memory skills are those that allow a person to remember visual details. Students can improve their visual memory by paying close attention to colors, types of dress, weather conditions, number of people, scenery, etc.

Sequencing Events

Ask students to take notes while they are watching the video and pay particular attention to the events as they occur. Later, have students review their notes and identify a central theme. Similar to a reading, the theme of the video is the main event. All of the other events are details related to this theme, presented in a certain order. Students' notes will generally show this order. Sequencing events allows students to recall specific details. It also helps them to understand the central theme of the video.

Visual-Detailing

Visual-detailing refers to identifying and listing individual or minute images in a video. Since we generally use both sight and hearing as we watch videos, we balance the two depending on our focus or concentration. When using visual-detailing, we make a conscious decision to allow our eyes to do the work to pick out key details from the video.

Lesson Planner Methodology

The *Stand Out* Lesson Planner methodology ensures success!

Stand Out ensures student success through good lesson planning and instruction. Each of the six lessons in every unit has a lesson plan. Unlike most textbooks, the Lesson Planner was written before the student book materials. A lot of learning occurs with the student books closed, so by writing the lesson plans first, we could ensure that each objective was clearly achieved. Each lesson plan follows a systematic and proven format:

W	Warm-up and / or review
I	Introduction
P	Presentation
P	Practice
E	Evaluation
A	Application

Warm-up and / or review

The warm-up activities establish a context and purpose to the lesson. Exercises use previously learned content and materials that are familiar to students from previous lessons.

Introduction

In the introduction step, exercises focus the students' attention on the goals of the lesson by asking questions, showing visuals, telling a story, etc. Instructors should state the objective of the lesson and tell students what they will be doing. The objective should address what students are expected to be able to do by the end of the lesson.

Presentation

The presentation activities provide students with the building blocks and skills they need to achieve the objectives set in the introduction. The exercises introduce new information to the students through visuals, realia, description, listenings, explanation, or written text. This is the time to check students' comprehension.

Practice

Practice activities provide meaningful tasks for students to practice what they have just learned through different activities. These activities can be done as a class, in small groups, pairs, or individually. All of these activities are student-centered and involve cooperative learning. Instructors should model each activity, monitor progress, and provide feedback.

Evaluation

Evaluation ensures that students are successful. Instructors should evaluate students on attainment of the objective set at the start of the lesson. This can be done by oral, written, or demonstrated performance. At this point, if students need more practice, instructors can go back and do additional practice activities before moving on to the application.

Application

Application activities help students apply new knowledge to their own lives or new situations. This is one of the most important steps of the lesson plan. If students can accomplish the application task, it will build their confidence to be able to use what they've learned out in the community. The Team Projects are an application of unit objectives that involves task-based activities with a product.

In addition to each lesson plan following the WIPPEA model, each unit in *Stand Out* follows this same approach. The first lesson is always an introduction to the unit, introducing new vocabulary and the basic concepts that will be expanded upon in the unit. The following five lessons are the Presentations and Practices for the unit topic. Following the six lessons is a Review lesson, which allows students to do more practice with everything they already learned. The Team Project is an Application for everything they learned in the unit.

_____

_____

_____

_____

_____

_____

_____

_____

_____

_____

_____

_____

_____

_____

_____

_____

_____

_____

_____

_____

_____

_____

_____

_____

_____

_____

_____

_____

_____

_____

_____

_____

_____

_____

_____

_____

_____

Instructor's Notes

LESSON PLANNER METHODOLOGY   269

Instructor's Notes

_____

_____

_____

_____

_____

_____

_____

_____

_____

_____

_____

_____

_____

_____

_____

_____

_____

_____